THE TECHNIQUE
of
FILM MUSIC

THE LIBRARY OF COMMUNICATION TECHNIQUES

THE TECHNIQUE OF FILM EDITING
By Karel Reisz and Gavin Millar

THE TECHNIQUE OF DOCUMENTARY FILM PRODUCTION
By W. Hugh Baddeley

THE TECHNIQUE OF SPECIAL-EFFECTS CINEMATOGRAPHY
By Raymond Fielding

THE TECHNIQUE OF THE SOUND STUDIO
By A. Nisbett

THE TECHNIQUE OF FILM ANIMATION
By J. Halas and R. Manvell

THE TECHNIQUE OF FILM MUSIC
By R. Manvell and J. Huntley

THE TECHNIQUE OF FILM AND TELEVISION MAKE-UP
By Vincent J-R Kehoe

THE TECHNIQUE OF TELEVISION PRODUCTION
By G. Millerson

THE TECHNIQUE OF THE TELEVISION CAMERAMAN
By Peter Jones

THE TECHNIQUE OF TELEVISION ANNOUNCING
By Bruce Lewis

THE TECHNIQUE OF THE MOTION PICTURE CAMERA
By H. Mario Raimondo Souto

THE TECHNIQUE OF EDITING 16MM FILM
By John Burder

THE TECHNIQUE OF THE FILM CUTTING ROOM
By E. Walter

THE TECHNIQUE OF SPECIAL EFFECTS IN TELEVISION
By B. R. Wilkie

THE TECHNIQUE OF LIGHTING FOR TELEVISION AND MOTION PICTURES
By G. Millerson

THE TECHNIQUE OF
FILM MUSIC

First Edition written and compiled by

ROGER MANVELL and JOHN HUNTLEY

*with the guidance of the following Committee
appointed by
The British Film Academy*

William Alwyn (Chairman)

Ken Cameron, Muir Mathieson, Basil Wright

Revised and Enlarged by

RICHARD ARNELL and PETER DAY

Communication Arts Books
Hastings House, Publishers
New York 10016

First Edition 1957
Reprinted 1967
Reprinted 1969
Reprinted 1971
Revised and Enlarged Edition 1975

Italian Edition:
TECHNICA DELLA MUSICA NEL FILM
Edizioni di Bianco e Nero, Roma

Printed and bound in Great Britain by A. Wheaton & Co., Exeter

CONTENTS

	PAGE
Introduction to First Edition	7
Introduction to Second Edition	11
Acknowledgements	13

1. MUSIC AND THE SILENT FILM

Music and the Drama	15
The Early Cinema	19
The Special Relationship between Music and the Silent Film	21
Musical Arrangement and Special Scores	24
Music in the Film Studios	28

2. MUSIC IN THE EARLY SOUND FILM

The First Use of Sound	31
The Early Development of the Musical Film	36
The Animated Film	39
The Dramatic Film	45
The Documentary and the Avant-garde Film	46
The Idea of Music in Films	49
The Rise of the Symphonic Score in Films	53

3. THE FUNCTION OF MUSIC IN THE SOUND FILM

The Full Range of the Sound Track: Effects and Dialogue	63
Performed Music: Filmed Opera and Ballet	66
Notable Opera and Ballet Films since 1957	71
Performed Music: Filmed Concert and Cabaret	73
Filmed Lives of the Composers	78
The Musical	82
Functional Music	87
(i) Music and Action	90
(ii) Scenic and Place Music	108
(iii) Period and Pageant Music	126
(iv) Music for Dramatic Tension	135
(v) Comedy Music	150
(vi) Music for Human Emotion	159
(vii) Music in Animated and Specialized Films	170

(viii) Music in Animation 1955–1972   194
(ix) Independent and Avant-garde Films   196

4. THE MUSIC DIRECTOR AND THE SOUND RECORDIST
The Function of the Music Director   199
Procedure in Hollywood   204
The Development of Modern Recording Practice   206

5. THE COMPOSER'S VIEW   219
Further Points of View   233

6. FOUR FILMS SINCE 1955   245
The Devils   246
2001: A Space Odyssey   253
Second Best   254
Zabriskie Point   260

APPENDICES:
An Outline History of Film Music   265
Film Music Criticism   287
Select Bibliography   291

INDEX   303

INTRODUCTION TO THE FIRST EDITION

THIS is the second volume in the technical series on the film which the British Film Academy is undertaking in association with the Focal Press. Its subject is very different from that of the first book, *The Technique of Film Editing*. Editing is a fundamental part of the sheer grammar of film-making. A film cannot fulfil its function of presenting a drama from a continuous succession of viewpoints without editing; editing is a vital part of the dramatic structure of a good film.

When music is added to a film, the unique powers proper to another art are synthesized with the natural powers of the film. Music first came to accompany the silent film in order quite simply to absolve it from its silence, and it has remained ever since as a further emotional stimulant. Yet because film-makers are not normally musicians or composers, or composers by any means born film-makers, the ancient art of music has far too often been misapplied to the new art of the film.

This book has been written to help resolve the comparative lack of understanding of music by film-makers, and the lack of a proper recognition of the art and craft of film-making by many composers. The common term "background music" is, in our view, derogatory; it does not indicate the contribution a finely conceived score can make to a film. We prefer, even though it is an ugly term, the description "functional film music", because this at least implies what every good film score should become, a vital part of the dramatic structure of the production and not an emotional prop filling the sound track with false stimulants. We believe that composers who turn to the film as a new patron of their work require special qualifications (which they can acquire through study of the needs of the film-maker) as well as a special musical temperament, if they are to adopt a proper professional attitude to the exacting task of providing music for films. The film offers composers a new and exciting branch of composition; in the words of Dr. Vaughan Williams: "The film contains potentialities for the combination of all the arts such as Wagner never dreamed of."

We would like to emphasize that this book, like its predecessor *The Technique of Film Editing*, is not a manual of technical instruction. That is, it does not presume to teach composers how to write music for a film or film-makers what kind of music they require. With the help and personal experience of many musicians actively concerned in the art of composing for films, the writers explain how this branch of composition has developed in the past, and examine how it has been practised in recent years. The book describes certain principles of composition as they have been evolved by imaginative composers and film-makers in a number of countries (and more especially in Britain and the United States). Each new film requiring music sets the composer and the film-maker alike a new problem in composition. No book on the subject can tell them directly how to solve this problem; it can only show them how other composers and film-makers have resolved their particular problems. All we can hope is that some examination of the effects of good composition for films will assist those working on other productions to realize the contribution music could make to their films if it is rightly used.

*   *   *   *   *

This book is addressed at least as much to film-makers as it is to musicians. It is, in fact, addressed to everyone interested in the films, whether engaged in professional production or not. But it is also, of course, addressed to the musician, though it has been written with the smallest possible use of technicalities of a kind only the trained musician can fully understand. Our aim has been to provide a book which will help film-makers to get the best from the composers whom they invite to collaborate with them. This they can do by realizing exactly what music can contribute to their films, and by giving the composer the chance to create a functional as distinct from a background score. Music is a very powerful stimulant indeed to the emotional responses of the audience; well used, it adds tremendously to the impact a film has on those who see it. It is therefore in the interest of the film-maker to understand this capacity in music, and excite the invention of his composer rather than encourage or even force him to produce the inchoate kind of score which too often passes as film music and drowns the drama of a film with an excess of ill-defined noise. For we hold that the undisciplined exercise of the musical imagination, without true regard for the form it has to work in, is unprofessional. Just as the composer has had to learn how most effectively to apply his art to the theatre in ballet, opera and incidental music to the drama, so we believe he must learn how best to apply it to the film.

The plan we have adopted in this book is simple. First, we have shown how music for the silent film grew out of incidental music composed for the theatre, and how music for certain silent films began to establish the principles of composition which hold good today in sound film music. Next, in Chapter 2, we have tried to show how the first principles of sound film music composition were developed through the imaginative collaboration of composers and film-makers during the first few years of sound, up to about 1935. By the middle nineteen-thirties the possibilities of functional film music had been demonstrated, and we substitute for the historical approach to the subject an analytical one of contemporary achievements. Chapter 3 describes the present position of sound recording in its relation to music, the function of the Music Director in the studio, and the technical approach of various composers to the task of composition for films. Chapter 4 shows the various dramatic forms film music takes, and analyses in each case shot-by-shot and phase-by-phase a particular sequence in which we would claim that a composer has been successful in writing music of such a kind that it contributes fully to the dramatic effect of the film. In Chapter 5 we conclude by letting the composers themselves speak their minds on the subject of this new form of composition, and make recommendations to the film-maker on what they believe to be the most fruitful way of collaborating with him as fellow technicians.

We are very conscious of our great debt to the composers and film music directors of many countries who have given us their views in writing or at interviews. Without their most generous help the greater part of any value this book may have would certainly be lost, and its authority similarly lessened. Individual acknowledgements are made elsewhere in the book.

We are grateful to the Academy for its support during the period the book was being prepared, and to Mrs. Steele, the Executive Secretary of the Academy, and Miss Tessa Mills for undertaking the difficult task of typing the manuscript of this book. Finally, we would like to thank Mr. Kraszna-Krausz of the Focal Press, for his sympathetic co-operation during the time the book was being prepared for the Press.

William Alwyn

INTRODUCTION TO THE SECOND EDITION

SINCE publication of the first edition of this book in 1956, very considerable changes have taken place in film making throughout the world, and many of these developments greatly affect the uses of music—whether live, recorded or synthesised.

Technical advances in sound recording and the use of multiple track tape recorders have enabled composers generally to use fewer musicians for a required effect. As a result, the music director in charge of the music department of a studio and of the conducting of the score, has virtually disappeared, at least in the United Kingdom. The composer or arranger nearly always conducts his own music, even when larger orchestras are used, while the electronic composer, using perhaps only electronic devices and tape recorders, produces a finished tape for direct delivery to the film producer. Rising costs, both of services and of labour, have also forced a more economical use of resources. The sociological effect of this would tend to mean that nowadays, fewer musicians would be employed, that they would be more flexible and versatile, higher paid and quicker at the recording session. This perhaps poses problems beyond the scope of this book.

The role of music has changed too. Many directors do not believe in "mood" music, "chase" music and so on and only use music defined as "foreground" music. That is to say, it is used only as part of the visuals: when a radio is switched on, we hear appropriate music; if musicians are playing we hear them. Some directors will use music only for titles. Many others still use music for theatrical effect but, perhaps because of the influence of TV, it tends to be condensed and certainly very far from being symphonic or heavily orchestral.

During the past twenty years there has been a total revolution in the visual arts. This came with the flourishing of pop art, conceptual art, kinetic sculpture and so on. There have been experiments of all kinds in music as well. These seem to have settled down into the following streams:

1 *Pop.* This is surely by far the most far reaching trend, having had the most influence on film makers, especially in the English speaking countries. The explosion caused by the arrival of the Beatles had an effect not only on music but on the life style of a generation all over the world. As many pop groups were self taught, they did not read music. Film makers followed suit and films were cut to fit the tracks—synchronisation became less important. Nothing was notated. The sound engineer became part of the composition.

2 *Main stream.* A continuation of traditional musical thought.

3 *Electronic music.* A development produced electronically often without the use of human performances or "real" sounds.

4 *Improvisation.* Again a return to the instantaneous composition where composer/performers dispense with all but minimal instructions written down in advance.

5 *Theatre music.* Involvement of the performers and the audience in the *composition* of the music. The film invades as well, creating the mixed-media. This might be a throw back to the masque, with the addition of film and tape.

Apart from "musicals", musical comedies or operettas, many more films have been made about music, musicians and composers and special chapters are devoted to these.

It is not within the scope of our survey to include music for TV, but it is clear that this medium has enormously influenced both film making and the use of music, particularly so perhaps in animated films.

In other words, this book is a general survey, not an encyclopaedia, and it is important to apologize for the omissions dictated by the limited size of the project. Generally, the second edition follows the lines of the first, with one or two differences. There is no discography. So much film music is now available on disc, that a complete list would be unmanageable. The excellent discography in the first edition is mostly concerned with 78 rpm recordings, now obsolete in almost all cases, so we have not reprinted it here. Also, there is less musical analysis and perhaps more technical and critical discussion. Chapters have been included covering the underground and pop music.

ACKNOWLEDGEMENTS TO FIRST EDITION

THE Committee appointed by the British Film Academy to supervise the preparation of this book is responsible for the main arguments which it expresses. Members of the Committee have made individual contributions which are acknowledged in the text. Ken Cameron wrote that part of Section 4 which describes the practice of sound recording, and Muir Mathieson the description in the same section of the work of the Music Director in this country. John Huntley was in particular responsible for the film music analyses which make up a great deal of the book. Wherever possible these analyses have been made with the help and advice of the composer.

The Committee owes a deep debt of gratitude to the many composers who have assisted in the preparation of this book, and in particular to Sir Arthur Bliss, Sir William Walton, Dr. Vaughan Williams, Malcolm Arnold, Elisabeth Lutyens, Eric Williams, Louis Levy, L. Applebaum, Dag Wiren, Roman Vlad, Aaron Copland, David Raksin, Max Steiner, Hugo Friedhofer, Virgil Thomson, Miklos Rozsa and Bernard Herrmann. The Committee would also like to thank the recordists who gave their advice on Section 3 of the book, and in particular E. A. Drake. Gerald Pratley of the Canadian Broadcasting Corporation gave invaluable help in providing information for the list of disc recordings at the end of the volume, and has contributed a note on the consideration of film music apart from the screen.

Acknowledgement should also be made to the following writers, publishing houses and journals for permission to quote from material published by them: Messrs. Allen and Unwin (*The History of the British Film, 1906–14*, by Rachael Low), Sampson Low (*Music for the Movies*, by Louis Levy), Faber and Faber (*Film Music*, by Kurt London, *Secrets of Nature* by Mary Field and Percy Smith, and *Film* by Rudolf Arnheim), Victor Gollancz (*Voyage to Purilia*, by Elmer Rice), Longmans, Green & Co. (*Celluloid*, by Paul Rotha), Denis Dobson (*Cocteau on the Film* and Hanns Eisler's *Composing for the Films*), Phoenix House (*Came the Dawn*, by Cecil Hepworth) and also the Editors of *Cinema Quarterly*, *Film Music*, and the Journal of the Society of Motion Picture Engineers. Permission was given by Marion Leigh for material published by the late Walter Leigh to be reproduced; Mrs. Derek Hudson, daughter of Norman O'Neill, allowed us to quote from a paper published by her father in the *Proceedings of the Musical Association*; and the Society of Authors gave permission for the quotations made from Bernard Shaw's writings.

Finally, the Committee wishes to acknowledge the help it has received from the following Production and Distribution Companies in the preparation of special cine-frame stills used for the illustration of Section 4: the J. Arthur Rank Organization, British Lion Films, Ltd., Metro-Goldwyn-Mayer and the Robert Flaherty Foundation.

13

ACKNOWLEDGEMENTS TO SECOND EDITION

THE co-authors of the second edition are grateful to Ken Cameron for revising and updating the section on sound recording; Kenneth Wright for updating the section on performed opera, ballet and symphonies; Stan Hayward for writing the section on animated films since 1955; and Philip Malbon for hand-copying from the composers' original manuscrips the musical quotations from *The Devils* and *Second Best*.

Acknowledgments for quotations are due to:

Sight and Sound. Ted Gilling's interview with Bernard Herrmann.

Royal College of Music Magazine. Extracts from "Why Film Music?" by Kennethe V. Jones.

Hitchcock, by Francis Truffaut, A. D. Peters & Co.

The Making of Feature Films—A Guide, Ivan Bulter, Penguin.

Films and Filming. Gordon Gow's interview with Ken Russell.

National Film Theatre. Quotes from David Curtis and Simon Field.

Stills from *The Devils* are reproduced with the permission of Warner Brothers—Columbia.

The help and advice of the following is also greatly appreciated: Peter Maxwell Davies, Ermanno Comuzio, David Heneker, Tristram Cary, Steve Dartnell, Norman Spenser, Bryan Forbes, John Addison, Satyajit Ray, Gavin Bryars, and Mike Leigh.

1

MUSIC AND THE SILENT FILM

THERE has always been some form of association between music and the presentation of drama. A flute-player accompanied the classical Greek tragedy and comedy, entering the orchestra area with the actors of the chorus. The music he played was essentially simple, and completely subordinate to the speaking of the poetry. Plutarch refers to music in Greek drama as a kind of seasoning or relish. He could well have been describing certain forms of musical composition for the film some twenty-two centuries later.

Music and the Drama

When the theatre of the Renaissance began the development of modern drama which was to remain virtually unbroken to the present time, the place of music in dramatic production varied considerably with the form taken by the drama itself.[1] Music was obviously an integral part of the Elizabethan masque and of the operas first developed in Italy during the eighteenth century. But music, though present, could be completely divorced from the production itself, acting as an interlude or bridge during intervals in the performance, as it often does in the contemporary theatre. As drama began to free itself from poetry and the representation of heroic action, the need for music lessened, and the theatre began to become a place where the dialogue of the best plays was most often written in prose.

[1] An early example of what was apparently a most effective piece of incidental music was that noted by Samuel Pepys in February 1668 when he attended a performance of Dekker's and Massinger's *The Virgin Martyr* at the King's Theatre in London. ". . . *But that which did please me beyond anything in the whole world was the wind-musique when the angel comes down, which is so sweet that it ravished me, and, indeed in a word, did wrap up my soul so that it made me really sick, just as I have formerly been when in love with my wife, that neither then, not all the evening going home, and at home, I was able to think of anything, but remained all night transported, so that I could not believe that ever any music hath that real command over the soul of a man as this did upon me; and makes me resolve to practice wind-musique, and to make my wife do the like.*"

15

The film, however, began its development as a form of public entertainment at the end of the nineteenth century, during which the popular drama had sunk to a comparatively low level from which the dramas of Ibsen, Tchekov and Shaw, among others, were eventually to raise it by creating a new kind of theatre that at first appealed only to the intelligentsia. But the cinema was not catering for audiences of this kind, and it took its cue from the main forms of popular entertainment established during the nineteenth century. These included, in addition to the old-time music hall, melodramas of the sort represented by *East Lynne, The Lyons Mail, The Corsican Brothers* and *The Bells*. Spectacular productions of Shakespeare were put on by actor-managers who, whether they were great artists or merely barnstormers, knew that if Shakespeare's plays were to appeal to the popular taste, they needed a good deal of "dressing" in the way of striking presentation and the addition of the powerful emotional stimulant provided by what was called incidental music. Music was often specially composed to fit the dramatic needs of the stage, being used as a kind of emotional prop at salient moments in plays.

By the time the cinema was born, the pianist and the orchestra had been long established in the living theatre, quite apart from their essential work in musical comedy, operatic productions and vaudeville. In many significant ways the work of composition for the drama of the nineteenth century anticipated composition for the sound film. In the published *Proceedings of the Musical Association* for 1910–11 a paper by Norman O'Neill[1] on *Music to Stage Plays* provides us with an authoritative statement on the work of the theatre composer of the nineteenth and early twentieth centuries by a man who himself wrote many scores for plays. Much of what he says at this time is applicable to composition for films today. After stressing the close link between the composer and the theatre in the past, and particularly in the case of the Shakespearean theatre, O'Neill claims that it was Kean and Irving who were chiefly responsible for bringing distinguished composers into the theatre of the middle and later nineteenth century. Kean commissioned Hatton to compose for his Shakespearean productions, while Irving com-

[1]Norman O'Neill was the most celebrated theatrical composer of his day, working in the theatre from 1901 to his death at the early age of 58 in 1934. Had he lived, he would undoubtedly have composed music for the films; indeed a few months before his death Leslie Howard suggested to him that he might provide the score for *Smilin' Through*. His most famous theatrical compositions were those for *The Blue Bird, Mary Rose, A Kiss for Cinderella* and *Kismet*. He was musical director at the Theatre Royal, Haymarket, for over twenty years. A biography by his son-in-law, Derek Hudson, was published in 1945.

missioned German, Sullivan, Elgar, Parry, Stanford and Coleridge-Taylor for various of his productions.

O'Neill differentiates between three kinds of music for the theatre—interlude music, incidental music and special composition. Interlude music was used for bridging scenes and for performance during intervals. Incidental music included dances, marches, songs, "melodrames" (that is, music played behind speeches—for example, in the long monologue which forms the climax to *The Bells*), and motifs like a tremolo on the appearance of the villain or a sentimental theme for the heroine.

But it is the specially composed scores commissioned by the theatrical managers which excite O'Neill's imagination and which most clearly parallel in requirement and technique those composed nowadays for films. This will be seen in the passages quoted below. Meanwhile, we should note the terms in which he attacks the elementary "melodrame" music played while the actor spoke, with its primitive rendering of eight-bar phrases that were repeated until the actor had reached the end of his speech.

> The music is simply called in to bolster up the weakness of the drama. It is used to stimulate (by what I may call unfair means) the imagination of the audience, and to help the actor in what for him might be some rather dangerous moments. It is supposed to be easier for an actor to "hold" his audience under these conditions than it is when he has to do all the work himself. This is one of the reasons why this type has survived so long. I do not think audiences particularly care for it, for I have a high opinion of the theatre public; it is the actor who clings to this tradition of melodrama. Luckily we do not get much of it in our first-class theatres, but if one goes to the suburbs and provinces one will still find it, and I am afraid it will die hard.

The result of O'Neill's first ten years' experience is concentrated into his short paper for the Musical Association, in which he claims that:

> The composer today, who has knowledge and experience, will find much sympathy, intelligence, and understanding for his work in the theatre as he will elsewhere. Music is no longer treated in the haphazard way it was formerly, and every musical effect will be as carefully prepared and rehearsed as the rest of the performance.

O'Neill writes as follows about the correct procedure to be adopted when a special score is required for a play:

> When a play in which the music is to be an important feature is to be put upon the stage, the composer usually meets the author and the producer and discusses where it will be advisable to introduce music. The producer or "metteur en scène" of a play draws up a plan of the whole action in every detail, the scenic effects, and so forth, which he intends to employ. These will greatly determine the spirit and atmosphere of the production. It is not

17

enough for a composer only to know the play through and through, but he must also be in close touch with the exact spirit in which the work is to be given.

Where music is to accompany the dialogue he must, before writing any music, know the tempo of the speeches, the pauses and business to be introduced, so that his music may coincide in the minutest detail with the stage rendering of the play. He will otherwise find his musical effects clashing or coming in the wrong place. Where music accompanies the action and there is no dialogue, as for instance in a procession or entrances of characters, most careful adjustment is necessary, the producer and composer working together and arranging the time that any such effect or business will take on the stage. Where there is no dialogue, the stage business should be timed to the music. Where there is dialogue the music should be timed to the stage.

The composer should be in touch with the producer when the whole production is worked out on paper, and then make his own scheme of the music. The difficulties are many, and unless the composer is in sympathy with the producer the chances of a successful result are very small. It is essential they should work together and understand exactly the effects they each desire to obtain.

Of the special problems of putting music to speech, O'Neill writes:

The musical accompaniment to a speech should steal in and steal out so quietly, that the audience are no more aware of it than they are of some subtle change in the stage lighting. Bizet is most successful in his treatment of the melodrama in *L'Arlesienne*, the music often beginning with one or two pianissimo violin notes con sordini and fading away in the same way. I do not wish to give you the impression that in music for the stage melody has no place. On the contrary, no successful incidental music (or any other for that matter) can be devoid of melody and thematic material. I only feel that clearly defined tunes in conjunction with the dialogue are out of place. When a running accompaniment of music is required for a long stretch of dialogue, the exact time of each speech, the pauses, entrances, and exits, must all be carefully measured.

In illustration of this I will quote from a manuscript of a play to which I wrote the music. The scene opens with an Irish folk-song, at the close of which there are two lines of dialogue (twenty seconds) then a phrase of the song again, four lines of dialogue, at the end of which there is some business (half a minute), and so on. In this way I was able to time my music to the scene, throughout the whole of which music was played.

As soon as the actors were word-perfect we rehearsed with the pianoforte, and so the music grew with the production. Even if they took a sentence a shade faster or slower it was an easy matter to accompany them so long as they kept to the originally arranged scheme of pauses and business. Of course, final touches are always made at rehearsal, and for that reason it is as well to have as many rehearsals with pianoforte as possible before the play is taken with orchestra.

On a later occasion, Norman O'Neill re-read his paper, and added in manuscript an interesting note (which we quote by courtesy of Mr. and Mrs. Derek Hudson) on the various unusual combinations of instruments which the theatrical composer should be prepared to use to achieve specific effects. Again, one feels how remarkably he anticipated the practice of the imaginative composer of film music:

I cannot lay down any hard and fast rule as the character of music to be written should decide for the composer what combination of instruments is necessary to obtain the required effect. In *Mary Rose* 5 violin, 2 vla., 2 vc., 1 bass, oboe and flute, clarinet, harp and piano, a 16×8 ft. organ pipe, 3 voices and a saw! For a play of another type even some brass might be essential, and then much tact and skill must be used in scoring or the balance will go by the board. A modern musician will find plenty of opportunity for using his imagination and invention in spite of and perhaps because of the necessary limitations connected with the writing and performance of music for the stage.

It is not without interest that George Bernard Shaw, in a lecture he gave in the same year to the Musical Association, and which is recorded in the same volume as O'Neill's paper, spoke with great respect for the "tradesman" composer who works in the theatre. What he says applies equally well to the position of the composer in the film studio today:

> Until a composer has learnt how to turn out music to order for other people and for practical use, he will not be able to turn out work to his own order, no matter how many exercises he may have laboured through. And though this generation has many more opportunities of hearing orchestral music, and even of practising it, than existed thirty years ago, it is still true that the theatre is the only place where a young man who aspires to mastery of the orchestra can make himself what I call a real tradesman.

He had equal respect for the good musical director, or theatre conductor:

> In the theatre, when I want a piece of music for a certain purpose, I can get it. If I want it a certain length, I can get it exactly that length. If in the course of rehearsal I want it altered to suit some change in the stage business of my play, I can get the alteration made. The conductor does not say that his inspiration cannot be controlled in this way, and that he must work his movement out as his genius prompts him and as its academic form demands. He does not tell me that he cannot do what I want without eight horns and four tubas, half-a-dozen drums and a contra fagotto. He has to do it with one oboe generally. He is really master of his materials, and can adapt them at a moment's notice to any set of circumstances that is at all practicable. And it is precisely because he can do these small things when other people want them that, if he has talent enough, he can do great things when he himself wants them. This is the way of the true master.

The Early Cinema
(1895–1910)

When they were first commercially exhibited to the public, motion pictures were associated with cafés, fairgrounds, vaudeville theatres as well as lecture-halls. Ten years and more were to pass before the film began to establish itself as a specifically dramatic form of entertainment, though short action films were, of course, being made much earlier than this. The cinema, in fact, took some years to discover its potentialities, and until that time was satisfied to develop

19

its short topical and "interest" subjects, its travelogues, vaudeville turns and trick films, its short comedies, farces and melodramas as a side-show to other kinds of public entertainment.

Cecil Hepworth describes his own first tentative efforts as film-showman and lecturer, with his sister at the piano:

> I remember one little series which always went down very well indeed. It was called *The Storm* and consisted of half a dozen slides and one forty-foot film. My sister Effie was a very good pianist and she travelled with me on most of these jaunts. The sequence opened with a calm and peaceful picture of the sea and sky. Soft and gentle music (Schumann, I think). That changed to another seascape, though the clouds looked a little more interesting, and the music quickened a bit. At each change the inevitability of a coming gale became more insistent and the music more threatening; until the storm broke with an exciting film of dashing waves bursting into the entrance of a cave, with wild music (by Jensen, I think).[1]

Percival Mackey is perhaps typical of those who have recorded some impressions of the days of primitive presentation. At the age of fourteen, he became pianist to a fairground touring show which included, in one programme, a ventriloquist, a conjurer, a slapstick comedy act and a short film. The projector was operated by hand from the middle of the centre aisle in the showman's tent and a primitive illumination system was driven by two portable gas cylinders. Mackey received 2s. 6d. a week to provide a largely improvised piano accompaniment to the whole show.

Later, he joined the Royal Irish Animated Picture Company Grand Orchestra in Tipperary, organized by an early pioneer of the late 1900's, Arthur Jameson. The orchestra consisted of a circus trumpeter, aged 72, a drunken Irish fiddler of 45, and Mackey, now 18, on the piano; this group was occasionally augmented for special effects by a harmonium. The company provided a touring film show, which usually set up in village halls for one night only, and a great deal of improvisation took place, due to the absence of any kind of rehearsal. Subsequently, he took work as a cinema pianist at such sites in London as the Blue Halls, Harrow Road, and the Electric, Brick Lane, Aldgate (where it was customary for the conductor to swear loudly whenever one of the six musicians comprising the orchestra made an error).

From the very start, therefore, the vacuum of silence had to be filled by musical accompaniment, partly to distract the attention of the audience from the ugly mechanical clatter of the projector, and partly because the very liveliness of the action in the primitive silent films appeared unnatural and ghostly without some

---

[1] *Came the Dawn, Memories of a Film Pioneer*, by Cecil M. Hepworth.

20

form of sound corresponding to such visual vitality. When the Lumière family first tested the commercial value of their earliest films in the Grand Café on the Boulevard des Capucines on 28th December 1895 a piano accompanied the screening. Trewey gave the first public performance in Britain of the Lumière programme at the Polytechnic in Regent Street, London on 20th February 1896. Cecil Hepworth told the story, based on a statement made to him by Birt Acres, that the harmonium from the chapel of the Polytechnic was brought in and played during the screening. By April 1896 orchestras were accompanying the films exhibited at the Empire and the Alhambra music-halls.

It should not be overlooked that Edison first became interested in the potential commercial value of moving pictures when he thought that the public might be amused by watching the artistes whom he recorded for his phonograph give a synchronized performance in the motion picture. Throughout the period of the silent film there were constant attempts to link phonograph and gramophone recordings with moving pictures.[1]

In Britain, for example, in 1900 *Little Tich and his Big Boots* was produced with an accompanying gramophone disc, and afterwards films with sound were made of artistes such as Vesta Tilley, Lil Hawthorn and Alec Hurley. There are records of a 46-minute version of *Faust* and, indeed, many hundreds of these synchronized films were made during the first ten years or so of the century, all based on commercial gramophone records.

The Special Relationship between Music and the Silent Film

It was, however, through the live performer in the orchestra pit of the picture palace that music began to develop a direct and even creative relationship with the silent film. It is not without significance that the first important introduction of the composer to the film world came at the same time as the film began to associate itself with the theatre. In 1908 a company known as Le Film d'Art was founded in Paris, partly under the influence of Charles Pathé, in order to encourage famous actors of the theatre to appear in films derived from equally famous plays. The Académie Française and

[1]Throughout the silent period various gramophone sychronizers were developed for use with films. The first in Britain was the Chronophone, demonstrated at the London Hippodrome in 1904. Edison and Pathé also developed synchronizers, and later, in 1907, Hepworth's company launched the Vivaphone, which was successful for many years in producing short films of music-hall turns, limited in length by the playing-time of the gramophone disc. The quality of the sound remained poor, and the advancing technique of the film soon made it desirable for full-length productions to be accompanied by piano and orchestra.

the Comédie Française supported the idea, and the first production made by this company was *L'Assassinat du Duc de Guise* with a script by the Academician Henri Lavedan. Camille Saint-Saëns was invited to compose a special score for this film; it became his Opus 128 for strings, piano and harmonium, and consisted of an Introduction and five Tableaux, each part being carefully cued for the film.

In 1909 the first sheets of "suggestions for music" of which we have a record were issued with a number of Edison's films. In *The History of the British Film* 1906–14, Rachael Low writes:

The important music of the period was that of the piano, and it was here that artistic intentions were most clearly expressed. But although good advice to pianists was abundant as that to aspiring plot writers, for some years there was far too little effort to fit suitable music to the pictures. With the pianist playing from 2 to 11 p.m. for his 25s. or 30s. a week, and frequently doing odd jobs in the mornings, it was hardly surprising if an occasional comic rattled through to the sound of Schumann's *Träumerei*, or scenes of winter sports to Mendelssohn's *Spring Song*. Some earned more, particularly those good at improvisation, and £3 10s. a week is mentioned in one place; on the other hand a young girl might earn as little as 15s. Under such conditions many pianists had no money to buy new music and no time to learn new pieces, or even to see the films in advance of the first performance.

In addition to the pianos there were orchestras in the more prosperous halls, and automatic musical instruments with names which proclaim the same search for impressive showmanship as those of the picture palaces which housed them —the Clavitist-Violina, the Cinfonium, Cinechordeon, Biokestra and Orchestrion. The outburst of organs, zithers and bells from about 1910 onwards was considered marvellously artistic. At the same time the appearance of large and expensive machines for providing sound effects made many showmen enthusiastic participators in the artistic success of the films. The Allefex machine, put on the English market at £29. 15s. by A. & H. Andrews, in late 1909, included running water, breaking china and puffing engines in its many accomplishments, but was hardly more ambitious than the humble "artiste in effects" who sought realism with sandpaper and a tin tray.

The emotional value of "realistic" sound effects, like the emotional importance of the right kind of music, became an issue as a result of the well-intentioned efforts of the picture theatre staffs. Effects were to remain in their hands. But by the end of this period both renters and producers were taking a larger part in suggestions for music and even, for more important features and exclusives, provided music which had been specially composed.

These attempts to create a link between musical accompaniment and the mood and action of the film were by no means universal in the picture palaces which, by 1910, had begun to take over motion picture entertainment for the public. Louis Levy in his memoirs[1] recollects how the little cinema orchestras round the period 1912 were quite satisfied to play selections of light café music quite unrelated to the film on the screen—and, after a given period of the

[1]*Music for the Movies*, p. 12.

William Tell Overture, Rubinstein and Tchaikovsky, get up and leave the film and its audience to the deathly hush of silence. The producers of the films might agitate for a showmanlike presentation of their work, but in the end it was the exhibitor who determined how far the music was to be either a true part of the performance, or merely a polite embellishment to fill the embarrassing vacuum of silence relieved only by the half-muffled clicking of the projector.

The next stage was quite simply for the conductor, with his eye on the screen, to instruct his orchestra what particular selection he wanted while the film progressed, the pianist improvising as the players hastily turned the sheets on their music-stands. William Alwyn has the following amusing recollections of when, as a boy, he joined the players of a provincial cinema orchestra:

My flute teacher, the only one available in the provincial town where I was born, earned his living as a factory hand during the daytime and professionally as a musician in the evenings at the local "Picture Palace". My progress was so rapid that at the early age of eleven (this would be in 1916) I was taken "for the experience" (much against my Mother's wishes, who thought it beneath the family dignity) to sit with my teacher during an evening film performance and add my immature pipings to the general ensemble.

I waited for him outside the cinema, a small boy with a flute-case anxiously tucked under the arm, and punctually he arrived, scrubbed clean and very much alert, after his long day in the boot factory. We entered by a side door and stumbled into the auditorium, ducked under the curtain that screened the pianist from the audience, and here we were in a new world—a world that was to provide so much of absorbing interest for me as a composer in the future.

One by one the band arrived, the violin-leader, the cornet and the cello (this was our modest array) each nodding a brief acknowledgement to the pianist who continued rattling on with his musical accompaniment to the film with a nonchalance and skill that amazed me then and still, looking back over the years, seems a formidable accomplishment. In front of me on the music stand was a thick stack of music; *Poet and Peasant* and *Zampa* were in the better class, but a general stand-by was the works of a certain Kéla Béla (I think that was the name) whose music even then seemed to me to combine prodigality with the commonplace to a quite remarkable degree. There was, of course, a mixed bag of sentimental favourites and an album of specially composed film music designed to meet any known situation. Also on the desk was a piece marked *Theme* which I was told by my mentor to keep separate from the rest and at a given signal from the leader (two raps on the desk?) to abandon whatever piece I was playing and dive abruptly into this special theme.

At last, after much furtive tuning and whispering, we were all ready and the the leader at an appropriate moment lifted his bow, and off we started on the first piece on the desk. I was just beginning to get under way when another signal from the violinist left me stranded in mid-air (or mid-blow!) as my teacher expertly and rapidly whipped over the pages into the next piece in order on the desk and off we went again at a different tempo and so on till the next signal. It was a game of hare and hounds with one small terrier puffing well in the rear. The essential link in the performance was the pianist who bound this hotch-potch of music together with his rapid modulations and improvised chords.

23

It was some years before I repeated this breathless performance and then I was a young professional musician in London. By that time the art of fitting music to a picture had been brought to a high pitch of efficiency and in the big London cinemas, which employed expert orchestras of symphonic dimensions, more often than not, considerable time and taste had been spent in selecting appropriate music and the signalling for a change of piece was done by ingenious coloured lights on the music desk.

But the "Picture Palace" pianist of my childhood remained for long my hero—which speaks much for an early appreciation of genuine professional skill!

Another future composer for the films, this time an American, David Raksin, remembers a cinema orchestra in Philadelphia:

My father conducted music for the silent movies—usually scores compiled from the various kinothek libraries; but when necessary he would compose music for part of a film himself. As a boy, I sat beside him during Saturday matinées in the orchestral pit of the old Metropolitan Opera House in Philadelphia, and even in those days I talked of making film composition my profession.

Musical Arrangements and Special Scores

As the cinema grew in popularity, orchestras grew in size, gradually filling the orchestra pit beneath the screen in the converted music-halls and theatres which had "gone over to pictures". The music became a feature of the show in the bigger cinemas, and the Music Directors and Conductors held responsible and well-paid positions in the world of commercial music, often giving concert performances of light classical selections during intervals in the programme. Those who took their specialized profession seriously studied each film before it was screened for the public, and either arranged their own series of musical items chosen to fit the film or followed those supplied at extra fee by the producers of the more important productions.

One of the first examples of a score most carefully conceived for a film presentation which became in itself a great occasion was Griffith's musical arrangement for *Birth of a Nation*.

Birth of a Nation was given its *première* at the Liberty Theatre, New York, in March 1915. It was presented twice a day at fixed times and was divided into two "acts" with a standard theatrical interval between the two parts. Exhibition took place chiefly in well-established theatres, with the full orchestral facilities being used to perform what was rightly described as the first film to be accompanied by a "full orchestral score", built on symphonic lines. Thus, in London, the initial shows took place at the Scala and at Drury Lane Theatre.

The score itself was the joint work of D. W. Griffith (who had studied composition in Louisville and New York) and a composer and orchestral leader named Joseph Carl Briel. It consisted of an elaborately orchestrated assembly of original material; a mass of short, sometimes mixed quotations from Grieg, Wagner, Tchaikowsky, Rossini, Beethoven, Lizst, Verdi and the full range of "non-copyright" composers; and various well-known traditional tunes of the United States such as *Dixie* and *The Star-Spangled Banner*.

Examples of original music by Griffith and Briel included a prominent love-theme (for the Little Colonel and Elsie Stoneman).[1]

Another special section involved the Clan call, a strange sound produced on reed-whistles and horns, which was used as the Ku-Klux-Klan motif throughout the second part of the picture, sometimes in combination with other material such as quotations from Wagner's *Ride of the Valkyrie*, elements of *Dixie* and sound effects of galloping horses during the Ride of the Clansmen in the last two reels. There was also a special theme for the villainies of Austin Stoneman and Silas Lynch, a comparable musical line for the rise of the Negroes to power and an opening theme used for the historical sketch of the bringing of the African Negro to America. Scenes of the evacuation of Atlanta were accompanied by a setting of Grieg's *In the Hall of the Mountain Kings* from *Peer Gynt*.

Cueing was unusually elaborate and some of the more closely-scored scenes began to approach the techniques later developed in sound film recording. A series of scenes involving Lynch and Colonel Cameron, occupying two pages of the piano-conductor score (moderato) gave the following cues:

> Lynch's second time with Colonel.
> As Lynch's arm crosses chest.
> Offers hand second time.
> Lynch exits.
> Title "Lynch the traitor".
> Lynch swearing.
> The Union League Rally.
> Eye in door.
> Wait for door close.
> Lynch at speaker's table second time.
> First time: If I don't.
> Picture.

Although somewhat vague words out-of-context, the film composer of today will have no difficulty in recognizing the technique of the

---

[1] This tune underwent a strong transition when it was purchased outright from the Epoch Producing Corporation—Griffith's own company—and was re-orchestrated to become the signature tune of the *Amos and Andy* programme, originally a sound radio show and later a regular television production.

single "prompting" phrases which suggest the care that lay behind the preparation of the score.

The score for *Birth of a Nation* was a pastiche that, musically speaking, merits little attention today; historically, it set standards of orchestration and technique that were to remain in force throughout the silent period or until such time as the serious contemporary composer was willing to recognize the possibilities for sound in the new art that Griffith had so firmly established on the visual plane.

Griffith, however, was exceptional in his meticulous desire to achieve the right dramatic effect through the music he selected. For the most part, pianists and conductors of film orchestras had to piece together their own musical selections. To help them in this task, volumes of classified "mood" music began to appear as early as 1913, when the Sam Fox Moving Picture Music Volumes by J. S. Zamecnik were published.

The best-known of the many libraries of cinema music which appeared for use during the fifteen years left to the silent film after Zamecnik's publications was Giuseppe Becce's *Kinobibliothek* (or *Kinothek*, as it was called), first published in Berlin in 1919. This brought together many pieces of descriptive music, classified for mood and style, and often specially composed for the purpose by Becce himself. A feature of this library was the manner in which established pieces of music were re-arranged to adjust them to the requirements of collective use.

Even pieces which were characteristic in themselves could have their nature transformed in the melting-pot of compilation. There arose a new style, which absorbed all the earlier individuality of the single pieces in favour of a new collective character. This went so far that even the rhythm, tempo, key, form, instrumentation, and actually the melody of a piece of music had to be re-modelled.

This arbitrary treatment made the use of renowned works of great masters, which appeared in increasingly large quantities in the repertoires of film musicians, a knotty problem indeed. On the one hand, serious music was indispensable; on the other hand, often enough it was not allowed to retain its own character. Change it its form was the least significant thing which could happen to it.[1]

Louis Levy, whose experience in cinema orchestras began before the first World War, writes in his autobiography *Music for the Movies*:

The first real step taken towards the development of a true technique of music for the movies was started by films being given a preview to the conductor (or as he was sometimes ingloriously known, the "fitter"), with the object of making some attempt at fitting the music to the mood of the film to

[1]*Film Music* by Kurt London, p. 54.

be shown. Things began to happen immediately this need for such artistic synchronization became apparent. I personally would see a film several times to fit an appropriate musical accompaniment. During this period the exhibition side of the industry was growing enormously, palatial "picture houses" were springing up all over the country, often in converted shops, The boom in "pictures" had begun, and larger orchestras were being introduced. The whole cinema industry was taking shape as a respectable place of entertainment . . .

Music publishers began to notice the new field of development open to them, and some of the more enterprising publishers soon engaged composers to specialize in incidental music for the film, and to compose numbers to fit all cinema moods. So there came to be some tangible commercial return for musicians who took a serious interest in the development of film music; without such a motive, of course, art atrophies.

With the aid of the classics, popular music of the day and special stock incidental music supplied by publishers, the music to silent films around the 1920's became a recognized adaptation of art. The public was quick to notice this, and the degree of ability of the local cinema's musical director to "fit" his pictures played an important part in the box-office receipts. Theme tunes were then introduced by me for the first time. It became the custom for the same piece of music to be played for the same hero or heroine, another piece for the villain, and yet another theme for the comedian!

Among the more celebrated film scores of the later silent period are those by Edmund Meisel for Eisenstein's films *The Battleship Potemkin* and *October*, by Darius Milhaud for Marcel l'Herbier's *L'Inhumaine*, by Arthur Honegger for Abel Gance's *La Roue* and *Napoleon*, and by Dmitri Shostakovitch for the Russian film *The New Babylon*.

It is one of the tragedies of film history that Meisel's scores for Eisenstein's films, perhaps the most famous of all those composed for silent productions, seem to have been irrecoverably lost. All who heard them in performance recollect their power, which led to their being banned in some cases when the films themselves were permitted to be screened without the emotional stimulus of Meisel's music.

Ernest Borneman (writing in 1934) had the following interesting comments to make on Meisel's method of scoring these silent films:

Meisel analysed the montage of some famous silent films in regard to rhythm, emphasis, emotional climax and mood. To each separate shot he assigned a certain musical theme. Then he directly combined the separate themes, using the rhythm, emphasis and climaxes of the visual montage for the organization of his music. He wished to prove by this experiment that the montage of a good film is based on the same rules and develops in the same way as music. The result of this experiment was that some so-called "good" films did not in any way produce music, but merely a chaos of various themes, unordered and unorganized. Others of the films which he chose, however, resulted in a kind of strange rhapsody, unaccustomed and extraordinary to the ear, but nevertheless not without a certain musical continuity. By far the best result was from Eisenstein's *Potemkin*. (*Sight and Sound.*)

A published copy of a piano score by Meisel has recently come to light, namely his music for Walter Ruttmann's famous documentary film *Berlin*, produced in Germany in 1927. Without showing any marked individuality, the Meisel score impresses by its highly professional approach, and by its courageous use of contemporary German idioms. It is the logical development of the silent film music accompaniment considered in the light of the contemporary music of his day. The cueing is close (a page of score is reproduced on page 58), the orchestration, judging by the indications in this piano reduction, is ambitious and scholarly, but it is the frank employment of contemporary idiomatic resources which impresses most when re-examining the score today. One can easily understand why this "new" film music made such an impact on audiences at the time.

Meisel's outstanding film score was for *The Battleship Potemkin*. Hanns Eisler makes the following comment on this composition in his book *Composing for the Films*:—

Meisel was only a modest composer, and his score is certainly not a masterpiece; however, it was non-commercial at the time it was written, it avoided the neutralizing clichés and preserved a certain striking power, however crude. Nevertheless there is not the slightest indication that its aggressiveness impaired its effectiveness to the public; on the contrary, its effectiveness was enhanced.

Music in the Film Studios

If the emotional stimulus of music was important in the presentation of films to the public, it was soon found to be equally important in the studios themselves. In a letter to the writers, Maurice Elvey, who began his career as a film director in 1913, made the practical point that music was used "in order to counteract the noise in the studios—after all, you often had two films being made on the same stage". But the chief reason for introducing music to the studios was, of course, to help the actors to create the correct mood and atmosphere in the particular scene they were playing.

In 1916 George Pearson wrote an entry in the notebooks he always kept over the years he worked as a film director: "I have come to the conclusion that every studio should possess a piano." Only by its means, he felt, could the right degree of emotion be raised in the actor, and from 1916 onwards he engaged a small staff trio to work in his studios. This trio was made up of piano, violin and viola. They had a wide repertoire of mood music, and Pearson always indicated to them in advance the kind of music he needed. The work of this little orchestra was frequently supplemented in the

28

studio by gramophone records. After the actors had been taken through a movement rehearsal before the camera, and the mechanics of the scene had been worked out, the trio was brought in to assist in the development of the emotional rendering of the scene. The music was kept very subdued, and the players were screened off. Pearson claimed to the actors that the emotional stimulus of the music affected the quality of their work tremendously, and greatly assisted in any quick change of emotion in a scene, which would be carefully timed by the musicians and reflected by an appropriate change in what they played.

George Pearson was possibly the first director to employ an orchestra in the studio, and he kept one on the permanent staff from 1916 until the sound film arrived. Music, he said to the writers, was the "emotional dialogue of the silent film". Maurice Elvey also believed in the importance of using music to help his actors. "In California," he writes, "I always had a trio even on exteriors to help with the creation of the mood." His trio was made up of piano, violin and guitar.

Anthony Asquith, however, after using a studio orchestra at Cricklewood when he made his first film *Shooting Stars* in 1927, and again for his second production *Underground*, abandoned its use altogether for his third film, *Cottage on Dartmoor* (1928), which was the kind of subject where one would have thought a studio orchestra could have been very helpful. This film was later released after the arrival of sound with a special score recorded in Berlin under the supervision of Victor Peers with every attention paid to careful synchronization with the action.

When an important film directed by Pearson was trade shown, a full orchestra was brought in. It was Pearson's practice to rehearse the film with the conductor. He often discussed with Louis Levy, who was frequently the conductor on these occasions, whether the music used in the studio during the making of the film would also be effective for its public presentation. After these discussions, a final carefully-cued musical continuity was made up, and this was distributed with the film for the guidance of the conductors of cinema orchestras. One of the most sensational trade shows George Pearson can remember was for his film, *Ultus, the Man from the Dead*, which took place early in 1916. The exhibitors were brought by charabanc from Central London to the Gaumont Studios at Shepherds Bush. There they were ushered on to one of the studio stages which was entirely hung with black drapes in the shape of a vast coffin. Every so often a voice intoned over a loud speaker the line from Dante: "Abandon hope all ye who enter here". In front of the screen at the head of the coffin was a full orchestra, and the film opened with Schubert's *Unfinished Symphony*, which was at that time little known to the general public. The effect was all that publicity could desire, and this was possibly the first occasion on which a large orchestra was brought into a film studio in Britain to accompany a film at a private presentation of this kind.

2

MUSIC IN THE EARLY SOUND FILM

THE true arrival of the sound film was the arrival of sound-on-film. This came after a brief interim period when sound was provided in the form of gramophone discs synchronized with what was really a silent picture and amplified in the theatres. In America, Warner Brothers produced *Don Juan* with music synchronized on disc, and this film had its *première* on 26th August 1926.

The First Use of Sound

The sensational demonstration of synchronized sound was, of course, *The Jazz Singer* (first shown on 6th October 1927) since it introduced in certain sequences lip-synchronized singing by Al Jolson. The cinema-going public all over the world flocked to hear Al Jolson cry: "Say, Ma, listen to this!" and launch into the hit tune of *Mammy*. The first genuine American talking film was *The Lights of New York*, shown in 1929. It was an undistinguished picture, quickly followed by others at a time when producers were anxious not to be left behind in the rush for sound.

Britain was fortunate that her first true production in sound proved to be a film of some distinction—Alfred Hitchcock's *Blackmail* (made at Elstree, and first shown in June 1929). *Blackmail* was originally shot, in its entirety, as a silent picture, but its completion coincided with the widespread use of sound in American films arriving in this country in 1929. It was therefore decided to re-shoot the picture in sound, salvaging as many shots from the original as possible, but remaking such scenes as involved synchronous dialogue or effects. The musical accompaniment had already been considered on the basis of a "live" orchestral accompaniment in the cinemas, and *Blackmail* offers a recorded example of a silent film score, with only occasional, if interesting, concessions to sound film technique. Hitchcock used his sound track most ingeniously at certain moments in the film, and especially in the famous "knife" sequence—the first instance in the history of the sound film of sound used to achieve a specific dramatic effect beyond the straight reproduction of speech. However, an analysis of the sound-track of the first reel shows how closely *Blackmail* followed silent film technique.

The first reel (about 800 feet) consists almost entirely of original silent material, with music and a few odd effects added. The British censor's certificate describes the film as "Blackmail (synchronized)". The musical score is composed of material supplied by Campbell and Connelly, compiled and arranged by Hubert Bath and Harry Stafford. It is played by the British International Symphony Orchestra conducted by John Reynders.

The music is based on a simple, four-bar dramatique[1], repeated twenty-eight times during the first reel in various guises. This descending passage is first heard in the title music under an intense string agitato, leading to the first shot of a van wheel, in full close-up, followed by shots of a Scotland Yard police van, fitted with radio. The main musical line is constantly announced on full strings or brass, as the agitato is maintained. The van stops outside the entrance to the dirty courtyard of a tenement block; two detectives enter a doorway and proceed up a flight of steps inside one of the houses. The theme is played twice on strings pizzicato, with suitable mysterioso embellishments. The wanted man is in bed. A gun is on a table near by, and a sharp chord points his attempt to seize it. He is forced to dress, and the music continues to hint at the main theme. They hustle him into the van, and drive off to a heavy restatement which is held until the police station is reached.

Scotland Yard is introduced by the central theme, this time on full orchestra. The man is taken to the inspector's office and an interrogation commences, set entirely to music; the main theme is again played, coloured by a reference to the title music agitato phrase. An identification parade follows, and then the man is taken to the Charge Room. No dialogue is spoken but, most daringly, a section of the main tune is used on full brass to synchronize with the sharp statement of the police officer and the arrested man's equally sharp reply. Finger prints are taken, and the detained man is pushed into a cell, accompanied by a heavy, melodramatic version of the last four notes of the main theme, played as a descending phrase on full brass.

The detectives go on their way to the wash-room in the Yard and we hear snatches of their conversation (un-synchronized) as they talk of family problems. The main theme slowly changes into a light-hearted, flowing form, as the two men responsible for the arrest, their job done, go off duty.

The music itself is an exact version of the kind of sound that used to accompany films in the largest West End cinemas of the late 'twenties. It is repetitive, naïve in content, highly atmospheric and based almost entirely on a simple "theme and variations" pattern. As reel one of *Blackmail* has only six sound elements in it (a flap of a van being dropped, a stone thrown through a window, car hooters, the click of a cell door, some men's chatter and the unsynchronized dialogue at the end), the music proceeds without interruption across all kinds of scenes, both with and without speech.

During the period 1929–30 other countries, including France, Germany, Italy, Sweden and Russia, made their first sound films. The first French productions with sound-track were, in fact, made in England whilst the studios in France were in process of adaptation for sound film production. The first sound film to be made in France was René Clair's *Sous les Toits de Paris* (released in 1930), again a film of distinction, with music composed by Raoul Moretti and Armand Bernard, in this case made by a director who was in theory opposed to the introduction of sound to films.

[1]A charming silent cue-sheet phrase for a "mystery" theme.

Like many film-makers who regarded the film as an art, Clair felt that sound in the form of the continuous reproduction of dialogue would rob the film of its distinction as a medium achieving all its effects visually through moving pictures. The passages he quotes in his book *Réflexion Faite*, taken from his writings at the close of the period of the silent film, constantly lament the loss of the popular poetry of the dream world of silent images and its replacement by the raw realism of the "talkie". "Words," he wrote in 1929, "used like this destroy the workings of the imagination: the presentation of actuality must be conventionalized as it is in the theatre, and was in the silent film." He soon observed that sound unlimited, unselected, becomes a bore, including sound in the form of music, which even today (he adds in an aside dated 1950) "is in the greater number of films used far too frequently and in a quite arbitrary way".

Nevertheless, Clair's first film, like Hitchcock's, made its own particular pioneer contribution to the first stages in the dramatic use of sound, for example in the remarkable sequence of the fight with knives in a back street beside a railway embankment in the middle of the night (see page 39).

Soon other sound films with imaginative direction began to be produced, such as Anthony Asquith's *Tell England*, G. W. Pabst's *Westfront 1918*, Lewis Milestone's *All Quiet on the Western Front*, and the first Russian sound film, Nikolai Ekk's *The Road to Life*. One of the first films in which music was used constructively was *The Blue Angel*, directed by Josef von Sternberg in Germany in 1931, with a score by Friedrich Hollaender.

The early sound films were of two main kinds: those which used music continuously in the manner established in the cinemas for silent films, and those that in effect dispensed with music altogether. The first kind employed synchronized music on disc and, as soon as it was technically possible, music recorded on the sound-track of the film as a continuous flow of accompaniment after the style of the cinema orchestra itself. All that the latter did, in effect, was to record and so standardize the musical background to productions which still employed the old technique of the silent film.

No one thought how tragically the new films with their recorded tracks would affect the employment of thousands of musicians who had worked in the cinema theatres. Only too often little groups of these men had to take their instruments on to the streets and beg for a living. This unforeseen result of the change-over to sound put many thousands of instrumentalists out of work in 1929, and established a more or less permanent antipathy towards any form of

33

recording in the minds of those Unions which guard the welfare of the professional musician.

The second kind of sound film used music very sparingly or not at all. At their best these new films used dialogue and sound effects with such vigour and reality that an entirely new art of motion picture-making was born—films such as *Quick Millions, The Front Page* and *Kameradschaft*. At their worst they were 100 per cent talkies—shot following shot of talking faces, or the camera placed in the theatre stall as play after play was photographed for the screen. Stars of the silent cinema who were ineffective when it came to the speaking of dialogue disappeared for ever, and actors and actresses trained in the living theatre took their places.

The film, indeed, had to be rediscovered by the film-makers. What they had now was a new dramatic medium at their disposal.

As a dramatic medium, the silent film operated in the world of the deaf-mute, supplemented by a musical accompaniment, of course, for those who could hear. Directors of imagination performed feats of technical ingenuity to imply by means of visual action or suggestion what would normally be directly conveyed by words—the titleless German film *The Last Laugh* managed to do this, but at the cost of slowing the pace of the action interminably. Characterization was reduced to terms of observation though it is true that the range possible was great in rare films like *Greed* or *The Passion of Joan of Arc*. What was most noticeable about the silent film was its otherworldliness, its dream quality, its elemental simplicity in terms of comedy, farce, melodrama, tragedy. The broad emotions of these simplified dramatic situations were underlined by the mood music played by the pianist or the orchestra, and later on the all-pervading Würlitzer organ. This is nicely suggested by Elmer Rice in *Voyage to Purilia*[1], a satire on the strange world of the movie theatre, published in 1930.

It is difficult to convey to the terrestrial reader, to whom music is an accidental and occasional phenomenon, the effect of living and moving in a world in which melody is as much a condition of life as are light and air. But let the reader try to fancy himself lapped every moment of his existence, waking or sleeping, in liquid, swooning sound, for ever rising and falling, falling and rising, and wrapping itself about him like a caressing garment. The effect is indescribable. It is like the semi-stupor of an habitual intoxication: an inebriety without intervals of either sobriety or complete unconsciousness. It is insidious and irresistible; the hardest head and the stoutest organism cannot withstand it. And I dare say that more than once in this record of Purilia, the sensitive reader will catch echoes and overtones of that omnipresent harmony; now pathetic, now gay, now ominous, now martial, now tender, but always

[1]Reproduced by kind permission of Victor Gollancz.

awakening familiar memories, always swellingly mellifluous, and always surcharged with a slight but unmistakable tremolo.

Only in the presentation of action was the silent film all-powerful —as, for example, the Russian epics like *The Battleship Potemkin*, or the American Westerns and slap-stick farces showed in their very different ways. Music could help establish the atmosphere of the places, interior and exterior, as the action moved about.

The first immediate gain in the sound film was the human voice; the second was the addition of natural sounds. It was inevitable that the film had to pass through a phase in which human speech and natural sounds were introduced for their own sakes. These were the novelty; music as such was not. The first imaginative developments were therefore almost exclusively in the realistic dialogue picture. Singing, however, merely because it combined words and music, exploited the new sound film for the public, and the musical film was soon introduced—in America and Germany particularly, and in France, as we have seen, in the films of René Clair. But most straight dramatic films, after the first relatively brief phase of a continuous synchronized musical background, tended to dispense with music as far as possible in favour of continuous dialogue.

During the first decade of the sound film, the ten years 1929–39 before the war, developments were, in fact, more rapid than they seemed at the time. The dialogue film (at its worst, the 100 per cent talkie) had to develop into the true sound film—that is, the fully-balanced production which allows the film's greatest asset, the intimate eye of the camera, to observe the action to the greatest dramatic effect, with dialogue, natural sound and music constantly in reserve to forward plot and character. The silent film had discovered the fluidity of the film's photographic form—the revealing close-shot, the build-up of successive shots through skilful editing. The true sound film needed to develop this technique farther with an equally fluid use of the sound track. Fluidity was lost in the long scenes of unbroken dialogue correct for the stage, but far too heavy and slow for the visually dynamic drama of the screenplay. In this quickly moving action, this subtle observation of the people and the places of the drama, music could play a much more intimate and a much more emotionally effective part than was possible in the continuous musical flow of the silent days. Music for the film, like the dialogue itself, needed to learn a new discipline, a new relation to the film drama, the movie, the picture screen-play. A very great deal was done in this direction in the ten years before the war, and was done in a number of film-producing countries.

35

The Early Development of the Musical Film

The early development of musical films has been described in some detail by Kurt London in his book *Film Music* (English translation, 1936). He distinguishes, in the general rush to produce musical films of many kinds during the first phase of sound, a number of different forms—the operetta (William Thiele's *Drei von der Tankstelle* and *Die Privatsekretorin*, from which the English film *Sunshine Susie* was derived), the drama with little dialogue but musical accompaniment (Clair's *Sous les Toits de Paris* and, much later, Chaplin's *Modern Times*), the transcription of opera on sound-film (which he rejects as impossible artistically), and, finally, concert-films, in which orchestras are seen in action. He makes no mention, however, of the earlier American musicals which were already establishing their own distinctive style with *Broadway Melody*, *King of Jazz* and *Forty-Second Street*.

Sunshine Susie (1931), featuring Jack Hulbert, was one of the more successful British musicals, as well as one of the first to be made in this country. Hollywood techniques of "shooting to playback" were not yet in use, and the songs were recorded at the same time as they were filmed. The conditions for recording in the studios at that time have been vividly described for us by Louis Levy, who was musical director for the production:

We were soon to find the difficulties caused by shooting the film and recording the sound simultaneously. Quite apart from many practical difficulties, there was the major artistic point that the artist on the set and the band perhaps twenty yards away off set were so divided that the performance suffered. The tonal quality in some cases was appalling owing to the poor acoustic conditions caused by the presence of so much paraphernalia in the studio.

In silent film days we had all the apparatus we needed in the studios, with miles of cables, banks of arcs, and great screens (known in the industry as "niggers") to reflect light and help shadow effects. These screens played the very devil with the sound, and artists who came to us after some experience in the BBC studios of those days (which, goodness knows, were primitive enough compared with studios today) were aghast to discover that we had made almost no provision for damping reverberation. Sound waves could echo and re-echo among the complex battens, flies and stage-like contraptions of the film studio.

Of course, it was untrue that we had not visualized such difficulties, but the various factors which combine in the production of a film even under ideal conditions do result in the process never being easy. There is too big an army of men and machinery to muster for the whole thing to be trouble-free. It was just that film studios already have become so complex that we subconsciously jibbed at adding to their equipment. Already things were too complicated.

During those pioneer days it was an exception for film camera and sound-recording apparatus to work simultaneously without one or the other breaking down. Just to record one song I have had to work for twenty-four hours, battling with almost every sort of mechanical, studio, and finally human tendency to break down! Things are so much easier today that we forget, some of us, what a strain it was for the first artist in sound films. There is a lot of nonsense spoken about acting temperament and strain, but this sort of studio strain does introduce a new factor which can leave its mark even on a hardened and experienced artist.

Screen stars in the first days of sound films had to watch their marks of limitation (chalked marks on the studio floor, or memorized lines of limitation in relation to the camera and microphone), memorize their action and sing, all at the same time. The nerve strain must have left its mark on some of our pioneer musical stars.

When shooting a song, for instance, we never enjoyed the luxury of running the whole thing through. Instead, we did it in the old silent manner of cutting after a few seconds of recording, to get a new camera position. After the first few bars the director would shout "Cut". Then a new set-up with new positions would be given, and then we would shoot and record a few more bars.

That is how the whole thing was done until completion—a fairly hopeless condition as anybody who has seen a modern movie in production will know. But you must remember that in those days some of the people had already had about twenty years' experience of silent film-making, and they could not at once see how or why those methods needed scrapping in favour of a new method which even then was only just in process of evolution.

In *Sunshine Susie* even the incidental music was made in this bar-by-bar fashion. When we had decided on a piece of music to accompany any one scene, the band would play off-set while the actor went through his actions or lines in time with the music. All the time, through one short scene, it was "cut"—"cut" —"cut". It is a wonder that we ever managed to produce anything at all. But we did, with much use of celluloid, electricity, time and temper—and money. The last factor did not matter much, for despite all our worries and all my insomnia, these early efforts were good box-office.

One of the first films to break the standard "song-and-dance" routine of the back-stage musical was the German production *Congress Dances* (1931). Using the play-back method, Erik Charell shot Werner Richard Heymann's song *Just once for all Time*, in which Lilian Harvey rides in a carriage through the city streets and on to the Royal Palace. First, the melody is foreshadowed during the track-in to the glove shop where Crystal works as an assistant. She describes her adventures with the Prince on the previous evening, but the other shop-girls are sceptical and laugh at her scornfully. As the girls are fighting at one end of the shop, a messenger arrives from the Palace with a command to take her to the Prince. "Your carriage awaits," he announces. Crystal steps into the carriage amid the surprised and envious stares of her friends. The main melody starts again and the carriage moves off.

There follows a continuous tracking shot lasting in all for 2 minutes 22 seconds, during which the carriage travels through part of the town, past a market place, under an archway and up to the outskirts of the city. Crystal sings the whole of *Just once for all Time*, and the crowd begins to join in. The remainder of the sequence takes Crystal over a river bridge, across the open country, into the

Palace grounds, across the entrance hall, up the staircase, into two large rooms, and on to the ceremonial bed prepared in her honour. The music is continuous throughout, often with synchronous lyrics. Some idea of the fluidity of the whole effect may be obtained from the following shot list:

1. Long track, mostly in medium or medium-close shot, with one large pull-back during the market-place scene.
2. The carriage comes out of the city; an oblique view, as the horses break into frame, followed by the carriage.
3. A long track as the carriage heads out towards the country.
4. A medium shot of the carriage, with Crystal singing.
5. The carriage passes over a bridge across a river; groups of boys and girls pick up the song as it goes by.
6. The carriage passes a group of girls washing clothes in the river; they pick up the song.
7. The carriage crosses the sky-line, whilst groups of lovers are seen on the banks of the river in the foreground. They also pick up the thread of the song.
8. The carriage passes across the sky-line in long shot.
9. The carriage passes a crowd dancing in the woods to the sound of an organ-grinder's music; they perform to the main theme song.
10. The carriage passes through the gates of the Palace; Crystal is still singing.
11. The carriage swings round in front of the Palace and stops. The music picks up the theme gaily as Crystal enters the Palace. The camera pulls back as she comes through the main doors.
12. Footmen bow as Crystal comes into the hall; she swings gaily round them, still moving to the theme tune, which is now on orchestra alone.
13. The camera cranes across the hall as she waltzes up to the steps.
14. From the top of the stairs, Crystal swings into view; the camera pulls back to follow follow her to the main reception room.
15. Crystal enters in long shot, whirls round, sits for a moment at a desk, leaps up, crosses to where a little monkey is sitting in a cage on the wall (the camera follows all the movements, ending in close shot). The music continues throughout, setting the pace for both camera and actress.
16. Crystal at a window; she throws it open.
17. Long shot of the grounds below; a large crowd of children is dancing and singing the main theme in a sunlit garden.
18. Crystal moves away from the window and explores the room still further; she finds another door and goes through.
19. Crystal enters the bedroom. A line of maids pull back curtains to reveal a vast wardrobe. The camera follows as she goes to a fine dressing table. Still moving to music, she runs out of frame right.
20. The camera is already craning in and down as Crystal leaps on a magnificent bed. She jumps up and down to the pointing of two large drum beats, and finally throws herself up in the air, landing with a thud in the mass of soft pillows and rich eider-downs. The music rises to a climax as the camera cranes to a close shot of her happy face. Fade Out.

The imaginative use of the play-back method to achieve the maximum freedom of movement during the delivery of a main theme song was well demonstrated in this early example from the UFA studios.

René Clair's early sound films, as Kurt London points out, had little dialogue but a correspondingly large share of music. The first of them, *Sous les Toits de Paris* (1930), was, in fact, the first sound film to be made in France. The way in which the music was used as an accompaniment to the atmosphere and action of these films was similar to its use in the silent period. It went, of course, much farther than this; the films were permeated by their theme songs which built up associations in audiences that were cumulative in their emotional effect. The music began to assist the action, interlocking more closely with it, bridging dialogue scenes, developing climax. The charm, the sentiment, and the humour of Clair's films have secured their survival and *Sous les Toits de Paris* remains one of the best of this brilliant series of comedies.

Sous les Toits de Paris (music by Raoul Moretti and Armand Bernard) was the French interpretation of the "Theme Song" picture, realized in terms of René Clair's highly imaginative treatment. The picture is dominated by the atmosphere of the music of Paris—the street-singer, the battered acoustic gramophone playing the *William Tell Overture*, the accordion band of the little dance halls. In particular, it stems from the famous crane shot that starts in the streets as the ballad singer leads the singing of *Sous les Toits de Paris*. The audience is taken from a close-up of the singer, up across the cobbled street (with glimpses of varying reactions at first, second and third floor windows), ending amidst the quaint chimney-pots with a view of the whole of Paris. The same device is used at the end of the picture, giving a pleasing sense of shape to the rather rambling story.

The musical structure of the film consists of two main theme songs, a number of secondary vocal strains, some gramophone versions of popular classics, simple atmospheric café dance music and a quantity of lightly orchestrated incidental music. Thus, in the last reel of the film, Albert is seen after his release from prison. The sound of voices singing one of the secondary themes is heard as he moves dejectedly along the pavements.

Casually, he enters the café where he used to take his girl. The villain of the film is dancing with her; both are unaware of his presence. Suddenly, the girl sees him. She abandons her partner for Albert. The band plays the second central waltz theme of the picture. They dance in the intimacy of a full close-up, the camera swaying with them in perfect unison with the music. Incisive drum taps accentuate the growing enmity of the villain and his gang, as they gather to confront Albert.

The music stops; Albert is challenged by Fred. They leave from a back door of the café, as a new accordion waltz starts up. In an alleyway outside, the realistic music of the café fades and is replaced by a lightly-scored string dramatique, very much in silent film tradition. This slowly fades and is lost as the street fight begins, accompanied only by the sound of shunting goods trains, distant locomotive whistles and the passing of a fast passenger train; the complete effect is reminiscent of the imaginative use of sound in Hitchcock's *Blackmail*, notably in its contrast to the action.

The villains are rounded up and hustled into a nearby police station, accompanied by a light musical parody in the "cops and robbers" style of the silent film. Albert and his friend Louis escape to a bar; here they argue over the girl, both wishing to win her favour. Dialogue is cut to the minimum by a simple device. Whenever the camera views the scene from outside, music replaces speech. The bar has large glass doors and windows, so that the action can be viewed easily from the street; old-fashioned glass-lettered announcements for wines and beers on the windows add to the atmosphere and help compose the shots. One argument is conducted to a scratched record of the *William Tell Overture*, introduced realistically as the turntable and horn of the machine are shown in some detail. Variations on the main waltz theme are introduced as incidental music to the action during a dice-throwing contest for the girl, viewed almost entirely from outside.

The Animated Film

The brothers Walt and Roy Disney founded their studio in Hollywood in 1923, and created silent cartoons about the adventures of Oswald the Rabbit. Walt Disney then created the character of Mickey Mouse, and was at work on his third Mickey cartoon, *Steamboat Willie*, when *The Jazz Singer* was enjoying its first success. Disney at once held up release of the series until he was in a position to add a sound-track to *Steamboat Willie*. This then became the first Mickey Mouse cartoon to be shown to the public and was released on 19th September 1928 in New York. It was an immediate success; audiences were delighted when Mickey and his girl-friend Minnie improvised on the theme of *Turkey in the Straw* after the goat had swallowed the score. Mickey turned everything to account with rapturous ease—even the anatomy of Claribel the cow. Soon Disney was in a position to enlarge his studio output and add the *Silly Symphony* series to the films about Mickey. The first of these was *Skeleton Dance* (May 1929), animated to the music of Grieg.

In the only fragment of this film available for examination in Britain, the sound-track contains no dialogue, only effects and music. The night scene in the churchyard is set by a conventional misterioso theme, overlaid with owls hooting, the church bell chiming midnight, a dog howling and an eerie flapping sound for a group of bats. The first skeleton makes his appearance to the familiar Saint-Saëns tune.

Then three more skeletons appear, and the quartet starts a simple dance, set to a string and bassoon rhythm. Suddenly, one of the skeletons places another member of the group on the ground, removes his thigh-bones and plays on the other's spine like a xylophone, adding trills by quick ripples around the rib bones. The music consists of a setting for xylophone and small orchestra of the main tune from *March of the Dwarfs* (Part 4 of the Lyric Suite, Op. 54 by Grieg); it is this music that dominates the rest of the film and provides by far the most ingenious section of the whole cartoon.

The most celebrated of the early *Silly Symphonies* was *The Three Little Pigs* (1933) and its theme song *Who's Afraid of the Big Bad Wolf* showed the power of the film to popularize a hit tune on a world scale; it joined the successful tunes from the early musical films (such as *Broadway Melody* and *You Were Meant For Me*) as song numbers which the combined forces of radio, film and commercial disc recordings could make popular on an entirely new scale. The so-called mass media of film and radio came into operation almost simultaneously at the turn of the decade. The popularization of theme tunes associated with films had been foreshadowed early in Pat Sullivan's *Felix the Cat*—everyone sang *Felix Kept on Walking*.

An isolated cartoon film in an entirely different style was made in France during 1934 by Anthony Gross and Hector Hoppin. This was *Joie de Vivre*. Its fantastic theme of the chase of two girls by an apache on a bicycle was matched by an equally fantastic graphic style as the girls dance through industrial landscapes and countryside made up of simplified line drawings. This early experiment in close synchronization revealed the value of a precise musical pattern in animation.

Tibor von Harsanyi, the composer, used a very unusual form based on the pattern of ABC—Trio—CBA, each extension of the original theme being timed with mathematical accuracy. The orchestral style is sharply outlined, like the sketch for some fuller work, yet it is ideally suited to the black-and-white line drawing technique of the artists, with its mixture of idyllic and industrial settings, ending in the signal cabin of a railway, where the girls and their young man perform an ecstatic ballet with the levers and cause havoc among the trains. Modern cacophonous sounds are interpolated by high-pitched brass, but the shape of the cartoon material is always held together by a strong beat to be found in the musical accompaniment.

The first genuine experimental film score was composed for another animated picture made in France, Berthold Bartosch's *L'Idée* (1934), a half-hour film based on a book of woodcuts by Frans Masereel, with a magnificent score by Arthur Honegger, introducing the electronic instrument the Ondes Martenot.[1]

L'Idée is essentially a political film—the idealized representative of the masses, like some kind of creative artist, conceives the Idea of liberty in the form of a naked female figure who inspires him in his struggle and whose cause he serves.

The financiers and business men, failing to clothe the Idea to their own taste, condemn it. Its creator tries to stir the masses to accept the Idea, but he is arrested, tried and shot. But the Idea lives on, and moves men to revolt against tyrannical authority. The revolt fails, but the Idea remains, waiting the time of its acceptance.

Bartosch (who also worked with Lotte Reiniger on the backgrounds to her silhouette films) represented his action by means of two-dimensional cut-out figures, varying from white through all degrees of grey to black against backgrounds placed at different levels from the camera, thus giving depth to the scenes. The result has been described as the first animated film with a serious theme.

Honegger's music is notable for its vicious simplicity, bold orchestration and high degree of synchronization. The musical line is always clear; the main body of the scoring is for a small group of strings, trumpet, occasional solo woodwind and the Ondes Martenot, an electronic instrument previously used by Honegger in concert-hall experiments such as *St. Joan*.

The sound-track opens with a timpani roll and a trumpet flourish, recorded in a peculiarly harsh tone characteristic of all the brass sections. A sustained anticipatory string passage leads up to the first appearance of the Idea, introduced by a long elegiac solo on the Ondes Martenot, occasionally pointed by a slight string accompaniment. Whenever the Idea appears suddenly in the film, the ethereal sounds of the electronic music are heard in variations on the main theme announced in the opening solo. The only exception is when the creator is confronted by the Idea at the moment he contemplates suicide; the melody is heard then on a solo saxophone.

[1]Ondes Martenot: an electronic instrument of great versatility, first introduced in 1928. It combines the principle of the Thérémin with a keyboard, adding additional devices for vibrato and glissando effects as well as a left hand control for the introduction or removal of filter circuits affecting the upper partials. Honegger used it in his concert music at about the same time as this film was made.

References to the busy streets of a modern city are accompanied by a paraphrase of early jazz styles or a rhythmic phrase for bassoon and strings; at one point a striking series of Ondes Martenot glissandos is used for crowds rushing along the pavements. Clashes between Authority and the Idea are frequent. During the trial, a funeral march with muted trumpets and timpani beats is set against a steady solo violin phrase representing the Idea. When the creator speaks to the crowd, a slow, solo saxophone conveys his message, which is picked up by the audience as a deep, rising rumble on the lower strings.

After his death, the Idea goes on spreading, to a musical rhythm set by a printing press that pours out hundreds of copies of her picture to rushing strings and a synchronous click of Chinese blocks. Tension rises between Authority and the masses, while financiers try to enslave the Idea by offering her the wealth of the world; the music rises to a peak of brass, strings, piano chords and high-pitched shrieks of anguished glissandos on the Ondes Martenot. The military advance to drum taps and trumpet, beautifully intercut in track and picture to a rising string crescendo for the masses.

A great clash occurs; the soldiers fire in a quick succession of string chords, stabbing Martenot "bullets" and sharp cymbal crashes against a sustained side-drum roll, and the people are mown down. It might be represented visually thus:

····· = Drum roll   ↘ = Ondes Martenot   ✳ = Cym. crash

The military return to an almost gay, triumphant drum-and-trumpet theme, intercut with a dead march as coffins are carried in procession. Authority gloats and pays homage to the power of money, but the vague outline of the Idea still shines against the firmament, moving slowly out into space as the Ondes Martenot gives a final major statement of the hymn-like main theme.

In the case of Disney's films, the music soon went beyond the stage of a general rhythmical relationship of sound to picture (as in *Skeleton Dance*, for example). Soon the most exact and detailed timing was observed, the animation closely tied to the score, and the score to the animation. Hence the significance of the phrase "Mickey-Mousing" in film musical terminology; it means the exact, calculated dove-tailing of music and action.

It was the cartoonist, and Walt Disney in particular, who first exploited the full possibilities of closely synchronized music in the sense that the animator, by the nature of his craft, was forced to work to the basic 24 pictures per second of the sound film. If a composer wrote a bar in 4/4 time at M.M. = 120 (120 crochets to the minute), one bar would last for 2 seconds, or 48 animation frames. The idea was extended to dialogue and effects, so that they too became "orchestrated" to the kind of discipline usually restricted to music.

The Disney films packed a vast quantity of material in a very short space of time, and made every element of the track count. *Mickey's Moving Day* is a typical Disney short film of its day; in a scene in which Mickey Mouse, Donald Duck and Goofy move house under threat of the sheriff (for non-payment of rent), the following material appears in the space of 40 seconds:

"We gotta move" (Mickey Mouse).
String tremolo (one measure equivalent of the dialogue).
"We gotta move" (Donald Duck).
Six-note phrase on strings—flourish of one long—four shorts—one long. (One measure equivalent of the dialogue).
"We gotta move" (Goofy).
Six-beat phrase on strings and woodwind—long—tacet—trill—boom. (One measure equivalent of the dialogue.)
"Ha! Ha!" (Goofy).
Flourish and four string beats.
Eight beats (two bars) of strings and bassoon theme.
Four beats (one bar) and four hammer bangs overlaid on the beats. (Theme as before.)
Four beats of string and bassoon theme. (As before.)
Four beats based on: Crash/"Phew"; Bang; Boom; boom (timpani).
Piano clangs, with run up scale; reversed, twangy, echoed.
Piano clangs: miscellaneous.
Piano clangs, with run down scale; reversed, twangy, echoed.

The remainder of the sound-track is equally complex and occasionally contains more material in the equivalent space of time than in the example given above. Yet the result for the audience remains fresh and stimulating, despite the possible impact of what appears at first to be an excursion into mathematics rather than film-making.

An interesting parallel to Walt Disney's early technique in the sound film cartoon is described by Mary Field and Percy Smith in their book *Secrets of Nature* (1934). This early attempt to edit live action photography in a manner similar to the closely synchronous cartoon film was to be developed later by Disney himself in his post-war nature films, the True Life series.

The *Secrets of Nature*, in their silent days, usually had special musical settings arranged for them and, when they became "sound-films", the greatest attention was devoted to their accompanying music. At first well-known works were used, but, after a time, the policy of using original music written for the picture was adopted.

There were two reasons for the change. The first was that first-class music is too good to be an accompaniment to anything. It challenges notice; detracts from the importance of the film; and, for many people, has associations which interfere with the interest of the picture. The second reason was that the *Secrets* are full of short sequences and changes of rhythm; and to select extracts from classical music to synchronize with all these changes of mood meant to make a potpourri from the works of masters which was not acceptable even to elementary students of music.

Occasionally in a longer film, such as *The Changing Year*, a sequence will demand to be accompanied by some well-known work. In that film the hay-making sequence seemed to have been photographed in order to be fitted to the first movement of Beethoven's *Pastoral Symphony*; but this is an exception. Water-fleas, cheesemites, badgers and seabirds all seem to have more star value in their films when their movements are emphasized by simple original music and not overshadowed by great works.

The musical setting for the *Secrets* has always been done by W. E. Hodgson, who, as conductor of the orchestra at the Marble Arch Pavilion, was a famous maker of musical settings even before the days of the "talkies". Unlike many musicians, he appreciates the fact that the musical setting is to enhance the film

43

and not to overwhelm it. He has great skill in selecting and fitting pieces of music to accompany different scenes and he has a marvellous knack of finding himself cues in the films by which to time his music, a most important and useful gift when the change of melody has to come on a change of picture or when one special chord has to synchronize with one short action. In nearly every one of the *Secrets* there is a special sequence from which all commentary is rigorously excluded and in which orchestra and film can blend together in a glorious orgy of sight and sound.

Usually these sequences have been carefully planned from the beginning of the editing. The final sequence of the unfurling of the maidenhair fern in *Nature's Double-Lifers* is one example, and so is the romping scene of the baby badgers in *Brock the Badger*.

Sometimes, however, the best pieces of synchronization are done on the spur of the moment and are the result of very quick and ready co-operation. One example of this is the now well-known "dance of the nightingale" in *The Nightingale*. The picture had been prepared to include only a small section of the scene showing the bird jumping on the bough. Commentator and orchestra were both well rehearsed and we were just about ready to synchronize and were waiting for the red light and for the recorder's command to "Turn 'em over".

Suddenly Hodgson remarked, "The bird looked as if he was dancing at the end, didn't he?" Everyone was interested. The film was put through again and, sure enough, the nightingale was dancing. Quickly Hodgson dashed to his library for suitable music that would fit the movement; the film was hurried off to the cutting-room and the two scenes of the dancing action were hastily lengthened and cross-cut to give a rhythm. The commentary was altered and speech was completely removed from this section of the film in order to leave the sound-track clear for the music; and, in breathless hurry and excitement, the dance was synchronized. It earned for the film a cartoon, all to itself, in *Punch*, a very high honour for a very short film.

Music and commentary are quite enough to put on to the sound-track, and "effects" are not usually included in the sound of the *Secrets*. In some of the earlier "sound-films" we recorded some animal noises, but the orchestra and the commentator and the lions roaring appeared to be too much sound for one nature film to carry. We were all of us sorry when the animal-imitators no longer haunted the studio, for they are very amusing people. Life however was more restful without their practising of cocks crowing and laughing jackasses laughing, and tigers growling, which noises they would make industriously both in and out of season, when they were not actually recording. One of these animal-imitators was asked how he came to take up such a queer profession and replied: "Well, I've always been fond of animals—I started life as a butcher."

After the ex-butcher had left us we relied upon the orchestra to give us any effects we needed. The bassoon supplied the shrieks of the baby cormorants, the quarrelsome squeaking of the young bitterns, and the hiccoughs that attended over-eating in both the bittern and the short-eared-owl families. In theatres all over England these musical "effects" nearly always raise a laugh and often are applauded, yet they never clash with the musical setting or, comic as they are, fail to harmonize with the general tone of the films.

The two most difficult films to synchronize were *Daily Dozen at the Zoo* and *Playtime at the Zoo*, both of which tried to reproduce the Walt Disney technique, but with real animals instead of cartoons. A very great deal of material was taken at the Zoo of the animals in actual movement, and the actions were filmed from every angle and with every lens so as to allow for cutting on an extravagant scale. The material was viewed by the composer and the music for each sequence was then specially written. The total time of playing was next found with a stop-watch, and then we counted the number of seconds between each emphasized beat of the music. As film is shown at twenty-four pictures to the second, it was a matter of simple arithmetic to work out the number of pictures that would have to come between the beats. To get this exact number, the scenes were cut on action, which enabled us to remove any superfluous "frames".

The work looked simple enough when we planned it but actually it was infuriating to do. For instance, Daisy, the bear who does slimming exercises, had to touch her toes at the seventy-eighth picture twelve times in succession and the kangaroo, hopping to the tune of *Pop goes the Weasel*, had to spring from the ground at every twenty-sixth picture.

A desperate argument arose over the otter, who turned somersaults through the water in waltz-time. Hodgson insisted the otter was not moving in rhythm. I, who had painfully counted every forty-four frames between the somersaults, was convinced that the timing was correct. It then turned out that I had been counting from the time when the otter left the water, while Hodgson was emphasizing the beat when the animal hit the water. As a result of this variation, the sequence had to be recut to make twenty-two pictures between the otter leaving the water and striking the water, and another twenty-two before it left the water again. It was a piece of work to bring tears to the eyes—and, for a time, I bitterly regretted that I had ever had the idea of making real animals move to music.

The Dramatic Film

We have seen that music for normal dramatic sound films was at first either an extension of the old silent film pattern, with the score "flooding" over the action to the point of musical saturation, or was reduced to a minimum in favour of the dialogue. Here we must at once distinguish between the use of music "realistically" as part of the action itself, and the use of music "non-realistically" as part of the background effects for the establishment of atmosphere. *Kameradschaft*, for example, uses no background music during the action, but in the scene where a group of German miners go into a French café, the music for dancing is supplied by the musicians who appear on the screen. This is termed realistic music, or music occurring within the action. Its dramatic and atmospheric effect is totally different from that of music which steals up on the action of a film non-realistically, giving an additional emotional colouring to a scene that has no intrinsic musical content of its own.

The controlled use of these two main forms of music in films gradually superseded the blind use of a continuous background score, and called for the services of composers prepared to take the trouble at the same time to learn and to invent a new discipline of musical composition. To this day, however, the old traditions die hard, and there is often too much rather than too little music used in the normal dramatic film. It wells up to cover both the good and the bad in a film's action, adding too often a spurious emotional

45

grandeur of pathos or tension to scenes which do not possess enough of these qualities in themselves to satisfy what is known to be the needs of audiences who long to "lose" themselves in the emotionalism of a picture. The temptation is always to dress up a film with music, whether it needs the dressing or not. It was soon realized that scenes which proved weak in dialogue or in acting could be emotionally strengthened in this way, and throughout the quarter-century of sound film production there must have been few films which did not use music during at least a third of the action. The previous well-established tradition of the continuous use of music to accompany the silent film influenced, therefore, both film-makers and their audiences, leading them to feel something was missing when the music stopped playing. It is still an advanced film technique which uses music sparingly in a film, and yet it is the sparing use of music which has so often proved by far the most effective dramatically.

The disciplined use of "realistic" music in an early sound film is exemplified in the German production *The Blue Angel* (1930), directed by Josef von Sternberg, with Emil Jannings and Marlene Dietrich.

The musical score, by Friedrich Hollaender consists of the main theme songs, sung by Marlene Dietrich, including *Falling in Love Again* and *Blonde Women*, and various settings of a German chorale (cf. the bird-catcher's theme from Mozart's *The Magic Flute*—Papageno's tune). There is no "background" music as such, although the film has an Overture for the opening titles, consisting of an arrangement of *Falling in Love Again* and the Chorale tune.

From then on, music is used naturalistically. The professor (Emil Jannings) whistles a few notes from the Chorale tune to the bird cage as he takes breakfast. The elaborate chiming clock over the gates of the University also plays the same tune as the clock strikes eight. In the Blue Angel café, the stage band punctuates the action realistically, even to the extent of being motivated by doors opening and closing as the stage area is approached. Marlene Dietrich's songs are, of course, naturalistic. In the class-room scene, children's voices start and end as a window is opened and closed.

The Professor arrives at the door of the University. He pulls a bell cord and the bell sounds inside. A limping caretaker, with a bull's-eye torch, opens the door. The Professor brushes past him and goes upstairs to his old classroom. As he enters, a very quiet sound of a slow string bass beat is heard, gradually swelling to a sustained, expanding string tremolo that covers scenes of the caretaker coming up to the door and entering the room. He finds the Professor dead at his old desk, his hand gripping the front edge as he lies in an attitude of desperation. The music resolves into the Chorale tune, the main melody picked out on muffled chimes against a background of flowing strings and harp arpeggios. The film ends in a long tracking shot back through the classroom as the clock outside strikes twelve.

The Documentary and the Avant-garde Film

The avant-garde film-makers of France and Germany practised every conceivable kind of experiment with theme, camera and cutting in the years just before the introduction of sound; when the film gained its sound-track, conditions naturally became very much more difficult for the experimental film-maker without substantial resources; the number of avant-garde films produced was substantially less. Stringent budgets, however, forced composers to score for a very small number of instruments and this in turn led to experiment in achieving the greatest possible dramatic effect with small resources. But if the avant-garde branch of production declined almost to the point of extinction, documentary film production increased, and in many respects maintained the attitude of experiment which was the essence of the avant-garde film. Among the more experimental films made during the first years of the sound-track were *Le Sang d'un Poète* (Jean Cocteau, 1931; score by Georges Auric), *Zéro de Conduite* (Jean Vigo, 1933; score by Maurice Jaubert) and *L'Idée*, while the documentary films included *Rising Tide* and *Contact* (Paul Rotha's films of 1933, with scores by Clarence Raybould), *New Earth* (Joris Ivens, 1934, with score by Hanns Eisler), *L'Hippocampe* (Jean Painlevé, 1934, scored by Darius Milhaud) and Walter Leigh's compositions for Basil Wright's *Son of Ceylon* (1934) and the G.P.O. Film Unit's *Pett and Pott*.

We will take, as examples of experiment with the sound-track, sequences from two of these films, *New Earth* and *Zéro de Conduite*.

New Earth, Joris Ivens' documentary on the Zuyder Zee land reclamation project, has music by Hanns Eisler. The score is based on the principle that machinery is accompanied by natural sound and men by music. The orchestra includes strings, woodwind, trumpet, banjo, saxophone, accordion and jazz-type percussion; the musical pattern is divided into three main tempi. First, there is an allegro, for the general work of the men on the project; this is also used in the titles and as a source from which the rest of the material flows. Secondly, there is a blues, used notably in scenes of men carrying or handling heavy pieces of equipment such as pumps or pipelines. Thirdly, there is a five-note, descending phrase, played furioso across the final closing of the gap.

The opening title allegro introduces strings, woodwind, trumpet and banjo in a manner influenced by the jazz of the nineteen-thirties; there are strong beats on the side drum, often set against accordion phrases, to express the idea of hundreds of men at work as the Zuyder Zee project begins. A long sequence of dredging by machinery is accompanied by well-recorded sounds; later a stongly syncopated blues theme appears. As the men strive frantically with crane, shovel, barge and tug to fill in the gap, the music sweeps in with a wild furioso, and the accordion ripples down its five-note phrase over and over again, backed by a savagely incessant saxophone. At last, a large title announces "CLOSED"; the saxophone and trumpet thrust forward a triumphant statement of the main allegro melody, and the film ends on a resolution of all three streams of musical development.

New Earth is notable for its success in integrating the highly individualistic style of Eisler into a documentary which, at first sight, must have appeared to offer little musical scope.

Zéro de Conduite opens with the shouts and cheers of boys at play, which slowly mix into the singing of the school song, composed by Maurice Jaubert, with words written by Charles Goldblatt. As the titles end, there is a return to the cheering and shouting.

The first shot is of a window of a railway train. The music sets a strong train rhythm, which is sustained throughout the opening sequence. At first, it is heavy, almost a blues tempo. A schoolboy sits alone and sad; a plaintive oboe passage appears across the bass rhythm. The train slows down, entirely in music.

A second boy boards the train; the rhythm picks up once more in the music, becoming faster as the first boy brightens up in the presence of a colleague. Over the brisk bass, a gay flute tune ripples out as, from unfathomable pockets, come all kinds of toys and gadgets. A toy flute is roughly matched to the existing flow of music on the track; similarly a toy trumpet introduces a professionally-played sound to parallel the mood rather than provide a realistic imitation. Balloons are produced and blown up musically by Jaubert, with suitably expanding brass phrases. The final trick comes as large cigars are flourished, and the clouds of smoke from the open train window mingle with the smoke inside; and strong brass slurs punctuate the action. As the train jerks to a standstill, a sleeping youth falls to the floor of the compartment. "Il est mort!" shouts one of the boys; he has fallen with a heavy, musical thud. The natural sounds of the station flood in on the track, the boys get out of the train. The game is ended; the fantasy world becomes a real station platform. The sequence ends as abruptly as it began. The music is finished.

Jaubert's contribution to this picture is imaginative. Apart from the sequence described, it consists mainly of the songs sung in the school, "attack" music for the riot, a charming "miniature" trumpet march for the procession in slow-motion through the dormitory (with an interesting use of wordless voices), and a number of drum flourishes for various pointers in the school routine.

Walter Leigh's score for *Song of Ceylon*—one of the most advanced sound-tracks of the early period—will be considered later in this chapter.

A film in which music, and indeed, sound in general, was treated highly experimentally was V. I. Pudovkin's *Deserter*, with music by Y. Shaporin. Pudovkin himself in his book *Film Technique* (1933, translated by Ivor Montagu) writes about his attitude to the use of music in his first sound film: "Music", he says, "must in sound film *never be the accompaniment. It must retain its own line*". He then analyses a sequence in *Deserter* in which a demonstration by workers in a large industrial city is, after a period of success, broken up through the intervention of mounted police. A struggle rages round the workers' red flag, which, after their defeat, is nevertheless raised again and the demonstration re-formed. Of the music Pudovkin writes in *Film Technique*:

The course of the image twists and curves, as the emotion within the action rises and falls. Now, if we used music as an *accompaniment* to this image we should open with a quiet melody, appropriate to the soberly guided traffic; at the appearance of the demonstration the music would alter to a march; another change would come at the police preparations, menacing the workers—here the music would assume a threatening character; and when the clash came between workers and police—a tragic moment for the demonstrators—the music would follow this visual mood, descending ever further into themes of despair. Only at the resurrection of the flag could the music turn hopeful. A development of this type would give only the superficial aspect of the scene, the undertones of meaning would be ignored; accordingly I suggested to the composer (Shaporin) the creation of a music the dominating emotional theme of which should *throughout* be courage and the certainty of ultimate victory. From beginning to end the music must develop in a gradual growth of power . . . What role does the music play here? Just as the image is an objective perception of events, so the music expresses the subjective appreciation of this objectivity. The sound reminds the audience that with every defeat the fighting spirit only receives new impetus to the struggle for final victory in the future.

48

The Idea of Music in Films

Early statements on the use of music with sound films were comparatively rare in British writing for the screen, but some seem particularly interesting when they are read again today. Paul Rotha in his second book *Celluloid* (1931) reacts strongly against the dialogue film of the period—"speech is fundamentally foreign to the cinema" (p. 86). He wanted to see a bolder development of wordless sound and music on the track:

> Every month brings a new and more stimulating Disney sound cartoon to the cinema and still, after all this time, no director or producer has learned the obvious lesson from these superb masterpieces of sound and visual rhythm. Such a magnificent example of what lies to be achieved in the sound medium as *The Skeleton Dance* passes by unheeded. We hear the chariot race in the synchronized version of *Ben-Hur*, the machine-guns in *All Quiet on the Western Front*, the aeroplanes in *Hell's Angels*, the accordion in *Sous les Toits de Paris*, the footsteps in *The Virginian*, the drum-beats in *The King of Jazz*, and yet we are incapable of perceiving the superiority of sound over speech.

And again:

> It is imperative that experiment and study should be pursued by theorists in the employ of big companies until a film is produced in which a story is told purely in terms of moving screen images, set to a mechanically-recorded score of real or distorted sounds interwoven with creative music.

Alfred Hitchcock, interviewed by Stephen Watts for *Cinema Quarterly* (1933, Vol. II, No. 2) claimed that films should have their music scores completed before going into production. Music is part and parcel of the film, and its use in the development of the action and the establishing of atmosphere should be determined while the film is being planned. This has never been the normal practice in the studios, but Hitchcock's observations show real appreciation of the need for a close integration between the music and the other elements in film-making, both in picture and sound. While he thinks it wrong for the audience to be actively conscious of the music, none the less it should have a direct effect on their reaction to the film. He gives an instance from his own film *Waltzes from Vienna* (1933):

> There is a dialogue scene between a young man and a woman. It is a quiet, tender scene. But the woman's husband is on his way. The obvious way to get suspense is to cut every now and then to glimpses of the husband travelling towards the house. In the silent days, when the villain was coming, you always had the orchestra playing quickening music. You *felt* the menace. Well, you can still have that and keep the sense of the talk-scene going as well. And the result is that you don't need to insist pictorially on the husband's approach.
> I think I used about six feet of film out of the three hundred feet used in the sequence to flash to the husband. The feeling of approaching climax can be suggested by the music.

It is in that psychological use of music, which, you will observe, they knew something about before talkies, that the great possibilities lie.

In *Waltzes from Vienna* Hitchcock claims that "naturally every cut in the film was worked out on script before shooting began. But more than that, the musical cuts were worked out too". In certain sequences the images were deliberately cut to conform to the rhythm of the music. And frequently, Hitchcock adds, music can supplement cutting, more especially in quiet scenes where its comment on mood and tone can sometimes be more subtle than the interplay of images which is so important in moments of violence.

Film music and cutting have a great deal in common. The purpose of both is to create the tempo and *mood* of the scene. And, just as the ideal cutting is the kind you don't notice *as* cutting, so with music.

The closer form of integration between picture, music, and other forms of sound was also noted early by the German writer Rudolf Arnheim, whose book *Film* was published in English translation in 1933. He wrote:

Music has been very cleverly used in some sound films. A great future probably lies before the combination of sound music and tone music, i.e., acoustic accompaniment of which it cannot be said exactly whether it consists of natural sounds or is achieved by means of instruments. The introductory bars to Granowsky's *Song of Life* consisted of a slow simple melody whose individual notes went parallel with the cuts. The montage thereby achieved a forcefulness that was intended by the director and which would have been hard to realize by optical means only. In Wilhelm Thiele's film *The Ball* the jeering laughter of the servants is cleverly worked into the refrain of the dance music. These represent attempts to create a closer union between sound film and music, to admit music as an intergral part of the production instead of leaving it as an external appendage.

Most valuable is the article *The Musician and the Film* written for *Cinema Quarterly* (1935, Vol. III, No. 2) by the late Walter Leigh shortly after he composed the music for *Song of Ceylon*. He complains of the unnecessary, obtrusive music which is only too common in the cinema, then as now, and the restricted view of the sound-track taken by almost all film-makers at that time—the pedestrian stretches of dialogue, the flat reflection of the picture in the sound. Discipline, he claims, is just as necessary in devising the sound-track as it is in devising and cutting the picture. He explains an all-important principle underlying sound film-making in the following passage:

When watching a stage play, we select for ourselves, out of sounds which proceed from various parts of the stage, those which we are to listen to, such as dialogue and revolver-shots, and disregard entirely all the unimportant sounds such as the footsteps of the actors, clicks of cigarette-cases, striking of matches, and shutting of doors. But in the cinema, all sounds, proceeding as they do from a single point, the loud-speaker, are listened to with equal attention, with the result that sometimes a particular sound, say of footsteps, may be charged with sinister meaning that is quite unintended. Every sound in a film must be a significant one; there is no room for extraneous sounds. Therefore the effect of each sound must be properly and carefully calculated.

Walter Leigh realized that the composer must "approach this new problem of film-sound as a fresh art with many unexplored possibilities, which is only now starting to make its own conventions."

The composer approaching the film problem for the first time will be struck by one especially important fact, namely, that in film-music more than in any other kind of music the greatest virtue is economy. A phrase of five bars lasting twenty seconds suitably fitted to thirty feet of picture may express as much as the whole slow movement of a symphony. One minute is quite a considerable length for a piece of music in a film. The academic principles of leisurely formal development are therefore of little use in the composition of film-music, though they may well be employed in the construction of the whole film and its sound-score. The same need for economy applies to the instrumentation; four instruments may well provide a better effect than forty, and a piece that sounds painfully thin and ridiculous in the concert-hall may be perfectly satisfactory over the microphone.

It may be said without presumption that the peculiar powers of the microphone have, with the exception of one or two isolated experiments of which little notice has been taken, not been exploited to much advantage up to the present. The most obvious possibility is that of balancing, by placing at suitable distances from the microphone, those instruments whose normal volumes are entirely unequal. The film-composer has to recognize that the much-despised "canned" quality of film-music is actually its most important characteristic and greatest virtue.

Leigh as a composer accepted the fact that the composer's interest should lie in the combined effect of all forms of sound on the track. He distinguishes between synchronized natural sound, natural sound in counterpoint and sound effects used "so to speak musically, for direct emotional purposes". Natural sound in counterpoint uses sound *allusively* for special emotional effect—take the train sounds which accompany the efforts of the elephant to fell the trees in *Song of Ceylon*. Sound effects can be used musically, the "subtle use of noises for their own sake, to create certain atmospheres in the same way as music does, has still to be developed, and it is undoubtedly in this field that the most creative advances and the richest discoveries will be made".

At the close of his article, Walter Leigh shows how he experimented with sound as a whole and music in particular in the case of Basil Wright's film *Song of Ceylon*:

In the film *Song of Ceylon*, an attempt has been made to make use of the above suggestions in constructiong a sound-score which has a definite shape,

51

and not only is an accompaniment to the visuals, but adds an element which they do not contain. The film has, in fact, been cut throughout with an eye to the sound-score. Its form is musically conceived; an analysis of its four movements would read like that of a symphony. Each sound has been selected for its seeming inevitability, as harmonies are in music. Even the commentary is calculated as an effect and not as a necessary nuisance.

The chief aims of the sound-score are simplicity and clarity. The audience's difficulty in co-ordinating sight and sound has been recognized, and confusion has been avoided as far as possible. Two kinds of music have been used: the native singing and drumming for realistic purposes, and the western orchestra in an attempt at a palatable combination of Sinhalese and European idioms, for atmospheric and emotional purposes. The two extremes, music and synchronized natural sound, are used respectively for emotional high-spots and points of rest.

Non-synchronized sound is used a great deal for various specific purposes. An example is the distant bark of a dog heard during a shot of a native building a hut; the implication of the dog is a hint at village life not far away, and the effect of the combination of picture and sound in their context is to foreshadow a contented domestic life in the house now being built. The sound of a train is continued over a shot of an elephant pushing down a tree, and slowed up to correspond with its efforts. Morse and radio announcers reciting market prices are heard over shots of tea-pickers, sounds of shipping over the gathering of coker-nuts. Sinhalese speech, being presumed to be unintelligible to the audience, is used purely as a sound with its obvious connotation, except where a close-up of a speaker demands synchronized speech.

One or two experiments have also been made with the microphone. The vibrations of gongs have been picked up by swinging the microphone close to the gong after it was struck. Some percussion instruments are used whose virtue is only discernible through the microphone. A particular attempt is also made at an instrumentation suitable for "canning". All the natural sounds have been artificially produced in the studio, occasionally by very unlikely means. That it shows examples of a few of the possibilities offered by an entirely new approach to the whole problem of sound is the chief claim of the film.

Thus by 1935, barely five years after the sound film had become general in the cinemas, certain film-makers and composers had already begun to realize the opportunities for experiment open to them on the sound-track. In 1934 Cavalcanti had been invited by John Grierson to come over from France to supervize the development of sound in the documentaries he was producing for the G.P.O. Film Unit, and during that year Muir Mathieson became full-time Music Director for Sir Alexander Korda's productions.

Their influence was to be all-important in British production, more especially because they realized that the film needed the services of the best composers in the country. When Benjamin Britten composed the scores for *Night Mail* and *Coal Face* (1936) and Arthur Bliss that for *Things to Come* (1935), the period had begun when it became customary for British film-makers to invite leading composers to work for films and, with the guidance of men like Mathieson and Cavalcanti, learn the new technique of the film score.

The Rise of the Symphonic Score in Films

As we have seen, it was about the year 1935 that certain standards in relation to film music had begun to take root in the sound film. René Clair's freshness had established a tradition for the French that would be hard to break, Honegger's score for *L'Idée* put the case simultaneously for electronics and the simple sound, Walter Leigh determined the approach of British documentary to music with *Song of Ceylon* and *Pett and Pott*, and America had *Forty-Second Street*, *Broadway Melody* and an Academy Award to the Columbia Music Department for the score in *One Night of Love*.

By 1935, the symphonic style of music score for films had begun to be developed. Prokofiev composed one of the first scores in this manner for *Lieutenant Kije* (1934), and Flaherty's *Man of Aran*, with its symphonic score by John Greenwood, was heard in the same year. At Denham Studios, Arthur Bliss was called in to work with Alexander Korda and his Music Director, Muir Mathieson, on Britain's biggest pre-war production, H. G. Wells' *Things to Come*. Simultaneously, Max Steiner was working in Hollywood on the score for *The Informer* (1935). He was also writing for a major symphonic effect—and using a very large choir. So, by the end of 1935, two major film scores had appeared, both with "heavenly choir" finales, and both soon to be adapted for concert-hall performances and recorded for the gramophone. With less publicity (and less success) William Walton had in the same year obtained his first experience of working for films with *Escape Me Never*, and this was followed in 1936 by his first score for a Shakespearean film, Paul Czinner's *As You Like It*, with Elizabeth Bergner and Laurence Olivier.

By 1936 Benjamin Britten, Erich Wolfgang Korngold, George Antheil, Virgil Thomson, William Alwyn and Arthur Benjamin had all written film scores. In short, the symphonist had entered the motion picture business, and the contemporary style of composition for films had begun.

We will conclude this chapter with some description of the two scores which drew the attention of film-makers, composers and public alike to the importance of the composer as a member of the film-making team—those written for *Things to Come* and *The Informer*.

Immediately after *Things to Come* had been completed, H. G. Wells wrote as follows:

The music is a part of the constructive scheme of the film, and the composer, Mr. Arthur Bliss, was practically a collaborator in its production. In this as in so many other respects, this film, so far at least as its intention goes, is boldly experimental. Sound sequences and picture sequences were made to be closely interwoven. This Bliss music is not intended to be tacked on; it is a part of the design. The spirit of the opening is busy and fretful and into it creeps a deepening menace. Then come the crashes and confusions of modern war. The second part is the distressful melody and grim silences of the pestilence period. In the third, military music and patriotic tunes are invaded by the throbbing return of the air men. This throbbing passes into the mechanical crescendo of the period of reconstruction. This becomes more swiftly harmonious and softer and softer as greater efficiency abolishes that clatter of strenuous imperfection which was so distinctive of the earlier mechanical civilization of the nineteenth century. The music of the new world is gay and spacious. Against this plays the motif of the reactionary revolt, ending in the stormy victory of the new ideas as the Space Gun fires and the moon cylinder starts on its momentous journey. The music ends with anticipations of a human triumph in the heroic finale amidst the stars.

It cannot be pretended that in actual production it was possible to blend the picture and music so closely as Bliss and I had hoped at the beginning. The incorporation of original music in film production is still in many respects an unsolved problem.

To this Bliss replied:

My argument is that in the last resort film music should be judged solely as music—that is to say, by the ear alone, and the question of its value depends on whether it can stand up to this test.

In support of the idea of a completely filmic score, however, Bliss admitted that:

While I was writing my *Things to Come* music, I felt that I was to some extent surrendering my musical individuality to the needs of the film itself; so, as a kind of mental purgative, I wrote my *Music for Strings*, which, of course, is absolute music.

In spite of the internal contentions that existed at the time, the music for this film has become world-famous and is consistently quoted whenever the history of film music is discussed. Bliss produced a concert suite, which was recorded on three gramophone discs, with the London Symphony Orchestra conducted by the composer. The March theme was played regularly over the radio, especially in the late 'thirties, and concert performances of the suite still take place. The original recording for the film sound-track involved fourteen full orchestral sessions at the Scala Theatre, London. In addition to a full symphony orchestra, an extra percussion orchestra, including several experimental instruments, and a large choir were added for a number of sessions. The conductor was Muir Mathieson.

The opening of the film includes scenes of Christmas. A group of children are playing with their new toys and the music is gay, being scored for woodwind, strings and harp. Gradually the camera closes in to reveal that the toys are the toys of war—model guns, tanks and bombers. The music of the children is slowly swamped as a deepening menace creeps in, depicted in the music on the brass, which becomes progressively more dissonant.

54

The famous March theme is heard first as the World War commences and troops are mobilized. It is very heavily scored, with a large percussion section. Further strong musical sounds are used for the scenes of the enemy's first attack.

(Reproduced by kind permission of Novello and Co. Ltd.)

After war on a vast scale, the world is in ruins and pestilence breaks out, spread by a desperate foe; music underlines the emotional nature of the scenes. There follows a period of reconstruction and a sequence in which new machines rebuild the cities of the future. Bliss produced some remarkable orchestral sounds to suggest the great, hidden power of the equipment, using the humming effects of large masses of strings in unison, with alternate sections bowing or playing pizzicato.

The final scenes in the picture show the departure of a space cylinder to the moon. The space gun fires and the rocket, with two young people inside, starts on its journey into the sky. In a large observatory, their parents see the cylinder as a very small speck against a starry background. Cabal speaks: "For man no rest and no ending. He must go on—conquest beyond conquest . . . All the universe—or nothing . . . Which shall it be?" A flowing string melody plays under the scene, until the two men stand looking at the great mirror of the telescope. As the last lines are spoken, a full choir, singing word-lessly, gives out the final statement of the Epilogue theme, and the film ends with this expression of human triumph amidst the stars.

In the United States, Max Steiner inaugurated a similar musical tradition with his score for *The Informer*. As with Bliss, Steiner came to films after a formal, academic training in music. Born into a Viennese musical family, he composed and conducted from an early age before entering the theatre, where he conducted his first opera at the age of fourteen. After a period in England, Steiner settled in America in 1914, and went to Hollywood in 1929. He received an Academy Award for the score he composed for *The Informer*.

As in the case of *Things To Come*, *The Informer* contains a March Theme. It is associated throughout the film with the inevitable tragedy that hangs over the head of Gypo Nolan (Victor McLaglen), a Dublin slum-dweller who informs on his friends during the Irish troubles of the earlier part of this century. Appearing first as a heavy, rhythmic beat for brass and side drum, often against a distant, shimmering effect on strings, the main theme is broken into fragments, which are used for independent development to express such ideas as Gypo's love for his girl or the temptation suggested by a poster announcing the reward offered for information about Gypo's friend.

Other material is introduced to suggest the rebellious feeling of the Irish in 1922; a glimpse of a folk-tune is sometimes heard on French horns, answering the hated patrolling of military forces. A hymn theme is introduced early in the score and forms the basis of a finale similar in treatment to that of *Things to Come*.

Gypo has been dismissed from the revolutionary party and finds himself facing starvation. He is ignorant and simple-minded; his thinking has always been done for him by other people. Alone, he soon betrays his friends and receives the reward. But he is unable to conceal his default; he is caught and tried by the men who were once his companions. He is condemned to death through the rough justice of a revolutionary committee. The march theme returns with renewed anguish, announced by heavy brass chords. Vengeance overtakes Gypo, who seldom comprehends what is happening, his problems resolved in the end by the action taken by others. Cutting across the savage march comes a woman's voice, echoed and set against a sweeping string background, singing a penetrating, soaring arrangement of the *Ave Maria*; the restless theme of Gypo is finally resolved.

55

SAM FOX
MOVING PICTURE
MUSIC

By J. S. ZAMECNIK

VOL. 2   **PRICE 50 CENTS**

CONTENTS

		Page
Triumphal March		2
Indian Love Song		3
Indian War Dance		4
Indian Music		5
Japanese Love Song		6
Oriental Dance or Scene		7
Oriental Music		8
Love Scene		10
Plaintive Music		11
Spanish or Mexican Scene		12
Five Dances		
I	Russian Folk Dance	13
II	Minuet (Court Dance—Louis XIV Period)	13
III	Italian Tarantella	14
IV	Spanish Fandango	14 and 15
V	Zulu or African Dance	15
Weekly (Pathé, Gaumont etc.)		
Part 1	European Army Maneuvers	16 and 17
Part 2	Funeral March	17
Part 3	Paris Fashions	18
Part 4	Aeroplane or Regatta Races	19
Part 5	Marathon, Horse or Automobile Races	20
Part 6	Exhibition—(Flower, etc.)	21
Part 7	Explosion or Fire Scene	22
Burglar or Sneaky Music		22
Hurry Music (for Combats, Struggles, etc.)		23

Published by Sam Fox ◆ Pub. Co. *Cleveland, Ohio*

LONDON—LEIPZIG—VIENNA—ZURICH—PARIS. – BOSWORTH & CO.

The Title Page from an early Mood Music publication. The Sam Fox Moving Picture Music books were first published in 1913 and rapidly became popular with silent film music pianists in many parts of the world. The titles give a number of pointers to film history, notably in the references to the newsreels of the day; Pathé and Gaumont were already in existence, mainly on a weekly basis. The fact that two pages are devoted to "European Army Maneuvers" is interesting in relation to the date of publication, as is the charming combination of "Aeroplane or Regatta Races".

A page from the music score for Birth of a Nation, composed and arranged by Joseph Carl Briel and D. W. Griffith. A piano-conductor score and a full set of band parts were issued by the Epoch Producing Corporation (Griffith's own company) wherever the film was sent. There are 226 separate music cues included in the score, six of which are shown in the page reproduced above. The main scenes are grouped together under headings ("The Union League Rally") and each section contains individual cues based on specific incidents in the plot; the makers recommended a minimum of three full rehearsals before an orchestra accompanied the film in public.

MUSICAL SUGGESTIONS—By Arthur Dulay
"SEA FURY"

	Theme 1 — — —	L'Angoisse (from Fig. 1)	(Theme 1)	—	Porret	De Wolfe

Space below is for Musical Directors' own Notes and Cues.

	Sub-title or Action.	Style.	Music Suggested.	Composer.	Publisher.
1.	At Screening		L'Onde Tragique (Letter A)	Gabriel-Marie	Piena
2.	After water thrown	Broad	Vision Tragique	Dyck	Liber
3.	Sail ahead *	Agitato	Affolement	Ourdine	Piena
4.	Captain sees black cat	Sinister	Theme 1		
5.	It was the Captain's boast *	Quiet tense	" Rosamunde "	Schubert	Hawkes
6.	See crew eating	Agitated melody	Atlantide	Reynaud	Piena
7.	They bring food to Captain	Tense	A Vain Hope	Patou	Hawkes
8.	Mate draws revolver	Dramatic	Madame Roland	Fourdrain	Piena
9.	Deck scene	Agitated	Dialogue Dramatique	Brusselmans	Liber
10.	Mutiny !*	Dramatic agitato	Hate and Love	Samehtini	Piena
11.	They make rescue	Tense agitated	Jerusalem Delivree	Hovelacque	Piena
12.	Girl carried in	Sad dramatic	Bonheur Evanoui	Dyck	Liber
13.	Mills alone	Dramatic	La Mer Sombre	Fosse	Lafleur
14.	Kum !*	Hectic	On the Briny No. 4	Carr	Paxton
15.	Boy brings food	Agitated	Invocation	Mezzacapo	Liber
16.	Struggle on deck (note shot)	Jolly	Repeat No. 14		
17.	They hit man	Dramatic tense	La Haine	Delmas	Liber
18.	Captain enters	Tense	Agitato Misterioso	Popy	Liber
19.	Captain sees cat		Theme 1		
20.	Crew attack Captain	Dramatic	Destruction	Brusselmans	Liber
21.	Segue	Tense agitated	Ombre Complice	Marie	Piena
22.	After men leave	Agitated melody	Heures d'Angoisse	Delmas	Liber
23.	On deck	Dramatic	Ouverture Dramatique	Zerco	De Wolfe
24.	To men used to kicks*		On the Briny No. 2	Carr	Paxton
25.	Mills talks to helmsman	Tense Agitated	Incidental Symphonies	Schubert	Lafleur
26.	See men again	Jolly	Repeat No. 24		
27.	Bosun by wheel	Tense	L'Espionne	Delmas	Liber
28.	The dog watch*	Tense	Svengali	Somerville	De Wolfe
29.	Drops keg over	Dramatic	Le Lac Maudit	Staz	Liber
30.	Eight bells*	Tense movement	Mystere	Delmas	Liber
31.	Bosun talks	Tense	Misterioso Dramatique	Borch	Lafleur
32.	Bosun goes down into hold	Tense	Treachery	Latour	Liber
33.	The story's changed *	Dramatic	Tragico, Con Moto	Drigo	Lafleur
34.	Throws cat out of boat	Dramatic	Guilt	Ewing	Elkin
35.	Negro and boy on board	Semi agitated	Romantique (Piu vivo)	Smetsky	De Wolfe
36.	Men in boat seen	Tense agitated	Dramatic Hurry	O'Hare	Lafleur
37.	The wind ! the wind !*	Excited	Confession	Tschaikowsky	Liber
38.	In the night*	Stormy	" The Flying Dutchman "	Wagner	Feldman
39.	When day came*	Prayerful	Tout S'Apaise	Dyck	Liber
40.	A ship! a ship !*	Agitated	L'Exultante Tendresse	Marie	Liber
41.	Segue		Pleurs (Trio)	Messier	Liber

*Denotes sub title. All other cues scene or action only.

NOTE.—If you have not the compositions suggested in the third column, you may easily substitute accurate music by following the DESCRIPTIVE ACTION OF EACH SCENE AND TEMPO.

An example of a Musical Suggestions Sheet of the type sent out by film distributors in order to assist the local music directors in the cinemas. It is the work of Arthur Dulay, one of the most distinguished of silent film accompanists, who began his career in 1914 at the Pyke's Circuit cinema in Windmill Street, London. Today, he is resident pianist at the National Film Theatre in London. It will be noted that cues are given either for action or for sub-titles, depending on where the change of mood occurs, and that the music ranges from specially composed Mood Music pieces to the works of Schubert, Wagner and Tchaikowsky. Musical Suggestions Sheets were first issued by the Edison Company in 1909 and were used during the silent film period as an alternative to the expensive process of issuing a full score. A number of early talkies were made in which silent film material was synchronized to gramophone records of the items listed in Suggestions Sheets. The method is still employed in the distribution of silent amateur films, both for direct accompaniment on gramophone records and for the preparation of tape-synchronized musical backgrounds.

A page from Giuseppe Becce's *Kinobibliothek*, first published in Berlin in 1919. The method was to produce a catalogue for film situations, which are listed under general headings ("Katastrophe") and then broken down into a number of sub-headings. Main themes are quoted in each case, along with a cross-reference to other sources of similar material. Many of the pieces were by Becce himself, but this particular page covers works by Massenet, Puccini and Rachmaninoff, following the pattern set by the Musical Suggestions Sheets.

A page from Wolfgang Zeller's score for Prince Achmet, the first full-length animated film, produced in Germany between 1923 and 1926. It is the work of the silhouette artist, Lotte Reiniger, working in association with Berthold Bartosch, Alexander Kardan and Karl Koch. Cueing was so important that the score contained a series of frame-size reproductions incorporated into the manuscript; four of these little silhouette pictures can be seen in the page reproduced above. (From the private collection of Hans Feld.)

A page from the score for Gypsy Blood, a film version of the "Carmen" story directed by Ernst Lubitsch in 1921 The film score was arranged by a distinguished team of silent film music specialists, including Dr. Hugo Reisenfeld, Carl Edouarde, James C. Bradford and Joseph Carl Briel. The reproduction above shows the particular type of cueing mark used by the Synchronized Scenario Music Co., who specialized in the preparation of film music scores. The title page contains the following warning: "The score, as herein contained, is accurately adapted to the photoplay for which it has been prepared. It must not be marked, erased, torn, rearranged, mutilated or soiled. If it is, a charge to cover its cost will be made against the lessee of $2.00 per page mutilated or damaged by marking or otherwise."

A page from Edmund Meisel's music for Berlin. The film was made by Walter Ruttmann in Germany in 1927, using a script prepared by Carl Mayer. Meisel's work on the Russian classics, notably *Battleship Potemkin*, made him perhaps the most celebrated of all silent film composers. The highly-detailed nature of his cueing may be gained by the page reproduced above, which is taken from the accompaniment to scenes of a train entering the suburbs of Berlin in the early morning. (From the private collection of Hans Feld.)

3

THE FUNCTION OF MUSIC IN THE SOUND FILM

THE musical score specially composed for a film performs many and varied functions, all vital to the film itself. Broadly speaking, there are two main forms of film music—"realistic" and "functional" music. First, we shall deal with realistic music, leaving functional music until later in this Section.

Realistic music is the controlling factor in the dance-film (ballet-film or musical), the film-opera, or the sequences in which any form of musical performance appears in the action (the cabaret, the café, the concert hall, a sequence involving singing and so on) or controls it "off-stage" (for example, the actor singing alone in the action, but accompanied by an invisible orchestra). Realistic music, since it forms part of the action, must be composed before the film is undertaken in the studio; functional music may be composed after the film has been shot and assembled in rough-cut.

But first we shall consider the sound-track as a whole, since music must normally add its particular dramatic effect to other forms of sound already recorded along with speech and dialogue.

The Full Range of the Sound-Track: Effects and Dialogue

We have established that by 1935—some half-dozen years after the introduction of the sound-track—many film-makers and composers had become fully aware of the dramatic powers of sound. Certain film-makers had begun to balance dialogue with sound effects, or both of these with music specially composed for the purpose. Writers such as Rudolph Arnheim (*Film*, 1933) and Raymond Spottiswoode (*A Grammar of the Film*, 1935) began to work out on paper the range and variety of the controlled uses of sound which were possible on the track, and the effect achieved by their relationship to the picture on the screen. The sound-track was analysed in terms of its main elements—sound effects, speech and music.

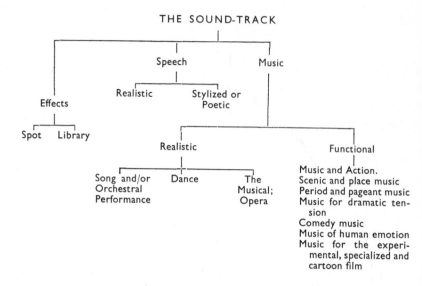

THE SOUND-TRACK

Speech — Music

Effects

Realistic — Stylized or Poetic

Spot — Library

Realistic — Functional

Song and/or Orchestral Performance — Dance — The Musical; Opera

Music and Action.
Scenic and place music
Period and pageant music
Music for dramatic tension
Comedy music
Music of human emotion
Music for the experimental, specialized and cartoon film

The effects themselves ranged over the natural sounds produced by the action or the background to it and the sounds which it was more convenient to dub on subsequently, making use of the library of sound effects which every studio was compiling—the recognized sounds of nature and the world around us. To these could be added sound produced artificially or distorted by mechanical means—the echoes, the reversed sounds, the electronic sounds—or even in the films of Norman McLaren the drawn sounds which never existed until they were painted as shapes on the track. A whole bag of sound tricks, like the winds of classical legend confined by Aeolus in a leather pouch and given to Odysseus, were at the command of the ingenious film-maker, and the problem at times became, like that of Odysseus, not to let too many of them out at once! It has been a constant complaint among composers that some carefully calculated moment in their score has been drowned out of existence by the rising howl of wind or even the slam of a door, whereas, of course, in the properly balanced track, the composer and film-maker should have worked together to weld the sound effects and the music as complementary pieces of dramatic sound.

The composer also had to study the varieties of speech which both the dramatic and the factual film were beginning to employ. In theory, the treatment of speech in the film can be even wider than it is in the living theatre, where virtually all speech is either dialogue or soliloquy except in those forms of traditional Oriental drama where a narrator is employed. The use of a narrator (or story-teller) is a frequent convention in the film, and has become a plague in the documentary.

Most dialogue in films is written in a naturalistic style—that is, in a form acceptable as representing normal human speech concentrated for dramatic effect and economy. The nearer this kind of naturalistic dialogue approaches sheer realism, the more obtrusive any form of association of speech with dramatic music tends to become—hence the film using almost no music at all, such as *Kameradschaft* and *A Walk in the Sun*. However, most films, though their actual dialogue may be written in a reasonably naturalistic style, soon involve situations in which some emotion is being expressed—amorous, sinister, exciting, tense and so on. A few bars of music can more readily establish these underlying emotions than words or even expressive acting. Music, in fact, can become the short cut to emotion. Although music is no longer used in a continuous stream to underline the obvious (as happened inevitably in the days of the silent cinema), it is nevertheless still used to excess in the sound film, its great dramatic powers dissipated because its effect is ever-present. The more banal the dialogue the more the words can be made to seem dramatically significant if "dressed" with a heavy musical backing. Used as an emotional prop, music can only too easily help the film-maker disguise weak acting and weak dialogue.

Not all films, however, are written in a naturalistic style; in many ways the effects of speech can be "heightened" in films as they are in the theatre. Various forms of dramatic eloquence can be achieved by the screenwriter according to the kind of scene he is constructing—some using dialogue bordering on naturalism, such as *A Walk in the Sun*, some written with a special stylistic wit, like *Kind Hearts and Coronets*, some even approaching expressionism, as in certain sequences of *Citizen Kane* and *Miss Julie*, or more rarely reaching out to special forms of dramatic poetry like *Orphée*. Many films achieve a latent poetry through the very economy and selection with which significant naturalistic speech is used; notable examples of this are certain dialogue scenes in Humphrey Jennings's *Fires Were Started* or in William Wellman's *The Ox-bow Incident*, scripted by Lamar Trotti. Other films are deliberately non-naturalistic in speech—they are legendary (*La Belle et la Bête*, *Rashomon*), historical (*Ivan the Terrible*), or fantastic (*On the Town*).

Nor should we overlook the narrator whose voice appears in every kind of documentary film—the voice sometimes insistent and

65

prosaic, or sometimes quietly intruding a fact here, some necessary point of information there (*Louisiana Story*), or sometimes becoming a strong factor in building up narrative tension (*Desert Victory*) or argument (*The March of Time, World of Plenty*).

All the various forms of dialogue and narration used in films create for the composer special problems when speech and music are blended. On one occasion he may be setting the speech of Shakespeare; on another he may be "pointing" the action of a gangster melodrama or "underlaying" a chase sequence.

Music, therefore, must take account of the other elements on screen and sound-track, and normally it succeeds them, being created and added last unless it forms an intrinsic part of the action on the screen.

Performed Music: Filmed Opera and Ballet

The film has been constantly used to present established operas, particularly in Italy and Russia since the war. It should be made clear at the outset that it is not strictly relevant to the study of film music to discuss these productions, which vary in the quality of their presentation from mere recording of singing and action on celluloid to the brilliant employment of film technique to establish the dramatic atmosphere of the work.

Gian-Carlo Menotti's opera on film *The Medium* remains an outstanding example of successful filmed opera. It is true that great pageant-operas such as *Boris Godunov* or operas with a great deal of lively action such as *Carmen* lend themselves to some extent to presentation on film; there is always a great deal in décor or movement at which to look while listening. But these operas remain essentially of the theatre because their conception is rooted in theatrical display; it is more important that the actor interpret his role through his capacity as a singer than that he should try to superimpose on his performance those subtle shades of characterization which the close shots of the camera demand in normal film-making. Only when the opera itself has been conceived as an intimate study of character does it genuinely gain through the flexible interpretation possible on the screen. *The Medium* was on every count a good film, and the nearer we approached the singers the greater the effectiveness and the poignancy of their characterization became. It is, of course, significant that Menotti himself directed his opera for the cinema.

A daring experiment which succeeded was the modernization of *Carmen* in the film *Carmen Jones*, interpreted in an American setting

66

by an American Negro cast. Nothing was taken from Bizet's opera but the broad outline of the plot and the music. Acted with all the emotional power which Negro artists bring to the drama, *Carmen Jones* possessed the vitality of a well-directed American musical. The impact of the entirely new lyrics sung in contemporary American idiom was in striking contrast to the familiarity of the music. It is interesting to remember that Rita Hayworth's film *The Loves of Carmen*, in which Bizet's music was not used, could never replace the musical associations which Bizet's score had created, in spite of its quite new visual presentation of the story.

However interesting the arguments about the technical problems of presenting established operas on the screen may become, it is only the opera specially composed for the film which is really relevant to any discussion of film music. An opera composed specially for production through film must exploit the flexibility of camera presentation, the close-shot and freedom of movement in the action, and the possibilities in aural inventiveness which microphone adjustment permits. The film industry has not, as far as we are aware, produced a film-opera of this kind, though American television in 1951 commissioned Menotti to compose the short and beautiful Christmas opera *Amahl and the Night Visitors*, and in 1955 the BBC television service gave a similar commission to Arthur Benjamin.

The nearest approach to the operatic form specially devised for the film is, of course, the American musical itself—and this obviously derives from the comic-opera tradition of the theatre which intersperses scenes of action and spoken dialogue with set-piece musical "numbers", the form of operetta fully established last century by Gilbert and Sullivan. We shall discuss the film musical later in this Section.

The movement of dancers has always attracted the film-maker, even in the days of silent film. The American musical relies as much on its spectacular dance numbers as it does on its lyrics; but the musical needs choreography specially created for the camera and the screen. The ballet of the theatre is an elaborate and subtle pattern of movement designed to be seen on the open arena of the stage. The movement of the principal dancers must be watched against the background of the corps de ballet, and when they dance solo, pas de deux, pas de quatre, etc., their movements are intended to be seen within the unity of the scene as a whole—small figures dancing against the background of the setting within an enclosed area on a stage which they constantly traverse in a play of light and colour. The instinct of the film-maker, on the other hand, is always to break

67

down the action into fragments which will be seen from different camera positions, and subsequently re-integrated on the cutting bench.

This is obviously why ballet conceived for the total arena of the theatre stage appears so ineffective on the screen. The long continuous chain of movement is not intended to become subject to the cut-and-come-again methods of the cinema. The close-up or midshot of the dancing ballerina does not show a part of the ballet she is dancing—all it shows is a part of the ballerina herself! This may well be sufficient for plot purposes which lie outside the performance of the ballet, but it is not satisfactory as a film presentation of the dance.

The American musical has again shown us what can be achieved on the screen when a dance-number is devised specially for the camera. The choreography of the screen-ballet exploits all the possibilities of the cinema, making variability of camera viewpoint as well as the timing and rhythm of cutting part of the technique of presentation, indeed part of the dance itself. The dancers dance, the screen images dance, the cutting-rhythms dance. There is, indeed, no more dynamic form of cinema. There is all the difference between this integrated presentation of dancing and the long shots alternated by occasional close-shots of an established or pastiche form of classical ballet performed on a theatrical stage during the course of a film. Even though a composer may have been invited, as he sometimes is, to write a fragment of "pastiche" ballet music especially for a particular film, he is not composing true film music. What he is then doing is compose for the theatre within the framework of the cinema.

For television, the BBC has not only produced specially presented stage operas—larger screens and the general introduction of colour have of course contributed to their effectiveness—but has commissioned TV-conceived operas from several composers, including Britten (*Owen Wingrave*) and Bliss (*Tobias and the Angel*).

A continuing problem in the creation of opera and ballet for television is the presentation of existing stage works, the vast repertory of which includes some of the greatest, and also the most popular, music. Thanks to Jack Bornoff, Executive Music Secretary of UNESCO, with warm cooperation from the Austrian Radio (which, be it said, had no TV service of its own at the time), experts from many countries met in Salzburg in 1956 to discuss the presentation of opera in radio and on film, and of ballet also on film. The result was the renewal of the Conference on a triennial

68

basis, with the addition of TV, demonstrations being given on monitors. The City of Salzburg itself generously offered a prize for the best TV opera as so adjudged by an international jury. Ten countries sent entries, including Japan, then all on film. Even at that time, the use of electronic music was in evidence. Later, colour was used, and Salzburg has remained the venue for this triennial Conference to which producers and directors come from all over the world, and the City has not only continued but increased the value of the opera prize. Commercial films are also shown, e.g. the Czinner-Maxwell *Don Giovanni* in 1956 and Betafilm's *Der Junge Lord* (Henze) later, together with examples of symphonic music like Von Karajan's *Beethoven: Symphony IX.* The conference discusses many and various techniques and styles.

Film remained the best medium for the visual side of all this (the sound, on TV at least, usually being heard from a magnetic tape running in synchronization), and many opera films, with or without magnetic tracks, are, and will continue to be, shown on TV. The videotape has now widely replaced film in television work. It combines picture and sound magnetically on one tape. It is easy to edit, cut, dub, transmit, and transport. Tapes can be dubbed from film, but the reverse is unfortunately impracticable. The restricted number of lines comprising the visual image, when "blown up" for the large screen, fall far short of modern photography on our wide theatre screens. Yet, as many music films are co-produced with TV authorities (notably in Germany), they are naturally available in the cinema, but in Academy format, rarely in wide-screen.

A tremendous amount of thought has been expended on presenting "concert" and other performed music on film. Variations on the old Hollywood "de luxe" layout, based on normal concerts, with fancy lighting and often inappropriate and vulgar ornamentation and gimmicks, have been endless. TV has offered many imaginative attempts, dignified and less so, and recent symphonic films have ranged from concert halls and "doctored" studios to cathedrals and opera houses. What electric multi-track recording and camera lenses have together brought to music films is the cutting in of closeup shots of momentarily important performers—soloists or groups— into the general picture, linked by all-important close shots of the conductor, whose facial expressions and gestures, whist giving cues, add greatly to the unity of the whole and the entertainment of the audience. The latter, for whose benefit the film is made, normally sees only the back of the conductor. "Emphasis" microphones underline the sound needed for the internal closeups, and the

69

multi-stereo tracks of modern film are unfortunately of little value to TV sets, which devote their space to vision while the sound amplification and speaker are utterly unworthy of the beauty of the original. Hi-Fi reproduction in the home makes one painfully aware of this.

Early films immediately discovered the value of personality; hence the importance of "the star". This is true in music presentation also. Stokowski proved himself a "natural" for film, and the multi-microphone technique he championed is now accepted as a necessity. Being no longer regarded as a mere showman, the Maestro's fine musical qualities are once again, after many years, being appreciated—at the age of ninety! Possibly the best music specifically composed for film is still Britten's *Young Person's Guide to the Orchestra*. In this, the composer, camera and soundmixer worked in complete unison, the whole being linked by that compulsive and genial personality, Sir Malcolm Sargent.

André Previn is doing the same service for BBC-TV; it is significant that he had already learned his job, and was highly successful, in the world of film. Leonard Bernstein, himself a notable conductor-presenter, is now filming for Betafilm AG all Mahler's Symphonies in a collaborative venture involving London Weekend Television (Aquarius).

Argument still continues regarding playback *versus* direct techniques in both opera and even in symphonic music. (It seems universally accepted that ballet is most satisfactorily filmed sequence by sequence to pre-recorded track, either taken from stage performance by the same artists or conducted by an M.D. who knows exactly from experience all the tempi and modifications demanded by the choreographer /principals concerned). A leading employer of both techniques is BETAFILM A.G. in Munich, who have boldly extended their efforts to great symphonies and choral works (see list below). It is fair to mention that in Austria soon after World War 2 a film was made of a Bach *Passion*, but it was never shown publicly in Britain.

Sometimes singers who can act mime to their own re-recorded tracks (Bohème, Carmen—many opera houses these days have this possibility in mind in casting their roles). Others "doubled" as in the early opera films like Pagliacci with an impossible young and slender Nedda, dancing alone in the middle of a meadow. In *Aida* one hears the voices of Tebaldi and Stignani, but watches film stars like Loren and Formichi. Von Karajan extended playback technique even to the whole orchestra, as in his Beethoven Symphonies and the Prelude and Interludes to Carmen: Kubelik and Boehm believed this to be wrong and insisted on simultaneous filming and recording. (Kubelik's *Eroica* is a good example). Often the techniques are mixed within the one film.

In playback there is always that great problem of lip-synchronisation in close-up, which is most nearly achieved in Fritz Buttenstedt's use of three spare mike circuits in addition to the main two all-in mikes: one of the three is pretty certain to have picked up the phrase momentarily needed by the editor.

Of quite unique and outstanding quality is Arthur Rubenstein's *Love of Life*.[1] For more than three months, François Reichenbach and Bernard Gavoty followed the pianist (already 82 years old) on his "trips and stays". He chats and reminisces about his long life of music, many amusing, some sad. He plays: but musicians must wish the 91 minutes' film had been extended to 2 hours to allow time for more complete pieces and fewer promising but unfinished scraps. A master's film about a Master.

Notable Opera and Ballet Films Since 1957

Aida (Verdi) ca. 1958. Italy. With voices of international stage fame (Tebaldi, Stignani) doubled in vision by film stars like Loren and Formichi, Corps and Ballet of Rome Opera, cond. Morelli. Director unnamed in programmes.

Der Rosenkavalier (R. Strauss) ca. 1959. Germany. Salzburg Festival performance with original cast, stylishly presented on film by Paul Czinner: Vienna State Opera, conductor Von Karajan.

Madame Butterfly (Puccini) Italy. Japanese cast and ballet, Rome Opera Company conducted by De Fabritis: dir. Carmine Gallone.

La Bohème (Puccini) ca. 1968. Germany. Freni, Raimondi, Panerai with La Scala Opera, Milan, dir. Zeffirelli and Von Karajan, cond. Von Karajan.

The Merry Wives of Windsor (Nicolai) ca. 1960. Yugoslavia. Norman Foster as Falstaff with Zagreb Opera. Dir. Norman Foster. Mainly American Cast, cond. George Tressler.

La Traviata (Verdi) ca. 1964. Italy. Dir. LaFranchi, starring Anna Moffo, Companion Film, Lucia di Lammermoor. (Donizetti) (not released G.B.).

Fidelio (Beethoven) ca. 1964. Two versions from Germany. Hamburg Opera Co. dir. Liebermann, both Hamburg State Opera

[1]*Love of Life* ca. 1969 France. (Miden Prodn). Dir. Reichenback and Patris.

German Opera, Berlin, dir. Sellner, cond. Boehm more imaginative than former.

Carmen (Bizet) 1968. Salzburg Festival Performance filmed by commuting to Munich studios. Directed and Conducted by Von Karajan. Vienna State Co. and Phil. Orch. international (?) cast. Von Karajan, like Hitchcock, makes brief appearance in crowd in Act 1. Ernst Wild's imaginative camera work supplemented by Francois Reichenbach's interjected close-ups, good in opera but irritating in orch. interludes. (Orch. playback. Interesting: the 3 Preludes to Von Karajan's *Der Rosenkavalier* of 10 years earlier.)

I Pagliacci (Leoncavallo) 1969. Germany. Dir. edited and cond. Von Karajan: La Scala Company with international cast.

Cavalleria Rusticana (Mascagni) 1968/9. Germany. Dir. Ake Falk, cond. Von Karajan: as *I Pagliacci*.

Cosi Fan Tutte (Mozart) 1971. Germany. Dir. Vaclavkaslik. Vienna Philharmonic International cast. Cond. Boehm. Excellent presentation of Baroque production—overdone perhaps in costumes and filming of an intimate *stage* work.

The Barber of Seville (Rossini) 1972. Germany. Dir. Fritz Buttenstedt. La Scala production with cast including Berganza, Prey, Alva, Dara, Montarsolo; cond. Ab Ado. Brilliant.

Háry János (Kodaly) 1965/6. Hungary. (Mafilm-Hungarofilm). Charming reconstruction of the legendary story with the internationally famous music (not strictly an opera). Part stylised, part realistic. Good example of using original music without maltreating it. Actors miming to opera singers, English sub-titles. All State resources. Cond. Ferencsik; Dir. Miklós Szinetár.

The Marriage of Figaro (Mozart) 1969. Germany. Earlier version, in German, heavily cut. Ca 1960. Berlin State Opera Orchestra. Doubled cast. Compere with Germany. Hamburg Opera Company. (Liebermann), full version, filmed on stage. Imaginative use of camera backstage during Overture.

The Mikado (Gilbert & Sullivan) 1969. England. D'Oyly Carte Company filmed in Golder's Green Hippodrome. Dir. Stuart Burge. Birmingham City Symph. Orch. cond. Isidor Godfrey.

The Firebird (Stravinsky) and *Ondine* (Henze) England. Dir. Czinner in Covent Garden Opera House. Royal Ballet with Margot Fonteyn.

Romeo and Juliet (Prokofiev) England. Dir. Czinner in film studio using the original stage sets. Royal Ballet with Margot Fonteyn. Much "action", dancing excellent, chief criticism was that some needed modifying for film.

Swan Lake (Tchaikovsky) 1965. Germany. Filmed in Schonbrunn studios with Vienna State Ballet and Fonteyn and Nureyev. (Nureyev choreography). Vienna Philharmonic Orchestra cond. Lanchbery.

Giselle (Adam). At least two interesting contrasted versions: 1956. England. Bolshoi Ballet with Ulanova and Fadeyechev, filmed in Covent Garden Opera House on stage after Royal Performance using tapes recorded during the performance. Session continued all through the night. Shortened version (63 minutes). Dir. Czinner. 1970. Germany. In Bronson studio Madrid. American Ballet Theatre with Carla Fracci and Erik Bruhn. German Opera Orchestra pre-recorded Berlin, cond. Lanchbery. Full length (95 minutes) sumptuous, realistic production, dir. Hugo Niebeling.

Concert and Religious Music
Beethoven. All *Symphonies.* Several *Mozart* and others, e.g. Dvořák. Germany. Filmed in Berlin, Vienna, Munich, completed Munich. Conductors, Von Karajan, Kubelik, Boehm, some direct, some playback techniques.

Verdi. Requiem. 1970. Germany. Filmed in La Scala, Milan with the Opera House resources and international cast. Cond. Von Karajan. Dir. Clouzot.

Bach. Mass in B. Minor. 1970. Germany. Munich Bach Choir and Orchestra in Monastic Church, Diessen am Ammersee, cond. Karl Richter. Dir. Arnbom.

Mahler. Complete Symphonies being filmed by B.F. in various venues, e.g. Ely Cathedral, cond. Leonard Bernstein.

Performed Music: Filmed Concert and Cabaret

The composer is sometimes required to write original music for concert performance within a film when, for one reason or another, established music will not fit the dramatic situation. The result may be a composition which eventually becomes well-known in its own right, like Richard Addinsell's famous *Warsaw Concerto*, composed for the film *Dangerous Moonlight*, which was an essentially romantic British picture about a Polish pianist serving in the Air Force during the war, a part played by Anton Walbrook. The piece is not typical of Addinsell's normal work, but he made a brilliant job of writing this short pastiche in the style of Rachmaninoff required for the concert performance which occurs in the film. It is not, of course, a concerto in the proper sense of the term, but in the space of a very few minutes it gives a vivid impression of the concerto form with all the romantic bravura associated with this kind of music.

The exact stages in the progression of this work have been noted down by Muir Mathieson, Music Director to the production:

Terence Young, writer and director, was on duty at an Army camp in 1940. While listening to a piano concerto from an American short-wave radio station he sketched out the idea of a Polish concert pianist who fights with the Air Force during the German invasion, escapes to England and joins the R.A.F. The finished script called for a short descriptive work for piano and orchestra that would give the impression of a concert pianist playing a concerto in the recognizable style of a romantic composer like Rachmaninoff.

Richard Addinsell was given the task and, over a period of six months, he produced a nine-minute tabloid concerto which was originally untitled. No credit title was given to the work nor was the name of the pianist who "doubled" for Anton Walbrook on the sound-track. It was only when the film appeared at the Regal Cinema, Marble Arch, that inquiries began to come in regarding the nature of the work. Neither records nor sheet music had been issued at the time, so arrangements were rushed through for a publisher.

There was no time to make a special gramophone record and, in the hurry, an "N.G. take"[1] of the music track that had now become known as *The Warsaw Concerto* was used for making the commercial disc. As I have often pointed out, the pianist, Louis Kentner, and the London Symphony Orchestra are out of step at one point towards the end, but this technical error seems to have given the work an added value as it creates a rather curious effect of its own!

Another good example of this kind of special concert hall composition for a film occurs in another British production, *Men of Two Worlds*, directed by Thorold Dickinson. Sir Arthur Bliss composed for the opening scene a short concert-piece which is introduced as a work by the African Kisenga, who is the hero of the film. The camera tracks along through the audience at one of the London picture galleries which were used during the war years for lunch-time concerts. It finally reaches the platform where Kisenga is preparing to play the cadenza to his concerto, and the camera cuts into a close-up of his hands, dark against the white keys, as the cadenza begins. In it you can hear the reverberation of those African drums—a living musical memory in the composer's mind. The piece is called a "Baraza", the Swahili word for a tribal council. This miniature concerto is perfect in its musical form. It is divided into three short movements together with the cadenza, and, like the Epilogue to Bliss's music for *Things to Come*, ends with a fine choral effect.

There is no form of inset musical performance which the action of some film will not eventually require. The old-time music-hall and the contemporary night-club are among the more recurrent scenes

---

[1]"N.G. take" is a rejected recording.

in our films. A scene in a cabaret gives the composer and lyric-writer the chance they always need to launch a new number in isolation on its own merit, as distinct from forming part of a major score for a musical. This does not normally represent any very specialized form of composition to them, except that the mood of the music and the sentiment of the lyric must sometimes reflect the situation in the film. It is only film music in so far as it is just required for use in a film. Otherwise, such songs follow the routine pattern associated with commercial "numbers" of their kind.

Musical interest is much stronger in those few films (like *Muscle Beach* or *Jammin' the Blues*) in which a real attempt is made to integrate jazz and other forms of popular music to the technique of film-making. In these cases the music takes the precedence and the film-maker responds pictorially to its rhythm and atmosphere.

The concert performance of established music is frequent in films. The instinct of the film-maker is to study the main phases in the development of the music and feature on the screen the player or players most concerned, cutting back now and then to long shots of the orchestra as a whole or close-shots of the conductor. When one of the leading characters is a soloist (as in *The Seventh Veil* or *The Magic Bow*), a leading executant must deputize on the sound-track for the star who goes through the motions of playing on the screen. This is purely a technical matter which is no concern of the composer of film music, except that there is an ever-present temptation to the film-maker to use sections of established music of the more popular kind which are out of copyright, instead of employing a composer to create a score which can be integrated closely to the needs of the film.

The disadvantages of using established music in dramatic films are several. The chief disadvantage is that it has an artistic vitality independent of the film. Its familiarity to the public has already made it into a breeding-ground for emotional responses which may or may not help the particular atmosphere or situation in the film. *Brief Encounter* offers an interesting example of this, and there will always be disagreement about how far the wonderful acting performance given by Celia Johnson was helped by the frequent recurrence on the sound-track of Rachmaninoff's Piano Concerto No. 2. Another main disadvantage of using established music with a strong emotional appeal is that the timing of those sections of the score which the film-maker wishes to use can seldom be made to fit correctly to individual scenes in the film.

More recently, the growing popularity of classical music for the orchestra has led to innumerable biographical studies of composers which act as a framework for the screen presentation of the more popular themes from their works. Whether the motives for producing these films be commercial or cultural or both, it is doubtful if either the composer or the cinema is well served by these anthologies of musical bits and pieces, though this matters rather less when the subject of the film biography is a composer of music only on the more popular level. The musical quotations used in these films are usually far too fragmentary, and tend to be derived from the most familiar themes.

Two other kinds of film which feature "performed" music already established in the concert hall should be mentioned here—films which offer various forms of visual interpretation of classical music and instructional films which are designed to further the appreciation of music.

Anyone who visited the silent cinema with any consistency will remember the convention of matching mood music to scenic or travel films, or, for that matter, to those sequences in dramatic films which used a series of scenic shots to establish atmosphere. It became a favourite practice, particularly in the German *Kulturfilm* movement, to "illustrate" a performance of classical music with interminable landscape shots of a mood rather obviously similar to that of the composition played on the sound-track.

This is of some concern to the film composer because it represents the misuse of music in the cinema, and so makes his task more difficult when he is discussing original composition with the kind of producer and director who expect him to flood their pictures with a similar continuous flow of sound vaguely approximating in mood to what is being shown on the screen. This is the "background" as opposed to the "functional" employment of music, and it is all the more to be deplored because it debases the performance of fine compositions to the level of an accompaniment to sentimental scenic films.

Instructional films in music appreciation such as *Instruments of the Orchestra* and *A Beethoven Sonata* (a filmed performance of a Beethoven Sonata for Horn and Piano, made by Ken Cameron) have been concerned so far to demonstrate how music is created in performance (that is, how it is done) rather than to deal with the nature of music itself (why it is what it is). The team-work of an orchestra can be admirably illustrated in a film, the picture cutting from one to another section of the instrumentalists as certain instruments take precedence in the continuity of the performance. The

76

conductor, soloists and featured players become the stars in the visual interplay of musical action, and the music itself gives the film its dramatic continuity. An example of this technique is to be found in *Instruments of the Orchestra*.

Instruments of the Orchestra was made for the Ministry of Education by the Crown Film Unit in 1946. The music, which was specially written, consists mainly of variations on a theme of Purcell by Benjamin Britten; it is performed in the concert hall under the title of *A Young Person's Guide to the Orchestra*. Muir Mathieson directed the film, using the London Symphony Orchestra conducted by Sir Malcolm Sargent. The sound-track was recorded by Ken Cameron in Wembley Town Hall.

One of the satisfying elements of the film is its clarity. The full orchestra plays the Purcell theme, followed by separate performances from the woodwind, strings, brass and percussion. It is then played again on the full orchestra. Each section is taken in turn and the instruments are shown by means of a series of variations. Finally, as Sir Malcolm Sargent puts it, "having taken the orchestra to pieces, we must put it together again". Benjamin Britten provides a Fugue for this purpose, in which all the instruments play the tune in succession. At the end, the brass enters with the Purcell tune, whilst the rest of the orchestra continues to play Britten's Fugue.

The progression of the Fugue sequences is as follows:

I. MEDIUM SHOT into MEDIUM LONG SHOT. CAMERA ON CRANE. WOOD-WIND. (48 seconds.)
The shot opens with the piccolo announcing the Fugue theme:—

(Reproduced by kind permission of Boosey & Hawkes Ltd.)

The camera then moves along the woodwind line, reaching each instrument as it starts to play the theme: piccolo, flutes, oboes, clarinets and bassoons. The camera finally moves round to give a general view of the complete woodwind section in action.
2. LONG SHOT FROM ABOVE. CAMERA ON CRANE. STRINGS. (50 seconds.)
The camera is very high up, looking down on the violins as they play the theme. A fast pan to the violas. A fast pan to the 'cellos. A slight tilt up the frame reveals the double basses at the rear of the main string body. A slight diagonal tilt down brings the harp to the centre of the picture, between the double basses and the 'cellos. The camera swings upward across the strings to reveal the brass section on a rostrum at the back of the orchestra.
3. MEDIUM SHOT FROM BELOW. CAMERA ON CRANE. BRASS. (22 seconds.)
The camera is slightly below the line of the brass, giving them a powerful appearance. First, the horns; fast pan to the trumpets; fast pan to the trombones and tuba.
4. LONG SHOT into VERY LONG SHOT. CAMERA ON CRANE. PERCUSSION into FULL ORCHESTRA. (45 seconds.)
The camera is already craning and tracking as the percussion appear on a rostrum at the back of the orchestra and on a level with the brass. After 12 seconds of percussion, the Purcell theme enters on the brass as the rest of the orchestra continues to play the Fugue. The camera cranes and tracks slowly back as the music rises to a crescendo.
5. EXTREME LONG SHOT. FIXED POSITION. FULL ORCHESTRA. (20 seconds.)
The camera takes in the full orchestra from afar for the Coda. The "End" title fades in rapidly on the last beat.

The skilled use of the camera to match the music has made this film one of the most successful experiments in the field of musical education by means of the cinema.

The lives of composers have over the years received extensive treatment on film, ranging from Poland's *The Young Chopin* in 1951, *The Story of Gilbert and Sullivan* made in Great Britain in 1953 and a number of films made in Hollywood including such films as *The Song of Schéhérazade* (the supposed life of Rimsky-Korsakov), *A Song to Remember* (a life of Chopin with Cornel Wilde as Chopin and Merle Oberon as the writer George Sand). Disney, too, produced his non-animation romantic story of the young Beethoven, *The Magnificent Rebel*, starring Carl Boehm as the young composer.

All these films are remarkable for their near sentimental treatment of the composers, their lives and their music. Music appears as more an emotion-boosting accompaniment to a good and at times tearful story. Who can forget the drop of red consumptive blood on the ivory keyboard in *A Song to Remember*? Little was attempted to reveal the real life of the composer through his music, or period in the composer's life with the sound track of music which had affinity to it.

Andrew L. Stones' two films *The Great Waltz* (on Strauss) and his *Song of Norway* (on Grieg) continued this basic Hollywood formula that music and romance equals money.

It is perhaps totally impossible to film music, perhaps incorrect to attempt to supply images to accompany great music. There is, too, the problem of historical accuracy, which is not confined to composers' lives. John Huston's *Moulin Rouge* is an historically inaccurate life of the painter Henri Toulouse-Lautrec, but yet still breathes the smell of Lautrec's milieu and art.

One is tempted to ask whether the life of a composer is vital to the understanding of his music. Is a knowledge of Beethoven's deafness vital to the enjoyment and understanding of his later music?

In 1955 Aram Avakian edited footage of Igor Stravinsky at a recording session conducting his *Story of a Soldier*. It appears that because the footage shot covered the action rather badly, it made it near impossible to edit it in a "classical" way.

Avakian did the then totally novel editing procedure of both jump cutting (which Jean-Luc Godard would make appear his own in his first feature *A Bout de Souffle* in 1959) and splicing together passages regardless of continuity. What moves this film out of being simply a film about a recording session into being a filmed musical life and work of Igor Stravinsky is the feeling of the edited end-product. The film seems to mirror the angular, near cubist nature of the music. Avakian recalls:

I intercut it and followed what I felt was the cubist nature of the music. . . . The nature of Stravinsky and his music seemed to dictate that kind of cutting— all those fantastic time changes every four bars. The way I cut the film, it didn't matter that Stravinsky had his coat off in one shot, on in the next, then had a towel around his neck in the one after that.*

It is the editing style which, coupled with the music, expresses much of the musical nature of this thirteen minute film, and turns it into a portrait of the man, Igor Stravinsky.

In Jean-Marie Straub's *Chronicle of Anna Magdalena Bach* (Italy-Germany, 1968) it is the visual compositions that Straub and his director of photography, Ugo Piccone, use which express much that the music of Bach also expresses. Straub uses a near static camera in long takes with occasional tracks in or out. The take length is dictated by the length of the music. The compositions are heavily baroque, mirroring the nature of the music—perspective is heavily weighted on one side of the frame in an asymmetric composition. The diagonals are often contrasting yet lead the eye inward toward the centre of action. There is a simplicity as opposed to a multiplicity of subject interest.

Basically ready in 1959 to make the film, Straub had to wait nearly ten years before he would find backers, for Straub refused to make compromises except perhaps in finally shooting the film in black and white. The script, written by himself and his wife Danièle Huillet, is in period German. It is not the actual diary of Anna Magdelena Bach, for she did not keep such a book. It is a compilation of phrases from Johann Sebastian Bach's own letters and other related documents from the period, but the facts are all historically accurate.

The film covers the life of Bach from his marriage in 1721 to his death in 1748. Shot on location at numerous settings (where they still existed) Bach himself visited, the film was shot totally sync. The sound, even on the music has no generalized accoustic balance (unlike most films which include choral and orchestral music). Straub's sound recordist Paul Schöler (with Louis Hochet and Lucien Moreau) used a single microphone set-up (here again most unusual for music recordings). The microphone was placed near the camera thereby creating a sense that the music was actually being performed (as it was during the filming) and brought the

Movie People interview by Fred Baker and Ross Firestone. Lancer Books, New York 1973, pages 162–3.

audience into much closer participation of the performance. This "act of music making" which in Richard Roud's words "is one of the subjects of the film".* Gustav Leonhardt, the musician, played Bach and unlike other "lives of the composers" is actually playing the music heard on the sound track.

This film is a feature-length film which is really about music—Bach's music. It is also a love story of Anna Magdelena and Johann Sebastian, and could even be seen as a documentary film about musicians dressed up in period costume, wearing wigs and playing Bach's music.

Ken Russell and Igor Talankin each directed different feature films, which were, curiously, both about the life of Peter Ilyich Tchaikovsky (1840–1893). Where Straub strove religiously for some sort of accuracy (foresaking the romantic perhaps for the documentary) Russell often took strange liberties with Tchaikovsky. In Russell's words:

The thing is that the private lives of artists up until the present time were very carefully shielded. Tchaikovsky is a pertinent case in point. His brother Modeste wrote the official biography and burnt all the letters from Nina, the wife, and destroyed the diary of Tchaikovsky in which he had written about his homosexual liaisons with various people. So, as I say, it has become detective work. One may be totally wrong, but I always find in most of the films I do that the facts are more extraordinary than anything I can make up. Why I think the Hollywood biographies are all boring is because they all follow the same path. The Liszt and Chopin films were almost identical.

In an attempt to find the creative urge and torment of the composer, Russell pivots his whole film around Tchaikovsky's marriage to a nymphomaniac, Nina, and suggests further complications by claiming Tchaikovsky was a homosexual, inventing a liason for him with a totally fictional character Count Anton Chiluvky. Despite Russell's efforts to understand Tchaikovsky the man and Tchaikovsky the composer it is for just these reasons that the film takes such liberties with the music and history.

Konstantin Bazavov has written that the film lacks "any sense of the inner torment of the composer's neurotic sensibility which he poured into his increasingly subjective and emotional music." Perhaps Tchaikovsky's most deeply felt music, the *Pathétique* (Symphony No. 6 in B minor), which is in Russia associated with

*Richard Roud's *Straub*, Secker and Warburg's Cinema One Series, published 1971. For other works on Straub see Roud's *Minimal Cinema: Chronicle of Anna Magdalena Bach*, pages 134–5, *Sight and Sound*, Summer 1968; Andi Engel's chapter on Straub in *The Second Wave*, Studio Vista, London 1971; and Andi Engels' long interview with Straub in *Cinemantics*, No. 1, January 1970.

death, is used over the scene when Nina and Tchaikovsky are on a honeymoon train ride which turns into a shaking, jolting ride of two nude drunks, both sexually frustrated and dissatisfied. The *1812 Overture* serves for a comic strip success sequence. Perhaps Tchaikovsky's own use of cannon and gun fire in this piece could be seen as verging on kitsch, but for Russell this piece is heard to a barrage of garish visuals—streamers, cheering, cannons decapitating those who have tormented Tchaikovsky. The Allegro of the First Piano Concerto in B flat minor (which is played on the sound track by Raphael Orozco) comes in a scene which starts in a concert hall and Tchaikovsky (Richard Chamberlain) is seen to be actually playing the piece. To achieve this, rare indeed in such films of composers' lives, but not rare in Straub's *Chronicle of Anna Magdelena Bach*, Richard Chamberlain was apparently tutored for six months. From the concert hall the scene moves to scenes from his past life, showing the drift of his mind, finally, still to the sound of the Piano Concerto, the scene drifts into lyrical scenes shot in slow motion—swans, summer, the bank of a river . . .

Mosfilms with Dimitri Tiomkin, the American composer and arranger born in Russia, produced in 1970 another version of Tchaikovsky's life called *Tchaikovsky*, directed by Igor Talankin. This version treats Tchaikovsky and his music in a very different manner. There is little emphasis on the unhappy marriage and no mention of homosexuality.

Of the film Igor Talankin has written:

We did not set ourselves the aim of analysing the nature of music. We merely attempted to show by means available to us how music is not devised but erupted from the depths of the artist's soul.... There are two main "characters" in our film—Tchaikovsky and music. They make a single whole. Yet it is a conflicting whole. Now the composer conquers the music, now music gains the upper hand. He was destined to become a musician since early childhood. And it is the burden of genius, the anguish of creation, the price which the composer pays for the delight he gives his listeners, that we wanted to tell about in our film.

And the co-producer, arranger and conductor Dimitri Tiomkin:

In my film life of Tchaikovsky the star is the music. The interest of the man Tchaikovsky is that he wrote this music—why he wrote it, the state of mind that caused him to write it. When he is composing the Fourth Symphony, it is the Fourth Symphony that matters. At the end of the picture when Tchaikovsky is dying and we have the Sixth Symphony (the *Pathetique*), I am dropping all the illustrative element. After a film of three hours—three hours of creative and psychological study—I think we have the right to show music to the audience *au naturel*. I should like to have the screen in darkness, but it might be a little dangerous, so, with no fancy montage, no camera tricks, we shall just see the orchestra and listen.

The *Pathetique* in *Tchaikovsky* is associated most movingly with death. Quite a different treatment from Russell's. It is somewhat surprising that out of the some three hundred and forty minutes of music that Tchaikovsky did compose these two films use many of the same pieces. Both films use the *Eugene Onegin*. Russell puts it over a scene of Nina, hatefully writing to Tchaikovsky, her rage and nail biting frustration. Talankin uses this with scenes of Tchaikovsky in the midst of composing the work at a cafe table, amidst cafe table meetings and conversation, lit by the cafe and streets lights.

With an art form as subjective as music, and with composer's lives often so scantily documented, it is obvious that their lives should receive such diverse treatment. Ultimately it is the viewer, the listener who must decide, in a very personal way which film has expressed for him visually the musical essence of the work, or which has expressed justly the composer's life and the relationship of his music to that life.*

The Musical

We have already seen how the musical film, and more especially the American musical, developed during the early nineteen-thirties. The original back-stage musical (with spectacular numbers elaborately presented to the limits of the studio's resources) was not the only form; the romantic musical-comedy of the kind made famous by Fred Astaire and Ginger Rogers gave the film operetta its contemporary slant. Most American musicals today have contemporary boy-and-girl themes, though some, of course, go back to the period of the pioneers. The accent is always on youth—youth in the Services, youth in show-business, youth in all its glamorous vitality forging its way to fame among the pitfalls and opportunities of modern life. There is no form of American film-making which so vigorously reflects the popular American outlook on life. Most musicals, again, are adaptations from stage-shows—some (for example, *Call Me Madam*) undergo a less radical transformation for the screen than others (such as *On the Town*).

*For further discussion on the subject see Gordon Gow's "Shock Treatment". *Films and Filming*, July 1970. The quotations made by Ken Russell were taken from this article.
The quotation by Tiomkin was taken from *The Making of Feature Films—A guide* by Ivan Butler. Published in England by Penguin Books.

The highlight of the American musical is always the "number", whose theme is normally made familiar to the public before they ever see the film. Such actuality as the story possesses gives way when each song begins and invisible orchestras accompany the singers. Realism may be abandoned altogether, and the décor burst out into displays of spectacular design and colour, like those for the ballet sequence in *An American in Paris*.

The original concert hall work for *An American in Paris* was composed by Gershwin in 1928 as a result of undertaking some composition for an early sound film with a Parisian background. He had previously written *Rhapsody in Blue*, commissioned by Paul Whiteman for a Symphonic Jazz concert in 1924; the orchestration had been carried out by Ferde Grofe. When the New York Symphony Orchestra asked for a piano concerto in 1925, Gershwin began to orchestrate his music personally, as he did in the case of *An American in Paris*.

The main theme of *An American in Paris* in its original concert hall form is "a busy Paris in Spring". Taxi horns (with their augmented fourths), characteristic phrases using repeated notes, brief moments of contemplation, a trumpet blues (against an accompaniment with every other bar in double time), and a syncopated main theme make up the chief elements in the pattern. This and the concerto are the most interesting of Gershwin's concert hall works.

For the purpose of the film ballet, Johnny Green, Conrad Salinger and, in particular, Saul Chaplin, all of the MGM studio staff, re-orchestrated and re-edited Gershwin's work extensively, lengthening some themes and juxtaposing others so that the material might be arranged into five main parts. A feature of the whole film ballet was the close link between the colour on the screen and the music. In each sequence décor is derived from the style of one or other of the post-Impressionist painters.

1. Busy Paris. The first sequence retains the basic pattern of the original work. Pizzicato strings and full brass announce the theme; a huge square, reminiscent of the Place de la Concorde and dominated by a fountain, is full of traffic, policemen, soldiers, visitors-about-town, and gaily-dressed girls. The taxi-horn theme appears a number of times. The dominant colours are the red dresses of a group of girls, and the red, blue and gold uniforms of the hussars, who break in with their madiche tune at regular intervals. The backgrounds are designed in the style of Raoul Dufy's paintings; Gene Kelly appears dressed in black and Leslie Caron in white. As night comes, red remains the dominant colour.

2. The Flower Market. A quiet moment for a pas de deux between Gene Kelly and Leslie Caron takes place in a small setting amongst flower stalls on the Left Bank, derived pictorially from the styles of Manet and Monet. The music consists of gentle woodwind and violin solos, with celesta, occasional muted trumpets and a slow linking passage for horns. The colours are various pastel shades of blue; a red rose, symbol of love, supplies the solitary splash of bright colour.

3. The Gay Whirl. In a street set like a painting by Utrillo, Gene Kelly meets a group of G.I.s. Everyone changes into brightly-coloured blazers; Kelly is dressed in red. Gaily-clad children are seen in the Jardins de Luxembourg, a set based on the style of le Douanier Rousseau. Leslie Caron and a group of girls are in bright multi-coloured dresses. The men represent modern America; they perform vigorous tap-dance routines. The girls present classical ballet; they execute pirouettes and bourrées courus, but they dance in modern Gershwin time. The hussars express tradition, maintaining their march movements like an old music-hall ballet.

4. Tempo Blues. There follows a very sharp transition to the blues, which through excellent recording, gives great scope to the trumpet and rhythm accompaniment. The backgrounds are in deep yellow and orange, with Gene Kelly and Leslie Caron appearing as black silhouettes. The action returns to the fountain set, and the dancers are seen bathed in red light against a deep blue-green, orange and finally blinding white light.

5. Finale. The orange and reds intensify, the music changes to a very fast, heavily-scored section leading to the Toulouse-Lautrec sequence. Kelly appears in the guise of Aristide Bruant, dressed in pale orange. Then the Can-Can girls enter in traditional white frilly petticoats, with red and black stockings; Leslie Caron wears a flaming orange skirt. The music grows more and more wild as the picture explodes into a whirl of colour. Suddenly, on a held chord for full orchestra, the great crowd disappears from the square. The colours change abruptly, leaving only pale blue and green. All reds disappear, except that of the solitary symbolic rose, towards which the camera moves as the final chord rises to a sustained crescendo.

Few composers have equalled the attack of Leonard Bernstein's style in this type of musical, as represented by his score for *On the Town*. His vociferous brass and thundering percussion provide natural material for the broad and glorious outcry of the MGM Studio Orchestra. There is integrity as well as great orchestral skill in his work, for Bernstein is as much a composer of the concert hall and ballet stage as he is of Tin Pan Alley. With the exception of the title number, his score for *On the Town* seems almost deliberately to avoid including a melody that people can whistle. In consequence, the straight numbers are its weakest elements; *You're Awful—Awful Nice to Know, Dear* seems to be wrested from an unwilling hand, anxious to get on with the next ballet. This characteristic is equally true of his second venture in the same style, *Wonderful Town* (which, at the time of writing, has only been seen on the stage); the impact again comes largely from the range of musical idea and the orchestral colour rather than from memorable songs.

The title number with which *On the Town* opens avoids a clear-cut tune. It is based on an often-repeated series of short notes, similar in style to Gershwin's theme in *An American in Paris*. There is no attempt to present the singing as anything but an occasional interlude in the forward drive of the ballet; the primary function of the music is to suggest the sledge-hammer pulse-beat of a great city. No one is likely to be inspired by the actual words of the frequently-stated main lyric:

> New York! New York! It's a wonderful town;
> The Bronx is up and the Battery's down;
> The people ride in a hole in the ground;
> New York! New York! It's a wonderful town.

Yet the complete unit of the brass figures, drum beats, xylophone frills, heavily-syncopated passages and the jingle of the words form one of the most impressive openings to a musical so far devised.

Bernstein's most characteristic style is to be found in the *Prehistoric Man* sequence, which offers great scope for the drum effects in which he delights. In this, as in many other scenes, the playback system has been used with considerable imagination. By recording the whole of the sound-track before shooting commences, the skilful musical director can endow the picture with pace and range. Thus, the scene of a crane-driver singing on the dockside at five o'clock in the morning when the film opens was shot on location; his voice is given the right degree of modulation and feeling in the recording studio, and the visual interpretation creates a wonderful feeling of freedom as the camera cranes along the actual Naval Shipyard in New York. The opening number for the three sailors carries a similar feeling of spaciousness by virtue of the fast cutting and exceptional use of playback in such difficult locations as the foredeck of a Staten Island ferry boat or the top of a Fifth Avenue bus.

The 1950's saw a whole range of musicals built around the latest, perishable, teenage idol. With the rise of the pop group in the 1960's this trend continued, tailored around the group itself. Often the film contained a slender story-line. It was the songs that counted. The most general trend over the whole period from the 1950's onwards was the translation of stage successes on Broadway and London into film musicals. *West Side Story* was one of these Broadway smash-hits to be turned into a film, but much of its brilliance was lost in the film version. New York's urban jungle background removed the bite and credibility it had on stage, and this was despite Daniel Fapp's, cool and steely, award-winning photography. *West Side Story* is notable for its eleven Academy Award Oscars, which included one for Leonard Bernstein's music and for Jerome Robbins' choreography.

Hit musical film of all times must surely be Rogers' and Hammerstein's last show together, *The Sound of Music*, aptly dubbed "The Sound of Money" because since its release in 1965 and up until 1972 it grossed over seventy-five million dollars. Directed by Robert Wise, *The Sound of Music* is memorable for its sharp editing. *Cabaret* emulated this in 1971—with its Visconti-like use of long drifting zooms. *The Sound of Music* collected Oscars for its editing by William Reynolds, for Ted McCord's photography, Irwin Kostal's scoring, Jane Corcoran's sound recording and for Robert Wise's direction.

In 1967 George Sidney, a veteran from Hollywood, came to England to direct England's first big musical *Half a Sixpence*. It had been, like *West Side Story* and *The Sound of Music*, a stage hit with Tommy Steele in the lead role. David Henneker, who composed the music recalls his experience on the film:

One of the greatest thrills for me was how George Sidney brought me in right from the start and, long before shooting, we used to meet together with Gillian Lynne, the choreographer. George would talk about the film and dissect the character of Kipps and what H. G. Wells had meant by a certain passage in the original book.

At least a year before final shooting every note and movement of the routine would be discussed by George, only later to be re-discussed when he brought in the top music man from Hollywood, Irwin Kostal, who had just won his third consecutive Oscar (the three being for his musical direction on *West Side Story*, *The Sound of Music* and *Mary Poppins*) to orchestrate and generally take over the musical direction. From then on I worked continually with Irwin, and, as shooting started, saw less of George.

A great deal of re-writing took place during the making of the film. Some of the re-writing was last minute panic work for me. For instance it was discovered that one of the songs that had been in the Broadway version, Tommy Steele's "11 o'clock number" in the second act, was not reconcilable with the new choreographic idea that had been thought up for the particular number. The one thing that could not be altered was the fact that we had H stage (the biggest and most expensive stage not only in Shepperton but in Europe at the time) for just five more days. The song and the choreography had to be altered. This meant a new song had to be written by the next day to give Gillian Lynne time to re-choreograph the number, rehearse it with the dancers, and also to give Tommy Steele time to learn both song and dance for it.

In 1969 *Hello Dolly*, yet another Broadway hit was turned into a film. It is remarkable, perhaps, for its planned production budget of around twenty million dollars, which makes it to date one of the most expensively planned budgets for a film. 1971 saw another adaption, *Cabaret*, directed by Bob Fosse with music by John Kander.

The setting is Berlin in 1931. The cabaret scenes of the film in the 'divinely decadent' Kit Kat Klub are at times electrifying. They rely heavily on close-ups of performers and audience. Less successful is the cross cutting to scenes outside the Klub. When the film opens up to the lives of Sally Bowles and Brian, outside the Klub, then the film is at its weakest. In Kander's stage original these scenes had contained musical numbers, but the film does largely without them. Like so many musicals (*Finian's Rainbow* excluded) the filmed musical falters when the director tries to make the film more than a musical. The action without song seems all too often without substance. *Cabaret's* editing style is highly complex and includes a large number of different camera angles. It is interesting to compare this complex, multi-camera set-up, with its resulting rapid editing of most of the musical numbers, with George Cukor's 1957 musical *Les Girls*. Cukor's musical numbers in this film are shot and edited in an extremely simple and economical way. The editing is at times hardly perceptible. Cukor sometimes uses only two cameras to cover a number, and even goes further in the edited version by going without close-ups. The whole number might be seen in one long shot. Cukor admits that this was not generally his planned intention. It was only after seeing the rushes of the two camera set-up that he realised what he had planned would be better achieved in one long shot.

Functional Music

We now reach what we regard as the most important section of this book—the analysis of examples of film music which in varying degrees represent the close and sympathetic working of the composer with the film-maker.

It seems singularly unfortunate that music which performs an important definite function in the film should ever have been termed "background" music. No one, except perhaps the most extreme balletomane, would suggest that the music written for a ballet functions solely as a background to the action on the stage, or that the operatic singer is supported by a background of music. The music of a ballet or an opera is an integral and complementary part of the art-form itself. It would be pushing the analogy too far to labour this point and, indeed, absurd to maintain that because opera cannot exist without music, and ballet is unthinkable without, at least, the rhythmic basis of music in the construction of its dance patterns, so the film cannot function without some form of musical accompaniment.

There have been many films made without the help of music, some of which have been eminently successful and effective precisely because of a studied absence of music and a compensatory reliance upon sound-tracks which side-stepped the too facile musical background. (After all, some films are basically realistic in conception—the word "some" is used advisedly as it would be an extremely dubious argument to advance that the art of the film is fundamentally a transcription of real life seen through the eyes of the camera—no art can claim to be an art if it is wholly real.) On the other hand the film without music could sometimes have been improved by the judicious addition of appropriate music.

Although, unlike ballet and opera, the film can dispense with music entirely, the practised craft of the film composer (and one should add, to some extent, the conditioned reflexes of the cinema audience) has made music a vital ingredient in the production of a film. When the editing stage is reached music allows the producer to linger in certain scenes to an extent he would not dare without the knowledge that music would subsequently support the visuals; music, indeed, allows the producer to suggest and express emotions and associations which would have been impossible to achieve by pictorial means alone.

Music is used with memorable effectiveness in the famous sequence of the charge of the French knights at Agincourt from *Henry V*. The originality and force of Sir William Walton's music fills the screen with a mounting excitement that could never have been achieved with natural sound effects alone. Its very unrealism moves audiences to believe in its living reality by playing insistently upon their emotional responses. Here music succeeds triumphantly and the sequence once experienced becomes unthinkable without the score. But this fine piece of film music is still classed under the generic title of "background" music, the same classification as that used for a piece of trite chase music in a serialized Western. It is wrong that film composers should be saddled with this unfortunate term, particularly as serious musical criticism increasingly tends to regard it in a derogatory sense.

Since Walton wrote the excellent score for *Henry V*, chase music has become a cliche that is best avoided. John Addison in *Tom Jones* introduced music only after the killing of the stag in the hunt scene. The whole of the hunt is accompanied solely by sound effects. The end result certainly does not lack excitement.

"Background" music in relation to the film is a misleading term and, in any case, does not describe its functions. "Integral" or "complementary" music might serve better, but the term "functional" is preferable, since the word implies the work a thing is designed to do. It is a proper and practical description of this newest branch of musical composition.

Functional music has a more complex relation to the action than realistic music since it is not an overt part of it. Here music "points", underlines, links, emphasizes, or interprets the action, becoming part of the dramatic pattern of the film's structure. For convenience in studying this boundless field of dramatic musical composition, we have divided it into various phases as the composer's approach to the work of composition is affected:

Music and Action.
Scenic and Place music.
Period and Pageant music.
Music for Dramatic Tension.
Comedy music.
Music of Human Emotion.
Music in Cartoon and Specialized Film.

In practice, film music begins to be functional at the point where it ceases to be mere background music, and takes its proper place in the dramatic structure of the film. As we have seen, the composer is normally introduced to the film when it has reached the stage known as the "rough-cut"—that is, when he can see it realized on the screen with its dialogue; in fact, it lacks only the sound effects and the element he must supply himself, the dramatic stimulus of music at those points in the action where the director feels the need for it. Often the director thinks he needs more music than is, in fact, good for the film; music can be so rich in emotional stimulation that too much of it surfeits the dramatic appetite of the audience. This is particularly true of music used too continuously for background effect.

But functional music must, by its very nature and definition, perform some necessary part in building up various kinds of dramatic effect, and the general rule might seem to be that the greater the economy with which music is used the greater the dramatic effect it will achieve. This is, of course, a controversial point. The first consideration of both director and composer is, therefore, to decide where music should not just as much as where music should be introduced. Some directors have in mind the future presence of music on the sound-track as they plan and shoot a particular sequence; others reach a decision as they supervise the editing of the film, sensing the need for musical support to carry and sustain the emotion of particular scenes and particular moments.

However a director discovers his need for music, the composer's own instinct in the matter should not be overlooked since, if he is a good composer of film music, he will know what his future score can achieve successfully at each point of the film where he is asked to assist. Once the passages are chosen and timed, he must go away and become a musician-actor, assuming the musical character of the film and creating music in the right dramatic mood for it. As the distinguished Italian composer of film music, Roman Vlad, put it when we consulted him: "The real creator of a film, in my opinion, is the director. I always try to compose the music which he would were he a composer."

In describing "functional" film music in the seven groups above, we do not want to imply that these are in any way strictly separate kinds of composition. But in the nature of the composer's work for films one or other of these functions may tend to be uppermost in his mind as he emphasizes an action, establishes the mood of a place or a period, or underlines and comments upon the human situation which a particular dramatic moment in a film may stress.

Normally film music should not become too complicated. It must enlighten, not baffle the audience (unless this is required for a deliberate dramatic effect). It must grip them, help them create the mood which is most in keeping with the needs of the film, and in doing this, it will have to stress now one, now another element in the drama. It is for this reason, as well as for convenience in presenting a variety of examples of film music for analysis, that we have adopted the succeeding divisions.

(i) Music and Action

David Lean (as director of the film) made the following advance note for the music he wanted to accompany the scene in *Oliver Twist* when Fagin introduces his methods of picking pockets to Oliver, who has just become a new recruit to his gang.

"The boys have sat down to supper with Fagin, and after the Dodger has brought out his spoils for the day, Fagin raps the table with the toasting-fork and says 'To work'. I should like music to accompany the whole scene of Fagin donning his hat, taking the walking stick and walking round like an old gentleman, and finally having his foot trodden on and his pockets picked, causing him to search frantically for his lost wallet and watch, which makes Oliver laugh so much. I think the music should start immediately after "To work" and end on the dissolve to Oliver lying asleep. This is to me almost the most important piece of music so far, and I should like to transform the scene into a comic ballet, with only one angry jar in it—the moment when Fagin gives the two boys who have failed to pick his pocket successfully a kick. This is important because, although I should like to emphasize the comedy in Fagin, I also want to retain his viciousness which is to develop more and more. In other words, Fagin as a character starts off in Oliver's eyes as an amusing old gentleman, and gradually this guise falls away and we see him in all his villainy."

Sir Arnold Bax's music does full justice to Lean's requirements. It is highly rhythmic, starting lightly and ending in a rich, vulgar tune. Three chords open out into the main idea, which begins on the strings; the development is interrupted with string chords and a rising phrase for trombones. The fun increases with a tune for the horns, with off-the-beat accompaniment by the full orchestra, going on to the trumpets and trombones as the noisy climax is reached, and a coda, based on the opening theme, brings the musical sketch to an end. At the recording session at Denham with the Philharmonia Orchestra conducted by Muir Mathieson, the music (shot as "4M1" —that is, the first section of music in reel 4) was first recorded straight through and then an additional sharp roll on the side drum (shot as "4M1—X") was recorded to obtain the vicious effect of the kick mentioned in Lean's notes.

The closest form of integration between music and action is known as "Mickey-Mousing" and is practised most obviously and consistently in cartoons and musicals. It is also closely associated with comedy. But in the normal dramatic film the *direct* reflection of the action in the music can easily become too obvious, and therefore banal and vulgar. It is interesting that both René Clair (in his book *Réflexions Faite*) and Jean Cocteau (in *Cocteau on the Film*) discount this particular use of music in film; in *Cocteau on the Film* there is a remarkable comment on the use of music by Cocteau in one of his dialogue-arguments with André Fraigneau:

"A.F. Let us now speak of the place you give to music in your films. The score of *La Belle et la Bête* is important, and was composed by Georges Auric as was the music of all your other films.
J.C. Nothing, it seems to me, can be more vulgar than music synchronism in films. It is, again, a pleonasm. A kind of glue where everything gets stuck rigid, and where no play (in the sense of 'play' in wood) is possible. What I like is accidental synchronism, the effectiveness of which I have had occasion to observe again and again. The best example I can cite comes from a ballet, not a film—*Le Jeune Homme et la Mort* where at the very last moment I decided to use Bach's *Passacaglia* so as to make the dances, based on jazz rhythms, take on an unexpected grandeur. Already from the second performance on, the dances 'inclined' towards the music, the conductor 'inclined' towards the dancers, and everything fell into place, so well, alas, that people refused to believe that the choreography had not been based on Bach.
A.F. But how can you hope for such accidental synchronism occurring with a score specially composed for a particular film?
J.C. I provoke it. Very often Auric gets annoyed, but he always ends by agreeing with what I've done.
A.F. How do you provoke it?
J.C. By re-shuffling. I've been using that method ever since *Le Sang d'un Poète*, when I shifted and reversed the order of the music in every single sequence. Not only did the contrast heighten the relief of the images, but I even found at times that that "displaced" music adhered too closely to the gestures and seemed to have been written on purpose.
For *La Belle et la Bête* Georges Auric wrote his score for one image after another, which made it almost impossible for me to break a single rhythm without being discourteous to the composer. The music was so beautiful that I felt that Auric, who is against explanatory music, had deliberately used the method of contrasts, slow choruses fastened on quick action, and so on. But

on the other hand when with *Orphée* I picked up, after twenty years' interval, the thread of *Le Sang d'un Poète* in which I had played the same theme with one finger as it were (I know I'm repeating myself but I can't help that), I took the most irreverent liberties with the composer. I recorded Auric's music without the images (to a chronometer) and for example put the scherzo he had composed for the comic home-coming scene into the chase through the deserted house. Or, even better, I recorded Eurydice's lament, by Gluck, meaning to use it only for the wireless in the cottage. But when I cut into Auric's music at the first shot of Heurtebise's entrance, I noticed that the first and the last note of Gluck's music fitted exactly with the first and last images of the scene, and I shamelessly took advantage of that little miracle.

Miracles of that kind are fairly common with people who calculate only by instinct. The same thing happened, for example, in *Les Enfants Terribles*, where I found that Bach's andante coincided faultlessly with the scene of Paul in the nocturnal hall, from the moment he comes in up to the moment when he lies down.

Another disrespectful liberty I took: I made a record of the drums of Katherine Dunham's band, and superimposed it on the final orchestra of *Orphée*, going as far as occasionally cutting out some of the orchestral music and leaving only the drums. I am telling you this because I heard Auric say on the radio that he approved of what I'd done, and recognized that these director's cuts gave added force and presence to his music."

Music, however, can subtly comment on the action without marching in exact step with it. An excellent example of this is Sir William Walton's music for the play scene in Sir Laurence Olivier's film production of *Hamlet*. The play scene is almost entirely musical on the sound-track, the play itself being performed in mime.

The players make their entry, accompanied by their own small group of instrumentalists, who sit in an alcove above. Here the composer suggests the idiom of the period, and uses an orchestra consisting of two violas, 'cello, oboe, cor anglais, bassoon and harpsichord. He opens with a sarabande, music in the slow, three-in-a-bar dance time which is frequent in seventeenth- and eighteenth-century music;

There is a sinister passage later to emphasize the entry of the poisoner:

As the camera moves round to show the reactions of the audience and particularly of the King, the stage music dissolves into a theme expressing a dramatic undercurrent as the tension rises in the Court audience. The camera, from its tracking, circular orbit, returns to the actors, and music reverts once more to the quiet accompaniment of the play. Then, at last, the actor-king has been poisoned, and Claudius's nerves break. The full power of the symphony orchestra rises up swamping the soft sounds of the oboe, 'cello, and harpsichord, and ending in a tremendous "crash chord". There is a moment's silence, and then the King cries in a loud voice, "Give me some light". He thrusts aside a torch, offered by Hamlet with a mocking laugh, and rushes from the Council Chamber. Complete confusion breaks loose as the cries of the courtiers for "lights" and the screams of the women are emphasized by the chaotic music. The sequence ends with Hamlet's hysterical singing.

In this example the music interlocks with the action, anticipating what is to come as well as reflecting rising tensions. The two threads of music (the "realistic" music of the instrumentalists in the scene, the "functional" music of the orchestra) offset each other, and the whole complex effect provides a commentary on the score which enriches its drama. Technically, the relationship was obtained by the music mixer, who provided a microphone layout in the studio which allowed the conductor to control both the small group and the full orchestra from one position, yet permitted the two sounds to be separated completely or mixed together at will.

The inter-relation of music and action in a film is the commonest form of film music that there is, along with music establishing mood. It is capable, however, of great refinement when the imaginations of film-maker and composer combine to use it well, and almost every great film score could furnish examples. In a sense, all film music could be very broadly defined as "music and action", for all film is concerned with action of various kinds at various levels of obviousness and subtlety. However, some composers may tend to favour emphasis of the general atmosphere underlying the action (its grandeur, its violence, its tension, its comedy, and so on) rather than reflect the detail of what is actually being done on the screen.

We are concerned at this stage with film music in which both atmosphere and points of action are reflected in the composition. Sir William Walton has described for us his attitude and method of work when composing for Shakespeare:

The value to a film of its musical score rests chiefly in the creation of mood, atmosphere, and the sense of period. When the enormous task of re-imagining a Shakespearian drama in terms of the screen has been achieved, these three qualities, which must be common to all film music, appear in high relief.

In the case of "mood" I would quote as an example the incidental musical effects in Hamlet's soliloquies which varied their orchestral colour according to the shifts of his thought. For "atmosphere" take the music of rejoicing after the victory of Agincourt in *Henry V*, which also illustrates the power to evoke a sense of historical period in a special way, for the contemporary Agincourt hymn which has been handed down to us was adapted to my purpose. Indeed the atmosphere of human feeling and the evocation of a past time are often combined, or made to blend from one to the other without any abruptness of transition. At the entry of the players in *Hamlet* (described above) I took the chance to suggest the musical idiom of the time by using a small sub-section of the orchestra (two violas, 'cello, oboe, cor anglais, bassoon, harpsichord) and then proceeded to make my comment on the action in my own personal idiom.

In a film the visual effect is of course predominant, and the music subserves the visual sequences, providing a subtle form of punctuation—lines can seem to have been given the emphasis of italics, exclamation marks added to details of stage "business", phases of the action broken into paragraphs, and the turning of the page at a crossfade or cut can be helped by music's power to summarize the immediate past or heighten expectation of what is to come. The analogy with printer's typography is useful, but beyond this, music offers orchestral "colour" to the mind's ear in such a way that at every stage it confirms and reinforces the colour on the screen which is engaging the eye.

The composer in the cinema is the servant of the eye, in the Opera House he is of course the dominating partner. There everyone, beginning with the librettist, must serve him and the needs of the ear. In the film world, however, from the first stage called the "rough-cut" where the composer first sees the visual images that his work must reinforce, an opera composer finds his controlling position usurped. He works in the service of a director. Since proportion is as important in music as in any other of the arts, the film composer, no longer his own master, is to a great extent at the mercy of his director.

A close and delicate collaboration is essential for the film must be served, but music must not be asked to do what it should not or cannot. After a while the composer who stays the pace acquires what has been called "the stop-watch mentality", a quality which I have heard deplored; but I am quite certain the habit, a peculiarly strict form of self-discipline, does a composer far more good than harm when he is working on his own for his own ends. Within or outside the cinema every second counts.

A film composer must have confidence in his director or collaboration will break down. In my three major Shakespearian films I have been particularly blessed in working with a director who knew precisely what he wanted at any given point not only in quantity but in kind. Laurence Olivier understands the composer's problems. He has a genius for thinking up ways of adding to them, or increasing those that already exist, but he never demands the impossible, and his challenges have invariably led me to be grateful in the end. In the deployment of his visual resources he is himself a dramatist and though a composer's task is never anything but difficult, the confidence inspired by such a director has certainly made things far easier than they might have been.

If the musical aspect of the battle sequences in *Henry V* and *Richard III*, for instance, is considered helpful to the general effect, that is due to an unusually complex and close collaboration of sound and screen from one bar or visual movement to the next, the outcome of much patience and exercise of technique certainly, but above all, I think, the fruit of mutual confidence and esteem.

Henry V was completed late in 1944. The music was written by William Walton and recorded by the London Symphony Orchestra conducted by Muir Mathieson. When the film appeared, a number of music critics published reviews of the score, including some detailed notes by Hubert Clifford, which appeared in *Tempo*, a journal issued by the publishing house of Boosey and Hawkes. Writing of Walton's approach to the score, Dr. Clifford commented:

The form of the film posed an awkward problem for the composer—the conflict between three periods. With the resources of 1944 (for the ears of 1944), the composer had to encompass a musical atmosphere of the days of Queen Elizabeth and those of Henry V. Walton's solution of the problem was as satisfactory as any stylistic compromise of this kind could be. Apart from the use in certain sequences of plain-song and organum and of the Agincourt Song, Walton's method was to divide the dramatic atmosphere and express it in terms of his own musical mind. The result was a happy absence of the ersatz, or the musical equivalent of Wardour Street Tudor. I had never previously been aware of the essential Englishness of Walton, but in *Henry V* there was an authentic English musical voice, just as English in its own way as that of Elgar or Vaughan Williams. More than that, Walton's music attained a virility and a dramatic range greater than that displayed by any other contemporary British composer.

One of the best-remembered scenes from the film is that of the charge of the French knights at the Battle of Agincourt and it is this section that we have chosen for a detailed analysis. Hubert Clifford recalls the reaction of the Press to this sequence when the picture first appeared:

> For sheer excitement—excitement that provoked the sophisticated Press-showing audience to an ovation—the crescendo of the French cavalry charge which commenced the Battle of Agincourt would be hard to surpass. I suspect the audience did not realize that they were applauding "t'other side"—but no matter. The gathering momentum of the charge was enhanced by the cunningly mixed sound-track. A long "cross-fade" brought the music to the foreground, interchanging in prominence with the harness and armour-clanking sound effects as the charge gathered its impetus. The director very wisely suppressed the effects and allowed the music its full head as the climax approached. The result was a tour-de-force which, with the action and the strident primary colours of the banners and the surcoats of the knights, drew a burst of spontaneous applause from the audience.

The action of the analysis that follows starts at the point when a line of drummers beats out a general call-to-arms in the French camp and the knights take their positions for the charge itself:

	1	**2**
ACTION	M.C.S. Line of French drummers, looking along the line, from a low angle.	L.S. Body of soldiers with long bows over the brow of a small hill.
DIALOGUE		
EFFECTS	(Drums.)	

	3	**4**
Shot 2 continues. L.S. body of soldiers with long bows over the brow of a small hill.	C.U. French drums: three drums in line, from low angle.	L.S. French knights moving into position
	(Drums.)	

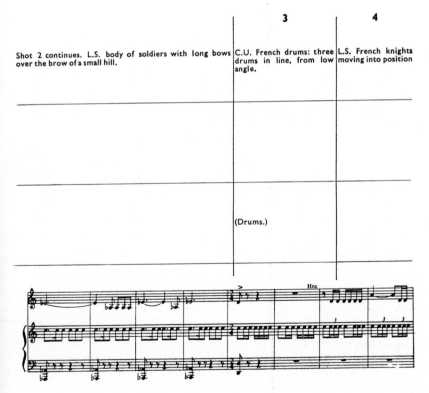

ACTION   Shot 4 continues. L.S. French knights moving into position.

DIALOGUE

EFFECTS

5	**6**
Insert. French banners dipping in salute. *Dissolve* to:	M.C.S. Water on ground; horses' hooves appear and break the pattern. A saddle cloth appears across the frame.
	Horses' hooves: slight clink of armour.

7

ACTION Shot 6 continues. Reflec-|L.S. Start of battle charge by the French knights. Camera tracking
tions of other horses in the|alongside.
water.
Dissolve to:

DIALOGUE

EFFECTS Horses' hooves; slight clink
of armour.

	8	**9**	**10**
Shot 7 continues. Start of battle charge by the French knights. Camera tracking alongside.	M.S. English archers raise bows in readiness. Low angle.	M.C.S. King Henry on horse-back. English standard in back-ground.	L.S. The battle charge by the French knights. Camera tracking alongside.

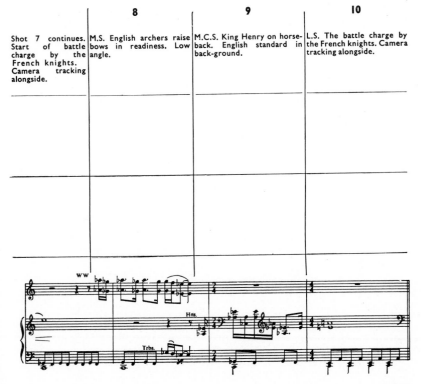

Shot 10 continues. L.S. The battle charge by the French knights. Camera tracking alongside.

ACTION   Shot 10 continues. L.S. The battle charge by the French knights. Camera tracking alongside.

Shot 10 continues. L.S. The battle charge by the French knights. Camera tracking alongside.

103

ACTION   Shot 10 continues. L.S. The battle charge by the French knights. Camera tracking alongside.

ACTION   Shot 10 continues. L.S. The battle charge by the French knights. Camera tracking alongside.

Shot 10 continues. L.S. The battle charge by the French knights. Camera tracking alongside.

Shot 10 continues. L.S. The battle charge by the French knights. Camera tracking alongside.

ACTION	**11** M.S. English archers at the ready.	**12** C.S. King Henry.	**13** L.S. The battle charge, viewed from behind the English lines, with stakes in the foreground.
DIALOGUE			
EFFECTS			

Shot 13 continues. The battle charge, viewed from the English lines, with stakes in the foreground.	**14** C.S. English archers at the ready.	**15** C.S. King Henry. He gives the signal to release the arrows.	**16** C.S. English archers fire a great flight of arrows.	**17** M.S. English archers watch the flight of arrows go away towards the French lines.	**18** L.S. Flight of arrows curve across the sky and strike amongst the French knights Seen from the English lines.
				First sound of arrows.	Arrows.

(ii) Scenic and Place Music

Since about 1920, programme, or purely descriptive music, has come to be discredited; all concert hall music, in fact, had to become abstract in order to be fashionable at the highest level. It may well be that one of the causes of this movement (apart from similar tendencies in the other arts, and notably in painting) was the growing use of descriptive music in the theatre and cinema. Composers, rightly or wrongly, wanted to disassociate their work as radically as possible from the banalities of the worst kind of programme music, with which the ears of the public were being flooded by theatre and cinema orchestras using the over-worked styles and idioms of the impressionist composers of the nineteenth century.

As the quality of the music specially created for the sound film rose with the introduction of an increasing number of distinguished composers to the film studios, the composition of descriptive music specifically for the concert hall has in recent years begun to come back into fashion. The concert hall may, indeed, owe something to the cinema after all, though in making this return to more direct forms of description in musical idiom it must be recognized that similar tendencies have shown themselves also in painting.

The various patterns of music which have been evolved in various parts of the world form a rich source of association in films. Indian and Japanese film music offers examples. It is interesting to note that, in the case of the Japanese cinema, motifs from the austere, monotonous, traditional kind of music are given modern forms of orchestration in films presenting traditional subjects. Most Japanese films about contemporary subjects use Westernized music.

Indian music even for those who have not had the opportunity or taken the trouble to understand its particular technical subleties, can start a considerable emotional response in Western audiences. Western composers have for long enough produced pastiches of Eastern music especially for the theatre and cinema, and this form of composition can exist both on a merely vulgar level and on various levels of the imaginative use of Eastern musical associations. There is no need to give examples of the former; there is plenty of bizarre bazaar music to stand for this. Walter Leigh's subtle suggestion of Eastern themes in his score for *Song of Ceylon* represents a true understanding of this kind of composition.

Composers whose imagination responds to the idea of places they may never even have visited can, on occasion, create music which is more evocative of atmosphere than the work of the national composers themselves. Bizet's score for *Carmen* and Debussy's *Iberia* are examples. Film scores which have attempted to bridge the styles and idioms of different nations and races include that for Robert Flaherty's *Elephant Boy* (John Greenwood), Elisabeth Lutyens's score for *World Without End* and William Alwyn's scores for *Three Dawns to Sydney* and *Daybreak in Udi*. The music used in Thorold Dickinson's African film *Men of Two Worlds* combines a reconstruction of genuine African drumming and chanting with Sir Arthur Bliss's special compositions which bridge African and Western forces in musical expression; it was created for the leading character in the film, an African composer with a Western musical training. The piano concerto from the film called *Baraza* has already been mentioned above (see p. 74).

The zither[1] music in *The Third Man* is a famous example of the use of a local instrument to establish the atmosphere of the place where the action of a film is set. The few melancholy, haunting notes from the zither were enough to create a romantic nostalgia for the legendary Vienna vainly trying to recapture after the war the remnants of its gaiety in the face of the new social evils represented by Harry Lime's criminal activities. The persistent zither is like traditional Vienna fighting back post-war realism, and its impact at first hearing in the film itself was very powerful.

Sir Carol Reed is an example of a director who always thinks in terms of music whilst shooting a picture. His method is to try and evolve some kind of central musical idea which will serve to emphasize the main theme of the story. In *The Way Ahead*, he imagined a series of silences followed by the sudden introduction of the vast sounds of war, from which should develop a simple but impressive military march. William Alwyn provided the necessary music. *Odd Man Out* turned on the various wanderings of the main character, the wounded rebel, Johnny MacQueen, and Alwyn provided the theme of *Johnny's Walk* before the film went into production. (See pp. 139–49.) *The Fallen Idol* needed a motif for the great house in Belgrave Square, and *The Man Between* used a characteristic phrase on a saxophone for the echoing ruins of Berlin. *A Kid for Two Farthings* used a little, repetitive tune for the kid, combined with a theme representing the Westminster chimes.

[1]The zither consists of a large group of strings mounted on a fretted sound-board and played with both hands. A plectrum is worn on the right thumb and normally used to carry the melody, using a set of five metal strings as in a guitar. Harmonies are normally provided by using the bare fingers of the left hand to pluck on a group of about thirty gut strings, colour-coded for easy identification. The metal strings produce a sharp, brilliant sound, whilst the softer accompaniment is created by the gut strings. It is a feature of the folk song and dance accompaniments in the mountain regions of Austria and Bavaria.

From the first moment when Sir Carol Reed heard Anton Karas playing his zither in a Viennese café, the Harry Lime theme was born in his mind. Unfortunately, its very infectiousness partially defeated it; for the radio mercilessly played the main themes of the music (which actually had little intrinsic quality once they were separated from their functional relation to the film) long before the majority of audiences had the opportunity to see *The Third Man* itself.[1] In addition to two main themes (the *Harry Lime Theme* and the *Café Mozart Waltz*) the score contained variations and improvisations on certain well-established melodies such as *Unter dem Lindenbaum, Alter Lied, White Chrysanthemums* and other traditional material.

The associative power of solo instruments was until recently probably too little developed in the film, whether introduced "realistically" (as in the superb sequence in Humphrey Jennings's *Listen to Britain* when the Canadian soldier plays his accordion in a train held up at night) or used "functionally" (as in the opening and closing sequences of *The Oxbow Incident* (*Strange Incident*), where a solo accordion using an American folk air both plays in and plays out the establishing music for the isolated settlement of Bridgers Wells in the Nevada of 1885, anticipating and closing with its melancholy notes the lynching tragedy which is the subject of the film).

[1] The main theme allocated to Harry Lime travelled through every stage from an enthusiastic inception to a decadent music-hall joke. An account of its gramophone record history illustrates the process only too clearly.

The proposal to publish the music was originally rejected by nearly every music publisher in London, and raised no enthusiasm amongst the gramophone companies. Eventually a representative of Chappell's thought the Harry Lime tune might have possibilities and agreed to print it. When the first intimations of a potential success reached the Decca Company, they decided to issue a sound-track recording of the *Harry Lime Theme* and the *Café Mozart Waltz*. The violent impact of the general release resulted in a boom for the Harry Lime tune, and the record sold 4 million copies. By this time, the E.M.I. group had become aware of the possibilities and issued an ingenious imitation of the original Decca recording, made by the "Café Vienna Quartet". The craze was launched.

The *Harry Lime Theme* soon appeared as a foxtrot at the Hammersmith Palais, a Beguine by Roberto Inglez, and words were added in a version called *The Zither Melody*, recorded by the Five Smith Brothers. The next step came when the E.M.I. group realized that perhaps some of the other music in the film had commercial possibilities; they therefore issued a record of *That Dear Old Song* and *Casanova Melody*, two of the tunes not written by Anton Karas but incorporated into his score. Decca countered by issuing the original sound-track of *That Dear Old Song*, and an item written independently of the film but dedicated by Karas to Sir Carol Reed.

The phenomenal success of *The Third Man* music was soon repeated in Canada and the United States, with more recordings. First came a version played by Alvino Ray on a guitar, followed by a guitar and orchestral version of the two principal tunes by Guy Lombardo and his Royal Canadians. Ethel Smith produced an arrangement for the electric organ. Back in England, the craze had been picked up by Max Miller and George Formby, both of whom made a version called *Come Hither with your Zither*. A toilet roll was produced in Switzerland which played the *Harry Lime Theme* as it unrolled.

The accordion is an instrument full of rich sentimental association with various countries—the lonely, melancholy airs of America, and the gay café atmosphere of France. (The use of such solo instruments as the harmonica, which have little or no association with particular countries or places, has recently become popular in films; for example, Larry Adler's music for *Genevieve*.)

But folk melodies are one of the finest sources of all for film music which must suggest the atmosphere of particular places and peoples. They can be used to enrich every kind of setting from Scotland and Scandinavia to the great regional territories of the United States and Eastern Europe—in every setting, that is, where folk music has become fully established and recognizable.

The use of folk melodies has enabled American film music composers to free themselves from the more inflated kind of composition which mars only too many Hollywood scores. An early example of this was *The Plow that Broke the Plains* (1936). Virgil Thomson's use of folk songs, American national melodies and traditional dance tunes has never been more strikingly illustrated than in this picture made over twenty years ago.

The prologue narration sets the scene in the Great Plains Region of the United States:
"This is a record of the land . . . of soil, rather than people—a story of the Great Plains: the 400 million acres of wind-swept grass lands that spread from the Texas Panhandle to Canada . . . the grass lands . . . a treeless wind-swept continent of grass stretching from the broad Texas Panhandle up to the mountains of Montana and to the Canadian border."[1]
The music for this section is like a hymn of praise to God's works.
The film then shows how a vast exploration of the entire area followed the discovery of the Great Plains:
"First came the cattle . . . an unfenced range a thousand miles long . . . an uncharted ocean of grass, the southern range for winter grazing and the mountain plateaux for summer . . . for a decade the world discovered the grass lands and poured cattle into the plains. The railroads brought markets to the edge of the plains . . . Land syndicates sprang up overnight and the cattle rolled into the west."
The suggestion of cowboy songs is heard in the strumming of a guitar; the orchestra takes up the theme, giving it an increasingly impressive and spirited presentation as the screen gradually fills with men and cattle.
After the cattlemen came the settlers who set up homes on the Plains and began a programme of cultivation:
"But the railroad brought the world to the plains; new populations, new needs crowded the last frontier. Once again the ploughman followed the herds and the pioneer came to the plains. Make way for the ploughman! Many were disappointed. The rains failed . . . and the sun baked the light soil. Many left . . . they fought the loneliness and the hard years . . ."
A banjo tune expresses the pioneering spirit of the settlers, but the gay music becomes increasingly discordant as the story unfolds.
A brief spell of violent prosperity was produced by the first World War; it was a "great day of new causes—new profits—new hopes. 'Wheat will win the war!' " The sequence starts with a line of tractors advancing to side drum beats and timpani rolls, interrupted by an explosion. A bugle sounds a Call to Arms. The tractors continue to

[1]All the quotations are taken from the film commentary itself.

111

advance, accompanied by drum rolls and discordant horns. The bugle call is repeated. As the tractors go to work on a vast scale and newsreel shots of Army tanks at the front begin to mingle with the agricultural scenes, the brass of the orchestra plays a series of variations on the theme of *Mademoiselle from Armentières*.

Despite the advent of the tractor and remarkably high figures of wheat production after the first World War, the seeds of depression were already being sown. The commentary at this stage gives no hint of this fact:

"Then we reaped the golden harvest . . . then we really ploughed the plains . . . we turned under millions of new acres for war. By 1933 the old grass land had become new. Wheat lands . . . a hundred million acres . . . two hundred million acres . . . more wheat!"

It is the music which carries the full expression of potential failure that lurked behind these apparent successes. A beautifully orchestrated "low-down" blues in the nineteen-twenties style makes the point very clear. A mournful clarinet and a "blues" trumpet (occasionally muted) provides the speculative melody against a background of percussion rhythm, timpani beats and taps on Chinese blocks. Cymbal rolls, terminating in timpani beats, add a grim warning of trouble to come; the muted trumpet leaves its melancholy theme and begins to snarl discordantly as the hopeless tide of false hopes sweeps on to inevitable disaster.

The stock markets crashed and the Depression came; so did the drought:

"A country without rivers . . . without streams . . . and little rain . . . Once again the rains held off the sun-baked earth. This time no grass held moisture against the winds and sun . . . this time millions of acres of ploughed land lay open to the sun."

A dignified theme treated in canon runs through this sequence, alternating with a march-like episode suggesting the irresistible revolt of nature against thoughtless exploitation.

The ruined settlers of the man-made dust-bowl began to move westwards at the rate of 30,000 a month (1936) forming a hopeless band of humanity in constant search of a day's labour in other men's fields:

"Baked out—blown out—and broke! Year in, year out, uncomplaining they fought the worst drought in history . . . their stock choked to death on barren land . . . their homes were nightmares of swirling dust day and night. Many went ahead of it— but many stayed until stock, machinery, homes, credit, food and even hope were gone. On to the West! Once again they headed into the setting sun."

As old cars, loaded with the simple possessions of miserable, itinerant families, roll in an endless procession to a primitive camping ground, Thomson employs a slowed-down tango for full orchestra to point the tragedy. This apparently incongruous rhythm is used with such skill that it produces one of the most moving moments in the film.

Later Aaron Copland, one of America's most distinguished composers, worked on *Of Mice and Men*, *Our Town* and *The Red Pony*, as well as other American feature and documentary films, using folk melodies to establish the atmosphere of the places and peoples in the film. Copland decided to turn his back completely on the more inflated kind of Hollywood score. He realized that sheer contrast is in itself dramatic, and that audiences, expecting to be bathed in floods of musical sound the moment the picture began, would have their senses alerted instead of dulled by a pattern of sound which was lean and sparse. *Our Town*, the film based on Thornton Wilder's play about the simple, typical life of a New England community, inspired in him a very original style for a film score. It is austerely tuneful, with an appealing little opening theme which somehow manages to reflect the religious values which are implicit in the life of New England, the simplicity of faith, the neighbourly goodwill.

112

Copland also composed a fine score for *The Red Pony*, the film made from Steinbeck's story about a little boy called Jody who forms a deep friendship with a pony given him by his father; the film also portrays very closely and sympathetically the sentiment of simple family life on a Californian ranch. Though Copland's music for *The Red Pony* derives from the American folk melodies, it is more austere than they, with less of their easy sentiment. It establishes perfectly the spirit of the place and the people—the working life of the farm at daybreak, the wagon teams of Jody's grandfather driven "clear across the plains to the coast" in the days of pioneer "westering".

In a conversation with the writers, Copland explained that he preferred seeing the film with the director and producer, deciding with them where music is needed and then creating the score by screening and re-screening each sequence where music is required using a cue-sheet and working with a piano. He considers, too, that composers should be "cast" for a film like a director according to the nature of the subject. He is known for his interest in folk traditions in music, and so was invited to compose for *Of Mice and Men* and *Our Town*.

On a grander scale of orchestration is Victor Young's score for *Shane*; this more nearly than either Copland's or Thomson's special forms of orchestration corresponds to Hollywood's normal development of folk melodies in scores for films dealing with Western and Pioneer subjects. *Shane* is a story of the settlers who had to fight for their land against the violence of the men who had first opened up the great territories of the West and wished to rule them with a reign of terror. Young's score matches with rich, nostalgic melodies the magnificent colour photography of Wyoming, with its great plains bordered by misty blue mountains along the horizon, which is the setting for the film's action.

The composer of film music must always be prepared to use foreign idioms when they meet the needs of the drama. In *The Rake's Progress*, for example, William Alwyn uses a combination of calypso and rumba during the sequence when the Rake, after his disgrace at Oxford, is sent to a West Indian coffee plantation to learn the business. The setting for the office buildings, the laboratory and the living quarters of the plantation were built in the studio, so that a responsibility was placed upon the composer to enhance as far as possible the work of the director, art director and lighting cameraman in creating the hot, steamy atmosphere. William Alwyn uses a short work for full orchestra founded on two West Indian dance rhythms.

113

The calypso melody is heralded by a simple, repeated phrase, introduced by the flutes:

pp

and appearing in various guises on the strings, oboe, clarinet and brass. It is occasionally intermingled with a four note echo on muted trumpets:

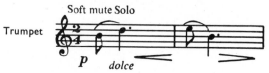

Wire brush percussion, harp and piano add further colouring to establish the languid setting of the plantation.

The gentle atmosphere is suddenly interrupted by a brisk montage showing the Rake being introduced to the various stages of coffee production. The music changes from the first shot to a rumba piu mosso giocoso. Jazz mutes are used by trumpets and trombones, while the main melody is stated vigorously by a solo clarinet, against a heavy rhythmic accompaniment. Later the full orchestra enters, establishing the original calypso tempo and, after further statements on flutes, clarinets, trumpets and strings, the section ends quietly on a single pizzicato beat.

Most scenic and place music in films is impressionist in style, interpreting simply or subtly, as the case may be, the human emotions which are aroused by the sight of expansive scenery, the sea and the places built by man. Many films provide examples of this kind of score—Clifton Parker's *Seascape* music for the Crown Film Unit's documentary *Western Approaches*, Alan Rawsthorne's themes for the wartime *Burma Victory* and *Waters of Time* (Basil Wright's documentary of the Thames), John Addison's Thames music for the opening of the feature film *Pool of London*, John Ireland's score for Ealing Studios' Australian production *The Overlanders*, Elisabeth Lutyens's music for *Eldorado* (John Alderson's film of British Guiana), Sir Arnold Bax's composition for the documentary *Malta G.C.*, Leonard Bernstein's dock music in *On the Waterfront* and Prokofiev's great musical landscapes in *Ivan the Terrible*.

A remarkable example of this impressionist kind of score is that composed by Dr. Vaughan Williams for *Scott of the Antarctic*. This film told the story of Captain Scott's last expedition in which he and the four men who finally accompanied him to the South Pole lost their lives. Here the music must bestow the touch of nobility on the men who, however ordinary they may seem to be in speech and action, are taking part in an adventure which requires patience and heroism and the highest degree of human loyalty. The huge vistas of blue sky, crystal snow and glacier ice reflecting the wonderful colours made by the sunlight, are both a lure and a threat, a siren land to which Vaughan Williams gives a distant woman's voice singing wordlessly to keep the men moving deeper and deeper into its wastes. But there is also in the music the deep growl of cracking ice. At the end of the film the choral effect returns to imitate the tearing wind which rages round the isolated tent where Scott and his companions write with frost-bitten fingers their last letters to their families.

The score has several main themes, later recorded for the gramophone—Prologue, Pony March, Penguins, Climbing the Glacier, the Return, Blizzard and Final Music. These themes were subsequently developed by Dr. Vaughan Williams into the *Sinfonia Antartica* for concert hall performance. We will confine ourselves here to comment on the Prologue for the film score itself.

The actual shots involved are as follows:

1. The Antarctic. Seen from the sea, forbidding frowning cliffs and mountain, jagged and snow-covered.
2. They stretch into the distance, rampart of the unknown continent.
3. Closer, there are tortured shapes of ice. Everything is motionless, a sense of complete desert.
4. The frozen shapes are impressive, above all, in their utter silence.
5. Beyond the mountains the Polar Plateau stretches away, broken only by an ice-hummock.
6. Suddenly a violent blizzard sweeps across it, blotting it out.

Two basic ideas run through the Prologue. First, the composer "points" the freezing temperatures of the Antarctic, with frigid sounds on the lower strings and a cold-steel effect of single, unconnected xylophone notes (Theme A). Secondly, there is the sense of emptiness, of mile upon mile of snow and ice, without life; a terrible feeling of loneliness cuts the Antarctic off from the rest of the world. This is expressed musically by a solo woman's voice, singing wordlessly; the voice was recorded at a great distance from the microphone producing an echo from beyond the horizon.

The section is divided into four parts. Theme A is heard first, swelling up from the depths of the orchestra. A string tremolo and the introduction of bass-drum beats herald the second section, as the echoing, solo voice enters against a further group of women's voices. The music is dimensional, with a foreground (the drum), middle distance (voices and strings, imitating the sound of the wind) and an horizon (the solitary vocal effect). Section three is introduced by a single note on the xylophone, as strings and brass rush in with a crescendo effect of Theme A. Finally, there is a return to voices and strings in a fourth section, punctuated by a single gong stroke in place of the drum. The wind machine appears in the last few bars, mingling with the voices in a final plaintive whine across the snows.

The main analysis in this section is given to the opening sequence of Flaherty's *Louisiana Story*, for which Virgil Thomson composed an outstanding score:

The film was made in 1948 and is based on a story set in the Bayou marshlands and forests of Louisiana, showing the impact of modern industrial development on a small boy's primitive world in swamp-ridden backwoods where nature reigns supreme. The screenplay was by Frances and Robert Flaherty, the photography by Richard Leacock and the editing was carried out by Helen van Dongen. The sound recording was the work of Benjamin Doniger and the music was played by the members of the Philadelphia Orchestra conducted by Eugene Ormandy. It is essentially a film of atmosphere rather than dramatic narrative and in this respect the music plays an essential part.

The Opening Sequence for Robert Flaherty's film *Louisiana Story* provides a remarkable example of the power of music to assist in setting the atmosphere of a particular place. Use is made of folk music but the original material has been cleverly re-set in the manner of *The River* and *The Plow That Broke the Plains*. Frederick Sternfeld, in an article for *Film Music Notes*,[1] explored the manner in which Thomson had made use of tunes taken from Irene Therese Whitfield's collection of Louisiana French Folk Songs:

> In the first scene, the score is the binding agent that gives continuity to the atmosphere which surrounds lotus-leaves, birds, snakes and the boy in his pirogue.[2] Music follows the camera, though not mechanically. Its motion sublimates the motion of photography, and the result is cinema in the original sense, not stills. The composer's tunes are of such versatility and are handled with such ingenuity of orchestration that they accompany with perfect propriety shots of beautiful flowers, weird alligators and the terrifying machine of the marsh buggy. The treatment of the folk songs is equally deft. Whitfield's collection gives only the melody, leaving to Thomson the responsibilities and opportunities of harmonization and instrumentation. The two solo statements in the English horn and viola respectively that introduce the boy in his pirogue are moving in their delivery and in their nuances of melody and timbre.

The source material used in the Opening Sequence is taken from two tunes found in the Whitfield collection:

On the following pages, the first seven shots are described in relation to the music; in order to illustrate the manner in which the music links the visuals, the next seven shots are reproduced by photographs against the appropriate quotations from the score. Unfortunately there is no method in which to represent the essential juxtaposition of camera movement to musical movement that makes this sequence so effective.

[1]Volume VII, No. 1. September-October, 1948.
[2]A pirogue is a special type of canoe dug out from a single piece of wood.

ACTION   After a very slow fade in, during which the camera pans upwards slowly, the shot opens on air enormous lotus-leaf undulating slowly. The leaf itself and mud-patches form black reflections in the water surface in which also bright clouds are reflected. Tiny animals skim over the surface of the water.

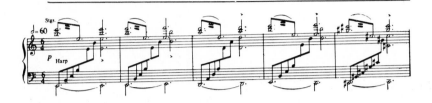

2   **3**

ACTION   L.S. Black, silhouette-like form of an alligator swimming very slowly. White clouds are reflected in the water.

L.S. The surface of the water with reflections of several lotus-leaves and branches with a strange bird on one branch. Camera pans up, revealing the scene as viewed by reflection.

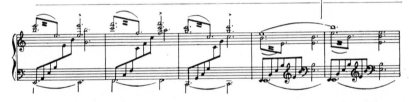

4

ACTION   Shot 3 continues. The surface of the water with reflections of several lotus-leaves and branches with a strange bird on one branch. Camera pans up, revealing the scene as viewed by reflection.

L.S. The surface of the lily-pond. Lotus-leaves are scattered here and there in the water. An alligator crawls slowly on to a cypress log.

ACTION	**5**	**6**	**7**
	C.U. Lotus-leaf, covered with dew drops.	C.U. Dew drop on leaf.	M.L.S. Bird on branch of tree.

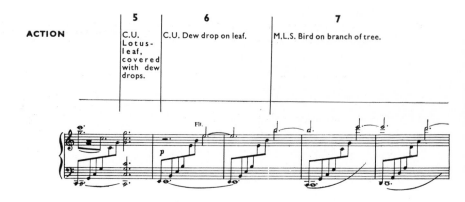

8

ACTION L.S. The forest in the swamp. The trunks of trees are standing in the dark water, silvery Spanish moss dangles from the branches. Shot from a floating raft which moves slowly, while the camera itself pans very slowly in the opposite direction. After a time, a small boy can be seen, paddling in a pirogue. He disappears and reappears again far behind the enormous trees in the foreground.

ACTION Shot 8 continues.

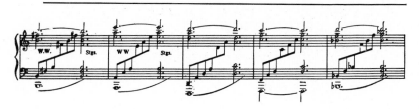

118

Shot 8 continues.

Shot 8 continues.

9

Shot 8 continues. L.S. The forest in the swamp. The shot terminates as the small boy once again disappears from view behind the great trees.

L.S. The forest. The camera moves in to the Spanish moss, as if passing through a Japanese screen.

ACTION Shot 9 continues. L.S. The forest. The camera moves in to the Spanish moss, as if passing through a Japanese screen.

DIALOGUE

EFFECTS

120

C.U. Swirl in the water caused by the boy's paddle, off-screen.

M.L.S. Boy in the pirogue, back to camera. He is proceeding cautiously, stopping at times, looking around.

Commentator: "His name is Alexander—"

Commentary Starts

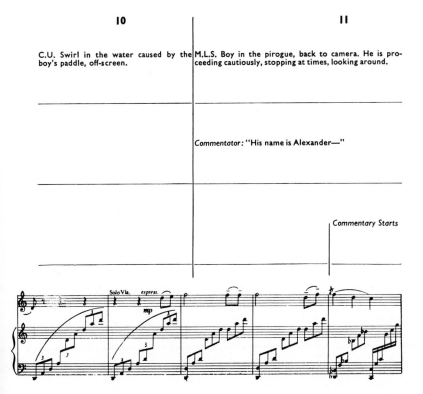

Shot 11 continues. M.L.S. Boy in the pirogue, back to camera. He is proceeding cautiously, stopping at times, looking around.

DIALOGUE

Commentator:"—Napoleon—Ulysses—Latour."

EFFECTS

Shot II continues. M.L.S. Boy in the pirogue, back to camera. He is proceeding cautiously, stopping at times, looking around.

Commentator: "Mermaids—their hair is green he says—swim up these waters from the sea."

ACTION   Shot 11 continues. M.L.S. Boy in the pirogue, back to camera. He is proceeding cautiously, stopping at times, looking around.

DIALOGUE   Commentator: "He's seen their bubbles—often."

EFFECTS   *Commentary Ends*

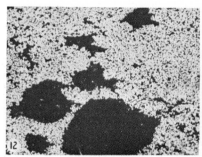 

12 | **13**

C.U. Bubbles coming up to the surface, disturbing the tiny little leaves.

M.S. The boy bends low to pass underneath the low-hanging Spanish moss. He paddles away from camera.

Commentator: "And werwolves with long noses and big red eyes come to dance on moonless nights.

Commentary Starts

(iii) Period and Pageant Music

Music is frequently required to develop a period atmosphere or to build up the grandeur of some pageant or spectacle set in the past. Just as Western composers have invented certain musical conventions when they want to suggest the idiom of Oriental or African music, so there are conventions which suggest periods of the past, for example, Elizabethan or Tudor times, and, far less accurately from the strict point of view of musical documentation, Roman or classical times. What may be illuminatingly achieved in the musical suggestion of period by William Walton in *Belshazzar's Feast* or by Honegger in *King David* may emerge on a much lower level of musical expression in the scores for biblical or gladiatorial screen epics. But the genre of composition remains, and every composer of film music will find eventually that he must compose in an idiom suggestive of the past. Walton's music for the play scene in *Hamlet* (already discussed above in the section on music and action), is also a good illustration of music which evokes the Tudor setting proper to a Shakespearian production.

A similar evocation of the past was required in the score for *Henry V*[1] by the same composer. The music for the opening of this film ("London 1600") is developed as follows:

A single bar of one held chord on muted violins heralds the arrival of a Globe Theatre playbill, announcing the production of a new drama, *The Chronicle of Henry V*. It comes out of the sky, twisting and turning in the breeze, to the accompaniment of a seven-bar flute roulade:

As the text is held on the screen, the full orchestra enters with a triumphant fanfare lasting for twelve bars.

The handbill fades and a vast panorama of London in 1600 appears. From the mass of little Tudor inns, almshouses, shops and dwellings crowded around and on London Bridge, there rises a stirring sound embodying the spirit of the people themselves; two bars for tuba, harp, 'cellos, basses and side-drums fit the mood exactly, introducing the simple rising and downfalling pattern that infiltrates the shape of the whole sequence:

---

[1]Reproduced by kind permission of the Oxford University Press Ltd.

126

As the camera moves across London from south to east, the orchestra, backed by a large choir singing wordlessly, rises slowly and majestically through *pp* to *ff*, until the camera is facing the Tower of London across from London Bridge. As the camera moves backwards and downwards, the music now falls away through *mf* to *pp con moto* throughout, until the top of the Globe Theatre comes into view on the South Bank. From the uppermost platform of the octagonal-shaped building, a festive flag is raised to a rising phrase on horns and trumpets. It finally ripples in the breeze to a long woodwind flourish over which the flute presides. The flag is tied in position and the master of ceremonies takes up a trumpet on which he sounds a solo fanfare to announce that the theatre is in session. Then, on a cue, the band of musicians in an alcove above the stage commence a lively overture while the audience gathers below in a bustle of excitement and preparation for the play.

This overture is in 4/4 march tempo, being scored for flutes, oboes, bassoons, horns, trumpets, full string complement, and a marked rhythmic accompaniment provided by the tabor,[1] playing mezzoforte throughout. It ends abruptly, leaving only the busy chatter of the theatre audience as they wait for the play to begin.

Equally effective is the atmosphere created by the traditional music of the Russian Orthodox Church in the Coronation scene from Eisenstein's *Ivan the Terrible*:

The sequence opens on a close-up of the crown, shaped like an ermine-covered skull cap with a flashing jewelled cross on top and other precious stones set in the material itself. The Archbishop enters in a long shot and the congregation bow as he passes. These two shots are accompanied by a great clamour of ancient Muscovite bells. A large choir, singing wordlessly, introduces a series of long, sustained sounds that give depth to the scene. The camera reveals a series of beautifully composed shots of statesmen and courtiers. Some deeply resent the crowning of Ivan but others are favourably disposed towards him. The bells are heard once more as Ivan enters:

1. Long Shot. The Archbishop moves in procession to the throne, which is placed on a small dais and approached from two sides by a thick carpet. The camera cranes down as Ivan suddenly enters from the right of the frame.
2. Long Shot. The congregation bows to the assembled company. There is a burst of sound from the choir, which mingles with the bells.
3. Close-up. The crown.
4. Close-up. The Archbishop bends to kiss the crown. Choir only.
5. Medium Shot. The blessing of the crown. The choir sings continuously for the remainder of the scene.
6. Close-up. The envious faces of the mother and son who had schemed to get the crown themselves.
7. Close-up. A view of the back of Ivan's head. Ceremoniously, the crown is placed upon it. There is another great burst of sustained sound from the choir.
8. Close Shot. Ivan's consort.
9. Close-up. The crown on Ivan's head.
10. Medium Shot. The Archbishop takes up the sceptre and begins to speak. The choir stops and almost immediately resumes softly, under the speech.
11. Close-up. The sceptre is placed in Ivan's hand.
12. Medium Shot. The Archbishop presents the orb.
13. Close-up. The orb in Ivan's hand.
14. Close-up. The crown on Ivan's head; he bows in acknowledgement to the Archbishop.
15. Close Shot. The Archbishop gives a blessing. The soft sounds of the choir end on the word "Amen".
16. Medium Shot. Bass singer, richly dressed and dramatically lit from below. He begins to sing alone, in a very deep, powerful voice. First main phrase of solo.
17. Close Shot. Bass singer. Second main phrase of solo.
18. Close-up. Bass singer. Third main phrase of solo.
19. Medium Shot. Ivan turns away from the Archbishop. Voice continues.

[1] The tabor is a small drum of indefinite pitch, originally used in folk-dancing accompaniments; it has a dry, dull, percussive sound.

20. Long Shot. The coronation scene. A shaft of sunlight cuts across the scene from a high window. The rising monotone of the song continues.
21. Close Shot. Bass singer. The shot is held roughly for one measure. Voice continues.
22. Medium Shot. Bass singer. Roughly one measure.
23. Very Long Shot. The coronation scene. Voice continues.
24. Very Long Shot. The vast congregation in the body of the cathedral. Voice continues.
25. Long Shot. The coronation scene. Two men stand behind Ivan; they are presented with bowls of golden coins. The bass voice continues to rise in intensity and pitch. It is suddenly cut off by the full choir fortissimo as we cut to:
26. Medium Shot. The coins begin to flow across Ivan's head as the bowls are ceremoniously tipped up. Full choir.
27. Close Shot. Group of three: Ivan and two men pouring the coins across his head Full choir.
28. Close-up. Coins cascading on the marble step below Ivan. Full choir.
29. Close-up. First man pouring coins from ornamented bowl. Full choir.
30. Close-up. Second man pouring coins from ornamented bowl. Full choir.
31. Close-up. Ivan's head, as the coins flow across it. Full choir.
32. Close-up. Woman's face smiling; she is a supporter of Ivan's triumph. The bass voice takes over again from the choir.
33. Close-up. Second woman's face smiling. Bass solo continues.
34. Close-up. Ivan's head, as the coins flow across it. Bass solo continues.
35. Close-up. Ivan's consort. The full choir takes over from the solo voice.
36. Close-up. Coins cascading on the marble step below Ivan. Full choir.
37. Long Shot. Ivan standing on the dais. The bowls are empty. Full choir, giving way suddenly to the joyful tolling of a single, deep-throated bell.

The sequence depends for its effect upon the lavish setting of the Russian cathedral and the pageant-like grouping of the characters, the powerful emotions roused by the masterly use Eisenstein has made of the bells and the choir, and the extraordinary vocal range of the bass soloist.

The scores devised by Roman Vlad for Luciano Emmer's short Italian films on the works of such artists as Giotto and Bosch, in which he attempts to re-create the religious atmosphere of medieval times, are an interesting experiment in developing period atmosphere. These, however, were specialized films and the music for them is discussed later. Vlad's score for the Anglo-Italian film production of Shakespeare's *Romeo and Juliet*, directed by Renato Castellani, represents the composer's main contribution to period music in a feature film.

One of the specialists in this class of composition for films is Miklos Rozsa, whose scores include not only those for *The Lost Weekend* and *A Double Life*, but also for *Quo Vadis?* and *Julius Caesar*. That for *Quo Vadis?* is specially interesting as a score for a film in the "colossal" tradition, which demands that a composer should be prepared to enter without any reservations into the spirit of the occasion. The music for *Quo Vadis?* was recorded at Elstree Studios by J. B. Smith and E. A. Drake under the supervision of A. W. Watkins; the Royal Philharmonic Orchestra and the BBC Choir were conducted by the composer in association with Marcus Dods of the Sadler's Wells Theatre.

128

In notes specially written for this book, Miklos Rozsa has made some very interesting comments on his approach to the task of composing the music for films set in the past.

I think that the musical score should fit in with the style created by the period of the picture. When utmost stylistic care is taken in the production of a period piece, and thorough research is made for historical facts, costumes, architecture, language, coiffure, etc., I think that the musical score should not destroy this unity by introducing stylistically a completely foreign element. It has to be stylized, as the very nature of dramatic music excludes the verbatim usage of music of periods, which were utterly undramatic; but with the melodic, rhythmic and harmonic elements of the past, the modern composer can create a dramatic language of his own, which fits the style of the screen-drama. Berlioz states somewhere that he had to change his style for every dramatic subject he undertook.

Elsewhere (in *Film Music* Vol. XIII, No. 1), Rozsa has commented on his score for *Julius Caesar*:

If it had been merely an historical film about *Julius Caesar* I would have undoubtedly tried a reconstruction or approximation of the Roman music of the first century B.C. However, it is more than that. It is a Shakespearian tragedy, and, with its language, a true mirror of Elizabethan times, and it is principally this language which dictates its style. In Shakespeare's time, as they had few scruples about stylistic correctness, the music was undoubtedly their own—Elizabethan. Should I have composed it in Roman style, it would have been wrong for Shakespeare—should I have tried to treat it as stage music to an Elizabethan drama in Elizabethan style, it would have been anachronistic from the historical point of view.

I decided, therefore, to regard it as a universal drama, about the eternal problems of men and the most timely problems about the fate of dictators. I wrote the same music I would have written for a modern stage presentation: interpretative incidental music, expressing with my own musical language, for a modern audience, what Shakespeare expressed with his own language for his own audience 350 years ago. The example set by Mendelssohn with his music to *Midsummer Night's Dream* was obvious, as he wrote his own, highly romantic music which now everybody accepts as authentic, to this romantic play of Shakespeare.

To emphasize the Shakespearian stage drama I wrote an Overture, based on the main themes of the music, to precede the play. It was strong and stark, to set the audience in the mood of the following events. It was later replaced by Tchaikowsky's *Capriccio Italien*, which oddly enough, some people found more appropriate to precede *Julius Caesar*.

The four protagonists of the play are Caesar, Mark Antony, Brutus and Cassius. The first two represent the ruthless, ambition-filled, arrogant, Roman imperialists; Brutus, the honest, straightforward man who loves Caesar but loves his country better; and finally Cassius with a "lean and hungry look", who is filled with envy and jealousy of Caesar.

There are therefore three main musical themes based on this grouping of the characters:

Caesar and Antony share a single central theme, as both represent the same basic ideas in the play, Antony being "but a limb of Caesar". It is a martial theme, stern and "constant as the Northern Star", which first appears as Caesar's march when he and his entourage come for the "Course". There is an interruption from the soothsayer's voice, crying out "shriller than all the music". The first main statement appears against the following six shots:

129

	1	**2**	**3**
ACTION	V.L.S. Stadium. Day. High Angle. Armed guards force a lane, through which Caesar moves in procession. Musicians come first: brass and drums.	L.S. The procession, from a different angle.	L.S. A section of the crowd. High angle.
DIALOGUE			
EFFECTS	Very heavy crowd noises, with cheering. Prominent drum beats.	Very heavy crowd noises, with cheering.	Very heavy crowd noises; heavy cheers.

Marciale

4	**5**	**6**
Repeat of Shot 1. Procession moves on towards tunnel.	Repeat of Shot 2. Camera cranes down to a M.S. of Caesar. Casca crosses r. into crowd.	M.S. Calpurnia crosses l. to Caesar. Antony in background; comes forward into three-shot with Caesar and Calpurnia.
	"Calpurnia" (Cr.). "Peace, ho! Caesar speaks" (Casca).	"Calpurnia" (Cr.). "Here, my Lord" (Cal.). "Stand you directly in . . ." (etc.).
Very heavy crowd noises, with cheering. Beats less prominent.	Crowd noises and music fade down for dial.	Crowd noises and music held softly under speech.

131

Shot 6 continues. Caesar's last words are "Set on; and leave no ceremony out". The march theme picks up once more, mixed with crowd noises. Suddenly there is a cry of "Caesar" from the crowd.

7. M.C.S. Caesar reacts to the voice.
   Soothsayer: Caesar (*over music and effects*).
   Caesar: Eh! Who calls! (*Over music and effects.*)
   Casca (*shouting down the tunnel against music and effects*): Peace yet again. (*The music stops suddenly.*)

8. M.C.S. Caesar. Cassius is in the foreground.
   Caesar: Who is it in the press that calls on me?
             I hear a tongue, shriller than all the music,
             Cry "Caesar". Speak; Caesar is turned to hear.

9. M.S. Section of the crowd.
   Soothsayer: Beware the Ides of March.
   Dialogue between Caesar and Soothsayer continues until:

13. M.S. Three-shot of Caesar, Cassius and Soothsayer.
    Caesar: He is a dreamer; let us leave him. Pass.
    There is an echoed shout of "pass" from the tunnel, Caesar signals, and, on a cymbal-dominated chord, the Caesar march theme resumes from within and beyond the tunnel that leads to the Stadium. The party moves inside for the ceremonies.

The theme of "gentle and most noble Brutus" is brooding, musing and sighing, portraying musically the man who is willing to sacrifice his friend (or was he his father?) who knows "no personal cause to spurn at him, but for the general good". The theme appears first under the titles as a canon, with motives of the Caesar theme interrupting it:

We hear Cassius's theme under his monologue after Brutus has departed at the end of the first discussion on a possible plot to kill Caesar. The music portrays the determined character of this envious intriguer who "reads much; is a great observer, looks quite through the deeds of men; loves no plays and hears no music".

132

This music leads to the street scene of thunder and lightning, fading out on the opening words of Cicero.

With the three main characters established, other material appears for individual scenes. Calpurnia's dream (this is only mentioned by Shakespeare but in the film we can also see it) concerning the murder of Caesar is accompanied by a dissonant muted brass figure in which high violin harmonies eject the Caesar motif. The nervous music follows the scene until Caesar addresses his own statue ("Nor heaven nor earth have been at peace"):

Before I set out to compose the music and before I saw the picture, I thought that no dialogue scene should have any music, as on the stage one uses music only for preludes and epilogues, transitions and entr'actes. The filmed stage-play, however, dictates new aesthetics and dramatic rules. Scenes with strongly dramatic content could be emphasized and brought nearer to our consciousness by the use of appropriate music. For example, as Artemidorus waits for Caesar before the Capitol, he reads a letter of warning. Caesar and the senators arrive and the tension mounts, for the audience knows that a trap has been laid by the conspirators.

The music which accompanies this scene is low; dissonant seventh chords are slowly creeping forward on a basso ostinato of timpani and brass pizzicati.

The whole assassination scene in the Senate and the oration of Brutus and Antony at the Forum are without music. These are not only the strongest scenes of the whole tragedy, but undoubtedly the most famous and greatest writing in the entire field of dramatic literature. Here every line is precise in meaning and does not need any help from any other medium. Music sets in only as a final punctuation, when the citizens of Rome rise in mutiny.

At Caesar's funeral, we hear the lament of women. It is a dirge in the manner of a Greek Nenia.

After the so-called pricking scene, when Octavius leaves, Antony remains alone, sitting on Caesar's chair and imagining himself as his successor. The brassy music brings back the ominous Caesar theme.

In Brutus's camp, the meeting of Brutus and Antony, their quarrel over their grievances are scenes of matter-of-fact realism and did not need any music. After Cassius and his captains leave, Brutus asks his servant Lucius to sing a song. Shakespeare only indicates "music and a song", and I thought that an Elizabethan song, because of its language, would be the most appropriate. I chose John Dowland's *Now, O now, I needs must part*, which was published in 1597 and might have been known to Shakespeare.

The famous scene in the tent, when the ghost of Caesar appears before Brutus to tell him that he will see him again at Philippi, is accompanied by a cold, glassy and shimmering sound, including a glimpse of the distorted Caesar motif again. It breaks off as the ghostly image of Caesar disappears.

The next musical section concerns the battle of Philippi. It starts with the frantic bugles of Brutus' array, after drum beats have heralded the attack by Antony's legions. The battle is an impression rather than a detailed and long débâcle; on a close-up of the victorious Antony, the Caesar-Antony theme is heard again.

Much of the above material has been connected with the problem of establishing and emphasizing the period atmosphere of the film, but the last section is principally concerned with the emotional aspects of the death of Brutus. (Detailed notes covering this part of the production will be found on pp. 121–2.)

(iv) Music for Dramatic Tension

Music building up or reflecting dramatic tension has its primitive origins in the old musical effects of the silent film days. Tension deliberately plays on the nerves of the audience when some climax of violence or threat is anticipated, but the moment of its release is unsure. Music can introduce the feeling of tension into a situation while the images on the screen retain their calm.

A remarkable example of this is the musical device used by William Alwyn in his score for the official wartime documentary, *Desert Victory*; it is a case of the music adding an entirely new dimension to what is being done. Before zero hour for the great night assault on Rommel's defences, the tension of silent waiting is expressed through close-ups of the men's faces and shots of military equipment standing poised in readiness, while the eyes of the officers are concentrated on their synchronized watches. Alwyn uses a single persistent note which rises octave by octave until it feels like the stretched nerves of the waiting men, and snaps when the barrage breaks loose in the wild crescendo of a great storm.

In a later film in this series of official documentaries, *Burma Victory*, the music by Alan Rawsthorne is combined with sound effects in a fine atmospheric sequence early on in the film, when General Wingate's Chindits were landed by air in Central Burma hundreds of miles behind the Japanese lines. In the dawn the gliders, which have successfully survived the fearful, hazardous flight over mountains eight thousand feet high, land in the clearing, their only audience birds of prey waiting for the fruits of disaster. Here Rawsthorne's music combines with the animal cries from the jungle to help spread an atmosphere of tension over the pictures on the screen.

In a different way Malcolm Arnold, who frequently works closely with his director to combine sound effects with music into a deliberate pattern, uses music to build up tension during the opening sequence of *The Sound Barrier*. The film starts with a clear sky above the cliffs of Dover, but as the camera turns we find ourselves beside the tail of a crashed aircraft on which appears a swastika. Soldiers are lounging on the cliff; we hear a mouth organ gently strumming; there is a Spitfire high in the sky. Then the music on soaring strings takes us up to the pilot who is full of the happiness of flight on a clear day, his machine racing across the sky. He goes into a dive— and suddenly the music changes into an ominous chattering sound. The plane is buffeting as it hits the sound barrier and the pilot tries frantically to pull it out of the dive. This is a fine piece of composition blended with the sound effects of the action.

A very different example is the ominous and very fully orchestrated music that opens Orson Welles' film *Citizen Kane*, the score for which was composed by Bernard Herrmann and is a tour de force matching the film itself. It is typical of Hollywood's very strong, direct use of music to establish fear and tension.

The film opens with the RKO Radio Pictures main title, in which the name of the company is spelt out in rapid Morse. Two simple titles on neutral backgrounds follow in silence:

1. Mercury Production by Orson Welles.
2. Citizen Kane.

The screen remains in darkness for about four seconds, whilst an ominous sound is heard from the brass of the orchestra. There follows a slow fade-in on a forbidding sign mounted on a heavily-meshed steel wire fence: "No Trespassing". Then a series of slow dissolves takes the audience gradually nearer and nearer the vague but vast outline of the main tower of Xanadu, Kane's private palace:

Shot 5. Wire mesh of steel fencing, viewed from very close. The camera is moving slowly upwards. Dissolve.

Shot 6. Another section of the fence; the camera moves slowly upwards. Dissolve.

Shot 7. Another section of the fence. The camera is still moving upwards. Dissolve.

Shot 8. The heavy embellishments of a wrought-iron gate. Dissolve.

Shot 9. At the top of the gate is a massive, wrought-iron emblem of the letter K.

Shot 10. A long shot of Xanadu in swirling mist; a cage of monkeys in the foreground. Dissolve.

Shot 11. A medium shot of the prows of two gondolas on a lonely artificial lake shrouded in mist. Dissolve.

Shot 12. A long shot of part of the grounds with statues of black, mythical beasts in the foreground. The main building can be seen in the distance through the mist. Dissolve.

Shot 13. A golf course sign in the foreground. The main building can still be seen through the mist. Dissolve.

Shot 14. An imitation Greek temple and artificial ruins. The main building is again there in the misty background. Dissolve.

Shot 15. A closer view of the main tower of Xanadu. There is a single window that sends out a great stream of light. Dissolve.

Shot 16. A closer view still of the window; suddenly the light goes out.

Starting with the brass, the music builds up the heavy, oppressive atmosphere of this darkly-illuminated scene. After tense horn chords, the contra-bassoon enters to create an eerie effect with the brass, similar to the sounds produced by Prokofiev in his music for *Alexander Nevsky*. As the Kane emblem appears (shot 9) the music seems to snarl the very sound of the letter, like some code invented by the devil. As the texture of the music thickens, vibraphone, strings and woodwind enter more freely, leading to a series of soft drum rolls that slowly become more insistent. The "Kane" motif is heard frequently on the horns. As the lighted window is approached, the music rises to a climax, ending in a sharp, frightening crash when the light goes out.

The scene now moves to the interior of the tower:

Shot 17. Medium shot of the window, viewed from inside. The light comes on again.

Shot 18. A snow storm fills the entire screen. Suddenly, it is possible to discern a little model house through the whirling flakes. In a process shot, the camera pulls sharply back to reveal that it is a glass snow-toy, held tightly in a man's hand.

Shot 19. Close-up of the toy in the man's hand.

Shot 20. A very big close-up of a man's lips; in a deep, resonant voice, they utter the word "Rosebud".

Shot 21. In slow-motion, the snow-toy falls from the hand of the recumbent man and appears to glide and bounce down a few steps.

Shot 22. In normal time, the snow-toy smashes to pieces on the last step.

Shot 23. Long shot of a nurse entering through a heavily-carved wooden doorway.

Shot 24. Through a concave distorting mirror, the nurse is seen to move forward into the room.

Shot 25. From low down and close in, there appears to be the body of a large man, lying on a kind of dais-bed. The nurse lifts the limp arms of the dead man and crosses them over his chest. She then takes the corner of a sheet and draws it across the body and face.

Shot 26. The light is seen at the window again, as in shot 17. The scene fades out.

After a moment of silence, the music creeps back at the end of shot 17, rising once more to a climactic crash as the snow-toy crashes on the ground. A sharp chord precedes the word "Rosebud", giving it greater significance. A hymn-like line is introduced from the entry of the nurse (shot 23), introducing a sustained feeling of reverence; the final fade out is paralleled by an orchestral diminuendo.

Of particular interest is the musical pointing of the light and the smashing toy, as well as the use of the Kane motif, which is heard at various times throughout the film and plays a prominent part in the musical structure of the Finale.

This Finale also has a tremendous dramatic effect with the shock that comes from discovering the secret hidden for ever from the characters who are searching for it.

A group of journalists are discussing the mystery of "Rosebud", Kane's dying word. In the echoing hall of Xanadu the newspaper men compare notes for the last time. The special investigator for the film magazine *News on the March* admits defeat, his voice as he speaks echoing through the palatial hall: "I don't think any word can explain a man's life. I guess Rosebud is just a piece in a jigsaw puzzle. A missing piece. Well, come on everybody. (Footsteps.) We'll miss the train."

The music starts under the last two words with a slow, ominous passage for muted brass and strings; a grim horn figure is prominent. Woodwind enters, bringing a more plaintive mood, until interrupted by a sharp chord on muted horns. Just over a minute from the start of the sequence, the camera has reached the end of a very long crane shot moving over the vast accumulation of Kane's possessions, and a man feeding a small furnace shouts "Throw that junk". A little wooden sledge is flung into the fire, and the word "Rosebud" painted on it appears for a moment before the heat buckles and splits both paint and woodwork. The full weight of the orchestra, dominated by a fortissimo string statement of the main theme, hurls this vital moment at the audience. The word is gone, and a shot of the exterior of Xanadu follows, with a column of black smoke rising from a tall chimney. Twelve great orchestral chords bring the drama of *Citizen Kane* to a close.

Before presenting in this section the analysis of the final sequence of William Alwyn's *Odd Man Out*, we would like to quote a passage written by Miklos Rozsa for *Film Music Notes* on the use of the multiple stereophonic speakers provided by the MGM sound system to build up a particular effect of tension in *Julius Caesar*. The advent of stereophonic techniques has given the composer an opportunity of using the devices of opera and the concert hall by freeing him from the restrictions of single-source sound. Miklos Rozsa explains how he handled musically the scene of the death of Brutus at the time when the armies of Antony and Octavius are advancing.

The last music starts after Cassius dies and continues from here to the end of the picture. The themes of Cassius and Brutus appear again in a subdued, low and depressed manner. Brutus appeals to his friends for death and they refuse him. He asks his servant Strato to hold his sword whilst he runs on it. He dies with the words on his lips: "Caesar, now be still; I kill'd not thee with half so good a will."

137

Throughout these scenes I wanted to give the impression that the victorious armies of Antony and Octavius are continuously advancing and coming nearer and nearer and nearer. This scene, however, is the culmination of the tragedy, when its noblest character, Brutus, like a Greek hero in a Greek drama, faces his inescapable fate. I wrote, therefore, two entirely different scores, contrapuntally worked out, but in content completely independent. The one, which represents Antony's nearing army, is a march based on Caesar's theme and is scored for brass, woodwind and percussion instruments. The other, which plays the scene in the foreground and underlines the tragedy of Brutus, is scored for strings only. Thus there is a complete contrast of colour between the two, apart from their emotional rhythmic and thematic differences.

The new stereophonic technique, with three loudspeakers behind the screen, came to my help. As the direction of the approaching army is from the right corner of the screen, we put the march track on this loudspeaker and the string track on the two others, screen centre and left corner. Thus there is complete separation of the two scores, which were recorded separately, and geographically the listener immediately feels that the army is marching from the right corner of the screen.

As Brutus dies the march becomes louder and louder and as Strato runs out from the scene it completely overpowers Brutus's string music and dominates the whole screen.

This juxtaposition of two different moods is not entirely my innovation, as Bizet already most effectively used it in the third act of *Carmen*, when Escamilio enters the arena and Carmen remains alone with Don Jose. In the background we hear the gay, bullfighter music which is interrupted by the orchestra with sombre comments about the impending drama in the foreground.

138

ODD MAN OUT
(Britain, 1946)

Directed by Carol Reed. Screenplay by F. L. Green and R. C. Sherrif, from the novel *Odd Man Out* by F. L. Green. A Two Cities Film, made at Denham Studios. With James Mason, Robert Newton, Kathleen Ryan, F. J. McCormick, Denis O'Dea Maureen Delany, W. G. Fay and Fay Compton.

Music composed by William Alwyn. Musical direction by Muir Mathieson. Recorded by the London Symphony Orchestra. Music recordist: E. A. Drake.

Johnny MacQueen is the leader of an illegal political organization in Northern Ireland. To get funds, he leads a raid on the cashier's office of a mill, is wounded during the getaway and fails to escape with his comrades. For eight hours the police hunt him through the city. One of his companions tries to decoy the police but fails. Various citizens succour him tentatively and often fearfully, anxious to push him on as soon as they can. One betrays him and other members of his organization. All the while, his girl friend, Kathleen, searches for him in desperation. Father Tom, a Catholic priest, is also anxious to speak with him before the end. In the vicinity of the dockyard, Kathleen eventually finds him, terribly injured, and tries to organize their escape. . . .

I

ACTION L.S. Approach to Dock Square through a covered way. Father Tom catches up with Shell, who is wrestling with a shoe that has come off in the snow.

DIALOGUE *Shell:* "Father Tom, me shoe came off
Father Tom: "Where is she?"
Shell : "The lace busted; she went on."
Father Tom: "Which way?"
Shell: "I couldn't keep up with her, but we'll get her now."

EFFECTS

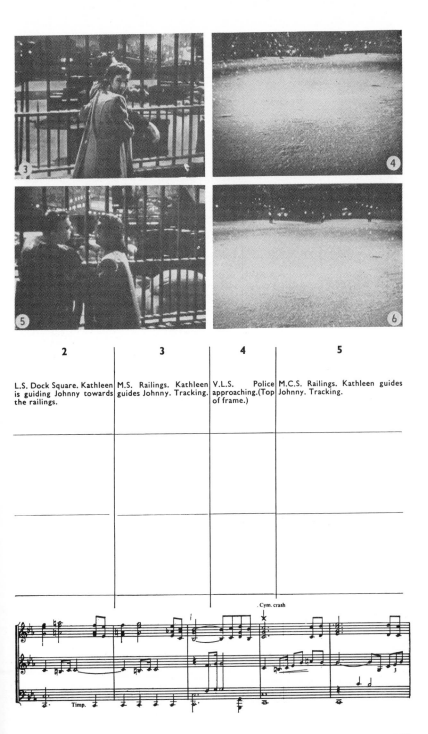

2	**3**	**4**	**5**
L.S. Dock Square. Kathleen is guiding Johnny towards the railings.	M.S. Railings. Kathleen guides Johnny. Tracking.	V.L.S. Police approaching.(Top of frame.)	M.C.S. Railings. Kathleen guides Johnny. Tracking.

	6	**7**
ACTION	V.L.S. Police approaching. (Top of frame)	M.C.S. Kathleen guides Johnny along the railings; his steps are becoming progressively weaker. The camera tracks continuously to follow them.
DIALOGUE		
EFFECTS		

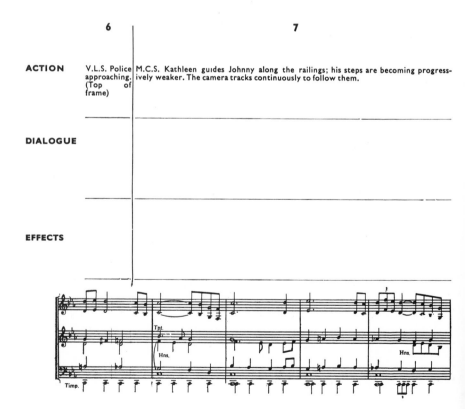

142

	8	**9**	**10**
Shot 7 continues. M.C.S. Kathleen guides Johnny along the railings, his steps are becoming progressively weaker. The camera tracks continuously to follow them.	C.S. Railings. Kathleen and Johnny.	V.L.S. Police approaching. (Top of frame).	C.S. Johnny has fallen back against the railings and hangs on grimly. Kathleen is beside him. Camera tracks in.

Johnny: "Kathleen, where are you?"
Kathleen: "It's all right Johnny, I'm here."
Johnny: "Is it far?"
Kathleen: "It's a long way, Johnny, but I'm coming with you."

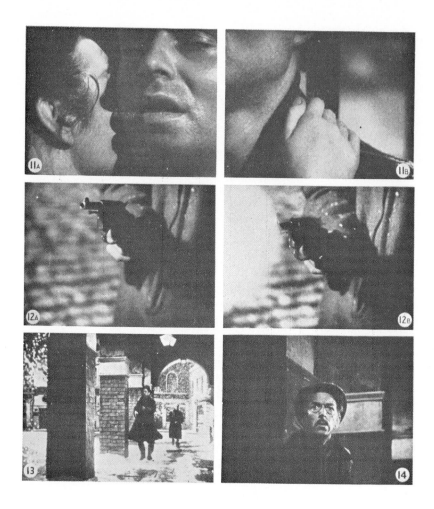

11	12	13	14	15
B.C.U. The faces of Johnny and Kathleen. The camera pans and tilts to show Kathleen's hand on his shoulder.	B.C.U. Gun in Kathleen's hand; fires.	L.S. Shell and Father Tom	C.S. Shell re-acting to shots.	C.S. Fathe Tom.
Kathleen: "We're going away together."				
Deep, breathy sigh from Johnny, recorded very close to the microphone.	Revolver shots.		Burst of revolver shots.	

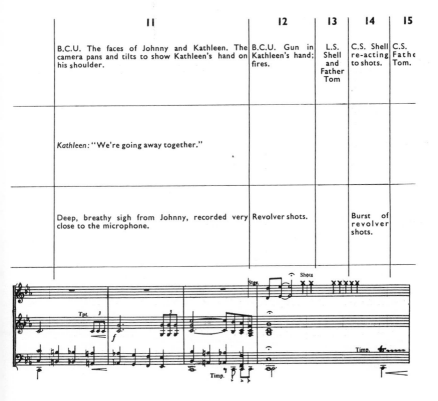

	16	17	18
ACTION	C.S. Shell.	L.S. Shell and Father Tom.	L.S. into M.S. Police cars and men move in towards the railings, where the bodies of Johnny and Kathleen are lying. The camera Tracks in.
DIALOGUE			
EFFECTS			Slam of car door.

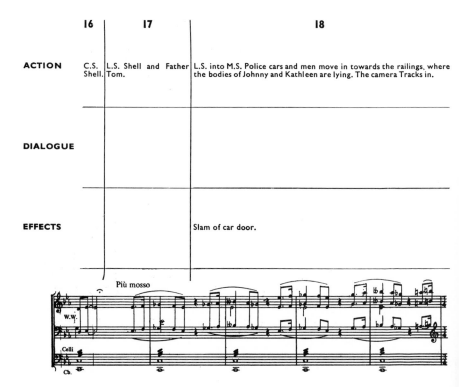

Più mosso

W.W.

Celli

Cb.

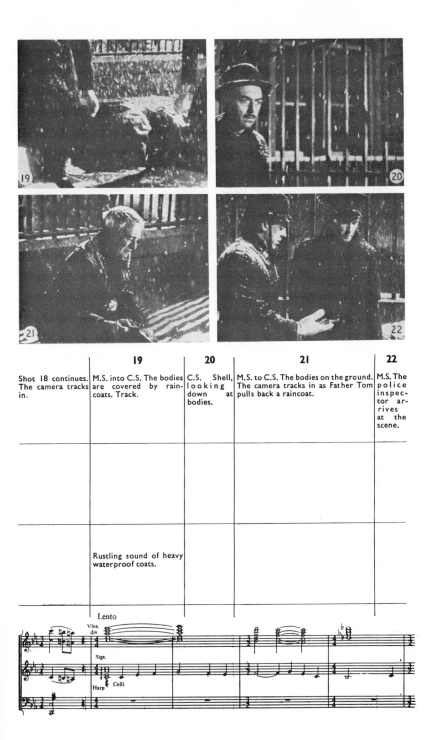

	19	**20**	**21**	**22**
Shot 18 continues. The camera tracks in.	M.S. into C.S. The bodies are covered by rain-coats. Track.	C.S. Shell, looking down at bodies.	M.S. to C.S. The bodies on the ground. The camera tracks in as Father Tom pulls back a raincoat.	M.S. The police inspector arrives at the scene.

Rustling sound of heavy waterproof coats.

Lento

		23	24
ACTION	Shot 22 continues He examines a revolver offered by a police constable	C.S. Father Tom overhears conversation, as he bends over the bodies.	M.S. to L.S. The Police Inspector stands over the bodies, gun in hand. Father Tom hears the siren and look towards the departing ship.
DIALOGUE	*P.C.:* "There's their gun, sir." *Inspector:* "Two shots fired."	*P.C.:* "Yes sir; that's when we had to fire back."	
EFFECTS	Click of revolver barrel being opened.		Ship's siren (long blast).

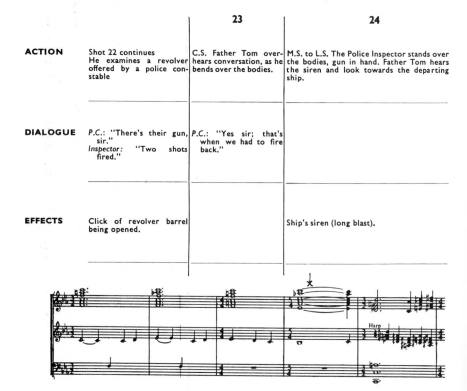

Shot 24 continues. As Father Tom moves off to the left, the camera pans to follow him. He rests his hand on Shell's shoulder and the pair go away into the distance. The camera pans and tilts up to the clock; it is midnight. The End.

Clock striking.

(v) Comedy Music

Music composed for comic effect often takes the form of the close alignment of music and action. For example, Richard Addinsell's score for *Blithe Spirit* makes special provision for the vagaries of Madame Arcarti, the spiritualist medium played by Margaret Rutherford. She rides through the little village on her bicycle, the tempo of the music nicely attuned to her somewhat irregular journey, scattering ducks as she passes over the bridge. A vibraphone is used to suggest her link with the spirit world; a trumpet calls her to go forward and do her duty.

Music is as quick to make a joke as it is to stir an emotion. Its lightning interplay with the comic action of cartoon films is proof enough of this; we shall comment on music for cartoon films in a later section. A special flair in the composer to make music for comedy is as important in film composition as the capacity to create dramatic scores.

It is, perhaps, rather surprising to find that a French composer, Georges Auric, who speaks little English, has been responsible for composing the scores of several of these comedies with their very British sense of humour. He was the composer for *Hue and Cry*, *Passport to Pimlico*, *The Lavender Hill Mob*, and *The Titfield Thunderbolt*, and it is interesting to see the manner in which Auric has adapted himself to the needs of this special kind of fantastic comedy.

Hue and Cry, for example, has very brisk title music, which is used to express the exuberance of the bunch of youngsters who are the main characters in the film and also during part of the melodramatic finale in which the villain stalks the young hero through a bombed building. For a short while, the atmosphere is turned from fun to fear; but the speed of the musical transition is a simple yet impressive demonstration of the power of music to assist the director. In *Passport to Pimlico*, a London suburb is temporarily transformed into a province of the ancient State of Burgundy. Here Auric used a contrasting British and French idiom to express the situation in musical terms. *The Lavender Hill Mob* offered a similar chance to compose in contrasting styles; the bank robbers start their activities in London, but visit Paris after their crime is committed.

It was *The Titfield Thunderbolt* which presented Auric with the most uncompromisingly national English comedy for which he has so far created a score. It is interesting to see how effectively he dealt with our country inns, and the old traditions of the local squire, village fête, and, above all, our British Railways! His music for the film seems at times like an amused yet rather puzzled Gallic comment on the peculiar English, adding a touch of French wit to the old-English world of afternoon tea and croquet on the lawn.

A musical joke of a very individual kind was that made by Larry Adler during the credit titles for *Genevieve*. Economy of effect was the main principle, and Adler's harmonica had all the virtuosity of Karas's zither in its relationship to the film. Here is what happens during the first hundred seconds:

0.00	First "Rank Gong" stroke.
0.04	Second "Rank Gong" stroke.
0.08	Complete silence; film titles proceed to announce cast and credits.
0.24	Vague flourishes on harmonica, as if tuning up.
0.32	First statement of waltz-like theme on harmonica, with piano accompaniment. The melody is developed a little.
1.25	A long diminuendo leads to:
1.32	Four final, high-spirited, unconnected harmonica squeaks.
1.42	Street noises; the Law Courts in the Strand.

The impudence of the instrument and the virtuosity of Larry Adler's playing were sufficient to give the film a disarming sophistication. Nevertheless, the harmonica is also an instrument which through its past associations expresses sentiment very easily, and a great deal of its effect throughout *Genevieve* was to offset the humour of the general situation with a nice balance of sentiment.

A gentler style of musical humour was to be found in William Alwyn's score for *The History of Mr. Polly*. For a short scene in which Mr. Polly goes punting for the first time, the composer succeeded in using a fairly rigid musical form with which to express the underlying atmosphere of the scene.

The Punting Scene consists of an incident in which Mr. Polly (played by John Mills) takes over a ferry service across a small river, watched by the Plump Woman (Megs Jenkins). His first attempt is not very effective. An old gentleman comes aboard, and Mr. Polly takes the punt pole ready for the journey. He finds both the pole and the craft very difficult to manage. During the tussle, Mr. Polly, the punt pole and the old gentleman end up in a sprawling mass at the bottom of the boat.

The scene is accompanied by a scherzo for woodwind; the material is presented in the form of a brief fugue. Mr. Polly's clumsiness is pointed by the oboe and bassoon; even the laughter of the Plump Woman on shore is captured by a series of rapidly descending phrases for various members of the woodwind ensemble.

Anthony Hopkins has contributed to the range of comedy music in films. In association with Peter Ustinov, he prepared the music for *Vice Versa*, which included an amusing parody on title music for silent films.

As the film opens, the famous Rank gong is accompanied by an impressive drum roll and a single ping on triangle. The Titles appear as rather battered lantern slides, accompanied by the orchestra tuning up in a noisy manner. The main tune is a vulgar "hurry music" theme, dominated by a raucous and inaccurate trombone, a tuba and a very out-of-tune piano.

151

A more subtle attempt at this kind of satire is to be found in *Muscle Beach*, a one-reel short film made by Joseph Strick and Irving Lerner. It consists of a rapid, impressionist report of a sunny day on an American beach, with the sun-worshippers assiduously exercising their muscles, practising acrobatics or indulging in sustained bouts of weight-lifting. The commentary, sung in a mixture of blues and calypso styles, makes its points in a gentle and unobtrusive manner. The sung commentary is by Earl Robinson.

PICTURE (Not cut on the beat)	SOUND (Singing, with guitar accompaniment)
1. C.S. Man exercising violently with large hand-held weights.	Just abdicate your Troubles; Eradicate your Worries; 'Cause it's the Summer Time;
2. C.S. (from behind). Man exercising violently with large hand-held weights.	It's the Time to Take it Nice and Easy.
3. M.L.S. (from below). Girl balancing on man's hands. She bends down to adjust her shoe.	Now I'm not saying that Clothes Don't Count;
4. M.S. Little boy on promenade, looking up to the sun through a spy-glass viewer which contains gaily-coloured views.	Or that Money Don't Help; Or that Bread Don't Count:
5. L.S. Man supported in air. Pan down to show group of men supporting him in pyramid style.	But if we all sat down to Write Our True Confessions
6. M.S. (from behind). Woman shielding her eyes from the sun and watching the group.	We'd have to own up that we Don't Own Much Possessions.
7. M.L.S. (from behind). Girl balancing in the air, supported by a man. She bends down, revealing a full figure.	Just a Body—That's What We've all Got—More or Less.
8. M.S. Man holding another man's wrists; he raises him up into the air from a lying position.	A Pauper can become a Prince in Disguise;
9. M.S. Girl runs forward and is grasped by the ankles by her partner, who throws her into the air in a flying motion; she is caught by a second man.	And fly through the Air the way a Seagull Flies: Like a Bird; Like a Plane; Like Superman.
10. L.S. Little girl watching.	(Dramatic pause.)
11. L.S. (from above). Girl being thrown into the air and caught by a man in a sharp, flicking motion.	A Little Practice; A Flip of the Wrist;
12. C.S. A girl turning somersaults in the air.	A Compound Fracture!
13. C.S. A girl exercising with large hand-held weights.	A Little Meditation; Some Idle Contemplation;
14. C.U. A perspiring and puffing man exercising violently with large weights.	For it's the Summer Time; it's the Time to Take It Nice and Easy.

A great deal of Hollywood's comedy music is linked with the cartoon world and it is interesting to note that a number of techniques associated with the animation studios are increasingly employed during the making of live-action scenes. For example, click-tracks are often used in scenes where there is a feeling of mechanical or physical rhythm to be imparted; this is often the case in the better type of comedy. The editor marks up all the points of action in a scene on a strip of blank optical sound film. Playing the strip through a Moviola or a sound projector produces a series of clicks which represents the rhythm of the action on the screen. The composer can then take the click-track and plot the music according to the rhythm of the clicks. In addition, the click-track may be played to the conductor and orchestral leader during the recording session to assist them in obtaining precise rhythmical effects. During the making of *Love Happy*, a film featuring the Marx Brothers, fourteen sequences were recorded by the click-track method.[1] The composer, Ann Ronell, has described her approach to the preparation of a theme for Harpo:

> The decision to score his sequences precisely was based on his being a silent comedian. Since he never talks, I let the music speak for him. He does whistle, however, and this peculiar fact gave me an idea of having him announce his own musical theme himself. Thus it is that Harpo's music in the score is his language; his gestures become rhythms, his movements are accents, his pantomimed thoughts find voice through the inflection of instruments whose colours express Harpo's spirited style. When it came to synchronization, I found the matter of the utmost importance. Paul Smith introduced me to the intricacies of the click track.

In the film, the main motif for Harpo appears first as his own whistle; it is picked up instrumentally by the piccolo and used frequently during the course of the action. A typical example is found in this material.

Part A of the Harpo motif is seen on the oboe at Bar 5; this is a duplicate of the theme originally whistled by Harpo. In addition, there is a whistled variation of the A theme which has been re-set to fit the visual action indicated in the click-track beat above the score.

[1]The following facts on the film *Love Happy* are taken from Film Music Notes. Vol. IX, No. 4. Score quotations by permission of Lester Cowan Productions, and the composer.

153

A British composer who has had considerable experience in the field of comedy is Malcolm Arnold. Through work on such films as *Captain's Paradise, The Constant Husband, Hobson's Choice* and *The Belles of St. Trinians,* he has evolved certain principles in the writing of film music which suit his own style. First, comedy music is not necessarily produced by the broad type of writing often associated with comic turns in the music-hall. Frequently more amusing effects are obtained by a contrast in mood to the visuals rather than a direct laugh in the music; the music, heard on its own, may not sound funny at all. Secondly, Arnold has found that a small orchestra is best suited to this type of work. Even in his dramatic work, he is a believer in the smaller ensemble for the microphone. For *Hobson's Choice* he used an orchestra of twenty-five, for *I Am a Camera* an orchestra of fourteen, and for *The Belles of St. Trinians* he had only twelve instrumentalists.

Hobson's Choice is the story of a prosperous Lancashire bootmaker, whose attempts to act as a domestic tyrant are largely unsuccessful. He spends much of his time drinking, and David Lean, the director, obtained a good deal of comedy from those moments when Hobson was at varied degrees of intoxication. Malcolm Arnold was brought into the film at the beginning. He pre-planned the music for a number of sequences, and one or two short scenes were shot and cut to the music. An example of this is the opening scene of the film; the individual shots and the full orchestral score are reproduced on the following pages.

HOBSON'S CHOICE
Opening Scene

Shot 1. A large sign, advertising Mr. Hobon's Boot Shop. It squeaks noisily in the wind. The camera cranes back to reveal a rain-swept street; Mr. Hobson's shop can be seen on the right-hand side. It is night-time and the street is deserted.

Shot 2. Interior of the shop. There is a sharp zip-pan, as the camera moves to a clock. It strikes 1 (a.m.).

Shot 3. Interior of the shop. The camera picks up a pair of ladies' boots. It pans slowly along the counter to reveal a pair of ladies' riding-boots, dainty ladies' shoes, ballet slippers, toddler's shoes, a pair of clogs and a mass of assorted shoes clustered on a rack. There is a zip-pan to reveal an annex of the shop; trees are banging against the skylight. The camera pans down to a chair. There is a zip-pan up to the door of the shop. Hobson bursts in to the sound of a loud belch. The music written by Malcolm Arnold for the whole of Shot 3 is reproduced on the following pages; the original music cues have been retained in the score.

154

Shot 3, Interior of the shop. The camera has moved sharply into position (1st bar) and is focused on a pair of ladies' boots. It pans slowly along the counter to reveal a pair of ladies' riding boots.

Shot 3 continues. The camera pans slowly along the counter and picks out other ladies' shoes; it eventually comes to a very dainty pair of ballet slippers.

Shot 3 continues. The camera pans slowly along the counter and comes to some shoes for toddlers, followed by a pair of clogs.

(Page 142). Shot 3 continues. The camera moves across a mass of assorted shoes and suddenly zip-pans to reveal the annexe of the shop; trees are banging against the skylight. The camera pans down to a chair. There is a zip-pan to the door of the shop, as Hobson bursts in.

(vi) Music for Human Emotion

All music is either the expression or the stimulant of human emotion. The significance of the title of this particular section is merely to indicate that branch of film music composition in which the emphasis is not on physical action, or a general response to period or place which the composer wishes to build up in the audience, or an effect of comedy or dramatic tension—but on the particular emotional feeling of the characters themselves. In the charming French film *Sylvie et le Fantôme* this is achieved by means which are surely the simplest ever used in a film—the Pipes of Pan. This little instrument manages to express most movingly the feelings of the love-lorn ghost.

At the opposite end of the scale is the music used by Akira Ifukube, composer of the score for the Japanese film *Children of Hiroshima*. Means had somehow to be found to express to the world the human reaction to the terrible experience of enduring the atom bomb. The main story is set in 1953; the explosion itself is a flash-back inset in a sequence when a young schoolteacher is seen returning to Hiroshima by boat some years after the war.

The film opens with a sad, grim theme on woodwind and strings, with long held notes on oboe and cor anglais against a background on 'cellos and basses. Scenes of the approach to Hiroshima follow, accompanied by a sustained effect on woodwind and the bass of the piano; this device is used in a variety of settings later in the score. The approach to 6th August, 1945, develops against a string and woodwind background that evokes the atmosphere of a Bach Choral Prelude. As 8.15 a.m. (the time of the explosion) approaches, the ticking of a clock becomes louder and louder, taking over from the music. The moment of the explosion of the atom bomb takes place in complete silence, with a sudden, blinding flash on the screen. A flower shrivels up. A bird falls to the ground. Men and women, stripped, blinded and bent with shock and pain crouch motionless like figures in a sculptor's frieze. Suddenly, a mighty sound of massed choirs and fortissimo piano chords breaks the silence with a sustained, dignified yet fearful cry of agony. As the climax of the terror subsides, a long diminuendo section prepares the way for the end of the flashback sequence and a return to the post-war story on which the main structure of the film is based.

Vaughan Williams's score for *Scott of the Antarctic* also uses a choral effect to reveal a great dramatic incident of human suffering. The massed voices of choirs are, of course, commonly used in films to give an effect of emotional "uplift"; there is nothing intrinsically wrong with this tradition except when it is wrongly or vulgarly used. In *Scott of the Antarctic* it is a momentary effect only. The desperate attempt of Captain Scott and his party to return to base camp after reaching the South Pole begins with a long trek across the snows. It is set to a heavily-scored section in slow march time, for the men are weary and progress is poor. As they huddle in a tent at the end of each day's travel, the rising wind is heralded by low moaning voices, interspersed with bass drum rolls and full brass statements of a blizzard theme. This torrent of voices and orchestral sound mingles with the roar of the wind and the flapping of the canvas tent, interrupted by sparse dialogue from the men and the reading of Scott's last letter home. As with many other sections of this picture, the music often expresses emotions that the men cannot reveal directly through their speech or actions.

Almost all films aim to be popular entertainment, and their music is correspondingly immediate in its appeal to sentiment or to the drama of the situation on the screen. For example, simplicity is the main quality of the sound-tracks of Chaplin's films, including the music. It is usually elementary, repetitive and immediate in its emotional appeal, and belongs to the theme song style of the late nineteen-twenties. The main theme in *Limelight* differs little from that of *City Lights*, written nearly fifteen years earlier. The audition scene in *Limelight* is a classic example of simplicity and timing. An empty stage and a hushed moment; a single command for "lights"; brief words of introduction; a rehearsal piano, acoustically correct and unhindered by "off-stage" orchestral embellishments. A tense silence as the dance ends; congratulations, factual and unemotional; lights off; the solitary abandoned figure of Chaplin in a corner. Then, to an emotional flash of music, the camera closes in on his saddened face.

Another great film-maker, John Ford, prefers direct and simple musical effects. The apparent ease with which he uses well-known tunes as primary emotional elements in the construction of his sound-tracks may suggest that this type of scoring should be more widely employed. Like Carol Reed's zither, it has, however, proved too dangerous a device to imitate, precisely because it is basically so simple; as a result, most directors apparently prefer to hide behind the shield of a hundred-piece orchestra playing music nobody knows. Using a simple tune which is immediately recognized means that the director assumes the tremendous responsibility of forecasting mass reactions to melody. The main argument for specially-composed scores is that the film-maker does not have to worry about individual emotional responses to music; he can, indeed, shape the pattern to his own ends at every stage.

Ford has mastered most of the problems. To be used successfully, the tunes should not be too fragmentated or they merely annoy; his characteristic "playing-out" of a scene to the full gives the music time to establish and develop naturally. Constant interruption by dialogue and effects will destroy the continuity of the music; Ford's love for the expressive power of the visuals guards against this fault. Finally, the method in which the tunes are presented demands the utmost care; Ford in this case has taken that unhappy product of Hollywood's Music Departments, the orchestrator, and given him an honourable place in the dubbing theatre. *Red River Valley* is not an easy tune to use in a dramatic context; yet, on the mouth organ and concertina, it fitted admirably into *Grapes of Wrath*. *Anchors Aweigh* can be a tiresome dirge; a change of tempo and muted brass setting made it a symbol of a special sort of courage in *They Were Expendable*. Ford is not even afraid to repeat a tune specially written for one of his own films, if the right occasion arises; when the mail wagons roll into view in *She Wore a Yellow Ribbon*, we hear an echo of the main theme from *Stagecoach*.

Perhaps *The Quiet Man* offered Ford the greatest musical challenge of all, if only to avoid *Danny Boy* and other such tunes which have been played to death in a hundred films of Irish sentiment. The inn scenes were carried along by *Colonial Boy*. It rarely interfered with the action, matching its tempo to scenes both dramatic and comic. A fleeting reference to *Galway Bay* came as a jarring lapse in Ford's usually impeccable taste for music. A clever orchestration of the rhythm of a tune more often associated with the Scots than the Irish (for scenes of John Wayne's walk back from Castletown) was among the best moments in the whole score.

A British example may be found in the use of African folk music by Sir Arthur Bliss in *Men of Two Worlds*. During the African location, recordings were made of a wide range of native music and the discs were passed to the composer before he began work on the score. The picture opens with a fanfare based on a genuine African drum rhythm. During the credit titles, a solo voice interprets a native folk song. The first shot is of the National Gallery in Trafalgar Square and a poster announces the performance of Kisenga's *Baraza* at a Lunch-time Concert. (This work is described on p. 65.)

There is also a sequence which shows Randall, the District Commissioner, flying to Tanganyika. Bliss was anxious to avoid the conventional "travel montage music", so he examined the scene carefully with Thorold Dickinson. After shots of the aircraft, of jungle scenery and matter-of-fact discussion between Kisenga and Randall, there appeared a shot of a snow-capped mountain. "That", said Bliss, "is the emotional peg on which the scene rests." Instead of a musical imitation of aircraft noise or of "travel effects". the music concentrates throughout on the appearance of Kilimanjaro, the great mountain of Tanganyika.

161

Kisenga returns to his village and is greeted by his mother and father. The two elderly natives who played the scene were not professional actors and it lacked the necessary emotion. Dickinson suggested that this was a case where the composer might legitimately be called upon to supply a missing emotion, and a suitably gay section for woodwind and strings helped to sustain the general feeling of rejoicing.

Kisenga teaches the children of the village to sing one of his own songs. Bliss took two African folk songs from the Tanganyikan discs and built them into one tune for the scene.

No location sound was used in the finished film; even the large-scale night scene was recorded at a special session at Denham Studios, in which the original African recordings were made the basis of specially-designed tracks.

Another form of simplicity of emotional appeal to match the sentiments of the characters are the theme songs used particularly in French and Italian films. The French, indeed, are famous for the creation of atmosphere and emotion through a simple theme song. René Clair established the tradition in such films as *Le Million*, *A Nous la Liberté* and *Sous les Toits de Paris*.

For *Un Carnet de Bal*, Jaubert (who had contributed so much as a pioneer to film music in France) used his *Valse Grise* as the main theme. It appears prominently as fluttering, eerie sounds that accompany scenes in which the central character, a widow in middle life, recalls her first ball when, as a very young girl, she danced with the men whose names she still has on the *carnet de bal* she has kept through the intervening years. The undulating images of memory are accompanied by the string tremolos and the quivering of the vibraphone; suddenly the picture becomes clear when an impressionistic scene of the ball as she visualizes it floods the screen. The sweeping waltz gives a picture of the great ballroom and the floating dresses of the women. Later on in the film, the theme is distorted to suit the emotions of the action; in the famous sequence with the epileptic doctor in the quayside tenement, it becomes dissonant and vicious, a sharply-pointed echo of something that once suggested beauty and gaiety.

An Italian score of great effectiveness is that by Alessandro Cicognini for Vittorio de Sica's film *Bicycle Thieves*. It belongs emotionally to the traditions of the Neapolitan folk song and of Rossini and Verdi. His power to move an audience is as simple and sure as that of Tchaikovsky. The screen is concerned with a contemporary realistic story, but Cicognini underlines the emotions in

162

the style of *La Bohème* or *Swan Lake*. Although the scores are entirely different musically, there is a comparison between Cicognini's music for *Bicycle Thieves* and the work of Vaughan Williams for *Scott of the Antarctic*; in both cases the composers are concerned with the expression of feeling that is not directly apparent on the screen.

There is continuous music during the last nine minutes of *Bicycle Thieves*. The situation is that the unemployed Italian worker, Antonio, has lost his precious, newly-acquired job as a bill-poster because a thief has stolen his bicycle. Most of the action of the film is concerned with his vain attempts to find the thief. After a clumsy and unsuccessful attempt to have a man he suspects arrested, Antonio and his small son Bruno walk away from the scene to the derisive shouts of his neighbours. The central theme is heard on the strings of the orchestra, as the two pass along the streets.

The rising sound of a great crowd begins to be heard, and the music changes to a sustained effect on the strings as the football stadium is approached. Outside the arena, hundreds of bicycles line the roadside; as the father sits down on the kerb, more bicycles flash past. The crowd comes out of the arena, punctuated by a rhythmic chiming effect on strings and percussion. Waves of tremulous sound rise up from the masses of bicycles that now fill the screen. The brass enters as the father sees an unattended bicycle by a doorway, and it is obvious that desire rises in him to steal it. Horns and strings combine to thrust out a stream of undulating sounds as Antonio wrestles with his conscience. When he decides to take the bicycle, the music rises to a climax, ending on a sharp chord as he snatches the machine.

Immediately a "chase" theme is taken up by the orchestra, softly at first, but becoming increasingly insistent as the crowd joins in the pursuit. The brass ends the agitato section with a sharp beat as the father is caught. When Bruno sees what has happened to his father, the main theme appears again, played soulfully on solo saxophone. Horn phrases accentuate the insults of the crowd as the father is eventually allowed to go free; then the main theme springs into prominence, being played three times as father and son go sadly on their way, the boy comforting his father by holding his hand. Eventually they are swallowed up in the crowd.

Three soft string chords bring the end title slowly into the face of the audience. The film is provided with a long playout, in which the central theme is given two full orchestral statements, almost as if it were the finale of *Tosca*.

A film in which music is used with great emotional discretion is William Wellman's *The Oxbow Incident* (*Strange Incident*). The composer is Cyril J. Mockridge.

It opens with conventional, heavily-scored title music, which introduces the main themes, including a vocal effect for a choir singing wordlessly. As the titles come to an end, the orchestral sound is very suddenly interrupted by a concertina playing *Red River Valley*, the folk music already mentioned above (p. 94). The concertina continues for a short way as the two main characters of the film ride into town, and it ends when they go into the bar.

In the last half of the picture, only six music cues are introduced, and two of these spring from the action itself. After the long arguments among the lynching posse concerning the guilt or innocence of the three men they are illegally trying for cattle thieving and murder, there is a lull in the action as the condemned men wait for dawn when they are to be hanged. One of them writes a letter to his wife. As the camera moves slowly through the group, the concertina begins again (though very subdued) to play *Red River Valley*. An old, religious-minded Negro, who is one of the minority of well-meaning men who have joined the posse in the hope of getting justice done and stopping the lynching interrupts the scene while he sings in a cracked and clumsy voice, *Don't Get Weary, Chil'lun . . . There's a Great Camp Meeting in the Promised Land*.

There is a further last discussion among the members of the posse; it is decided to take a last vote before proceeding with the lynching. As the men slowly separate into two groups, the majority for the lynching and the minority against it, the choral effect heard before in the title music appears once more. It is taken up by the orchestra, first with tremolo strings and bassoon, and finally by a mixture of the voices and full ensemble. There is a sharp chord and a percussion beat after the decision to proceed with the hangings is announced.

When the time comes to secure the nooses, heavy brass chords are heard, accentuated by drum beats. The horses are whipped away from under the victims; there are screams of anguish and terror from the strings, leading to thundering action when a man's nerve gives way at the last moment, and one of the victims has to be shot. After the hanging the entire party mount and leave the deserted spot as quickly as possible; only the Negro remains, kneeling down and wailing "You got to go through the Lonesome Valley; you got to stand by yourself, before your Lord".

Too late, the sheriff returns and meets the posse. He tells them that the lynched men were innocent. They all ride grimly back to town, and gather in silence at the bar counter. The letter from one of the hanged men to his young wife is read aloud, and two of those who were present at the lynching leave town to take money and what comfort they can offer to the man's wife and children. As the words of the letter end, the concertina is heard once more playing *Red River Valley*. It follows the riders up the main street from the saloon until they are out of sight, reversing the action which opened this tragic film. The full orchestra then sweeps in to establish a brief coda when the end title comes on to the screen.

So far we have considered examples of the more direct ways in which music can be used to bring the emotions of the audience into sympathy with the characters on the screen, or to reveal the nature of their experience when it would not be appropriate dramatically for it to be expressed directly in speech or action. A more complex interlocking of music, speech and natural sound is represented by a sequence in the documentary film *World Without End*, made by Basil Wright in Thailand and Paul Rotha in Mexico. In the sequence dealing with the cure of yaws by penicillin in Thailand, Elisabeth Lutyens's score identifies its emotion with the sufferings of the villagers.

The sequence starts with the agonized cry of a child suffering from yaws. The commentator states the nature of the disease and a terrible whining sound is heard as he speaks, recorded so as to leave the voice clear of interference. The effect is produced by the strings sustaining a very high-pitched sound against cymbal, side drum and tenor drum punctuations. After about three-quarters of a minute, it is broken by grim brass chords. The commentary resumes on its own, pointing out that, to the Siamese villagers, yaws is a disease without cure. A repeat of the brass chords reinforces his remarks.

Suddenly, there is a cut-away to a jeep, fighting its way along bad roads. For twelve shots, the music gives way to the roar of the car's engine; a close-up of the bonnet with UNICEF markings ends the insertion. The villagers assemble, a medical examination is carried out, a short lecture is given by a doctor, equipment is set up, penicillin injections are prepared and the children are inoculated. This three-minute scene is accompanied by a slow, rhythmic piece of music which is dominated by a solo clarinet or flute in a sad, pensive mood. The contrast between the businesslike work of the medical team and the state of the doubting and often terrified villagers and their children is emphasized by the plaintive tone of the music and the suggestion of reassurance.

The "backing" of speech by music is common in films. It may sometimes take the form of an attempt to aggrandize the passion which banal script writing and playing have been unable to produce unaided; in this case music in the grand manner may underlie the whole spoken scene. But the use of music underlying speech can be

164

well and imaginatively done, for example in the scene of Falstaff's death in *Henry V*.

A strong emotional effect is obtained by William Walton in this interpolated visual scene at the death-bed of Falstaff, during which the Hostess speaks off-screen the famous speech describing how he died. Using the passacaglia form, which is characterized by a short repeated passage in the bass (basso ostinato) upon which the main structure of the music is built, the composer was able to sustain the simple dignity and restrained pathos of the sequence. The section opens with the 'cellos announcing the ground bass. The violins and violas then enter Cantabile legato to build a simple melodic line, whilst the 'cellos continue to repeat the accompaniment, occasionally accentuated by the double basses. The division of the ground bass in even sections of four bars gives a marked sense of unity, and seems strangely appropriate to the long tracking movement of the camera as it approaches Falstaff's bed where he lies dying.

Sir William Walton's music for the soliloquy "To be or not to be" in *Hamlet* is an example of the extension of musical backing to speech into a form which might be called emotional "pointing". This he also did in *Henry V*, for example behind Leslie Banks's speeches as the Chorus, and, most effectively, behind the soliloquy of the King as he contemplates his sleeping camp on the night before Agincourt.

The sequence of the speech "To be or not to be" begins with shots of Hamlet on a high platform of a tower above the sea in Elsinore Castle. At first, the sound-track carries the roar of the waves on the rocks below. Slowly, a series of side drum rolls emerge into the foreground. The orchestra enters, swamping the sea effect with a long crescendo on trumpets, horns and strings agitato, punctuated by side drum rolls. A cymbal crash marks the climax. The camera moves back to reveal Hamlet, deep in thought; this is pointed by a furious descending passage for woodwind and strings, accentuated by a cymbal roll. A gentle diminuendo continues until only 'cellos and basses are left. The lines "To be or not to be: that is the question" are spoken against an andante sostenuto section for lower strings only. The music ends after the word "question", replaced by the sound of the sea, which runs like a fine thread underneath the lines:

> Whether 'tis nobler in the mind to suffer
> The slings and arrows of outrageous fortune,
> Or to take arms against a sea of troubles,
> And by opposing end them?

'Cellos and basses re-enter andante, playing quietly behind the next section:

> To die,—to sleep—
> No more; and by a sleep to say we end
> The heart-ache, and the thousand natural shocks
> That flesh is heir to, 'tis a consummation
> Devoutly to be wish'd. To die;—to sleep—
> To sleep! . . .

Then the full orchestra suddenly springs into a short furious crescendo, cutting off sharply into the next phrase: "perchance to dream". This musical punctuation lends great force to the speech and helps to develop Laurence Olivier's technique of delivering part of the soliloquy as thought and part as direct speech.

An unusually interesting example of a score in which human emotions ran high may be found in Hugo Friedhofer's music for *The Best Years of Our Lives*. In addition to winning the Academy Award for the best score of the year, this film attracted the attention of a greater number of music critics than is usual in film music. The detailed analysis that follows is based on the writings of the American composer Lan Adomian,[1] the Canadian writer and composer Louis Applebaum[2] and the American critic Frederick Sternfeld.[3] The nature of the composer's task was recorded in some detail by Lan Adomian when the film first appeared in 1947:

Any composer charged with the great responsibility of supplying a score for so important a human document as *The Best Years of Our Lives* would have to approach his task with the same honesty of purpose, with the same seriousness as did the writer, director, actors and all concerned with the making of this film. For, unlike most of its counterparts of the "twenties", *The Best Years of Our Lives* is not a picture of either disillusionment and Charmaines, or Rover Boy heroics and tough sergeants. The story of three returning veterans is uncommonly warm and human. It is a real and reasonable kind of humanity. And in reasonableness it seems to hold out a hope for the future that is both desirable and realizable. Such a story calls for a composer whose sensitivity will infuse the film with a poetic feeling which is only implied by the action. Mr. Friedhofer's score abundantly demonstrates that his talents and richly varied skills were equal to the responsibilities imposed by this film. The music at its best goes beyond underscoring or highlighting the action. Very often the music carries on at its own level. In the more extended passages the score appears to tell a parallel story in musical terms. Where the screen proceeds to carry forward its continuity in strictly realistic terms, the music frequently picks up from that point and completes the action, as it were.

The general plan to which Hugo Friedhofer worked in his score was analysed by Louis Applebaum:

A reading of the score reveals that Mr. Friedhofer, as many composers do, has chosen to work on the development, juxtaposition and super-imposition of leit-motifs more or less in the Wagnerian tradition. The material itself is definitely not Wagnerian in character, but the manner of its handling derives from the Wagner of the Niebelungen Ring. As a result, it is possible, in a few short quotations, to list practically all the root material out of which the score as a whole generated.

The most important of the themes is the one on which the Main Title is based. In the score it is called the "Best Years Theme":

Its simplicity, based as it is on the triad, its straightforward, warm harmonization, ably reflects the general theme of the film, principally as it concerns the

[1]Film Music Notes. Vol. VI. No. 5. 1947.
[2]Film Music Notes. Vol. VI. No. 6. 1947.
[3]The Musical Quarterly. Vol. XXXI. No. 4. 1947.

Harold Russell characterization of Homer. It has two main sections, each of which is used and developed separately in the course of the score. The first section (*A*) states the triad motif, the second (*B*) a chordal, almost hymnal phrase, both easily recognized and capable of developed treatment.

The second theme to appear is here called "Boone City":

It also contains two ideas: (*A*) a five-note motif with the characteristic leap of the major 7th to set it apart, and (*B*) a syncopated, moving, broken-triad motif. The *A* motif occurs often, and its major 7th interval manages to add interest to the melodic structure of the score. As will be seen later, it was eventually enlarged into a separate theme.

A third theme is once more chordal in structure. This one, associated with the neighbourly relationship between the families of Homer and that of his girl next door, is most interesting in its harmonization of a tune that is, like the others already mentioned, derived from the simple triad:

It seems to suggest strongly the feeling of much of Aaron Copland's recent writing. The remaining motifs are, fortunately, quite different in character. One, for Homer's girl, Wilma, is simple, delicate, folksey, almost plaintive, like the girl herself:

Another theme, in the style of Gershwin, underlines the relationship between Fred and Peggy:

The theme called "Peggy" follows:

Two or three dramatic sequences in the film received special treatment, with no reference to any of the principal motifs. There is, for instance, the hyper-dramatic moment in the tool shed when Homer, in frustrated embarrassment, is driven to smash the window. Use is made of a children's play-song, interestingly orchestrated and harmonized:

Orchestral colouring of a different kind, plus the full utilization of a minimum of musical material, in this case mostly the interval of the 4th, make an exciting moment of Fred's nightmare, his vivid memories of terrifying war experiences:

A sequence in which Fred Derry finds a vast dump of dismantled Flying Fortresses, climbs into one of the deserted planes and imagines himself back in the air has been analysed in detail by Frederick Sternfeld.

When the bomber scene begins Captain Fred Derry is ostensibly not on the screen. As his father reads the Distinguished Flying Cross award the music enters with the ascending second-motif from the earlier scene and continues with a treatment of theme *B* of the Prelude (see example 1):

It is given out softly until it reaches, as in the Prelude, the heroic chords of 1 *d*. Now the entire passage is played again, continuing as a counterpoint to the actual words of the award. But as citation and dialogue come to an end the sound-mixer increases the volume of the music which now expresses in full-fledged sovereignty, better than words, "the heroism, devotion to duty, professional skill, and coolness under fire displayed by Captain Derry". As the camera shifts to the line of junked planes the ascending second-motif looms more important, the interval finally (after eight repetitions) being extended to a fourth:

Now we see the interior of the dismantled bomber, as the ex-captain enters and the music gives us, for the third time in this scene, the half melancholy, half martial treatment of 1 *b* with its heroic conclusion (1 *d*). The obsession of reliving the deadly missions takes hold of the bombardier as we approach the climax, and while trick angles of the camera suggest an imaginary take-off, the progressive diminution of the ascending second-motif symbolizes the warming-up of the engine and, more than that, the accelerated heartbeat of a frightened individual. Here, the trumpet statement of 1 *b* against the final diminution of the ascending second reveals, if not the psychological origin of this scene, at least its potential substitute, the signal for taps. The tension increases as an inverted pedal on E-flat, sustained for ten measures, accompanies a close-up of the perspiring hero and leads to the quarter-note descent used earlier in the nightmare scene, being in rhythm and pitch (E-flat) a replica of the climax in

169

the earlier scene. The quadruple statement of this simple yet ominous five-note figure that has not been heard for almost two hours has a dreadful suddenness; yet it is nevertheless psychologically prepared.

(vii) Music in Cartoon and Specialized Films[1]

The easiest field for experiment in film music lies in the various specialized forms of production. There are few producers and directors whose films depend directly on the widespread support of the greater public who are prepared to let the composer explore an entirely experimental idiom. The general public consciously believe that they like easy and familiar airs or the impressive grandeur of the more obvious forms of symphonic music.

Although music which makes a new kind of imaginative demand on the response of an audience may easily excite their antipathy and so destroy the dramatic illusion which is essential to the success of the film, it should never be forgotten that the best film music is naturally the music which does its work without thrusting itself obtrusively on the attention of the audience. This means that the composer can often use experimental techniques in composition to excite the particular dramatic effects needed by the film-maker. The result may well be that the audience are quite unconsciously appreciating "advanced" forms of musical composition which, outside the context of the film, they would never be prepared to accept.

In the cartoon and specialized forms of film-making the restraints imposed by the need to excite popular sentiment are lessened. Documentary has always been a lively field for experiment; and the short films extending into the various forms of "art" or avant-garde production were a natural outlet for more advanced kinds of music. The cartoon film, with its flexible interplay between music and

[1]The special relation of music and film animation is discussed in the companion volume in this series by John Halas and Roger Manvell, *The Technique of Film Animation*, particularly pages 78–83, 237 et seq. and, on the specialised work of Norman McLaren, page 290 et seq.

effects, has trained audiences for thirty years to accept unusual combinations of sound as normal on the sound-track. We have aimed to show that this principle of the more advanced use of music and sound effects was already being worked out by pioneer film-makers and composers during the first half-dozen years of the sound film in the scores for such films as *L'Idée*, *Le Sang d'un Poète*, *Song of Ceylon*, *Night Mail* and *Coal Face*.

The cartoon film releases the film-maker from actuality; the cartoonist's world comes entirely from his imagination. He needs music to help keep the creatures of his fantasy close to the emotional sympathies of his audience, and to add wit and point to the action on the screen. The music for an animated film must be composed in advance of the animation. As soon as the main outline of the dramatic action for an animated film is complete, and the initial drawings for scene and character established in the form of a storyboard (the series of rough drawings giving a breakdown of the film shot by shot), the composer must create his score before the process of matching the drawn action to the rhythm and the timing of the music can begin. The animator has to have a music chart to guide him, giving a frame-by-frame relation of the picture to the sound.

Creating scores for animated films is a specialized branch of film music in which the composer must respond to the artist's particular visual style; contrast for example the visual world of *L'Idée* with those of *Joie de Vivre*, *Pinocchio*, *Animal Farm*, *Gerald McBoing Boing* and *The Unicorn in the Garden*. The very varied scores for these very varied films were composed by Arthur Honegger, Tibor von Harsanyi, Walt Disney's music department, Matyas Seiber, Gail Kubik and David Raksin.

The first Disney cartoon to use a song as major part of the structure was in 1933, when Frank Churchill wrote *Who's Afraid of the Big, Bad Wolf* for *The Three Little Pigs*. Over twenty repeats of the main phrase from the song were used in this ten-minute story. Since then, songs have been an integral part of all Disney's pictures, whether live-action or cartoon, and the studio has won Academy Awards with *When You Wish Upon a Star* from *Pinocchio* and *Zip-a-dee-do-dah* from *Song of the South*. In more recent films, such as *The Lady and the Tramp*, songs have been used as part of the main structure of the story.

The incident concerning the Siamese cats in *The Lady and the Tramp* is carried almost entirely by a number composed by Sonny Burke and Peggy Lee. It is constructed as a parody of Oriental music, using a rhythmic percussion accompaniment of drum beats, miniature finger-tip cymbals and a dulcimer-type xylophone. Most of the melody comes from flutes, strings and occasional bassoon, but the main line is produced by the chorus

171

of the two Siamese cats. Peggy Lee recorded both voices, making a tape track of one voice, playing it back and harmonizing it against herself to record a combined two-voice track.

The cats enter slinkily to the Oriental rhythm and sing:

> We are Siamese, if you please;
> We are Siamese, if you don't please
> We are former residents of Siam
> There are no finer cats than we am.

More rhythmic accompaniment follows their rapid survey of the house and its layout, and then they comment on the results:

> We are Siamese, if you please
> We are Siamese, if you don't please
> Now we're looking over our new domicile
> If we like, we stay for maybe quite a while.

Observing a goldfish swimming in a bowl, the cats make a rush for it, tussling with Lady, the dog-heroine of the story, in an attempt to pull the bowl off the table cloth:

> Do you see in that thing swimming round and round
> Maybe we could reach him in and make it drown
> If we sneak it up and pull it carefully
> There will be a head for you, a tail for me.

After a considerable battle, in which the table cloth is pulled to and fro to the music, the cats are thwarted and move to new ground:

> Do you hear what I hear? A baby cry!
> Where we find baby, there are milk nearby
> If we look in baby's bed there could be
> Plenty milk for you; and also some for me.

But Lady goes in pursuit. There is a fight and Auntie, a background human character, arrives to take the two cats away; as she carries them off, they link tails behind her to an ominous trill on woodwind.

In the UPA production *Gerald McBoing Boing*, comic outline figures are used with highly stylized movements which reduce human action to the simplest possible rhythms. Gerald is the despair of his parents since he cannot talk; he only speaks sound effects of which the most formidable is the familiar "boing" of the cartoon world, a noise made by a short length of strong wire spring attached to a sounding board. The composer, Gail Kubik, has only thirty seconds in which to set the scene of the film. The music is highly percussive and designed to put over the full impact of the "boings" produced by Gerald; the prologue opens with three sharp chords and ends with three "boings".

The orchestra is devoid of "middle tone" and starts crisply:

1   2   3

A miniature fanfare and variations, with frequent reference back to the three-chord motif, forms the main material of the overture, ending on a held trumpet note and a fast rhythmic phrase for viola, 'cello and woodwind:

The first section of the narrative is spoken over a soft repeat of the overture:

I. 1. "This is the story of Gerald McCloy
   2. And the strange thing that happened
   3. To that little boy."

The orchestra now springs to the foreground for two bars, using the left-hand of the piano to register its interruption effectively. The rhythmic passage reappears and the narration continues:

II. 1. "They say it all started when Gerald was two.
    2. That's the age kids start talking;
    3. 'Least most of them do."

Again the orchestra comes in sharply and the accompaniment is suddenly passed to the bassoon. After two bars the narration proceeds:

III. 1. "Well, when he started talking, do you know what he said?
     2. He didn't talk words
     3. He went 'boing-boing' instead."

One bar of lower woodwind leads to a triumphant

BOING—BOING—BOING

and the prologue is complete. The triplet device appears effectively in other parts of the film.

A short scene from a MGM Tom and Jerry cartoon entitled *Heavenly Puss* illustrates the complex planning involved in this type of production, even in normal "animal" animation. The film was made in 1948 and was directed by William Hanna and Joseph Barbera. The music was written by Scott Bradley.

The cat Tom is trying to enter Heaven.[1] Before he is admitted, however, the passenger agent for the "Heavenly Train" demands that Tom get a Certificate of Forgiveness from the much-abused mouse Jerry. To illustrate to Tom what would happen to him without the Certificate the agent lets him look at the hot place below (through a television set) where a red demon carries out intimidation on a violent scale. Tom is reminded by the agent that he has only one hour in which to get Jerry's signature, so he is returned to earth and awakens in his room.

[1]This material is based on notes by Ingolf Dahl, originally published in *Film Music*; the cue sheets are reproduced by courtesy of MGM.

A page from the "dope sheet" prepared for the MGM cartoon *Heavenly Puss*. (Reproduced by courtesy of Loews Inc.). The unit of the beat M.M. 88 is on these two pages translated in terms of 2/2 measures (except 202 which is in 3/2). On preceding pages changes in notation of the same beat to quarter note metres (2/4, 3/4) were made for musical reasons. Where the *unit* of measurement itself changes the composer starts a new recording sequence which is connected with the preceding section by the sound editor. On the following page, for instance, there was a change to a sequence based on the 12 frame beat, for which Bradley wrote a section in 2/4 time in the tempo of M.M.120.

174

A further page from the "dope sheet" for the MGM cartoon *Heavenly Puss*. Points of action that are to be emphasized are indicated on this detail sheet exactly on the spot (frame-wise) where they occur. The composer then has to place his musical accentuation on the equivalent metrical subdivision of the measure. For example, in measure 204, where Tom's spinning down to earth starts on the subdivision of the second beat; or in measure 208, where the music illustrates Tom's bouncing on the floor with a light accent on the subdivision of the first beat.

The rhythmic unit in this sequence is based on a 16-frame beat. As the music shown is written alla breve the half notes equal M.M.88. Reading upwards from the music, the following information may be obtained:

1. Length of actions, measured in frames.
2. Dialogue (in red).
3. Description of action.
4. Measurements of additional action.
5. Description of additional action. (e.g., the blast of flame from the crater starts on the 25th frame—musically speaking from the fourth quarter of the alla breve measure—and lasts for eight frames, i.e., until the next down-beat.)

There are no sound effects in the example shown but a space is provided. Onomatopoeia of the words that describe the highlights of the action, e.g., "Phoom" (bars 193, 204, etc.), "Eaa" (202), "Plop" (208) occur frequently; these are not audible vocal or sound effects but rather vivid verbal illustrations, for the benefit of the composer, of gestures, expressions and happenings.

The unit of the beat M.M.88 has been translated into music entirely in terms of 2/2 measures (except 202 which is in 3/2). The effect of the flame blasts from the crater (bars 193–200) are treated as a short pattern in five sequential two-bar phrases of very agitated "hell music" to express the over-all excitement of the scene, rather than to point up their individual elements of action.

The music thus carries out the following functions in relation to the cartoon action:

Bars 193–200	Flame blasts from crater.
Bar 200	Change of mood after crater effects.
Bar 201–2	Background to dialogue of agent.
Third beat of bar 202	Tom's startled gasp.
Second beat of bar 203	Tom's scramble to get away.
Bars 205–7	The spinning of his body in a cloud.
Bar 207	Smoke flash and bounce as Tom lands on floor.
Bar 208	He bounces back.
End of bar 208	Tom rising to sitting position.

In Britain Matyas Seiber, in association with John Halas, made a special study of music for animated films. From 1943 onward, he wrote the scores for a large number of Halas and Batchelor films including *The Magic Canvas*. In this case, gramophone records in which every bar of music was arrowed numerically and played separately were used in order to obtain the closest link between the visuals and the music. The records were played over by the artists who represented each instrument of the orchestra by a different colour crayon on a graph, marked out in frame numbers, bar numbers and musical pitch. After drawing in all the instruments on this chart, the musical sounds were transposed into a colour scheme that rose and fell according to the shape of the score. The animation was then carried out in accordance with the indication provided by the chart. Seiber was also responsible for the music of *Animal Farm*, the first full-length animated film to be produced in Britain.

In the field of documentary, the Shell Film Unit has always shown a lively approach to music. *The Rival World* was a film dealing with man's battle to hold back the insect world; it was sponsored by Shell and filmed in Africa, South America and London. Certain scenes

176

were accompanied by natural sound, but most of the sound-track depended for its dramatic effect on the use of music. James Stevens composed the main sections of the music, but for the more bizarre and repellent scenes "musique concrète" was used. Sections of the film were taken by the two directors, Bert Haanstra and Douglas Gordon, to the Paris studios of Pierre Henri. Natural sounds, suitable to the action on the screen, were selected and then altered in pitch and quality by electronic distortion until they were no longer recognizable. Three tape tracks were produced and mixed in the final stages of dubbing to form one master tape.

A number of Shell films have used music planned or composed by Edward Williams. In certain cases the music has been improvised during the recording session instead of preparing the customary score. A case in point was the music for *New Detergents*. After deciding the points at which music would occur, Williams organized the recording sessions with Lauderic Caton's West Indian Orchestra. The musicians were shown the film once and then invited to improvise while the film was flashed on the screen. The result is a pleasing effect of spontaneity in which the orchestra responds to the mood of the film in much the same way as the audience watching it. The picture was divided into two main montages, with a straightforward laboratory sequence in the middle; music was used only on the opening and closing montages, giving greater impact to the scientific exposition.

A specialized branch of film-making has grown out of the presentation on the screen of the graphic arts, painting and sculpture. The earliest films of the Italian director Luciano Emmer have been among the best of these special film studies of art, which either develop a short, more or less dramatic sequence out of the story-situation of a great work of art, or trace the development of a particular artist's career. The BBC Television Film Unit has produced a notable series of film on the works of, among others, Henry Moore and John Piper, and a history of British cartoon called *Black on White*, for which a gaily experimental piano score was composed by William Alwyn, who writes of his work as follows:

Many of the experiments with sounds used deliberately and consciously to produce what is now called "Musique concrète" were developed by composers in the British documentary movement during the nineteen-thirties through sheer necessity. The budgets for music on these early productions were usually very small indeed, often less than £20, which precluded the employment even of a small chamber group. The composer was literally forced to produce his "airs on a shoe string". These early documentaries contain many examples of effects such as a cymbal recorded backwards, and I myself remember recording the entire music for a film with a flute (played by myself) and a selection of wooden boxes on which I beat with various sticks to produce a passable imitation of African music and a very realistic (at least, I thought so then) accompaniment for a railway train.

From a similar force of circumstances (but this time not through under-budgeting but because of the difficult situation that at the time of production existed between the BBC and the Musicians' Union over the use of "live" players in films for television), the musical score for the BBC television film *Black on White* had to be dealt with in a similarly restricted manner.

The film traced the history of black and white cartoon drawing in Britain from Hogarth to the present day, and was presented generally with stills, the tracking camera, and the minimum of actual animation. The eye was allowed to travel over each picture and directed to salient points, and commentary, effects and music were used to underline the satire of the drawings. This material was arranged into a series of "period" pieces from the artists of the eighteenth century to contemporary cartoonists.

For this, with the help of a most efficient sound effects department, I gathered together sounds of a cracked bell, records of gunfire, a musical box, toy trumpets recorded in different keys, police whistles, and drum beats recorded by quickening the speed from a deep bass to a high treble, and so on. All these effects had to be moulded into the essential score—written for a piano which I played myself. The piano was chosen because I could adapt it to sound like a harpsichord (for Hogarth), or a grand piano (for a delicate Victorian drawing of a ballroom scene by du Maurier). The piano was re-recorded with distortion and mixed with the surface noise of a blank and scratched disc to produce the sound of an old record of a Charleston for a cartoon of the "bright young things" of the 'twenties.

Great care was taken in the composition so that when the piano was used as pure "background" it was treated as an instrument in its own right, using its own particular timbres and characteristics, and not as a substitute for the orchestra.

It was a very interesting experiment and the piano proved a highly satisfactory medium, not only for direct "pastiche", which was often demanded by the nature of the film, but in its ability to produce sounds which, although essentially "pianistic", were evocative and effective. The piano also "mixed" well, for example, with the tolling bell for the procession to Tyburn drawn by Hogarth in the "Rake's Progress" series. Naturally I was unable to resist the direct association of the film's title, *Black on White*, with the black and white keys of the piano. From such obvious connexions comes the stimulus to compose.

The dramatization of narrative paintings, which is in effect what Luciano Emmer and Enrico Gras have attempted, presents particular difficulties to both the film-maker and the composer. Emmer and Gras were among the first to develop an acceptable method of filming great works of art. This method is based on a selection of details from the work which, carefully ordered and timed, built up cumulatively to establish the atmosphere of the scene and its narrative element. Their composer was Roman Vlad.

Paradise Lost is one of the best examples of these films by Emmer and Gras; it is based on two large fifteenth-century triptychs by Hieronymus Bosch, now in the Prado Galleries in Madrid.

178

The film opens with a brisk, exotic overture based on the theme of the central panel depicting "The Garden of Delights". The scenes of the Earthly Paradise made by God are accompanied by a delicate thread of music for woodwind, piano and harp, emphasizing the atmosphere established by the commentary in the words "Each of these things was a miracle, for everything was just beginning".

The sentence "But all nature was in suspense, waiting for something still greater" is accentuated by a thin line produced on harp and piano alone, anticipating the coming of Adam and Eve. As the moment of realization approaches, a rising and falling phrase on the flutes appears, becoming increasingly insistent. Xylophone, bassoon and soft drum rolls appear in the texture of the music, ending with the appearance of the first human beings with the words "Adam and Eve, man and woman, looked at each other for the first time; they were both naked and were not ashamed".

Then follow the scenes of Temptation. "From all the trees and the fruits thereof they might freely eat, but not from the tree of Good and Evil". Two long, held chords on full orchestra (eight and nine seconds in duration) accompany the Serpent when he comes to tempt Adam. A long crescendo of orchestral sound accompanies the offering of the apple; at the same time, a Voice promises that to eat the forbidden fruit will cause Adam and Eve to live as gods.

There follows a long sequence showing the earthly pleasures which are in store if the law of God is broken. The theme, first heard in the overture, returns with vigour, creating a sweeping impression of sumptuous living, in which the two mortals are represented on a flowing, sensuous string tune against a background of abandoned orchestral effect dominated by a repeated trumpet note. Suddenly the gaiety is interrupted by a long timpani roll and ominous crashes on gong and full brass. The first sin has been committed; Adam and Eve are driven from the garden. An echo of the joyous string tune is heard as they move away into the mists of time; it is now sorrowful and poignant.

"And with the first sin, all sin came into the world." As the last notes of the Adam and Eve phrase die away, there is a sudden visual cut to the terrifying spectacle of Hell. For the next 2 minutes 18 seconds "all hell breaks loose", in the orchestra as well as the pictures. Great walls of sound stream out at the audience, the strings sustain a frenzy of whirling scale passages, the brass roars forth a series of indeterminate but powerful statements, culminating in scenes of fiendish torture conceived by Bosch in terms of sound itself as helpless humans are seen entangled in harp strings or captured in the bell of some vast, vague brass instrument of diabolical invention.

This rare and fascinating opportunity for the composer consists in essence of twelve shots, which Vlad has developed to the full:

1. A distorted kind of iron triangle is seen, played with an iron rod by a grim woman. A tortured human being is entangled in the framework of the instrument. The accompaniment produces an anvil-like series of beats.
2. A device like the end of a brass-viol is seen, with a series of tensioning handles attached to the sounding board. The sounds of hell are increasing in intensity.
3. A gigantic harp, with a naked man twined around the strings, is being plucked by the foul hands of a horribly distorted, devil-like figure. The man's arms are outstretched in a permanent cry of agony. A harp effect is produced on full orchestra, clangorous and dissonant.
4. A decorated drum is being rolled along and beaten by a hideous rat-like animal of elephantine proportions. Through a small square in the body of the drum can be seen the agonized face of a man. Great timpani beats occur on the sound-track.
5. A close shot of the man's face in the drum.
6. A figure like the fictional representation of a man from Mars is seen, blowing a great brass instrument of enormous proportions. Full brass, with strong trumpet attacks, are heard.
7. At the end of the instrument, in the bell which appears to have a diameter of about twenty feet across, the small figure of a man is seen, attempting to struggle out amid the great barrage of sound that causes the instrument to smoke like a volcano. An echo of the phrase used for shot 6 parallels the action.
8. As in shot 6. The first phrase is re-stated.
9. A man crouches in the shadow of the instrument, covering his ears with his hands in a desperate but useless attempt to keep out the terrible sound.
10. A man is seen, trapped in a large, bulbous pot, his hands raised above him in the neck of the vessel. He too is trapped in the overwhelming torrential torment of noise.

179

11. A great object like the bladder of a bagpipe, with tubes like drones hanging down on either side, thrusts its sound at ant-like men and women who are trying to escape from the suction cups on the ends of the drones.

12. Two massive human ears are seen, pierced by spears and divided by a great dagger, with insects crawling across the lobes, epitomizing a great torture by sound. The music rises to a huge cry of agony. A few brief shots of other nameless horrors follow and the film ends.[1]

As soon as the sound film became a reasonably accurate medium for recording and reproducing music, artists and film-makers began to experiment with various methods of expressing a wide range of composition in pictorial terms. This very personal form of film production depends for its effect upon whether the spectator is in sympathy with the interpretation offered; the ways in which individuals "see" music (if they see it at all) vary enormously, and many critics of this branch of film-making are quite unconvinced that this process of visualizing music on the screen has any justification at all.

Impressionist Photographed Images to Recorded Music

Among the first films to experiment in this new technique was a picture attributed to Eisenstein and Alexandrov. In point of fact, *Romance Sentimentale* (France, 1930) was made by Alexandrov alone, and the circumstances of its production have been described as follows by Jay Leyda:

> During their trip through Europe to America, Alexandrov and Tisse produced a short musical film, entitled *Romance Sentimentale*, in a Paris studio while Eisenstein was in London. Although the film was completed after Eisenstein's departure alone for America, the Parisian producer withheld the salaries of Alexandrov and Tisse, preventing them from leaving for America unless Eisenstein would attach his name to their film. He cabled permission.

The film bears the stamp of Alexandrov, especially in relation to his later work on such musical productions as *Jazz Comedy* and *Volga-Volga*. The changing moods of an old Russian song (set by Alexis Archangelsky) are played and sung by Mara Griy to a riot of beautifully photographed impressions of trees, sea, water and landscape. Extensive camera movement is used for fast-moving moments, alternating with calm scenes of mist-shrouded lakes and shots of dew-spangled vegetation. The music is unfamiliar and, as a result, the visual interpretation is acceptable and even stimulating.

The well-known German film-maker Walter Ruttmann, who had shown interest in the use of abstract visual effects during the making of his film *Berlin* (1927), attempted a screen interpretation of Schumann's *In Der Nacht* in 1931. Using a piano performance by

---

[1]This analysis is based on the English version of the film distributed by the British Film Institute.

Nina Hamson, he assembled closely-cut visual images, mostly of water, to form a visual parallel to the music. The technical quality of this film is good, although musicians may well dislike its artistic conception.

Patterns of moving water have always fascinated the man with a movie camera. In *Images Pour Debussy* (France, 1952), Jean Mitry took two of the Arabesques and *Reflets dans l'Eau* to make a three-movement interpretation of the composer's work, using images of reflections in the water. The first two sections use landscape and trees, including long sections of gentle movement produced by filming from a boat pushing its way through waving reeds. The last piece is set to dazzling images of the sun caught in reflection by rippling surfaces.

Kenneth Anger's *Eaux d'Artifice* (U.S.A., 1954) has been described by its maker as "an evocation of a Firbank heroine, lost in a baroque labyrinth, in pursuit of a night-moth. Fountains, cascades, a fan and . . . a transmogrification". The action is set to works by Vivaldi, in which black and white shots of various fountains in Italy have been dyed a deep green, producing a pleasant visual effect. The introduction of a human figure breaks the illusion, weakening the liaison between music and picture.

A simpler treatment of the "fountain" theme may be found in Renzo Avanzo's *Fountains of Rome* (Italy, 1953). Respighi's symphonic poem was recorded by the Rome Symphony Orchestra and presented with beautiful scenes of fountains photographed by Claude Renoir. However, the link between the rhythm of the pictures and the tempo of the music is frequently strained, although there is nothing wrong in principle with the practice of matching music to more or less appropriate pictures. In fact, innumerable films have been made which depend on the simple formula of linking scenic shots with programme music.

One of the more unusual of the "water" films is *Black Top* (U.S.A., 1952), made by the American furniture designers, Charles and Ray Eames. The action consisted entirely of the washing of a tarmac-covered school playground. By taking the camera close in, a flowing record was obtained of the sparkle of sunlight on the slowly moving mass of soap, water and bubbles as it rolled over the black surface. The shots were then loosely cut to the Bach *Goldberg Variations*, excellently recorded on the harpsichord by Wanda Landowska. A closer link between picture and sound might have improved the effect at which this film aimed, but its conception was bold and original.

A visual triumph for a time in this field was Jean Mitry's *Pacific 231* (France, 1949). Arthur Honegger's famous study in music of a train had originally been written with a film in view, but the project failed and it was some twenty years before Mitry revived it, shot some of the most exciting railway material ever recorded and put the whole woik together with considerable editing skill. The cutting of the picture to music was close, precise, and completely fair to the score.

Abstract Hand-Painted Images to Recorded Music

Even more speculative from the musician's viewpoint are the moving patterns, sometimes simply like stylized fireworks, which attempt to express music in terms of swiftly-mobile designs. Oscar Fischinger was one of the first artists to attempt this kind of film-making when he produced visual interpretations of one of the Brahms Hungarian Dances and the well-known *Mozart Minuet* (Germany, 1931). Brahms's music was visualized as a series of flat planes gliding towards the audience, interspersed with wriggling little scrolls that curled up and leapt off the screen at regular intervals. Mozart's music appeared to Fischinger in the form of large waves rising up in an endless procession. The same symbol was seen some twenty years later in the work he contributed to the Bach sequence of Walt Disney's *Fantasia*.

About the same time, Len Lye began to make his first mobile film to music, *Experimental Animation* (Great Britain, 1933), based on a South American dance tune. He used puppet-like figures, but in 1935 he made a completely abstract film in colour entitled *Colour Box*. This was adopted by the General Post Office Unit with a slogan for the parcel post. Over the next ten years he produced all kinds of music-pattern experiments, normally using dance tunes as the basis of his patterns. Working in the United States, he has been involved in such experiments as Ian Hugo's *Bells of Atlantis* (U.S.A., 1952), using in this case electronic music produced by Louis and Bebe Barron.

Among those who were influenced by Len Lye was the witty Scottish film-maker Norman McLaren. One of his earliest attempts at hand-painted abstract patterns moving to music was an advertising film called *Love on the Wing* (Great Britain, 1939); it was set to Jacques Ibert's *Divertissement*. On arrival in Canada in 1940, McLaren started work on his well-known series of charming, amusing, abstract films, including *Stars and Stripes*, *Boogie Doodle*, *Hoppity Pop* and many others. He has frequently used folk tunes in his Canadian films, for example in *Fiddle-de-dee* and *C'est l'Aviron*. In 1940 he made a semi-abstract version of Saint-Saëns's *Dance Macabre* in collaboration with Mary Ellen Bute.

Since then others have attempted to develop hand-painted abstract films drawn to music. Jordan Belson, working in the United States, has made a series, usually based on dance styles, such as *Mambo, Bop Scotch* and *Caravan*. Mention should also be made of Hy Hirsh's *Divertissement Rococo*, John Whitney's *Diversions*, Dick Ham's *Schizophrenia* and Mary Ellen Bute's *Polka Graph* (based on Shostakovitch's *Age of Gold* ballet).

Photographic Images to Artificial, Hand-Painted Sound

Attempts at creating hand-drawn sound-tracks have been in progress since the coming of the sound film; tentative proposals for this entirely new way of making sound had been formulated as early as 1922. Most film editors and sound recordists have at some time or another produced an artificial sound by making marks directly on to the film, or have compounded sounds which have had no existence outside the physical handling of tracks, tapes or discs. Serious work in this field has been conducted by various experimenters, of which perhaps the most successful is Norman McLaren. By applying an animation technique to the movements of actors, he produced "pixilation" and used it to tell a serious story in *Neighbours* (Canada, 1953). He built up a sound-track of hand-drawn musical effects, mixing them occasionally with normal orchestral instruments to give variety.

During the same period as these experiments, there has been the introduction of "musique concrète" to various types of documentary and art film. By mixing indeterminate sounds together in a rhythmic pattern, specialists in musique concrète like Pierre Schaeffer of Paris have provided a number of interesting accompaniments to films, often used in conjunction with orchestral material in the manner adopted by Norman McLaren. An example of this is the French film *Leonardo da Vinci; the Tragic Pursuit of Perfection*, made in 1953.

This film used sections of standard orchestral music and musique concrète as alternatives in order to express two contrasted aspects of Leonardo's character. The titles start on musique concrète, with a sound like the roaring of bells mingled with the wash of the sea, and impressions of distant voices are heard occasionally. A Latin plainsong slowly takes command as the titles unfold, and the strange rumblings of the artificial sounds give way to the ordered tradition of church music.

The opening sequence concerns Leonardo's spiritual character; it is accompanied by soft, dignified orchestral music, in which the harp predominates. Leonardo's first sight of the world presents him with death and the spectacle of war; he accepts the challenge

183

and prepares a great treatise on attack and bombardment by strange, visionary machines resembling the modern tank and mortar. The sequence is accompanied by musique concrète, composed of the clang and clash of war, reversed cymbal rolls, reversed explosions with their weird, elongated "woofs" and an extensive use of gliding frequencies, mixed with modulated Morse code oscillations. A chariot with scythes mounted on the wheels mows down men with great savagery in Leonardo's drawings; it is set to a swirl of high-frequency, master-oscillator glissandos and a whirl of meshing gearwheels.

The theme of peaceful living returns, and with it the gentle harp sounds heard earlier; the music is in the style of the sixteenth century, accompanying scenes from Leonardo's religious paintings. As soon as the thread of the story moves to mechanical or technical aspects of his work, the musique concrète returns; for example, there is a scene in which drawings from the sketch-books reveal a large number of fragments depicting whirlpools of water and coils of human hair; these are matched to a bell-like, tremulous, abstract sound. Again, there are shorts of various general designs for St. Peter's in Rome, which are accompanied by organ music; this merges into vague, clangorous bell noises as soon as detailed plans and elevations replace the broader concept of design and form.

A number of Leonardo's paintings perished within his lifetime, owing to his use of faulty materials. Reproductions of the pictures are shown, to the sound of Latin chanting. When the "leprosy" of decay spreads across them, a great wash of destructive noise sweeps in to accentuate Leonardo's failure. His sketches turn sour, pointed by a musique concrète assembly of native drum effects and dismally discordant noises.

Travelling to Milan, Leonardo became interested in various types of what would today be called industrial machines. He produced many sketches of cogs, gears, belt-drives, looms and engines; these are shown to an orchestration of clangs, clicks, whirrs and "bonks", mingled with staccato taps on native drums.

When Leonardo embarks on his famous flying experiment, the machine is launched to humming, pulsating sounds. "Did he fly? . . . Did he fall?", says the commentary. A figure descends on a primitive parachute, to a gliding frequency effect. Echoed clangs accentuate his failure. The deluge breaks loose; as the torrents pour across the sketch-book, the sound of wind and water is heard. At the height of the storm, the noise of piglets violently squeaking is introduced, mixed with the howl of a gale and occasional cries of human voices.

The film ends with a series of Da Vinci's best-known paintings, including his Madonna and Child, the Gioconda, the Virgin with St. Anne, the Lady with the Weasel and the Virgin of the Rocks. Normal orchestral music returns, carrying the pictures to a noble finale.

Hand-Painted Pictures to Artificial Music and Hand-Painted Sound

A great deal of experimental work in this field has been carried out by the Canadian artist, Norman McLaren. Certain of his films have involved the linking of artificial and instrumental music on one sound-track. The methods employed in the combination of orchestral and artificial music have often involved the construction of a basic score to which percussive effects are added by artificial methods. Thus, in *Blinkity-Blank* (1955), Maurice Blackburn, working with McLaren, was at first principally concerned with experiment in his own field before considering the synthetic material:

The group of instruments used for recording *Blinkity-Blank* consisted of a flute, an oboe, a clarinet, a bassoon and a 'cello. The music was written without key signature on a three-line stave (instead of the usual five lines); the spaces between the three lines were not used, therefore there were only three possible note positions to denote pitch:

184

If a note appeared on the top line it indicated that the instrument was to be played in its high register; a note on the middle line, in the middle register; and a note on the bottom line, in its low register. The limits of the registers were set beforehand for each instrument; inside that register, the musician was completely free to choose whatever note he wished.

The notes, however, indicated the precise time value and rhythmic pattern, time signatures and bars being used in the usual manner. It was therefore possible to conduct the orchestra and give some coherence to the group of instruments. Signs for the control of dynamics and signs for instrumental colour were used in the conventional manner.

The best results of this semi-free improvisation were achieved by taking the orchestra practically by surprise and recording without rehearsals, thus ensuring as complete a divergence of inspiration in each musician as possible, a complete disregard for all consciously agreed key signatures.

To create additional percussive effects, synthetic sounds were scratched directly on the film afterwards.

Animated Sound on Film

In view of its technical interest, we give as an appendix to this chapter Norman McLaren's own detailed account of the precise methods employed in the creation of artificial sound on film. It was published originally in the *Hollywood Quarterly* in 1953 (Vol. VII, No. 3) under the title "Notes on Animated Sound"; we are grateful to the editor for permission to reproduce it in full.

The Term Animated as Applied to Sound-Track

The term "synthetic sound" is generally used to cover a wide variety of new, non-traditional methods of making noise, sound effects, music, and speech, by electronic, magnetic, mechanical, optical, and other means; and it is not necessarily connected with the use of motion picture film. The term "animated sound" as used here has a much more restricted meaning and refers to a way of producing sound on film which parallels closely the production of animated pictures.

Since the technique as developed at the National Film Board of Canada bears the closest possible resemblance to the standard method of making animated cartoons, a brief description of it at the outset might be in order.

185

Black and white drawings, or patterns of light and shade, representing sound waves are prepared. These drawings are photographed with the same kind of motion picture camera as is normally used in the shooting of animated cartoons. In fact, they are shot in precisely the same way as the drawings of a cartoon; that is, one drawing is placed in front of the camera and one frame of film is taken, then the first drawing is removed, replaced with another drawing and the second frame of film taken, the second drawing is changed again and the third frame taken, and so on.

The only difference from normal cartoon picture shooting is that the drawings are not of scenes from the visible world around us but of sound waves, and they are not done on cards of a screen-shaped proportion but on long narrow cards. These cards are photographed not on the area of the film occupied by the picture, but to the left of it, on the narrow vertical strip normally reserved for the sound-track. When the film is developed and printed, and run on a sound projector the photographed images of these black and white drawings are heard as either noise, sound effects or music.

It is therefore logical to call the kind of sound produced in this way "animated", for not only is it made by the same method as animated pictures, but from a creative and artistic point of view it shares many of the peculiarities and possibilities of animated visuals.

But just as there are many techniques of animating visuals, so there are of animating sound. Some of these combine with or shade off imperceptibly into other methods differing in principle. In attempting to trace the history, I shall refer only to techniques that are a close parallel to visual animation.

History

Before the general adoption of the sound film in 1927, the possibility of the synthetic production of sound on film was already foreseen. In 1922, for instance, I. Moholy-Nagy discussed some of its potentialities in articles published in Holland and Germany. Later, Ernest Toch, the German theoretician suggested the direct writing of sound without traditional performers.

The first body of investigation and practical work seems to have been done in Russia at the Scientific Experimental Film Institute in Leningrad, where in 1930 A. M. Avzaamov, a musical theorist and mathematician, worked with the animators N. Y. Zhelinsky and N. V. Voinov on "ornamental animation in sound". Later this work was carried on at the Leningrad Conservatory by G. M. Rimsky-Korsakoff and E. A. Scholpo.

From a study of the available papers, their work appears to have been fairly extensive and along a number of different lines.

Avzaamov used a frame-by-frame method with a standard animation camera. Geometric figures such as rectangles, triangles, trapezes, ovals, parabolas, ellipses, etc., were the basic units for his sound waves. Pitch was controlled either by bringing the camera closer to or farther away from drawings of these shapes, or by preparing separate drawings for each pitch.

Volume was controlled by varying the exposure; harmony or counterpoint by multiple exposures, or by subdividing the sound-track lengthwise into sections, or by the very rapid alternation of several tones; portamento by a rapid series of micro-tones.

Avzaamov, who had set as his goal the freeing of his music from the restrictions of the twelve-tone tempered scale, and the creation of new tonal systems assimilating many of the scales of the traditional folk music of the Eastern and Southern Republics, achieved very accurate control over pitch and volume; his range of timbres was more limited; the fact that he used geometric forms like triangles and rectangles indicates he was using an empirical approach to tone-quality. He was not searching for complete flexibility in timbre, but rather for

186

a limited number of new tone qualities, arising naturally from simple graphic shapes.

Soon afterwards Scholpo and Rimsky-Korsakoff began the oscillographic analysis of natural sounds, and this in turn led to the building up of the music for a film by the assembling of small units of film, each bearing separate tones, into an edited whole of music and sound effects.

At about the same time, in Moscow, B. A. Yankovsky developed a system of animated sound in which he abandoned the frame-by-frame shooting of drawings on a standard animation camera in favour of continuously moving patterns (obtained from rotating wheels with cog patterns).

Animator N. Voinov's system was said to be the most practical of all the Soviet animated sound techniques. He had a library of eighty-seven drawings, graded in semitones covering slightly over seven octaves of the twelve-tone equally-tempered chromatic scale, with a fixed tone quality of great purity. With this he produced an interpretation of Rachmaninoff's *Prelude in C Sharp Minor*, and Schubert's *Moment Musical*.

Almost simultaneously with the Soviet experiments, a Munich electrical engineer, Rudolph Pfenninger, began work on his own system of animated sound. His researches seem to have been done quite independently of the Russians.

Pfenninger's method was rather similar to Voinov's and Avzaamov's. He had a library of cards each bearing the drawing of a single pitch, graded in semitones over a wide pitch range. In these drawings the basic units for sound waves were sine-curves and saw-tooth forms (using variable area); they were therefore not so arbitrarily chosen but were related to natural sound wave forms. To control volume he used variations in the amount of exposure (variable density).

About 1932 he produced an interpretation of Handel's *Largo*, a series of musical compositions as played by various musicians, and the musical sound-track for an animated cartoon film. He achieved great control over dynamic nuances. His method of making animated sound was clearly shown in a documentary film made in the early 'thirties called *Tönende Handschrift*.

About this same time, also in Germany, the Fischinger Brothers in Berlin were photographing geometric shapes on the sound-track, and I. Moholy-Nagy was boldly using alphabetical letters, finger-prints, and people's profiles as the basic graphic material for sound waves.

In England the New Zealand musician, Jack Ellit, experimented along lines similar to Pfenninger, and in 1933 pioneered in drawing sound directly on the celluloid without the use of a camera.

In the U.S.A. there has never been, either on the part of the Government or the film industry at large, any interest in the possibility of this kind of sound. It was only during the later 'forties that private individuals seem to have taken it up.

In California, the Whitney Brothers have developed a system differing in principle from European systems. It depends on the building up of the basic sound waves by the sine-wave motion of pendulums. The movements of several pendulums may be added together to produce the fundamental and overtones of a note. They can be made to operate a shutter in front of a light source, the fluctuations of which are recorded on continuously moving film. Their approach is therefore more radical. It has been applied in a number of their abstract films.

The sound-track is made by linking together mechanically twelve pendulums of various lengths by means of a fine steel wire attached to an optical wedge. This optical wedge is caused to oscillate over a light slit by the motion of the pendulums, producing a variable-area type of sound-track. The pendulums can

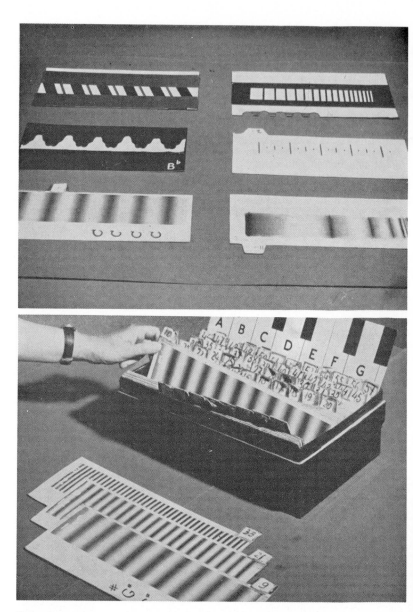

Above: Some of the patterns used to produce musical sounds of differing tone quality. Several methods are employed. The bottom left card uses variable density, the other cards on the left use variable area in different forms. The top and bottom right hand cards have rising-falling pitch, while all the others have even pitch.

Below: With a pattern of given tone quality a separate card is made for each semitone of pitch in the chromatic scale. Here, the pattern (a near sine-wave in variable density) has been repeated on each card; only its frequency differs.

188

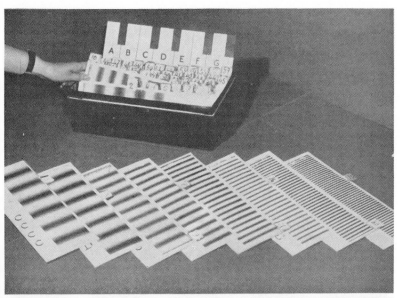

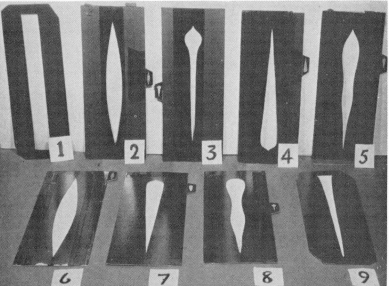

Above: The cards are conveniently assembled in a box, in which they range systematically from highest to lowest pitch. There are five parallel rows of cards, each row containing twelve cards and thus covering an octave.

Below: Some of the different types of envelopes or masks used for contouring the pitch within a single frame.

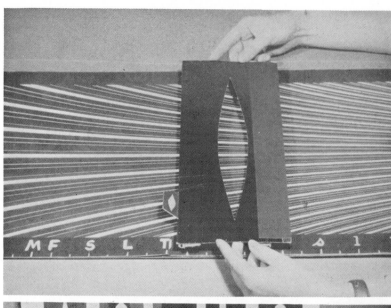

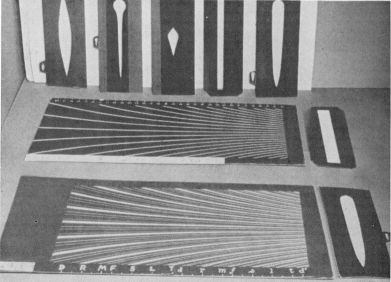

Above: Methods other than the box of cards for producing pitch are also used. Here is one for continuous gradations of pitch, so that *portamento, glissando, vibrato* and *microtones* are possible. It consists of a long card with converging lines, which slides under the tone-envelope or mask.

Below: Different kinds of striations on the sliding cards will produce different tone-qualities. The near card produces a very rich, complex tone quality, the distant card a much simpler timbre.

be operated together in any combination, or separately. The frequency of each can be adjusted or tuned to conform to any kind of scale by moving a sliding weight. Through the choice of pendulum lengths and driven speeds the full range of audio frequencies can be recorded. No actual sound is involved in recording the wave patterns generated by the pendulums. Only when the resultant film is projected at regular sound-projection speed is sound produced.

It is said that in recent years, the Englishman, C. E. Buckle, has worked out a system of synthetic sound.

In Ottawa, under Canadian Government sponsorship, the writer, with the assistance of Evelyn Lambart, has developed a system of animated sound, in general principle very little different from the Voinov and Pfenninger system, with a library of cards each bearing the representation of sound waves. However, a number of refinements have been incorporated, especially in relation to the contouring of tones, and the method has been streamlined to a point where it has become a simple and economic operation.

Love your Neighbour, Now is the Time, Two Bagatelles, Twirligig and *Phantasy* are successful examples of the use of the technique. Music for the first three was composed and photographed by the author, with the exception of the old-fashioned calliope section in *Two Bagatelles*. The music for the last two was composed and photographed by Maurice Blackburn, that for *Phantasy* being written for a combination of animated sound and saxophones.

Drawings of Sound Waves

What are the drawings of sound waves like, and how are they arrived at?

There are many different ways of producing them. For instance, it would have been possible to make them by recording (i.e., photographing) "live" musical sounds on to film sound-track, then tracing the resulting patterns from the track. However, to do this would be as pointless and creatively stultifying as to make animated cartoons by photographing live actors and tracing their outlines. Instead, in the films under discussion, a non-naturalistic approach was taken, with no particular attempt to imitate natural sounds or traditional musical instruments. New kinds of sound waves were made by using simple and easily-drawn shapes.

The drawings consist of a basic figure or simple shape, that is repeated over and over to form a patterned band. The figure may be no more than a white line on a dark ground or a single gradation of tone from light to dark, but, by virtue of its identical repetition, it builds up into a series of sound waves having a definite tone colour.

Each card in the library of drawings carries one such band of repeated patterns on an area 1 inch wide by 12 inches long. On some cards the basic figure is repeated only about four times within this area and this, when photographed on one frame of film, will sound as a musical note of a fairly deep pitch (about two octaves below middle A). For midpitches there are from twenty to thirty repetitions of the basic figure on each card, and for very high pitched notes as many as 120.

There is one card for each semitone of the chromatic scale, and in all, for the sound-tracks of the five films mentioned, sixty such cards were used, covering a range of five octaves, from two octaves below middle A to three octaves above.

These sixty cards were labelled with the standard musical notation and arranged systematically in a small box to form a kind of keyboard.

When the music was being shot, the box was placed beside the camera so that the composer (who would also operate the camera), desiring a particular pitch, would select from the box the required card and place it in front of the camera.

191

To get notes of a very deep pitch, the music was shot twice as fast as finally desired, and in the process of re-recording slowed down by half, and thus dropped one octave in pitch.

The Mosaic Nature of the Music

Because of the fact that a *picture* camera takes film intermittently by the frame (rather than running continuously as in the ordinary sound recording equipment) the sound-track has a mosaic nature; in other words it builds up out of small units each 1/24th of a second long.

If the duration of a note is desired longer, several successive frames of the same card are shot, thus building up a sustained effect, by a very rapid repetition of the same note, as in a harpsichord, a mandolin or xylophone; for a very short note, just one frame or at most two frames suffice.

For rests and pauses a black card is photographed.

Dynamics

Before exposing the film, however, the composer has to determine the precise volume or dynamic level of that note. This is one of the important new factors in animated music for, in the past, dynamic markings have never been written into traditional music scoring with any degree of precision.

The standard *pp*, *p*, *mf*, *f*, *ff*, etc., indicate relative, approximate amounts of volume, and are never applied to every single note in a score, and their final determining is left to the interpreting artist; but in creating animated music the precise dynamics of every note in the score is the job of the composer; in other words the composer must also be the interpretative artist.

To this end, 24 degrees of dynamic level were used (representing a decibel scale) and opposite each note in the score the number representing the desired dynamic level of that note was written.

For instance, 0, 1, and 2, represent three differing degrees of *ppp*; 9, 10, and 11, three shades of *mp*; 12, 13, and 14, three degrees of *mf*; 21, 22, and 23, three degrees of *fff*, and 24 represents a *ffff*.

Subdivisions of these 24 degrees were constantly being used (particularly in crescendos and diminuendos) but were seldom written into the score. In local or rapid crescendos and diminuendos only the starting and finishing dynamic marks were written and the type of crescendos and diminuendos (such as "arithmetical" or "geometric") were indicated by a small sketch.

The volume was controlled sometimes by manipulating the shutter or diaphragm of the camera and so affecting the exposure (variable density control) but more often by covering up the 1 inch-wide drawing until only ½ inch, or ¼ inch or other fraction of its width was visible (variable area control). Whichever method was used, the calibration was in decibels.

Tone-contouring

Not only did the composer have the last and precise word on dynamics but he was also forced to specify the exact tone-contour of each note; that is, what sort of attack, sustention and decay each tone was to have.

This is important because even more than the basic tone quality of the note, the contouring of the note affects the "instrumental" effect. In traditional musical sounds, for instance, a piano note has a very rapid attack, no period of sustention, but a long period of decay; its contour is like a mountain peak with one very steep side, and one gently sloping side. A typical organ note has an abrupt attack, a prolonged sustention and a rapid decay; a contour rather like a plateau with a precipice at one side and a steep slope at the other. A tap on a wood block has a sudden attack, no sustention and a very rapid decay. Wind instruments are capable of much less abrupt forms of attack than percussion

192

instruments. A violin, like the human voice, is capable of almost any kind of attack, sustention and decay.

And so the composer, by giving a particular contour to each note, affected what would traditionally be called its instrumental quality. In practice this was done by placing black masks of varying shapes in front of the selected pitch card bearing the drawing of the sound waves; in this way we obtained about six kinds of tone-contour.

In *Love Your Neighbour* there was considerable use of different types of tone-colouring, while in the other films only one percussive-type contour (wedge-shaped) predominated.

Tone Quality

In the sound-track of *Love Your Neighbour* the range and variety of sound effects and tone qualities were considerably enlarged by using several supplementary sets of drawings, some of which had rising and falling pitches for portamento and glissando effects. Some drawings, though very simple to the eye, had a very complex sound wave structure, rich in harmonics, thus giving very strident and harsh sound qualities.

Harmony

For several simultaneous musical parts either in harmony or counterpoint, three different methods were used. Either different drawings were superimposed on each other by several separate exposures, or the sound-track was divided lengthwise into several parallel strips and the different drawings shot alongside of each other in each strip. Alternatively each musical part was shot on a separate film and the various parts mixed together during re-recording.

Acoustic Quality

Animated sound produced by this method is normally completely "dry" or without resonance or echo. To achieve more resonance and to add acoustic quality two methods were used. The first, mainly for specific notes and localized or momentary effects, was done by shooting the same note on a rapid series of diminishing volumes (that is, the same drawing in smaller and smaller sizes); this simulates the natural effect of the sound waves bouncing back and forth from the walls of an instrument, room, hall, or cavern. The degree to which any particular note in the score can be placed in such an acoustical environment is controlled during shooting by the number and nature of diminishing replicas of the original drawings of that note.

To obtain the general or overall acoustical environment, varying amounts of reverberation and echo were added, either electronically or acoustically during a re-recording.

To sum up the various features of animated sound as developed to date at the National Film Board of Canada:

The composer has control over pitch (to the nearest 1/10 of a tone), over dynamics (to at least 1 per cent of the total dynamic range), over rhythm and metric spacing (to the nearest 1/50 of a second). The control over "timbre" (tone-contouring and tone-quality) is less flexible, but a variety of about a half-dozen types of tone-quality and tone-contour is possible, which by cross-combination give quite a range of "instrumental" effects.

Now that the initial research has been done it has been found in several cases more economic to make animated rather than live music, particularly for animated visuals. Close synchronization with previously completed visuals presents no problems, and subsequent changes and alterations to parts of the music can be made without the need to re-do the whole score, simply by re-shooting the particular notes affected.

Music in Animation 1955–1972

Prior to the coming of commercial TV, animation played a very minor role in film making. At the best it was an occasional entertainment filler before a feature: at the worst—and most often the case—animation was limited to diagram inserts, special effects, and decorative typography in credit titles. Large studios often had a one or two man animation unit as an appendage to the main studio and controlled from the outside. The music that backed such animation was aptly named "ricky-ticky" and was often one stage better than an old time piano accompaniment.

The first major development was the advertising jingle. The idea of a song only a few bars long was as new as that of a film only a few seconds long. The impact of animation gave it the edge on live action initially, and with music that could be closely tied in mood and rhythm, a unity emerged that is now accepted as a way of life. Developments in live action editing soon took over, and the boom in animation subsided almost until its current revival which came in with colour TV. In retrospect the animated films of the past such as Disneys, tended to use "catchy" tunes more than mood music, and this is probably because the animation is matched to the soundtrack as against the live action technique of writing music to fit the film after it has been shot. It is this catchy tune development that is basically the jingle form.

The second significant development has been a gradual evolvement of film titles into a specialised form of animation. TV promoted the extensive use of animated graphics of titles often accompanied by the theme of the program, but the best exploitation of this has been in feature film titles. *Around the World in Eighty Days* is an outstanding example of such graphics, where the music is the theme of the film. In the case of the *Pink Panther* the music theme and titles became a series of cartoons quite separate from the original film. Title theme and graphics (or special effects such as *Dr Who* titles) are now so totally accepted that it is difficult to realise that only fifteen years ago titling of programes had the lowest budget of any animation and in the BBC the Wurmser titles of very simple typography were common; now they have a large department that employs some of the best designers in the world, and use top composers to write the title themes. The animated signature tune has also become the standard introduction to personality programmes, and in particular, where the titles use animated photos of the shows personalities.

194

A third development, although well established in practice before TV, did not take on such a refined form until the "pop" era of the sixties; this is the use of films and effect lighting in "happenings" where a Pop group would use lighting to create visual impacts consistent with the aural one. It is the abstract hallucinatory effects achieved in this area that make it quite distinct from the previous forms. Here, the music is very dominant.

The lighting effects are seldom controlled or matched to the music, it is a step in the direction of environmental art where one is totally surrounded by the event. This use of lighting has gradually become more refined. In some cases the instruments themselves activate the lighting equipment and in others films or slides are projected in a continuing cycle. This last development has now incorporated animation to a high degree. The BBC program *The Old Grey Whistle Test* uses many old animated films, or specially made abstract animations to accompany pop groups. Stuart Wynne-Jones is a leading exponent in this type of animation, and much of the work shown is his. It is a very fast developing field for both animators and pop groups as there is much talk of video-discs of pop groups having this type of visual presentation.

Following on from lighting effects, special picture effects have been created by the use of electronic equipment. The TV programme *Top of the Pops* makes considerable use of effects such as feedback, colour polarisation, multiple images, etc, in effect, a form of live-action cartoon. Because both music and picture depend upon the actual electrical signal being sent, it is very easy to make the music control the picture in some ways. In the Philips Evuloun exhibition in Eindhoven, there is a machine looking like a huge beast that will come up to you if you whisper or speak slowly, but if you shout or speak harshly it will rear up and turn away. A great deal of work has been done in the field of computers to make machines operate by vocal signals to give visual outputs. The overall effect that there has been a way of thinking that goes towards the end of making the picture produce the sound (e.g. optical soundtracks) or the sound produce the picture. An interactive matching in parallel instead of adding one to the other in series.

The outcome has been something that is broadly classified as "cybernetic film" which means a film that exploits the characteristics of a machine to produce the image rather than capturing existing or produced images. Examples include computer animation, optical effects, multiple projectors or lens, processing and editing techniques. It is difficult to define it accurately, other than to say that on seeing a cybernetic film one is more aware of the film form than the film content. It is the form that the authors are experimenting with, and to this extent they use music to "stabilise" the film. To give something that the viewer can hang onto as the visuals go off into their own uncharted worlds.

It is the combined facilities of making music create the image: the development of sound and colour synthesisers along with electronic pattern generators etc, the growth of information processing techniques (and that is what art is) that has led to the existence of many devices offering instant sound and picture control and manipulation of a range that no artist or composer in history has ever had or dreamed of. Any pictures created in this way—picture by picture—are in effect animation. A total form of picture/sound that is symbiotic is about to emerge so that soon composers will be thinking in terms of colour, space, and movement, whereas animators will be more and more concerned with the effects of sound upon the final picture.

Independent and Avant-Garde Films

Jean Cocteau predicted that film making would become an art only when its technical requirements were as cheap as paper and pencil. As the traditional methods of feature film production rose in cost, good quality smaller cameras became relatively cheap. In the 1950's, as an alternative society was in the process of challenging tradition Hollywood was becoming increasingly rigid. New film makers appeared with little faith in either society's codes or those of Hollywood. They tackled the taboo subjects generally using techniques vastly different from those of their predecessors.

What was avant-garde yesterday is often conventional tomorrow. The "underground" film movement soon surfaced and even influenced conventional feature films. Andy Warhol, for one, soon turned into, and became ever increasingly part of, the new feature film system. Others had no desire to compete with the system. The theoretical structure of film became increasingly debated. A new wave of formalist film makers appeared, professing a highly structured formal system behind their work. This structure is often repeated in a structured approach to the music for these films.

The range of independent and avant-garde films is wide. Simon Field and David Curtis, writing in The British Film Institute catalogue to a festival of independent and avant-garde films in 1973 surveyed the range in this way:

196

There are film-makers using autobiographical diary form (Mekas, Sonbert), investigating the possibilities of narrative (Rainer, Wyborny), questioning the nature of the relationship between audience and film (the Heins, Le Grice, Landow), searching for film's basic syntax (Hammand, Frampton), dealing with landscape in film (Snow, Raban, Gottheim), working with erotic material (Noren, Dwoskin), and so on. This is to name only a few of the film-makers and to simplify and create areas that in the work constantly overlap and interchange.

In 1950 the novelist and dramatist, Jean Genet, directed his one and only film, *Un Chant d'Amour*, considered a classic from the underground. The film was silent. Gavin Bryars was commissioned in 1973 to compose a sound-track for the English print of the film. He resisted the initial intention of the distributor to create a synchronous sound-track of effects to match the points in the silent film where sound would inevitably result from an action. He created a structured musical piece that lasts the full length of the film. He believes that "music impinges most on film where it occupies its separate spaces." He broke the structure of the film into its component parts:

I broke down the film into the footage of each shot, relating scenes to one another both in terms of their content, who was involved, where it took place, its duration, pace and so on. This analysis resulted in a notation from which I could effect, firstly a 1:1 relationship with sound and film and from that I constructed larger scale time relationships by working out each component part.

It is noticeable that Bryars was struck, less by the overt homosexuality of the film than by its systemic construction. This is one example of a tendency in many independent underground films to work more with formal structure in all film's formal means. Music, film music in particular, is often composed according to a mathematical scheme but with film music it has seldom sought to underly and compliment the formal structure of the film. Kenneth Anger in his *Scorpio Rising* (1962) employs music of a totally different and more traditional conception. It could be called "period music". He uses rock 'n' roll songs of the American subculture which is also the subject of the film. His actual choice of songs and their location in the film is carefully selected. For example, *Blue Velvet* is used for a dressing scene involving dressing in *blue* jeans.

Gavin Bryars takes the whole nature of his structured music to further extremes in *Jesus Blood Never Failed Me Yet* which he co-directed with Steve Dwoskin. In this film the music came first. He had a recording of a tramp singing the hymn that titles the piece.

He made a thirteen bar loop of this and ran it repeatedly for thirty minutes. This tape length is equivalent to one thousand two hundred feet of 16 mm film. He added orchestral accompaniment very slowly throughout the singing and, at the end, slowly faded the whole music. The repeated nature of the song is mirrored in the structure of the film's visuals which consist of twelve one hundred foot takes (to make the total one thousand two hundred feet of the sound) of an old man walking in slow motion towards a camera held with a fixed frame. The elliptical nature of the music is mirrored in the visuals which are repeated, dissolving one identical take into another.

Another aspect of this film reflects the changing nature of film and film music. Film music has often been played away from the screen and the visuals for which the music was composed. Live performances of music played in conjunction with a film are somewhat rare, though as early as 1924 Eric Satie composed music and had it performed live to a film, *Entr'acte*, directed by Rene Clair based on some notes by the Dadaist painter Francis Picabia. *Jesus Blood Never Saved Me Yet* was "performed" live in The Queen Elizabeth Hall in London on 11th December, 1972. The visuals were screened together with the stereophonic tape of the original hymn in its thirteen bar loop form. An orchestra played Bryars composed music. Like *Entr'acte* this film is also available for distribution with an optically-striped track so that can be screened in conventional viewing circumstances.

The subject matter of both Genet's *Un Chant d'Amour* (that of homosexuality in prison) and Anger's *Scorpio Rising* (about homosexuality and motor bike gangs) is typical of the anti-traditional subject matter of some independent, avant-garde films. Steve Dwoskin's *Dyn Amo* (1972) deals with the plight of women as sex objects. Again Gavin Bryars composed music with an inner construction akin to the film's construction. Like the wide range of areas covered by independent and avant-garde films, the music that is sometimes found in these films has a wide range of functions. The "New Formalist" approach of Bryars based around the very structure of the visuals is one significant development which takes Eisenstein's formalist approach to sound and visuals onto a wider plane.

4

THE MUSIC DIRECTOR AND THE SOUND RECORDIST

The Function of the Music Director

FEATURE film production has now been organized into a distinctive pattern which may well be represented by the chart shown below.

```
                        PRODUCER
                     /      |      \
SCRIPT-WRITER  ——  ⟋   DIRECTOR   ⟍  ——  ACTORS
                        Design
                      Photography
                        Sound
                        Editing
```

The initiation of a picture and the overall financial responsibility for it lie usually with the producer. As the impresario of the film industry, he will guide a film through from beginning to end, either personally or by delegation of authority. The actual creative process of making the picture is the responsibility of three main groups, represented by the director, the scriptwriter (who may be a professional screenwriter providing original material, a novelist, or a playwright), and the actors (stars, featured players, small-part actors and crowds). In order to carry through the technical processes involved, this team is backed by the four technical branches of film production, i.e., design (including art direction, set construction, costume design, make-up, hairdressing, property work and set decoration), photography (including special effects), sound (including floor recording, effects, post-synchronization, re-recording and music), and editing (including assembly cutting, track-laying, laboratory liaison, and post-production processes).

The Music Director may be involved with each of these groups and technical branches at some stage in the process; indeed, on certain types of film, he will be on call from the first script stage to the preparation of the final married print.

199

Relation to the Producer

When a film is first considered, the producer may wish to consult the composer from the outset; arguments as to the value of this step are put forward in Section 5. If the film is predominantly concerned with music, the Music Director may well be one of the first appointments made in the mounting of the production, since his advice will be needed in the choice of songs or singers, dancers, musicians or orchestras. In his capacity as liaison between the composer and the studio, he will be consulted on the choice of composer, both from the point of view of cost and of suitability to a particular subject. At this stage a knowledge of the styles and capabilities of all the available composers is the main requirement of the Music Director, as well as information about their current commitments in the concert hall and opera house. Budget considerations may call for a discussion on the size of the orchestra. The director may also contribute to the discussion from the point of view of the "man on the floor".

Relation to the Scriptwriter

Preliminary discussions with the producer are usually followed by the arrival of a script. From this the Music Director can gain a more detailed impression of the film's atmosphere and style, and he will discover specific points that will shortly require his attention, such as songs and dances, or music from sources like a wireless set, a town band, and concert hall, theatre or night-club orchestras; the playing of a gramophone or even the whistling of a tune must be carefully noted. If lyrics are involved, it will be necessary to discuss them with the scriptwriter, or obtain the services of a lyric-writer. Where existing music is to be used (perhaps with some story or plot association), copyright investigations must be initiated immediately in order to find out whether clearance can be obtained and the music used in the film.

Relation to the Director

As soon as the director has indicated his proposed method of shooting individual scenes, any "live" music must be recorded ready for playback. As a director gets closer to his subject, he may wish to know many new facts from the music department—for example, the date of the first piano, whether a waltz could be danced in 1900, which Guards' band would be playing in the forecourt of Buckingham Palace, the size and composition of "dummy" orchestras, the exact methods of using playback, recommendations for specialized artists, such as mouth-organ or mandolin players, combinations for street bands or buskers to meet the needs of a particular scene. The answers to all requirements of this kind and even the supervision of shooting during complex musical sequences, will be among the services required of the Music Director.

On completion of the floor work, the director will wish to be associated with every stage of preparation, recording and re-recording of the music score, from its inception at the rough-cut screenings to the final mix.

Relation to the Actors

Where a musical film is being made, the relationship of the Music Director to the actors is so obvious as to need no further comment, beyond the fact that it will be part of his function to ensure that the performers are presented in the best possible manner, and that full advantage is taken of the many recording techniques to obtain the very best visual and aural presentation throughout the film.

In the case of presenting individual songs or performances for which actors not used to musical work may have to sing or play, the Music Director is responsible for explaining such procedures as shooting to playback and post-synchronization; he will often have to use tact and sympathy as he guides actors through these unfamiliar and rather elaborate technical processes. He may have to coach them or, in the last resort, explain as discreetly as possible that he must recommend a double be employed to record the sound-track.

It may be that the song or performance has been planned as a substitution process from the beginning. In this case, the actor must be introduced to the artist who is to record his sound-track (a piano concerto, possibly, or a complex violin passage) and undergo a period of training for the time when the visuals must be made to match with the playback disc. "Dummy" pianos or even "stopped" violins may be needed, and the actors will have to be coached in following, with expressions as well as with fingers, a short but often elaborate section of music recorded by his sound-track double. On the set, such carefully prepared scenes will need to be supervised by the Music Director during shooting, and so will the occasional ballroom scenes, Highland flings, xylophone solos or soulful moments around grand pianos, which recur so frequently in film production!

Relation to the Lighting Cameraman

The lighting cameraman may be concerned with a range of problems, from the over-polished console of an electric organ to the number of arcs required to illuminate the Royal Albert Hall for Technicolor exposure. In order to simplify shooting, the system of employing "dummy" musicians has been established, not only to assist the process of filming to playback, but also to ensure that the director has at his disposal on the set a group of players who understand and respond to the requirements of the camera. Muir Mathieson remembers the first time that he tried to persuade brass players to allow the studio to rub putty on their beautifully polished instruments to remove the glare; there was some consternation! Now musicians who appear consistently in films realize the cameraman's problems, and some may even keep special instruments for this purpose. Non-reflecting shirts and collars, good visual performance and the necessary adaptability to the requirements of the camera department are among the technical points understood by these specialists. This is particularly necessary when foreground action may mean that the director must rely on their full co-operation with a minimum of instruction.

When a full orchestra of players who are not used to appearing before the camera is assembled for a film such as *Instruments of the Orchestra* or for a purely orchestral sequence, it is essential that the Music Director evolves some method of rhythmic cueing for the cameraman in order to make certain that the camera is looking the right way at the right time during the performance, especially when a complex series of camera movements are involved.

Relation to the Art Director

The art director may consult the Music Director on a range of subjects, from how to obtain a seventeenth century harpsichord to the proper lay-out of the choir and orchestra in a church hall for a performance of *The Messiah*. Musical properties are in fairly regular demand for set decoration, and the music department will be well advised to know where almost any kind of equipment may be found, from barrel-organs (obtainable from one source alone in Britain) to such items as music stands and conductors' batons.

Relation to the Editor

As soon as the rough-cut has been completed, the liaison between film editor, Music Director and composer (who will by now have been selected and contracted for the picture) becomes an important part in the main music process. The composer is called in to see his first screening of the picture in as complete a form as is practical at this stage in the production. Because of the importance of this music screening, the producer will frequently attend together with the director and the film editor with his staff. Detailed notes are always taken of the decisions reached during the discussions which normally follow the screening of the completed film, and the second reel-by-reel projection. The composer and Music Director bring in fresh minds which can often re-invigorate the production team. After the arduous work on the floor, the production team may well have flagged and they welcome the enthusiasm of the newcomers.

The discussions about the music concern two main problems— where there should be music and what kind of music it should be. Each scene or sequence is considered in detail and the various members in the production group make their individual comments. Inevitably, these comments are based on very personal reactions, for film-makers, like film-goers, hold strongly differing views on the precise function of music in films; however, argument can, at this stage, be highly stimulating to the composer.

Having determined which sections of the film need musical accompaniment, the exact nature of the sounds to be produced for each section must be decided. This will eventually depend on the composer's ability to interpret musically what may be a series of non-technical suggestions from the producer or director, but these suggestions will certainly be amplified for him by the Music Director who, at this stage, brings to bear on the discussion his joint knowledge of the world of music and the technical requirements of the cinema.

To assist the composer, the editor and his staff prepare a series of exact timings for the action and dialogue of each section of the film in which music is to appear: the music department should ensure that these notes are not just a dull list of figures, but a reminder to the composer of his original reactions on seeing the film for the first time.

Relation to the Recordist

The second major phase in scoring a film begins with the recording sessions. After the score has been delivered by the composer, orchestral parts copied and the orchestra assembled in the theatre, the work of transferring each section of music to film or magnetic tape is carried out by the Music Director, who now assumes the role of conductor.

With the composer at his side, the score itself in front of him, the picture on the large screen at the back of the orchestra, and a well illuminated footage-counter or timing device in a prominent position, the carefully timed performance of the various musical sections is carried out, usually to a strict time schedule and occasionally in the presence of a restive producer and a tense director. The routine procedure of rehearsal, recording and playback is only broken when some serious problem in timing arises, or a complex readjustment in microphone lay-out is called for. Regular consultation with the Music Mixer is necessary to ensure that the complete intention of the composer is in fact being registered on the sound-track.

After the music sessions are completed, the editor and the sound department at once prepare for the final mixing of dialogue with music and sound effects. Occasional discussion may be held on the omission of certain sections of the music or the substitution of sound effects; additional music may even be called for in certain cases, where new scenes have been added or old scenes deleted. The attendance of the Music Director at the dubbing sessions has always been a matter of some controversy, as we have seen. Given a good dubbing mixer and an imaginative track-layer, the composer's intentions, which were discussed in detail at the preview of the rough-cut, should remain more or less intact; for the decision of the director of the film is final.

The final test comes at the première, and the Music Director, like his colleagues, will want to examine the results of his work under ordinary theatre conditions, watching the effect of a smoothly integrated score on the emotional reactions of the audience.

Procedure in Hollywood

The distinguished composer working in Hollywood, Hugo Friedhofer, has written for us the following detailed account of his method of work, which represents procedure in Hollywood as experienced by the composer. Individual composers naturally differ in the way they like to work, but Friedhofer's meticulous system not only reveals the complexity of the task of composition for films, but how a composer in a Hollywood studio collaborates with the Producer, Director, Editor and others working on the film.

My own method of procedure is as follows: (1) One or two screenings for the purpose of absorbing the style and content of the film, without any conscious consideration of the musical problems involved.

(2) A reel-by-reel screening, with repetitions if necessary, at which time the music cutter assigned to me makes notes concerning the various sections to be scored, which cues demand breaking down in complete detail, whether there are any sections which will ultimately be done to click-tracks, whether long scenes should be broken down into shorter sections at such points where there is a complete change of mood or pace, and if so, will overlaps or crossfades be necessary; in short, every facet of the technical *modus operandi* is carefully discussed and noted in detail.

(3) A conference with the film editor and the sound effects cutter in order to ascertain whether or not certain sequences shot out of doors, and in which the dialogue has been partially obscured by the sound of wind, running water, gunfire, automobile motor noise, etc., are to be replaced by clean dialogue; what kind of sound effect it will be necessary for me to take into consideration when planning music for such and such a scene, and so on.

(4) While all this extra-musical exploration has been going on, the sub-conscious mind has been hard at work, devising thematic material, determining the general mood, style and atmosphere of the score to be composed, weeding out incongruities and ruling out what Sir Donald Francis Tovey has referred to as "impossible projects", so that by this time I can safely say that the score has been composed, except (of course) for the sometimes heartbreaking process of finding all the right notes.

(5) A composer assumes that he has been selected to score a film because the producer and director have complete confidence in his professional knowledge, experience and skill. Personally it has always been my practice, once the general plan of the score has been formulated, to have a final conference with the producer and director, for the purpose of outlining (to the best of my ability) the style and format of the score, the sections which I feel should or should not have music, etc., etc., thereby precluding the possibility of any unpleasant surprises on the recording stage.

(6) By this time, cue sheets containing all the necessary detailed description of the action and dialogue, all timed to the split second are ready for me. All that remains to be done is to settle down to the task of putting notes on music paper.

(7) Excepting in those rare instances when there is sufficient time for me to orchestrate my own music, I sketch in complete details on from three to six staves, depending on the texture of the music. Orchestral colour is carefully indicated and subsequently discussed with the orchestrator assigned to me. The composition of a film score of average length (that is to say, one whose running time is somewhere between 40 and 60 minutes) takes me anywhere from four to six weeks to complete, exclusive of recording and re-recording.

Nearly half a century has passed since music, recorded specially and synchronized with the film, became an established addition to this form of entertainment throughout the world. Today the film composer is skilled in this specialized medium. He understands the exacting demands of the screen, and can exploit the potential subtleties and technical tricks and accept the limitations of the craft. Under the best of circumstances he is served by highly competent orchestras, fine acoustics, and recording techniques which are nearing a state of perfection. High quality microphones, the excellence of modern magnetic recording methods, theatre loudspeakers which are rapidly ceasing to be the weakest link in the chain, and now the "enrichment of the marvel of stereophonic sound", all combine to produce a result which verges on the original performances. The aim in using any sound recording and reproducing machine must surely be that the reproduction should be indistinguishable from the original performance. This aim is within sight. It was not always so.

205

The Development of Modern Recording Practice

The earliest forms of sound film had to make the best possible use of the tools available at the time. The transition from the silent to the sound film was so abrupt that there was no time for research engineers to develop the improvements which all knew were so necessary. In the light of present day knowledge it seems remarkable that the quality obtained during the late 1920's was as high as it was.

Edward Kellogg, in a paper read to the Society of Motion Picture and Television Engineers, modestly for one of the pioneers, puts the situation in a nutshell. "We tend," he says, "fortunately to forget the troubles that are past. Still more we forget the troubles other people had. We who took part in the development of sound equipment may be tempted to think that we made the talking picture possible. But if we gave the credit they deserve to the writers, directors, actors and their bosses, and to the patient guinea pigs who bought tickets, perhaps the only bouquet left to hand ourselves is to say that our stuff was not so bad as to make the talkies impossible."

Not long passed before what must have been a period of feverish activity produced substantial results. In 1931 Olson demonstrated the ribbon microphone in a form not substantially different from that used today, giving the recording engineer the double benefits of a response which was smoother than hitherto and a useful degree of directivity. About the same time the engineers of the Radio Corporation of America, the General Electric Company, and others developed methods of securing uniform speed of film transport, thus reducing greatly the evils of "wow" and "flutter"—the fluctuations of pitch that could render terrible otherwise good sound.

It was the same with the optical systems of recording machines, the mechanism of loudspeakers, and so on through the highly complex chain of events between the recording studio and the cinema auditorium. The system of recording on what we would now call long-playing discs and of attempting to synchronize them with the visual film, although it was the obvious first approach to the talkie, died a natural and fairly rapid death, and the photographic sound record on film alongside the visual frame took its firm place—the same place that it occupies today. The speed with which the film passed through the camera and the projectors was increased by half as much again to help the recording engineers achieve adequate high frequency response, and the American studios flooded the world with sound-tracks which, considering the short development period, attained remarkable fidelity.

Undoubtedly the most significant development in recording methods since talkies first appeared has been that of magnetic recording. And to be fair it must be said that the theory of this remarkable invention originated in Europe. Indeed it is reasonable to say that this has been the only fundamental change in recording technique, at least in so far as the talking picture is concerned, since disc gave place to film. Initiated, therefore, in Europe in more or less its present form, it spread rapidly to America after the second World War. It is now in the process of ousting photographic recording from studio work all over the world, and will certainly become more and more accepted in the cinema as the reproduction equipment becomes cheaper and more available. It is questionable whether the theatre audience fully appreciates the prime technical improvements of this method of recording over photographic methods—the increased frequency range possible, giving superior quality, more lifelike and natural response, and the higher signal to noise ratio, virtually removing the objectionable background noise and increasing the range from pianissimo to fortissimo.

The third main advantage, that of economy to the producer, is already greatly, though not yet fully, exploited in the studio. As long as the cinema public remains as uncritical as it is of sound quality, the advantages of magnetic quality will be appreciated most in the studio. With photographic recording a period of hours had to elapse, while the negative was developed and prints made, before the day's work could be checked. The hard and expensive toil of a company of musicians could easily be ruined by some unforeseen fault in film stock manufacture, or by errors in recorder operation or processing. With magnetic recording instantaneous playback is possible, and the final results are there for all to hear, immediately.

All these, however, are technicalities, and this book has no space for them. The theories and the technical complexities of sound recording are covered admirably by many of the books on the subject already in existence. Given the tools, it is for the sound recording engineers all over the world in the course of their routine duty to produce by their individual methods and with their individual preferences the best possible sound records of the material before them.

In almost any technical process, the answer to the question, "How is it done?", calls for a reply which is both straight-forward and fully explanatory. The reply may not necessarily be easy and may most probably be full of technicalities incomprehensible to the lay mind. Nevertheless, there is one and only one correct reply. But to the question, "What is the best way to do it?", there may be as many answers as there are people doing it.

How is music for the cinema recorded? This is easy to answer. The engineer places the right types of microphone in the right positions in an acoustically correct theatre with an ideally constituted and ideally placed orchestra. The microphones are connected to the correct type of sound recording channel, properly adjusted, and the engineer regulates the output of each microphone to the correct degree, making as he goes any necessary corrections or adjustments to his equipment. There are, however, in this simple outline a few variables, a little room for matters of opinion, and in the end there is always the problem of what is right and what is wrong.

To try to reach some common denominator, some general field of agreement on which this chapter could be based, a number of controversial questions were asked of several leading film music recordists in England. At least, it was felt, some measure of unanimity could be obtained on the acoustic conditions for a given type of orchestra; some agreement would be reached on certain routine techniques. This was an idle hope. The replies may all be the result of good solid experience obtained by doing the job under their own conditions. A wealth of knowledge may well have gone into each carefully considered reply. They may all be right. They are certainly all different.

To be controversial for a moment, let us consider the object of the exercise. We are assembled in a recording theatre with an orchestra, a composer, a conductor, and all the necessary and unnecessary members of the production team; a multitude of creative people all regarding themselves as artists contributing to an artistic result. In the opinion of some the one person, the only person, who should be regarded as the creative element present is the composer. It is the duty of the music director to ensure that the orchestra performs the music as the composer wishes and that the timing is as it should be. It is the duty of the recording engineer to see that the ultimate sound-track is a faithful record of the wishes of the composer. Suggestions should and will be made from time to time and from person to person. But it is the composer alone who knows precisely the effect he wants. He may not be right. He may be, and frequently is, completely wrong. But just as long as he is entrusted with the work of providing an artistic, imaginative, and fully satisfactory musical accompaniment to the visuals on which so much effort has been expended, then everybody else present must form part of a team to reach that end.

This point gave rise to one of the disagreements in the answers supplied by sound engineers. Should the composer be present in the listening room? Or is the engineer better qualified to produce the ideal sound by himself? It seems strange that there could be any doubt about this. How can the engineer, not being equipped with second sight, possibly know what the composer is aiming at? A subtle theme on the woodwind could easily be masked by a brass accompaniment unless steps were taken to avoid it. But if the one at the controls does not even know that the theme exists, and the composer is not there to tell him, the entire effect will be lost. Yet to this question, one half of the replies received preferred the composer to stay outside. Many of these replies came from engineers of great skill and reputation. It seems that they must have had unfortunate experiences in the past.

There are, of course, the composers who talk all through a take or who persist in hearing wrong notes which they themselves wrote. There are composers who are convinced that their music in the film should dominate everything else including the dialogue. There is the clicker of stopwatches and the beater of time, and perhaps the worst of them all, the composer who quite patently does not care at all and dreamily sits with his crossword puzzle. Nevertheless, it still seems odd that there are engineers who prefer to do without the guidance of the one man who can be of help when problems arise.

A question like that is virtually asking the engineer whether he thinks he should be a technician or a musician. It would probably be an ideal solution if he were both. But the combination of skill in both these crafts is, perhaps fortunately, rare. There are recording engineers who claim that their facility in reading a score is ample recompense for having to do without the guiding hand of the composer. They have been observed at work, frantically trying to follow the top line while their own less glamorous job goes by the board. A technician who is not also a musician finds it hard to conceive anybody reading intelligently the score of a completely unfamiliar work simultaneously with doing another not over-simple occupation efficiently. The score for a film may well be an involved composition. Although it can, and frequently does, have the sound of apparent simplicity, it may nevertheless include passages of considerable complexity for conductor and musicians. Very few composers would claim the ability to read a contemporary and complicated score at sight. Even fewer would regard it as possible to make intelligent sense of it at first reading with his attention divided by another equally important occupation. Yet there are engineers without musical training who claim such powers. There are people who might put an unkind interpretation on the claim.

Nevertheless, some recordists assert that they make a creative contribution to the final musical effect. Just as an orchestra can create an outstanding performance of a work, a competent music recordist can capture and re-create in another medium the life and excitement of that performance. If the musician and recordist, by their skill and musical appreciation, are able to give that extra quality to the final result, then, the recordist argues, each in his own way may be said to be part of the creative element.

The main problem which confronts the sound engineer is securing a balance between different sections of the orchestra which is satisfactory to the composer (and here we must remember that film music is generally a very different matter from concert hall music), and yet still conforms to the rules which the technical processes involved impose. This problem is largely one of microphone and orchestra placement. It could also be affected to some extent by varying the acoustics of the theatre, but it is rarely possible that appreciable variation is obtained. Orchestra positioning generally conforms to certain accepted arrangements. Both musicians and conductors prefer to establish a workable plan and stick to it. We are left therefore with one main variable: how many microphones to use, and where to put them.

The world of recording engineers again is fairly evenly divided on this subject. Theoretically, of course, if each section of the orchestra is covered by its own microphone, and balance is achieved by regulation of the amount of each microphone in use, then any conceivable balance is easily possible. This imposes, however, a close microphone method of working to ensure that the one in question receives all that it is meant to receive, and as little else as possible. Hence one tends to lose "room tone", and increased partition within the orchestra tends to spoil ensemble performance. There is no doubt that, given a theatre which is acoustically ideal for the chosen orchestra (and how few of them are!), an extremely good result can be reached with one well-placed microphone covering the whole orchestra, augmented by one or two close-range subsidiary microphones which are introduced only when additional emphasis is needed.

One of the fundamental differences between listening to an orchestra in a concert hall, and listening to a recording, is the fact that the visual sense plays no part in the latter. Indeed, in the case of the cinema performance (ignoring, of course, a film of an orchestra) the eyes are concentrated on the events upon the screen. The solo violin in a violin concerto, although playing an independent part, is also competing with a body of strings producing the same tone colour. The audience in the concert hall follows his performance because the soloist is there, in front of their eyes, prominent among the rest of the players. If he is competing with an accompaniment which is loud or fully scored, the visual isolation which is unconsciously available to the listener gives the sound adequate separation. And this is again augmented by the directional property of two ears, which can focus sound just as two eyes can focus vision. Obviously the microphone must compensate for the lack of vision in a recorded or broadcast performance.

A point which should be made is that dance band work needs a completely different technique. Here the problems of room tone rarely arise. The dance band of today likes the dry, tight sound given by many microphones operating a matter of inches from the instruments. The piano microphone will be placed literally inside the instrument, and the muted trumpets will be played with the mutes close to another microphone. And it is not exaggerating to say that a vocalist has spoiled a recording because her nose made a rubbing noise against the microphone casing.

These, however, are extremes. As usual, compromise is the true answer.

It is an interesting point that production companies involved in high budget films, and consequently having more time for recording available, more elaborately equipped studios at their disposal, and more money to spend on larger orchestras than smaller companies, present their composers and recording staffs with what is fundamentally a much simpler problem, and one that is much quicker to resolve. The small combination of instruments needs far greater care from the composer, finer musicianship from the players, and greater skill and patience from the engineer. In the large orchestra faults are often masked by weight of numbers; in the small combination everybody must pull his weight.

We have mentioned "room tone". Perhaps a short explanation is called for. When an orchestra is playing in an enclosed space the sound reaching the microphone, or for that matter the ears of the audience, can be quite clearly divided into two parts: the direct sound emanating from the instruments themselves, and the sound reflected from the walls, floor and ceiling. It is this second component, which contributes to what may be called "room tone"; it can make one hall sound different from another, and it is very often responsible for the richness and colour of a recording. This is not the place to enter into a discussion upon the physics of acoustics, but it is enough to say that the science is highly advanced, and acoustic physicists can accurately foresee the ultimate room tone of any existing or projected building. The dimensions and proportions, the nature of materials used on the confining surfaces, and the furniture all play a part in affecting this factor. The reverberation of a building is not quite synonymous with its room tone, but the two terms mean nearly enough the same thing for our present argument.

For normal orchestral work a degree—some say a fairly high degree—of reverberation is essential. And it must occur or be arranged so that this reverberation at different pitches conforms to the desired laws. Unless a film studio has a stage specially constructed for music recording and nothing else, it is unlikely that natural reverberation will be present to the right character and degree. This is where artificial means may have to come in. It is quite possible to introduce artificial reverberation, either by means of specially designed, highly reverberant chambers, or by electronic means, into recorded music at any chosen point and on any one microphone channel. It is an extraordinarily useful tool; useful not only, in small quantities, to add space and richness to the music, and to add apparently to the size of the orchestra, but also for trick effects. How lovely a cor anglais solo can sound if it is used with a degree of added reverberation and is accompanied by the rest of the orchestra recorded normally. And how impossible to achieve this effect in a concert hall. And what interesting effects can be obtained by instruments recorded very close to the microphone, with the inevitable tight sound, and then enriched by artificial reverberation. Groups have been developing this idea in recent years to great profit.

It is quite true that such devices are spurious, and it is equally true that, like all good ideas, they tend to be over-exploited to their own detriment; but, after all, everything in film work is spurious up to a point. The film business is full of masters of the art of fake.

It is rare that the economics of the film industry in this country today make possible the employment of a symphony orchestra of the proportions one expects in a concert hall. Indeed few recording theatres could cope happily with some ninety performers. Since, when a composer is scoring for an orchestra of normal symphonic proportions, he has need of all the colour he can get from wood and brass sections, it is inevitable that any reduction from concert hall dimensions must be made in the string sections. When perhaps fifty to sixty musicians are used it is still possible to have a complement of string players which does not sound impoverished, and judicious microphone placement can generally succeed in making up something of the difference. But when the maximum possible comes down much below that, and we are left with only three desks of first violins and maybe two of seconds, then technique—and results—have to undergo drastic modification.

Many experiments have been made in trying to give two or three violins playing in unison the apparent effect of six times the number. Reverberation chambers, multiple track recordings, even the use of electronic delay devices, have all been tried, and it is fairly safe to say that all have failed. Perhaps the best attempt at such an effect has come from recording the available strings, and recording them again to a playback of the first recording. And even then perhaps again. The resulting tracks are all mixed together synchronously. The result is very often an improvement, but at the best it is a poor substitute, and in any case, for obvious reasons, this sort of treatment is frowned upon by the Musicians' Union. The exquisite, shimmering, singing sound of a big body of strings can only be produced by using a large number. It has nothing to do with the physical volume of sound. Maybe it is due to the way the individual musicians play their instruments, maybe due to the interaction between the extreme harmonics produced by vibrating strings. And maybe it is because we do not yet know all there is to know about the physics of music.

The sound engineer must bear very much in mind, as of course must the composer, that the music track produced at the recording session will rarely be heard by the audience in its original form. It will be mixed with dialogue and sound effects; it will be played louder or softer to suit the dramatic demands of the film. And, worst of all, it may possibly be cut shorter or, by repeating sections, made longer to adapt itself to alterations in the picture. It might even be cut out altogether. Here, however, it must be stressed that composers of repute whose contributions to music for the cinema are of real and lasting value, are taking a firm stand. And rightly so. It is the privilege of the composer to insist upon firm guarantees that the film to which he works is in its final form, that the machinery of approval in all its stages has been gone through, and that the lengths he is given are unalterable, before he attends the screening.

It is a good thing, and it is now almost universal, for the music director to conduct the music as he listens to the dialogue through headphones as well as watching the picture on the screen. He can then exploit to the full the skill of the composer, and make use of phrases intended to be heard clear of any other sound. And, after a take, it is wise to play the recording back roughly mixed with the dialogue it will ultimately have to support. Sometimes the mixing engineer chooses to "flatten" out to a degree the increasing and decreasing volumes throughout a section. His prime reason is that in the final mixing stage it is possible to restore the original range without loss of balance, and by giving to very quiet sections rather more amplification than they warrant he can reduce the unwanted system noises that photographic recordings are heir to. And further, should alterations mean that the music is used in a position different from the original conception it is more likely to give an acceptable result.

Of course, alterations should not be made; engineers should not tamper with composers' intentions; and music should not be used in contexts other than those for which it was intended. But just as long as producers and directors and film editors are human, and just as long as there are exhibitors and distributors and censors who sometimes are not, things like this will happen.

The question of the ideal acoustics for a music auditorium is one that has induced considerable research, and very great divergencies of opinion still exist between the physicists and the musicians, with the recording engineers rather insecurely balanced on the fence between them. And it is a strange thing that some halls which seemed to meet with satisfaction among everybody were designed in the days before acoustics became a science. The Queen's Hall in London, the destruction of which during the war was one of the greatest losses to London's musical life, was a shining example. Maybe the somewhat elaborate Victorian construction compared with the cleaner, simpler lines of modern design was part of the secret; maybe the great use of timber instead of the more readily available materials of today, had effects not fully appreciated by the scientists. At any rate, to work in the Queen's Hall was a delightful experience for musicians, audience and recording engineers alike.

The acoustic designers' modern triumph, the Royal Festival Hall, built in London in 1951, is a vastly different matter. It has a hard, unyielding sound, which responds magnificently to a magnificent performance; but it will tolerate nothing less. A recording of a large orchestra, particularly when the hall is empty, with a well-chosen microphone at a distance, can be a thrilling sound. Strings have both "bite" and sonority, and brass can cut through with edge and definition. Criticisms have been made that extra bass resonance would be beneficial from a concert point of view, but for the recording engineer, who has other means at his disposal for coping with such possible deficiencies, the results can be delightful and invigorating.

London's only other major auditorium, the Royal Albert Hall, has become amongst musicians something of a joke. It is unfortunate that an audience cannot be assembled where a recording engineer can place his microphone, because the British Broadcasting Corporation, admittedly after years of trial and error, succeed in producing most excellent transmissions.

These halls, of course, are not normally available for the film recording session. Nor are they equipped with the elaborate projection and playback machinery necessary for efficient film recording. The major studios all have their theatres, either designed for music recording, or specially converted from ordinary stages, but one ventures to suggest that few if any of these in England are wholly satisfactory. A sweeping comment this, and one which will reap disapproval. The scientist can, in the experience of modern invention, produce any desired effect. One wonders whether we all know quite what we do want. The high fidelity equipment now easily available for radio and record reproduction in the home has not had an unmixed reception, because public taste has not altogether developed a liking for what the scientist says it should have. We do not all like what is good for us, and that is probably just as well.

It is usually the duty of the engineer to group the orchestra in the arrangement which experience has shown to be most suitable for his particular studio or hall. It is naturally a duty which must be done with the full agreement of the music director. In England some years ago it was fashionable to use a multi-microphone technique, in which, as has been stated earlier, considerable physical separation between different sections of the orchestra was necessary to enable each microphone to record only that section which it was intended to cover. The British recordist E. A. Drake, however, defends the use of the multi-microphone technique of recording as follows: "Unless one uses highly directional microphones—which from the point of view of room tone is not very desirable—one obviously does not expect to achieve complete sound separation between sections of the orchestra, but one *does* expect to pick up *mostly* string sound on a string microphone, and so on. The chief points I have against a single microphone pick-up are: in placing the microphone sufficiently far back to cover the whole orchestra, solo instruments in particular tend to sound 'thin' and to lose their characteristic 'timbre'; for the same reason (the distance of the microphone from the orchestra) there is a definite tendency to too much reverberation, with a consequent loss of attack and detail. This latter effect is also aggravated by the necessity of having to work at a higher level than usual on the gain control."

The multi-microphone technique certainly added to the facility of the engineer in obtaining correct balance. Almost any conceivable relation between one section and another was possible by merely turning a knob. It is now, however, accepted that such extremes become distasteful to the members of the orchestra, and inevitably performance suffers. The normal concert hall grouping, or at least a near approximation to it, is customary today when recording large orchestras. Perhaps rather more patience is needed in securing a good balance, but the result is worth it.

Undoubtedly music recording is at its simplest when it is least critical. The full symphony orchestra in the concert hall presents few problems to the engineer. A modern chamber work, with perhaps extreme delicacies of balance between first and second violins, and the ingenuity in getting just the right amount of string tone without introducing harshness, can present real difficulty. Indeed, solo instruments often tend towards complication. It is not easy to capture the subtle tones of the bassoon without introducing unwanted key sounds, or to secure the character of a guitar and yet avoid the slide on the strings. The shrill penetration of the piccolo has its problems for the engineer no less than the extreme bass tones of the organ which should literally be felt as well as heard.

The responsibility for the final music track must always remain divided between the composer and his engineers. The good film music composer will help both the film and the recordist—and incidentally himself—if he understands fully the technique of recording and exploits the knowledge. He must understand the potential uses of microphone technique and the facilities available for the modification of sound, and make use of them in his score. Equally he should realize the limitations of the recording medium, and temper some of his ideas. There is no use in writing for a solo muted viola to be heard very softly, and following it immediately with some vast fortissimo tutti, and expect to record the range as it appears in the studio. Enormous improvements are being made in the efficiency and versatility of present-day recording and reproducing media. But there are limits, and the composer must appreciate them.

216

Nor is it certain, and this is another question altogether, whether the audience in the cinema always relishes being shocked into sudden wakefulness by a violent crescendo of sound, no matter how skilfully it has been orchestrated or how lovingly it matches the visuals. For the majority of audiences the cinema is still a place of rest and relaxation.

In the experience of many recording engineers the majority of the composers of film-music still fail to realize that this is and must be an outlet for their art separate from the concert hall. And thereby they often make their own task infinitely harder. So often the orchestra is faced with pages of heavily scored music, with hundreds of semi-quavers chasing each other from bar to bar (pages of subtlety and genius, of invention and counterpoint) when the composer has been clearly told that there is a long intimate dialogue sequence on the accompanying track. Naturally, the final result is a mess, a mess of undistinguished, indistinguishable scratchings which do not help the film, and which certainly harm the composer. All that is necessary is very probably a simple tune on the 'cellos, or an easy melody on a clarinet. Perhaps many new composers fall into the trap because they fear they may not be giving the producer his money's worth. They write the simple tune, and then, on second thoughts, ruin it by over-embellishment. If there is time at the recording session, line by line these unwanted frills will come out, and a depressed and weary composer will see nights of over-zealous toil thrown away. He is fortunate if there is time to do this. If there is not, he will write less film music in future.

During recent years a somewhat different philosophy has crept into recording studios—particularly those which cater for the pop market. As magnetic recorders have developed from the conventional 6.25 mm. width of tape to 12.5 mm., 25 mm., and now 50 mm. widths, the number of parallel tracks which can be accommodated has risen to 24 and even 32. By using a great number of microphones a high degree of separation between instruments can be obtained, so that an ultimate balance can be achieved, after the band has left the studio, which satisfies the most demanding of tastes. Not only that, by recording on some tracks, and using these tracks for synchronous playback, the same players can overdub onto their own performances. This technique has been applied more generally to the record industry than to that of motion pictures, but these two worlds are drawing closer, and a film recording studio which cannot offer its clients at least a sixteen track recorder is likely to find things embarrassing.

This multi-track system naturally involves a more sophisticated form of control desk—a very costly item. A further problem is that the inherent noise of the magnetic track—low as it is compared with optical recording—nevertheless multiplies in direct proportion to the number of tracks used. If steps were not taken to combat this the end result might probably be inferior to that of the bad old days. But a remedy is usually developed for every ailment and at least one skilfully designed noise reduction system is now in general use. But still at great cost.

There are sound engineers alive today who sometimes feel that things are getting slightly out of hand. The sight of a multi-microphone set-up of upwards of nine microphones for a single drum kit for example is apt to make them wonder where it will all end. But the sound engineers cannot deny that the modern pop groups, skilfully recorded on many tracks, and even more skilfully reduced to a final stereo record, can produce a most exciting sound.

Further developments in technology will undoubtedly come. Twenty years ago who could have envisaged video tape? Who ten years ago envisaged video disc? These both are only ways of extending the high frequency recording ceiling even higher. The modern high quality condenser microphone is considerably smaller than it used to be; and can be made vastly more directional and therefore selective. What will happen next? Certainly sound recording is going through dramatic changes. The modest amateur cassette has now become a highly professional piece of equipment. The long playing disc can produce magnificent results, although one wonders for how long people will endure its bulk and fragility in the face of its magnetic competitors.

All this will force the cinema to raise its standards—for a start magnetic single track could be universally used. Alternatively, universal use of Dr. Ray Dolby's method of improving frequency range, signal to noise ratio, and distribution factor of the normal optical track could be brought into universal use. These changes will cost money, but if the cinema is to continue in a viable form, then its sound reproduction must at least compare with the type of sound which is common in most people's homes.

5

THE COMPOSER'S VIEW

I believe that film music is capable of becoming, and to a certain extent already is, a fine art, but it is applied art, and a specialized art at that.—Dr. R. Vaughan Williams, 1944. (*Royal College of Music Magazine*)

DR. VAUGHAN WILLIAMS could be said to represent the traditional composer's approach to the new branch of his art. He composed his first film score at the age of 69 for *49th Parallel*. He regards film composing as "a splendid discipline"; he considers the film as a great medium: "I still believe that the film contains potentialities for the combination of all the arts such as Wagner never dreamed of." On the other hand he also writes of film music:

Its form must depend on the form of the drama, so the composer must be prepared to write music which is capable of almost unlimited extension or compression; it must be able to "fade-out" and "fade-in" again without loss of continuity. A composer must be prepared to face losing his head or his tail or even his inside without demur, and must be prepared to make a workmanlike job of it; in fact, he must shape his ends in spite of the producer's rough hewings.

The late Sir Arnold Bax, who composed music for films, including the documentary *Malta G.C.* and the feature *Oliver Twist*, wrote despairingly:

I do not think the medium is at present at all satisfactory as far as the composer is concerned, as his music is largely inaudible, toned down to make way for—in many cases—quite unnecessary talk. This is, in my opinion, quite needless as it is possible to pay attention to two things at the same time if they appeal to different parts of the intelligence.

It is part of the purpose of this book to establish some meeting-point for the film-maker and the composer. Bax writes of film music which is incorrectly adjusted to its purpose, music which is treated as a noise to be faded up and down at the will of the film-maker. Dr. Vaughan Williams seems to mind this treatment less, indeed he anticipates it. But in a situation such as this either the film-maker is squandering the talent of great composers, or the composers themselves have not understood fully the nature of film music. It is, indeed, a situation quite different from that described by Paul Rotha, writing as a film-maker who has always realized the importance of the composer's work in his films, and used music so skilfully in his own films:

The old idea that music must fulfil the function of an undercurrent to the picture, just quiet enough to prevent distraction from the screen, being faded down when the commentator speaks, and faded up again when he has finished, this is as antiquated as the type of film for which it is still used. Modern music for sound film must be an integral part of the sound script, must on occasions be allowed to dominate the picture, must on others perform merely an atmospheric function and frequently it must be intermixed with natural sound and speech.[1]

The essence of agreement between film-maker and composer is that each should respect the nature of the other's art in order to secure the best possible result from the combination. Both, of course, will readily agree that this is so. But there is always the problem of the film-maker who wants to use music but lacks any real understanding of it, and the composer who is quite prepared to write music for films but has little or no fondness for or understanding of them.

The meeting-point between film-maker and composer is first of all a mutual recognition of the quality of each other's art, and a genuine attempt to try to understand it. The composer who does not like or respect films should quite simply not work for them. The film-maker who only wants a musical prop to gloss up the emotions of his picture should not expect a composer of imagination to produce music for him to turn on or off at will. The best results come obviously from mutual understanding. The composer must learn, as Dr. Vaughan Williams was willing to learn, the new discipline of composition for films. The film-maker must learn that music can be one of the greatest dramatic assets his picture can acquire, provided he is prepared to draw on the musical imagination of the composer, and create the right conditions for him to give his best services to the film as a film.

Most composers of distinction who have worked for films recognize the importance of the composer becoming a member of the creative team of film-makers. For the purpose of this book, several composers have given us their views on this point. We quote a number of them; most agree fully, a few less whole-heartedly than the rest.

[1]"Documentary Film", edit. 1952, p. 168.

David Raksin: It is always important to me to know what part the writer, director and producer expect music to play in their film. By the time I am assigned to it, they have usually been at work for several months, and have already developed attitudes toward the film that I must know about, if only to bring my own thoughts into focus. If we agree on the role of the music, such discussions are useful to all of us. If we do not, it is better to settle beforehand whether I ought to do the picture at all. And when the qualities of talent and insight are missing from these discussions, the nuisance can hardly be condoned as necessary.

Hugo Friedhofer: A composer assumes that he has been selected to score a film because the producer and director have complete confidence in his professional knowledge, experience and skill. Personally, it has always been my practice, once the general plan of the score has been formulated, to have a final conference with the producer and director, for the purpose of outlining (to the best of my ability) the style and format of the score, the sections which I feel should or should not have music, etc., thereby precluding the possibility of any unpleasant surprises on the recording stage. I believe that any composer who comes to the film hoping to find therein a vehicle for complete self-expression, is doomed to disappointment. The end product, the perfectly integrated whole, is the supremely important thing.

Roman Vlad: The real creator of a film, in my opinion, is the director; I always try to compose the music which he would were he a composer. This is why I consider myself an "artisan" when I undertake to compose music for films, by trying to forget my own internal world and identifying myself with that portrayed by the film. I therefore try to compose the music for that particular film, and not to impose my own film on it . . . I feel that collaboration with the director is indispensable, if one is dealing with a director who knows what he wants and who will leave the seal of his own personality on the film. When this is not the case, then it is preferable to be left free to compose without having to bear in mind anyone's suggestions. As I have said, I always try to "depersonify" myself, because a film is for me a matter of teamwork between technicians and artisans (if not always of artists). But naturally the "personal" element cannot be eliminated; it is important therefore that the team should be chosen beforehand in order to ensure the best possible harmony between the various personalities involved.

Max Steiner: The composer is definitely a member of a team, and any time a screen composer wants to be a "star" of a picture, his music is bound to fail. I have always tried to submerge myself.

Virgil Thomson: The spectacle with music must be a collaboration . . . Each technician must use his own technical imagination, but they must work for a common end and under the leadership of the director.

Miklos Rozsa: I do believe that film music is an integral part of a collective effort of many artists and technicians. The composer who refuses to co-ordinate his music to the requirements of this collectivity, refuses to serve the drama with his music and should therefore stay away from films.

Bernard Herrmann: Music is called upon to supplement what the technicians may have done, and mostly, what they've been unable to do.

William Alwyn: The composer should always realize that although, as a creative artist in his own right, he owes it to himself to write music which will

221

satisfy his own standards of criticism, it will be criticized ultimately purely on its relationship to the picture; he must be prepared, therefore, to work as a member of a group of technicians, each acting independently, but all with the same object in mind.

Malcolm Arnold claims that film music can only be regarded as a branch of the art of music when it is fully integrated to film, as it must also be in the case of opera or ballet. It then fulfils a true function, and is a form of artistic expression. Otherwise it is a hybrid form of applied art, which is no art at all.

The composers were next asked whether they found any opportunity for experiment or independent thinking in writing their film scores, and how far they felt themselves either restricted or stimulated by the producer's and director's views on how they should carry out their task. The answers were frank and to the point.

David Raksin: I always find opportunity for creative experiment and independent thinking in writing a film score. Many films present in themselves challenges that arouse the composer. And when it becomes necessary, as it must to every film composer, to cope with a movie that does not provide emotional or intellectual incentive, I undertake to provide these for myself. I may employ an odd combination of instruments, or a special approach to the picture's requirements; finding, for instance, the Great Plague of London photographed as an untidy interlude between untidier bed-chambers, I may elect to play it as the great affliction it really was. I may experiment with musical forms and devices; in one score I had enough cannons to start a minor Balkan uprising; in another I used a twelve-tone row whose first five notes spelled out the name of the picture's hero, which was not otherwise revealed until the last few seconds of the last reel. (When the studio's music executive asked what prompted me to choose so hazardous a course, I replied that it was in hope that the studio's top man would come charging out of the theatre after the preview crying, "Fire that saboteur, he gave away the secret of the picture in the main title!")

William Alwyn: A composer should always experiment, and any piece of music he is writing (whether it be symphony or opera, ballet or film) if he is absorbed in his work it will stimulate something, or some part of something, which has at least the symptoms of novelty. A film score can be experimental as a whole (on the rare occasions when the subject demands and the director is willing), but more usually it should give some small opportunity for new thinking and novelty in expression.

Dag Wiren: I very much prefer the following way of collaboration between the director and the composer. The director says when he wants music and what he wants it to express. Then the director and the composer discuss things each from their own point of view. The worst sort of collaboration is when the director leaves everything to the composer and then, when the music is recorded, changes everything and makes some sort of jigsaw puzzle with the music.

He adds that film music "gives one special possibilities to make experiments in orchestration".

222

Bernard Herrmann: Men such as Zanuck, Welles and Hitchcock have very stimulating ideas about the musician's responsibility and importance . . . The greatest inducement to compose for pictures, outside of the financial one, is the opportunity to experiment.

The majority of the composers questioned said that the film-makers, once it had been decided where music was required in a production, left them free to get on with their work without interference. Miklos Rozsa says of directors who know nothing about music: "If they are intelligent enough they know that their biggest contribution is to leave the composer alone." It became obvious that directors vary very greatly in their appreciation of music, and several composers said how glad they were to have worked with particular directors who had brought a real understanding of the contribution music could make to their films. As Aaron Copland put it to us, a director need not know music in the technical sense, but he must know what he wants from it dramatically. The scope for experiment is, in general, more restricted in the feature than in the documentary field.

Composers vary in their opinion as to the best time for their introduction to a film. Some prefer to get into the picture as early as possible.

Hugo Friedhofer: It is my conviction that far better integration could be achieved were it possible for the writer, director, cinematographer and composer to confer before ever one foot of film was exposed. There is still a tendency on the part of most film-makers to regard film music as being something which is, at the best, a crutch for weak scenes, and at the worst (for reasons not quite clearly determined) a somehow necessary and costly sound effect.

Roman Vlad: Methods vary from film to film. In really important ones, where the music plays more than a marginal part, work with the director, discussion regarding the style of the music, and the development of ideas proceed step by step with the shooting of the film. The real and definite work of the composer begins only when the editing is finished.

R. Vaughan Williams: I usually think of most of the music directly I get the script. I do not wait for the photography. I know this is wrong, but I can't help it.

David Raksin: If possible, I prefer to begin preliminary work in the script-writing stage, when musical considerations can still influence the shooting of the film. Usually, however, the composer is not called in until the rough-cut is ready for viewing. Having seen the film, I then discuss the musical aspects with the director, producer, and others concerned. Depending upon the film itself and upon those involved in the conferences, discussions may range from practical matters such as schedules and budgets to specific determination of placement of music, style, and the point of view that the music will assume toward the picture itself.

By the time my "breakdowns" have been prepared by the music cutter, I have usually come to some decisions on the nature and overall plan of the score which, in turn, affect and are affected by the thematic material I am writing. The character or range of a theme, for instance, may determine the colour of the orchestra, or conversely, the desired colour may determine certain characteristics of the material. Sometimes, when time for planning is not to be had, or when ideas have not had time to jell, I begin with what material I have, and write straight through the film, depending upon the necessary ideas to appear when I need them, and the structure of the score to evolve as I compose and as the interaction of music and film makes itself felt.

When identification with the subject of the film is necessary—and possible— in order to achieve the desired result, I try to identify. It is probably true that a capable professional should always be able to manufacture musical sounds appropriate to requirements. But ersatz emotion is much harder to disguise than real music is to write; besides, it is easier on one's conscience to be compassionate, for instance, than to simulate compassion, and consequently more practical. Style, period and content of the script and acting are the major factors which determine the style, period and content—therefore the sound—of the music through the kind of thematic material, development, instrumentation, style of playing, recording and re-recording characteristics deemed appropriate.

William Alwyn: I like to read the script and discuss the subject with the director and generally identify myself with the film at its inception. The main stimulus for the actual composition comes later at the first viewing of the "rough-cut". The dramatic impulse should be fresh and the inspiration come from *seeing* the film. Film music is visual music.

Aaron Copland said that he prefers to start thinking about the music for a film after reading the script, but other composers, such as Malcolm Arnold, prefer not to build up preconceptions of the film from the script, but to meet it for the first time in the rough-cut form as fully-realized drama. Arnold likes to wait even for the credit titles. Then he writes the score for the whole film straight through from beginning to end as a continuous piece of music. By this means he keeps its unity and sustains its development.

. David Raksin's interesting examination of his approach to the composition of music for a particular film also raised the important issue of how far the composer should attempt to identify himself with his subject. There was some difference of opinion here.

Hugo Friedhofer: I find that style, period and content are all powerful determinants. I do not mean by this that a completely eclectic attitude is indicated, or that it is necessary to compose music for a film dealing with the Crusades in an idiom lying somewhere on the far side of organum, and utilizing an orchestra consisting of nothing more recent than shawms, rebecs and citoles, with a choir of primitive and rather nasty sounding brass instruments thrown in for good measure. Let me say, rather, that I believe it is the business of the composer to determine exactly which aspect or facet of his personal idiom is best suited to the particular problem confronting him, to eschew any element which might possibly conflict with the style or mood of the film, and to write (within the limits of this self-imposed discipline) according to the dictates of his musical conscience.

224

Max Steiner: There is no general method as far as I am concerned. To me every picture presents a new and different problem. Some pictures require a lot of music and some of them are so realistic that music would only hurt and interfere. That of course is the most difficult phase of composing for the screen; not knowing where and when to place the music.

Elisabeth Lutyens: I like to feel first of all "audience reaction"—where one thinks, *seeing* the film silent, one is wanting or missing sound and why—and to supply it. It is the film itself that dictates or suggests the music, together with the orchestration—the two go together . . . The only film scores of mine or anyone else's, that I feel to be satisfactory are those that are the most completely identified and integrated with the film as a whole.

Virgil Thomson: I lay it out in "sequences". Then compose the music. Then play it on a piano with the silent film for the director. This is like a fitting at a tailor's. When it fits the mood of each sequence, I orchestrate. Then record. Then the director sometimes re-cuts the film a little. And we make the "mix".

William Alwyn: Every film needs a fresh approach. Unless one identifies oneself with the subject it will not be good music.

Dag Wiren: I just begin at the beginning and go on to the end. On the way certain themes emerge which may be used as leitmotifs though their character changes. I very much identify myself with the subject of the film and I try to give every separate film its own musical style.

Aaron Copland, like Roman Vlad, claims that particular composers should be cast for particular films, according to their known interests and styles of composition. He complains that in Hollywood the professional composer of film music has to create too widely, producing scores for any and every kind of film. Copland prefers to write only for the kind of film which suits him as a composer—such as *Of Mice and Men* and *Our Town*. Malcolm Arnold also says that the composer should turn down work for a film if he does not feel its subject to be within his range.

We asked composers to comment on the size and constitution of the orchestra which they considered ideal for film work. First of all conditions vary in the studios themselves; in some, where there is a full symphony orchestra of forty or more players under contract, the composer is normally expected to write for this combination of players. In other cases the composer is free to recommend a more varied, and probably a much smaller, combination. Different films obviously require different styles of music and groups of instruments, and the composer will also find that the production budget may restrict him. This can work two ways; the studio used to lavish conditions may not think it good for its prestige to use a small orchestra, whereas a documentary unit may be forced through sheer lack of money to ask the composer to work within a strictly limited framework.

225

Most composers, as we expected, wanted freedom of choice in this matter according to the nature of the film on which they were working and the style in which they had conceived their scores.

David Raksin: I have used all kinds of groups to suit the occasion and, sometimes, to accommodate the budget. In *The Man With a Cloak*, I composed most of the score for flute, oboe, clarinet, bass clarinet, bassoon, contra-bassoon, horn, trumpet, trombone, one percussion, harp, and solo viola d'amore. What I wanted was a dark and reticent colour. Budget was one of the problems in *Apache*; a lot of music, not very much money. About two-thirds of the score was composed for an orchestra of two flutes, oboe, English horn, two clarinets and bass clarinet, bassoon and contra-bassoon, one to four horns, one to three trumpets, three trombones, tuba, two percussion, piano, six violas, four 'celli, two basses and a tenor recorder. Big scenes of violence and bitterness for the most part, with one or two quiet moments; timbres that varied from dark to clamorous.

It is an industry practice to cut down the size of the orchestra during the period of recording, as the requirements of the individual picture diminish, so that the figures quoted here are usually for the largest group employed in a given film. Variants of the "symphony orchestra" were used in *Laura* (44), in *Force of Evil* (48), in *Forever Amber* (76), in *Carrie* (60), in *The Bad and The Beautiful* (47), among others. In *Suddenly*, the largest orchestra consisted of four horns, two percussion and thirty-two strings, with several sequences for strings only. In a recent film, *The Big Combo* (the title refers to a criminal syndicate), about one quarter of the score was written for a "standard" orchestra of forty; half for a brass orchestra of four trumpets, four trombones, one horn, and tuba, with sometimes an added percussion player, or a wood-wind or string soloist against the brass colour; the remaining quarter, including the main title, is scored for big jazz band: soprano saxophone, alto saxophone, tenor saxophone, baritone saxophone, bass saxophone, four trumpets (who are sometimes called upon to play in the extreme high register: written G and A, an octave above the staff), four trombones, tuba, one or two percussion, piano, amplified guitar, and string bass. Use of special combinations is, as I have indicated, primarily influenced by the requirements of the film itself, but a limited budget may also result in a search for a way of accomplishing with limited means the wishes of the composer and his colleagues. The spur of such necessity is all to the good.

One thing I find particularly stimulating in my work is knowing in advance who among our local virtuosi will play the music. High salaries paid in the Hollywood film industry have brought some of the world's greatest performers here, and I sometimes wonder if we are not a little spoiled by the technique, sight-reading and musicianship of our fine orchestras.

Such high-calibre artistry is especially gratifying in cartoon work, where demands are very great and ensembles very small—and really the most fun to work with. In *Madeline* (UPA), I used flute, oboe, clarinet, bassoon, violin, viola, 'cello and harp. In *Sloppy Jalopy* (UPA), a zany cartoon, I used flute, clarinet, bass saxophone, trumpet, trombone, piano, and one percussion. In *The Unicorn in the Garden* (my favourite, a Thurber story done by UPA), I used violin, viola, 'cello, harpsichord, clarinet doubling alto recorder, and soprano saxophone doubling bass clarinet. It is really too bad that the plush sound of a large orchestra is what most producers find indispensable; as matters now stand, it is still rather a risky business to score a big film with a small ensemble.

226

Bernard Herrmann: It depends entirely upon the picture, its scope, subject material and musical approach. I prefer to arrive at my own orchestral combination for each picture. I feel it is a great mistake to use the symphonic orchestra, as such.

Max Steiner: Too large an orchestra is cumbersome and too small an orchestra is ineffective for dramatic success. I employ on an average fifty musicians; sometimes more and sometimes less, depending on the requirements of the picture. There is no hard and fast rule.

Dag Wiren: Everything depends on the film. For some scenes I use only one or a few instruments, for others a symphony orchestra.

Miklos Rozsa: As MGM studios have an orchestra of fifty men under yearly contract, this is the basic orchestra that I am working with. I would always prefer a normal symphony orchestra, as this is a perfectly balanced instrument, but for economic reasons this is seldom obtainable at the studios. Of course there is room for experimentations with small groups for pictures where one instrument, be it a zither, harmonica or an accordion, creates more mood than a full symphony orchestra would. Again, it depends on the subject and mood of the picture and one cannot generalize, as one aulos could hardly have been enough for the scoring of *Quo Vadis?*, for instance.

Some other composers, in particular William Alwyn and Malcolm Arnold, say that they welcome the chance to use for maximum dramatic effect very small and unusual combinations of instruments. Arnold used only fourteen players for *I Am a Camera*, twelve for *The Belles of Saint Trinians*, and twenty-five for *Hobson's Choice*. Roman Vlad, while admitting that the use of the normal symphony orchestra, with special scoring suitable to the recording process, may be necessary for some films, claims that he prefers to use a chamber music orchestra for what he calls "phonogenic" reasons—in his view it quite simply records better ("the possibilities of obtaining a clearer sound are superior"). On the other hand Vaughan Williams, Hugo Friedhofer, Virgil Thomson and Aaron Copland prefer normally to use a symphony orchestra. None the less, Virgil Thomson agrees that it can be very satisfactory artistically to experiment with small combinations of players, but adds "the small combination lacks variety and breadth for a long film". Aaron Copland is also interested in the potentialities of electronic instruments and musique concrète.

This problem of the effectiveness of large orchestras on the soundtrack has now been modified by the introduction of the multiple track systems of recording. Stereophonic sound means a complete revision of scoring to take advantage of two or more entirely separate channels of sound working on the ears of the audience instead of an amalgamation of dubbed tracks issuing from a single source. A musical theme, for example, can be developed on one track while the dialogue is restricted to another. A spatial sense can be developed with music anticipating action coming, say, from a speaker on the left while the current action is confined aurally to a speaker on the right. The composer, in fact, can think in terms of the balance of effects from a variety of sources and positions instead of the balance of effects re-recorded together and issuing from a single source.

Composers vary considerably in their views about the way in which they should allow for the dialogue (which normally they know in advance of composition) and the sound effects (which may not in fact have been dubbed on to the dialogue track at the time they view the film). There can be, therefore, only too easily a hiatus between the dramatic conception of the composer in purely musical terms and the dramatic effect aimed at by the recordist when it comes to the final dubbing. Sound effects may break into musical effects, and instead of a finely balanced combination of dialogue, effects and music sharing in the achievement of a single dramatic impact, a purely technical compromise may rob a scene of its essential drama either by throwing away what has in fact been individually achieved by the various members of the production team or by insufficient liaison between the composer and the sound effects department in the first place. One composer complains bitterly:

There is no co-operation at all. The sound effects department's job is to supply all necessary effects, the more the merrier, the louder the better. At this stage no one thinks of the music. Later, in the dubbing room, some effects might be taken out for the music's sake, but as a rule the "reality" always triumphs over the irrational dimension of the music. The final sound-track should be a joint effort of a joint planning, before the picture is made. However, this is never the case. The writer writes the script, the effects man puts in the effects, and what is left over (or missed) on the sound-track, the composer fills in with his music. A co-ordination should start at the early stages when the photo-play is being conceived and written.

Some composers experienced in the team-work of film-making insist on establishing this liaison themselves; others seem to have little influence over the manner in which their music will be handled at the dubbing stage.

David Raksin: One must always cope with dialogue if the music is not to suffer too greatly in dubbing. I always work as closely as possible with the technical men, even to suggesting to the dialogue recorder on the set that a sequence which is eventually to have music ought to be recorded at a "hotter", more resonant level and characteristic than usual; good directors will co-operate in this—others may consider it an intolerable imposition.

When there is time, I plan my music with complete knowledge of what the sound effects cutter is preparing, and try to have a clear understanding among all concerned as to which component has the solo part on the sound-track. The music-recording mixer is apprised of the kind of pickup, balance and resonance desired, and of the "competition" on the dialogue and effects tracks, and I always work very closely with the re-recording mixers.

Still I feel that insufficient care is taken to integrate the sound-track, and too often music has a place so far below the salt that it is of no use to the film. In the picture *Carrie*, there were dialogue problems so severe that had they remained unsolved the effectiveness of the music would have been considerably limited. Fortunately, this film had a special director of the sound-track who was a technician with a musical background, and together we solved almost all of the problems, so that the music was able to carry its part of the emotional burden of the story.

Hugo Friedhofer: I feel that the composer should regard the visual element as a cantus firmus accompanied by two counterpoints, i.e., dialogue and sound effects. It is his problem to invent a third counterpoint which will complement the texture already in existence.

William Alwyn: The ultimate aim of a film composer should be to obtain a perfectly integrated sound-track in which dialogue, sound effects and music all play their appropriate part. This is rarely, perhaps never, achieved. Music is usually written after everything else has been completed, and although I can take every care to allow for the dialogue in the composition, I cannot always allow for the sound effects which are pre-conceived but dubbed on after the music has been recorded. I should welcome a much closer co-ordination with the effects department, as my most satisfactory scores have nearly always matured when this close and intelligent co-operation has existed (e.g., in *Odd Man Out*). The most disastrous results obtain when the composer and the sound editor, working independently, have the same effect in view; one negatives the other.

Roman Vlad: With the maximum care, in order to avoid troublesome overlapping. (Unfortunately "good intentions" often fail because of last-minute changes made by the director in the dialogue, which is sometimes cut, added to or modified at the last moment.) Sound effects are often necessary and amusing, but I prefer to do without them and keep the score itself purely expressive. Sound effects in themselves can often destroy this.

Max Steiner (who has composed over 300 film scores in Hollywood since 1930): In my entire career, I was only consulted by the scriptwriter about music prior to the finished product once, and that was for *The Informer*. We all won the Academy Award on that picture.

Elisabeth Lutyens: Dialogue, commentary, music and sound effects should all work together. It is ideal—though not always done—to work in closest co-operation with the sound effects department. I do not think sufficient care is taken by the composer, scriptwriter and the effects department to obtain a properly integrated sound-track—more's the pity; music and dialogue often compete uncomfortably to the detriment of both. I think these considerations should be discussed and borne in mind from the beginning, not left to the dubbing session to make the best of several bad jobs. This is not always the composer's fault, but the music is left so late, and everything is rushed after the music session for the film to be ready on a dead line.

Miklos Rozsa: The lighter the orchestration and the texture of the music for a dialogue scene, the more one would hear of it after the dubbing. It is absolutely no use to write involved counterpoint, fast figurations, heavy brass orchestrations or highly pitched sounds for such scenes. The dialogue is always considered sacrosanct and is naturally featured. The more involved the accompanying music is, the lower will it go in the dubbing, and therefore the more one loses of it. Music for dialogue therefore, should be sustained, more homophonic than polyphonic, not much higher than the third position of the violins and, if dramatically possible, void of all heavy and open brass.

Sound effects also should be taken into consideration, although the problem is not quite as delicate as with the dialogue. If there is too much noise going on on the sound-track, the music again fares best if it is not too involved. In a battle scene, I once wrote a fugato and the result was that the contrapuntal lines were completely swallowed up by the battle noises and one heard nothing of my brilliant counterpoint! A simpler, chordal music with a heavy brass instrumentation would have cut through, and served the purpose considerably better.

Aaron Copland goes so far as to compose actually with the film itself, instead of relying merely on his memory and a cue sheet. He works with a piano while the film is projected and re-projected, section by section.

Finally, it is interesting to learn from composers why they undertake composing for films at all. This raises the issue of professionalism, and takes us back to the statements made by Norman O'Neill and Bernard Shaw at the beginning of this book. Composers, like painters and writers, can be individualist artists, following the vein of their inspiration and creating only for performance in the concert hall. Or they can be artisans in the true meaning of the word, working for the theatre, for ballet, opera, radio, television and the cinema. If their command of their medium is a professional one, they will fulfil this "applied" function of their art with distinction, and not in any sense as hacks. They will enjoy this exercise of their profession because it offers them a challenge in musical expression. Some may even prefer to earn a regular income in this way, as others earn an income as teachers, conductors or critics.

David Raksin expressed this point of view to us with clarity and frankness:

As a composer, I consider myself fortunate to be able to make a living at something I would be doing whether I could make a living at it or not. I have sometimes wondered if it might not be wiser to do something completely different as a profession, and keep my music apart from all considerations except its own. But while I might prove proficient, and even successful at another occupation, I cannot see the point of spending even a part of my working life in exile, when my present profession provides me with the opportunity to live immersed in music and the other arts, and rewards me with the freedom to enjoy and assimilate them. Assignments which afford pleasure and fulfilment to the film composer are few and far between, but no more so than in the best of other jobs; here, at least, I am writing music and conducting it, as a working musician should—but all too rarely does.

Many other composers wrote similarly.

Only a minority of great composers can gain a livelihood today by composing entirely for the concert hall; nor have they been able to do so in the past without the financial help of a patron, unless they had private means. A composer may be tempted by the fee offered him to accept a music contract for a film, but unless he can bring to his work a professional enjoyment in the exercise of his talent, he cannot hope to be successful.

Roman Vlad adds another important point. He wrote to us:

> I compose music for films not only for amusement and financial reasons, but also because I feel that composers of "serious music" should not completely desert such an important field for the determination of the taste of so vast a public as that made up of cinemagoers. This public must not be abandoned to the exclusive dominion of professional film music composers and corrupters of the kind catering for the lowest desires of the audience, who (in the case of cinemagoers) are also the hearers, even though they are not always conscious of the fact. There is, therefore, an additional cultural reason which urges me not to abandon composition for the cinema, even though by doing so I feel more of an "artisan" than an "artist".

Sir Arthur Bliss, who composed one of the very first important scores for a British feature film (*Things to Come*, 1935), gives his opinion on most of the problems discussed in this section in a statement made specially for this book:

> I came to my first assignment (to write music for the films) with all the excitement and pleasure that contact with an entirely new medium brings. That was in 1935; the film was *Things to Come*, and the invitation to collaborate came from H. G. Wells and Sir Alexander Korda.
>
> Later, it was interest in some particular film that finally persuaded me to write the music. A conspicuous instance was the film *Men of Two Worlds*—I admired Thorold Dickinson's direction; the photography was beautiful; the story of the coloured West African pianist and composer appealed to me.
>
> There have also been at least two films where the pull was distinctly a financial one. So I suppose a graph would show a downward slope: enthusiasm and curiosity for the new thing—admiration for a particular picture—greed.
>
> I soon found out that music in the final synthesis took a very humble position. In opera its influence is paramount and all pervasive, in ballet it is, at least, of equal importance with the choreography and the décor, but in the films it is subservient, and at the first sign of opposition disappears out of hearing.
>
> Sometimes it is the invisible producer who exerts the restricting influence, concerned as he must be with what the lowest common denominator (the paying multitude) would like.
>
> Often too the director of the picture is too unmusical to imagine how greatly music could enhance and sometimes even save sections of his film.
>
> I have had unforgettable experiences with one director who, where music was concerned, was a certifiable lunatic, and I had to discontinue collaboration. On the other hand there are many others who instinctively understand the value of a musical score, though untrained themselves. They leave a composer free; and so work with them becomes pleasurable and worth while.
>
> Before I decide to write the music, I like to see as many of the early "rushes" as I can. I want to be brought in at an early stage, and have an opportunity for

round table talks with the others concerned. I like to feel I am sure about the "general treatment" before I start my score.

Heaven help me from having a director who works by "inspiration" and who changes his mind every time he hears of some success or some novelty elsewhere, and who switches from a tragic to a comic treatment as nonchalantly as if he were stepping out of his bath!

I like a full three months to prepare my score. I am told many composers today have their own orchestrator at the end of the telephone line. I am sure the most original composers do not; for on the films it is often the actual texture of sound made that is the important factor, and only the composer himself can manipulate this.

Abetted by directors who once thought that the bigger the orchestra the better the film, I started by using a full symphony orchestra. I soon found out my mistake. Indeed, the smaller the number of players, the better is the recording and the greater the variety of tone colour obtained. I now prefer a picked band of soloists, with which sounds can be fabricated in the most effective way for the film. I believe that the composer should not think of either concert hall or opera house in determining these.

Today you find yourself more and more in healthy competition with the sound effects technicians. I do not know whether they have already taken over musique concrète—if so, this determined and resourceful department is a threat to music's own independence.

I do not seriously think we are in danger, as pure musical sound will always have a wide importance on the films. It is powerfully expressive. It can bring nostalgia to a landscape, drama to any hour of day or night; it can express undercurrents of human emotion, when the actors involved show little of it outwardly. It can suggest what is going to happen, it can recall what has happened; most important of all, perhaps, it can make what has turned dead and dull in a picture come alive and exciting.

And yet, music must not obstinately obtrude, as at any time it can. Someone said that the best film music is that which is not consciously heard at all. There is a truth in the paradox. The music should do its work so smoothly and perfectly that it is only when you see the same picture run through in the studio without it, that you realize its irreplaceable importance.

Commenting on Bliss' statement that "many composers today have their own orchestrator at the end of the telephone line" John Addison says:

I wrote all my own orchestrations until *Torn Curtain* in 1966. Since then, when using an orchestrator, I write my "sketches" up to 7 or 8 staves, showing what every instrument is doing. Half my score for *Sleuth* was done this way and half without an orchestrator. I doubt that anyone can distinguish the method used for any particular cue. The only difference is in the saving of time.

Composers readily admit their delight in earning good money for composition, just as writers and other professional people are proud that their talents are well rewarded. But, as in the practice of all the arts, it is the composer's personal pride in the quality of the work he can achieve in films which makes him delight in it. Dr. Vaughan Williams is evidently right when he refers to the challenge the film offers to the imagination and craftsman's skill of the composer. Too many composers who are eminent in their profession have returned again and again to film work for there to be any doubt at all in our minds that composition for films is a branch of the art of music. As Muir Mathieson has put it:

All that remains is for it to be unreservedly recognized that music, having a form of its own, has ways of doing its appointed task in films with distinction, judged purely as music, and with subtlety, judged as a part of a whole film. It must be accepted not as a decoration or a filler of gaps in the plaster, but as a part of the architecture.

Further Points of View

The problems and difficulties of composing music for films are manifold, but not in the production of the music itself. Probably the most critical problem is that of communication of the significant meaning and intention of the director to the composer, in that the form of communication is verbal, sometimes graphic. The 'meaning' of music is so infinitely precise that no words can exactly express this meaning. (Kenneth V. Jones)

IN this section the views of producers and directors plus those of composers have been included. As Kenneth V. Jones suggests there is need for the closest collaboration and understanding between composer, director and producer. In many student films the director *is* the composer as well, often using electronic means. The synthesiser enables those who are not trained musicians to create their own sounds. Menotti, the composer, has produced and directed his own filmed opera *The Medium*. Pier Paolo Pasolini generally has a hand in the selection of the often highly controversial music for his films. The Indian director Satyajit Ray is perhaps the best example of the director who has turned to composing his own music. Ray explains the circumstances:

Before I started composing for my films I had worked with three famous concert virtuosi—the sitarists Ravi Shankar who composed for the *Apu Trilogy*, Vilayet Khan who composed for *The Music Room* and the sarodist Ali Akbar Khan who composed for *Devi*. None of the three had much experience writing for films, nor were they "composers" in the western sense. All three provided me with beautiful music, some of which I was able to use. The rest did not fit and had to be discarded.

Dissatisfied with this chancy procedure, I finally took to composing myself. That was in 1960. I was familiar with both Indian and Western classical systems, and in my music freely combined the two. I avoided counterpoint, being too exclusively a western concept, but made use of the notion of instrumental colour and key modulation, both unknown to the Indian system, and both intimately related to mood and atmosphere.

If the director is not himself composing the music it is the producer and director who have the prime responsibility for choosing the right music for the film, whether it is already written or whether it has to be especially composed. This raises the whole question of who chooses the composer for a film and what sort of "brief" the composer is given.

Norman Spenser, for many years on the production side of 20th Century-Fox suggests:

> With a talented director I think one should always decide with him on the music. It would be a sad day for a producer if he fell foul of the director at this stage in the film's production because the producer's wishes were carried out regardless of those of the director's. The opposite rarely takes place in the right set-up. The producer is ultimately responsible for the total film production and it is usually written into the contract with the director that there will be hopefully artistic agreement in all creative matters but in the event of a serious disagreement the producer's wishes shall prevail. Looking back at some films I do not know if this is a good thing or a bad thing.

The experienced British director Bryan Forbes suggests the type of brief he gives his composer. Forbes, like Fellini, who works regularly with Nino Rota, is a director who has developed a regular collaboration with a couple of composers. John Barry has worked for Forbes on five films.

> I ask the composer to give me music which will compliment the original emotion I have tried to put on the screen. I regard music as a very important additional ingredient which should never intrude between the audience and the image on the screen. Bad, crude "mood" music can distort totally and change what was hitherto a hard film. It can distort the director's original intentions.

Fellini believes that he cannot suggest the music he wants from Nino Rota because he is not a musician, but he does have a firm and clear idea of what he wants.

> Nino Rota sits down at the piano. I stand by his side and tell him exactly what I want. Naturally I do not dictate the themes to him. I can only guide him and tell him what it is I wish.

For many composers this near dictatorial method Fellini employs might be a nightmare. It does, however, manage to overcome the gulf that can often divide the composer from the director and producer. The problems lies, as Kenneth V. Jones suggests, in that communication is verbal. Ideally both the producer and director should have some form of musical knowledge. British director John Schlesinger is held by many composers in high regard for his knowledge of music. Ken Russell also is highly regarded by Peter Maxwell Davies. Russell is perhaps fortunate in that he had a training as a ballet dancer and this stood him in good stead for both communication with composers and also in filming his lives of the composers for television.

A producer or director with a specialized knowledge of music can say to his composer "your orchestration is too heavy for the delicacy of that shot". That will immediately communicate to the composer that either he is using too many instruments (therefore creating a muddy effect) or that this sonority, being too great, must be diminished in intensity from loud to soft. A very loud chord can be so intrusive as to make it impossible for the viewer to see delicate detail or even take in the image at all. A musically illiterate producer or director confronted with the same piece of music would probably say "There is something wrong with the music but I do not know what". The composer would not know exactly what he meant. By experience in dealing with layman's remarks he might be able to guess the problem. He might guess wrongly. A stylistic change might be made and the music remain at the same density, with the same weight and orchestrations. The producer or director would remain unhappy and frustrated. What he had wanted, without being able to express it, was a light score with the same style.

A very important element of film music, and often a grievance among composers for the screen, is when the composer is called in for discussions and commencement of work. Ken Russell contacted Peter Maxwell Davies a few months before shooting of *The Devils* began.

I do not think I had any influence on the shooting of the film. I certainly knew what was going on for I went to Pinewood Studios to watch them shoot. Ken Russell and I discussed as the filming was in progress the sort of music that was to go underneath the scenes. In that sense it was a sort of collaboration. I was not just presented with a final film and told to get on with composing music for it. I knew what I was in for right from the word go, and we discussed parts that would be better without music and parts that would be better with music.

For some parts of the film it was quite clear that music would have a large part to play, particularly the long visionary scenes in black and white which were pure fantasy and with very little dialogue at all. Again in the burning scene of Grandier at the end I knew that music would have to take over. There were some places where music was inappropriate, where the dialogue was clear and cold. In such scenes there was no need for any background at all.

I did not compose while they were shooting. I waited until it was all finished. I did sketch out some very basic raw material.

Producer Norman Spenser has this to say about the best time to call in the composer and the type of "brief" given to the composer.

The ideal time to call in the composer is when the script, the final script, is ready and before shooting starts. He can read the script and, talking with the producer and director, become acquainted with the basic theme and concept of the picture as a whole. From the script stage to the scoring is a period of around thirty or so weeks. This enables the composer to give the due amount of thought to the creation of the picture and also gives him time to write the music, have it orchestrated, and generally satisfy all concerned that the right musical approach is being adopted. I am afraid that all too often composers are called in at much shorter notice. Sometimes this is unavoidable. There are films in which balances and mood change from the script stage to the finished cut of the picture. This has to be taken into account. Sometimes problems obtrude to delay the time at which the composer can be engaged. This was the case in *Vanishing Point* when the musical director had four and a half weeks in which to write music, lyrics and record the entire music for the picture. Of course some composers work better under pressure but in my opinion the ideal is to sit down with the musician when the final script is ready and at least start his mind working in the right direction.

First the composer reads the script and talks to the producer and/or director. It is then that the general groundwork of the kind of music the film requires is laid down. Then he has to wait until the final cut of the picture when he views it with the producer and the editor. All the areas where music is required are noted. The editor then provides him with a list of the musical sections together with their finished length down to one third of a second. That is when the composer can really sit down to write. The general briefing varies, of course, with the film and the musical requirements. The important thing is for the producer, director and composer to have a meeting of minds on the kind of music required.

Bryan Forbes agrees with Norman Spenser:

Whenever the decisions have been within my overall control, I like to involve my composer at the script stage. I like him to come down to the set or location at frequent intervals during the shooting period and I try to show him key sequences as soon as they have been assembled.

There are many variations of approach. The music for a musical is all composed and often recorded before shooting takes place. With a film like Arthur Penn's *Alice Restaurant* the film was inspired by the words of an Arlo Guthrie song bearing the title "Alice's Restaurant Massacre". It was the lyrics of this song and the events about which Guthrie sings that inspired Penn to write the screenplay.

John Barry created a section of the music for Forbes' *Deadfall* before shooting. John Barry relates:

In *Deadfall* there was a sequence where a robbery is carried out in a house while the occupants are listening to a first performance of a guitar concerto at a hall in the neighbourhood. In this instance I composed a complete work which was recorded first, and the film was shot and edited to my timing. At some points the relaxed moments in the concerto were deliberately matched to contrastingly tense shots in the sequence, so that instead of merely underlying the action the music slightly characterized it. I found this very satisfying, but it is an unusual opportunity.

236

Whatever the role of the composer in forming even the shooting style or editing style of a scene, John Addison is convinced, as is Roman Vlad that "the real creator of a film in my opinion is the director." John Addison adds:

Some composers, especially of the Hollywood kind, evidently do not compose the music which the director would compose. I have heard some composers complain of "director's interference". How on earth can.a director "interfere" with his own film? He may know little of music technically, but he certainly knows what effect he wants it to have, and where. Moreover, he will recognize at once whether or not it is successful, when he hears it at a recording session. Getting inside the mind of a director is one of the most fascinating parts of the job. I always play the score to my director on the piano during the period of composition. This prevents misunderstandings or unpleasant surprises at the recording sessions. Any alterations or new ideas can be carried out in an atmosphere of mutual trust. Indeed, if the director gets a new idea at the recording sessions, suggested by hearing the music with the picture for the first time, it is a fascinating challenge to find a way of creating what he wants on the spur of the moment without wasting time or money.

It is very difficult to imagine in advance the exact effect of the final combination of dialogue tracks, effect tracks and music. Because of this, music cues may have to be lengthened or shortened or dropped, and sometimes music may be necessary where none has been written. For this reason I always attend dubbing, and I do not consider my collaboration with the director finished until the sound track is complete. Because I know my own score and the director's approach to the music better than anyone else, I can save time when making alterations with the editor.

Cocteau went too far in "re-shuffling" an entire score. This is quite unnecessary because music can be specifically composed to play against, or counterpoint, the picture. I also collaborate with the mixer on questions of balance. A music cue which does not at first appear to work in conjunction with the dialogue and effects may prove highly successful if the internal balance of the music is altered. For this reason it pays to reduce to triple-track rather than mono for dubbing.

Bryan Forbes tends to substantiate this idea that the director has the whole film mentally in his head.

As a generalisation I always know the type of music I have wanted on my films and very often during the editing stages I have laid-in music tracks just lifted from records to see whether they give me the effect I am after. This is particularly useful to the composer in arriving at the sound or instrument we are eventually going to use.

Sometimes I edit to music. It is impossible to be pedantic, but music does help in montage sequences and establishes a rhythm without which any film suffers. A great many otherwise excellent films are marred because they are badly paced in the editing.

The young Polish director Jerzy Skolimowski talks about his own musical abilities and attitudes towards music in a film, in particular

Le Départ which he directed and had music composed by Krzysztof Komeda:

As regards myself, I can only sing out of key but even a false note can inspire Komeda. *Le Départ* is a test case to how much music a film can take and we may have to use a great deal. In the future I intend to use less music in my films.

Skolimowski's intensions to use less music in films is gaining support from other directors. Robert Bresson and Luis Bunuel have virtually excluded music from their films save for the occassional piece under credit titles and music that grows out of the live action—for example where there is a band playing in a dance hall seen in picture then the music of the band will be heard just as one might hear the sound of a bird singing if a bird was in scene. Mike Leigh in his first feature film *Bleak Moments*, made in 1971, uses music which he claims "grows out of the action".

In *Bleak Moments* the main source of music is Norman in the garage. One of the central images in the film was Norman playing his very bad folk music. Although that was the original scheme there was a point during the editing of the film when Les Blair, the editor, and I thought about getting someone to compose extra music for us. We always knew we did not really want it. Because it was my first film there were a couple of times I wanted to experiment but I knew I did not really want music, incidental or background music.

The Hungarian director Miklós Jancsó has used no incidental music in his films since 1965. Strangely his films, without being in any way related to a musical, contain a great deal of music. All the music or songs in the films are performed live. Their presence in the film is tightly related to the plot and content of the scene. The words of the songs, as in Mike Leigh's film, have an important relationship with the events.

Mike Leigh points out a particularly important question in this context of songs in films. Does the audience see the words as expressing emotions and do they actually listen to the words and the meaning, and importance of them?

I wonder whether people listen to the words because they are conditioned not to do so. I have noticed that in the French subtitling for *Bleak Moments* the words of the songs are not translated because they are songs. In part the words are important because of their ironies. In the film we have Norman, from Scunthorpe, who has drifted down to London. He has been playing the guitar for only a short time. He finds himself in a very middle class house in south London. The songs he plays and sings are all about drug addicts, Greenwich Village and San Francisco—two places he definitely has not visited. All these things are important to the film and to Norman's character.

Another film where music in the film comes "out of the action" is *Vanishing Point* which was produced by Norman Spenser. It is what one might call in the "bike movie" genre of films—*Easy Rider, The Rain People* and *Zabriskie Point* are three other examples. A professional driver is challenged to make the distance between San Francisco and Denver in an incredible time. He speeds on his way pursued by the police and tuning into a radio station, Super Soul, the blind disc-jockey of the station spurs him on, dedicating records to him. There are scenes of Kowalski in his motor car listening to the radio station and scenes of Super Soul playing the records. Obviously music plays a particularly important role in this film even during the scripting stage. The producer of the film, Norman Spenser has this to say:

In *Vanishing Point* the plot required pop music to be coming from the loud-speaker in the car practically throughout the story. When we got down to details this worked out to the equivalent of eighteen different pop records being played by the K.O.W. Radio Station. Our musical director, Jimmy Bowen, solved this by requesting a screening of the final cut of the picture after shooting was finished to which we brought along some forty odd young pop musicians, composers and lyricists. This generated a flow of musical ideas and out of it finally emerged the eighteen songs and pieces required. Jimmy Bowen and I kept in constant touch throughout and he checked every section with me as he went along. The length of the separate pieces was not quite so critical as in a normal film since the beginning and end of any particular piece of music, and its length, was not tied up in quite such a detailed way with specific action. The basic "soul" type of pop music was generally used because we felt that in American terms this would be the kind of music played from such a radio station by a black disc-jockey. There was also the element of "protest" which would come from such a station and which, of course, was necessary for the theme of the picture.

It has already been mentioned that finance plays an important, perhaps ever increasingly important, role in film music. Sound track of films selling on record or tape help enormously to recoup large financial outlays. Even the choice of a big named composer could, like a film star, have a part to play in film music chosen. Norman Spenser has this to add:

The percentage of a budget that is spent on music varies enormously. On *Vanishing Point* we had a special financial arrangement in as much as the music as a whole was technically sub-contracted from the music director, and he, with his various writers and performers, retained a percentage of interest in the publishing rights and the soundtrack album rights. *Vanishing Point* cost $1.5 million to make and the total music cost worked out at around $50,000 (not counting the percentages). This sum was everything, fees, musicians, hire of recording studio and such like.

I am afraid that sometimes the so called "box office appeal" of a composer does enter into the choice of a composer but I personally doubt whether this kind of approach is really satisfactory. Bert Bacharach may have a big name but he might end up writing worse music for a certain kind of film than "John Smith". Names such as his can be added to the poster and publicity but in my opinion nothing succeeds so effectively as the choice of composer purely for the sake of getting the right dramatic result, and not for the smaller return of publicity from a known name.

Besides the introduction of a new range of sounds which the pop group with its electric guitars and drum kits provide, purely electronic music has become increasingly heard on sound tracks. Electronic music is often used in conjunction with conventional means of music making.

Conventional instrumental music can also be modified by a whole variety of devices. Satyajit Ray describes some of the methods and techniques that he employs and the reasons why he does so:

Whatever I have done has been done in the firm conviction that background music has no more than a functional role to perform, and whatever enhances the mood of a particular scene is valid no matter how it is achieved. This has led me to try out musical effects without the use of musical instruments, or with musical instruments whose timbres have been changed beyond recognition by doubling or halving their frequencies with the aid of a variable-speed tape recorder. I never improvise. Like my films my music too is precisely worked out. The method of achieving particular effects may be unorthodox, but I always work towards a definite concept.

Tristram Cary, Professor of Electronic Music at the Royal College of Music in London and a composer for many films has this to say about the use of electronic music in films:

Electronic music can be used anywhere really, but since the understanding of its scope and possibilities by producers and directors (i.e. potential commissioners) tends to be limited. Electronic music is usually asked for where a weird effect is required—for science fiction and the like. Often I have talked someone into instrumental music when he has electronic music in mind, and vice versa. One difficulty is that if the music is very "strange" in character it tends to go badly with dialogue, which drags it back to earth. So if the score is really odd in character the less talking the better.

The Swedish director Ingmar Bergman in *The Hour of the Wolf* did just this. In a nightmare-like scene, heavily over-exposed and also hinting of homosexuality where the artist is fishing on the rocks and an adolescent nude boy savagely bits his leg, Bergman removed all sound effects and dialogue. Where many directors might well have used the crashing of surf on the rocks plus music, Bergman employs solely a highly successful electronic piece by

Lars-Johan Werle. In the same film Bergman also uses the work of Mozart. Antonioni in *Red Desert* also mixes electronic and instrumental music. Kubrick does the same in both *2001: A Space Odessey* and *A Clockwork Orange* as does Steve Dartnell in *Second Best*.

Basically it can be said that few films employ solely an electronic music score. This might well be because both makers and audience are not yet attuned to such. Tristram Cary does not see anything "special" in electronic music.

Electronic music is not 'special' in any way, merely one of the valid methods of composing and realising music. All music starts with a sound in mind, and it may finish up as a tape or dots on paper or both. What I do try to avoid is using electronic methods in a quasi-instrumental fashion to save the producer money—making a rich sound in a generally melodic fashion because they want to save recording sessions. Certainly a combination of instrumental and electronic can work very well. I like to have some say in the rest of the soundtrack, and often work with the sound editor to make sure that the effects will work well with the music. In a non-realistic film, the right effects are really to be regarded as part of the score, and it may be important to make sure that, for example, a bell is on D-flat.

Alfred Hitchcock's film *The Birds* is significant for Bernard Herrmann's "music", though not a single note of conventional instrumental music is to be heard on the soundtrack. Hitchcock and Herrmann used purely electronic sound for the "music". Bernard Herrmann in an interview with Ted Gilling in 1971 suggests that it was not music at all.

Remi Gassman, a composer of electronic, avant-garde music, devised a form of sound effects. I just worked with him simply on matching it with Hitchcock, but there was no attempt to create a score by electronic means. We developed the noise of birds electronically because it wasn't possible to get a thousand birds to make that sound. I guess you could if you went to Africa and waited for the proper day.

Many scenes in *The Birds*, certainly the scenes of the bird attacks on the houses, are carried solely by the sound, the electronically created sounds of shrieks and flaps. Hitchcock, ever detailed in the planning of his films, says of the sound track for this film:

After a picture is cut, I dictate what amounts to a real sound script to a secretary. We run every reel off and I indicate all the places where sound should be heard. Until now we've worked with natural sounds, but now thanks to electronic sound, I'm not only going to indicate the sound we want but also the style and nature of each sound. For instance, when Melanie is locked up in the attic with the murderous birds, we inserted the natural sounds of wings, but we stylized them so as to create a greater intensity.

On the precise technique of composing and recording electronic music for film, Tristram Cary's method is a good example:

I normally conduct my own scores, and if time permits I like to sit in on the dub too. I do not use tick tracks but do ask for dupes to be marked up and usually go over the sections in the cutting room the day before the recording begins. Very short sections I sometimes have made up as loops and make numerous takes on a matching magnetic loop. Electronic music for films, because it is delivered in numerous pieces for transfer to 35 mm and then laid according to precise instructions. It is impossible to frame sync. in $\frac{1}{4}$ in. tape so this is done on 35 mm at the cutting room stage. To take an example, in *Sources of Power*, which was made for Expo '67 I made over six hundred separate sounds, all separately announced. The film is a three-screen film. All these six hundred sounds became nine sound tracks running in sync. to produce the three track stereophonic result.

One might well ask why should there be music in films at all? Many directors do without it. There are almost as many answers to this question as there are films made. Some of the answers that follow give a clear insight to why music is used in films. Successful film music relies just as heavily on understanding the intention behind the director's desire for the music as it does on brilliant compositional skill. Tristram Cary says:

Many films have been made without music, and it is not absolutely necessary except in special musical films. The general position is not really different from music with plays or any other drama, and this has a long and honourable history going back at least as far as ancient Greece. Indeed, music as an accompaniment to singing or drama is much older than the "concert", the idea of people sitting down and listening to music as such being quite recent.

For Federico Fellini music is essentially a "secondary element" in his films where a bizarre visual array excites the eye.

Music for a film is a marginal, secondary element that can hold first place only at rare moments; in general, it must simply sustain the rest.

Despite the very different visual style of the two Italian directors Fellini and Antonioni, their attitudes towards music in films is essentially the same. For Antonioni the function of music in film is as follows:

The only way to accept music in films is for it to disappear as an autonomous expression in order to assume its role as one element in a general sensorial impression.

Antonioni is perhaps suggesting that significant musical composition is not the prime importance in film music. It is essential, at least for him, that the music does not stand out on its own. Rather it should merge into the general impression that assails the audience. Satyajit Ray goes so far as to say:

A great deal of music in films today sounds over-articulate to me. I suspect this is the result of the tie-up with the gramophone industry. Background scores now come out as long playing records. Normally one would not expect them to have an existence outside of the medium they were meant to serve. I strongly resent the use of great and familiar music in the background of films. In nine cases out of ten it reduces the music to the level of the film, rather than raising the film to the level of the music, which is obviously the filmmaker's intention. There is nothing more disgusting than to find Mozart's B flat in G labelled as the Elvira Madigan Concerto.

In its purely visual, non-verbal aspect, the language of cinema still lacks range and precise. Music helps to clarify concepts which the filmmaker otherwise feels to be inadequately conveyed. The selective use of actual sounds can provide a rich and expressive aural background. Subtle, emotional states may have to be pinpointed with the help of music to avoid ambiguity. Where actual sounds have to be omitted for stylistic reasons, music may be called upon to fill the void, as well as to act as a signpost for the departure in style. The leitmotif approach is still useful. The recurrence of a theme or themes makes structural contributions apart from serving other immediate functions.

The French director Alain Resnais raises some perhaps contradictory ideas about music and film.

I won't admit that the image counts most; why not the other way around? It all depends on the subject, but a film which consisted entirely of a sound-track with nothing in the frame would still be a film as long as the rhythm of the splices was in harmony with the rhythm of the words or the music.

This is perhaps a lone cry from a director whose cinematic style has never ceased to influence. Generally those involved with film music agree with Kenneth V. Jones when he says

In most instances it stimulates yet another sense area, adding a new dimension of awareness and response.

Director John Huston is more precise:

I hate decorative music. I want the music to help tell the story, illustrate the idea, not just to emphasize the image.

This is very much in keeping with Huston's films with their impeccably tailored story line, told with the barest of essentials and a carefully conceived visual conception which in itself is totally appropriate and quite sufficient, yet essentially subservient to the powerful story-line. It is not inappropriate to leave the final words to Bernard Herrmann who has composed for some of the most historically important directors—Welles, Hitchcock and Traffaut.

The real reason for music is that a piece of film, by its nature, lacks a certain ability to convey emotional overtones. Many times in many films, dialogue may not give a clue to the feelings of a character. It's the music or the lighting or camera movement. When a film is well made, the music's function is to fuse a piece of film so that it has an inevitable beginning and end. When you cut a piece of film you can do it perhaps a dozen ways, but once you put music to it, that becomes the absolutely final way. Until recently, it was never considered a virtue for an audience to be aware of the cunning of the camera and the art of making seamless cuts. It was like a wonderful piece of tailoring; you didn't see the stitches. But today all that has changed, and any mechanical or technical failure or ineptitude is considered "with it".

Music essentially provides an unconscious series of anchors for the viewer. It isn't always apparent and you don't have to know, but it serves its functions. I think Cocteau said that a good film score should create the feeling that one is not aware whether the music is making the film go forward or whether the film is pushing the music forward.

6

FOUR FILMS SINCE 1955

It is no longer easy to categorize the types of music used in films. What has been called the symphonic approach has waned, preserved only by the Russian director Kozintsev with his use of Dmitri Shostakovich for his *Hamlet* and *King Lear*. A newer style of film music has appeared where music is an integral part of the film's content, not an emotional overlay which heightens tensions, locates a setting or suggests the emotions of the scene. Often natural sound effects are now used where earlier music did the job.

Four films have been chosen with four different approaches toward film music. The significant value of these films is not necessarily their exceptional merit as films but rather the merit of the relationship of music to the content of the film as a whole and scenes within the films in particular.

Zabriskie Point contains music which could be classed as "period music" for it is the music of the hippy-drug culture of America that is the subject of Antonioni's film. It is also music that grows out of the action contained in the film. For many contemporary film makers music is used only when it does grow out of the internal action within the film. An important aspect of film music is also represented by the music of *Zabriskie Point* and that is the commercial importance in itself of the music soundtrack. The sale of such on records or cassette tapes serves both as publicity for the film and as a means to recoup the huge production costs. The significance of Antonioni's use of music in the film is its very tight integration with the plot and content of the film. *Easy Rider* with its similar pop soundtrack had little or no inter-relationship between music and content. They were virtually two separate entities.

Stanley Kubrick in his *Space Odyssey: 2001*, like Antonioni, uses pre-recorded music for his film. This time it is not from the pop genre but from the concert hall classics and some avant-garde electronics. Kubrick's use of music defies classification. It is an example of contemporary directors using classical music for films quite alien in setting to the period of the music's composition. Ingmar Bergman and Pier Paolo Pasolini are two other directors who often use classical music with a strong period flavour in films located in a totally different period to the music. Pasolini for example uses the music of Bach in his film *Accatone*, a story about a pimp in the post-war Roman slums.

Ken Russell in his *The Devils* chose French seventeenth century music and the music of the young avant-garde composer Peter Maxwell Davies for extra musical passages. Maxwell Davies' music might conceivably be called "symphonic music" if the word "symphonic" is used in a very loose and contemporary sense. It is rather the eclectic nature of his music, richly flavoured with medieval religious structure and idiom, that makes Maxwell Davies's music particularly appropriate. It does have a very remote "period" flavour but the very contemporary nature of his music suggests the universality and contemporary nature of the film's content. If anything Maxwell Davies' music underlines the emotional forces at play in the film.

Director Steven Dartnell frankly admits he used music in his film *Second Best* "to help the audience stay with the story line". *Second Best* is set in a neutral time vacuum where setting and clothing do not tie the film down to any particular period. Richard Arnell's music further helps the creation of such a timeless film but also helps Steven Dartnell locate the film firmly around the earth which is the central core of the story.

The Devils

This film was directed by the British director Ken Russell. It is based on Aldous Huxley's book *The Devils of Loudun* and John Whiting's play *The Devils* which was performed by the Royal Shakespeare Company in London in 1961. The setting is France during the reign of Louis XIII, largely within the walled city of Loudun. France has been torn by religious dissension between Huguenot and Roman Catholic. With the suppression of the Huguenot minority virtually completed, Cardinal Richelieu, Louis' powerful minister, orders the destruction of the walled fortifications of all the provincial towns in an attempt to thwart further Huguenot uprising and to help centralize power by stripping local dignitaries of the means to defend themselves.

Even before shooting the film Ken Russell approached the young avant-garde English composer Peter Maxwell Davies to compose the music for the film. Russell's choice of Maxwell Davies is interesting and important. It perhaps gives an indication of the intent he had in the film music for *The Devils*. Maxwell Davies' musical style is richly coloured, at times pointillistic and usually tinged with his deep interest in the medieval. Maxwell Davies before actually composing his music for the film had decided that he would base the music on the medieval plain songs—an "Ave Maria" and a "Dies Irae".

John Addison, the composer of numerous film scores including that for the period film *Tom Jones*, believes that:

Phoney period music is another cliche convention which effectively destroys one's belief in the reality of scenes with accurate period costumes and dialogue. There is a case for avoiding "dramatic" music altogether in period films, but heightening the drama by clever use of source music. All the source music was historically correct in *Tom Jones*, but in the background score I concentrated more on the vitality and gaiety of the characters than the overall period flavour. I employed "modern" instruments like the saxophone together with "period" instruments such as the harpsichord. The result was not anachronistic.

Peter Maxwell Davies and Ken Russell used a similar approach. Ken Russell used what John Addison calls "source music". He chose seventeenth century music played by the Old Music Consort and Maxwell Davies' background music. It is interesting to see that Maxwell Davies also uses the saxophone and the harpsichord. Maxwell Davies says that he tended to identify something derived from the "Ave Maria" with Sister Jeanne but he is quick to add that that was about as far as he went in using something musical with which to identify the characters. (It is perhaps interesting to contrast this method of Maxwell Davies with that of Richard Arnell in *Second Best* where he deliberately identified instruments with characters throughout the film).

On the question whether Maxwell Davies' music, or John Addison's for that matter, is anachronistic many problems are posed. Maxwell Davies believes that his music is "very much twentieth century styling, firmly based on the plain song melody". He used in *The Devils* many period instruments such as the flute, piccolo, clarinet, regal, viola, violin and celesta yet he had no intention, nor was his brief for, "period music". His intention was "to underline certain atmosphere and tensions in the film without calling attention to the music at all." If a true period flavour was necessary Maxwell Davies believes that the film should have been made in black and white and in old French and Latin. "Being in

247

The *Devils* directed by Ken Russell. Maxwell Davies' music enters on the sound-track with the arrival of Mignon who interrupts the meeting of Jeanne and Madeleine. Jeanne was expecting Grandier not Mignon.

REEL 10   EXORCISM

Exorciso te,creatura diaboli (adaptation of)
[Blessing of the Holy Orb,
Mass of same,Maundy Thursday]

Hunter Ka   [French]

arrange fanfare I to be recorded as approaching from afar to close up.
(Echoey,inside cathedral)

♩• = 120

FANFARE 1:24" (cue "His Excellency the Duke of Condé) ♩=120:24 bars of ⁶⁄₈ @ ♩•=120

The Devils directed by Ken Russell. The Exorcism of the devil from Sister Jeanne.

The Devils directed by Ken Russell. The burning sequence at the close of the film. Sister Jeanne, frustrated watches Grandier on the way to the stake Period music and atmospheric sounds commence the scene, soon to be overtaken completely by Maxwell Davies' score.

black and white does stylize it much more and it would have been a great deal stronger as such. I am sure Warner Brothers, the distributors said no".

Large sections of the film are in black and white. They are visionary sequences, visions by Sister Jeanne of the Angels, prioress of the St Ursulan Convent in Loudun. She is one of many who is drawn by the powerful magnetism of Father Urbain Grandier. She imagines a variety of religious-erotic fantasies involving Grandier. These sequences are without natural sounds and are carried totally by Maxwell Davies' music and a few passages of dialogue. Maxwell Davies says:

> If you are going to do something as unnatural as having music against a scene, I think naturalistic sound effects do not make it any more natural. Music is a convention of the art form. In normal life when you see something there is no music. If one is going to use film music, it is a stylization and I think the sound effects should perhaps be stylized too.

The visionary nature of the black and white sequences, their mental turbulence, their mixture of the sexual and the religious finds a perfect fusion is the highly eclectic nature of Maxwell Davies score. He seems able to mix all the ingredients of the visuals in comparable musical terms.

Two of the colour sections of the film are most striking for their use of music. They are the final burning sequence and chaos of the nun's orgy.

From the start, at the script stage, Maxwell Davies realized that the climax of the film, the burning of Grandier, would have to be carried by the music. Russell's extremely graphic depiction of the burning and the torture sequence that precedes it, are harrowing. Maxwell Davies saw no reason to employ a full orchestra to achieve the full cacaphony of musical sounds that he creates for the climax. Through amplification and electronics a small group of instruments are made to do a great deal. Throughout the film he only used three percussion players, violin, viola, cello, double bass, trumpet, trombone, two saxophones, flute, piccolo, three clarinets, organ and celesta. Many of the players doubled up to play two or more instruments.

The burning sequence is a very painful sequence to watch. On a primitive level Maxwell Davies was not afraid to underline this. At one point during the music for this scene he stipulated that one of the percussion players should scrape his fingernails against a blackboard. "I put a microphone right up to it so it goes on to the

251

sound track together with the music. One does not hear the scraping as such unless one really listens for it. I think the effect is there and I think in a much more subtle way that is how the music works".

One scene where the fusion of "period" with "modern" approach was abortive was the scene where Sister Jeanne meets Madeleine through the grille of the nunnery. Madeleine has come for religious advice and this soon turns into a fight. The sequence after the fight consists of Sister Jeanne meeting what she thought was going to be the object of her dreams, Father Grandier, whom she has invited to become father confessor to the nuns. Sister Jeanne turns from the grille to find that it is not Grandier but the infinitely less attractive Mignon.

Maxwell Davies says of this scene:

Ken Russell knows a great deal about music, but he knows when talking about music that his vocabulary is limited. He might say to me "I want dark gloomy music there". We thought and talked it out and we would think we understood each other. I would get down to a writing session, record it. The music was probably what he expected or slightly different but he accepted it. There was one bit that did not work. We were both surprised that it did not for we had both been enthusiastic about it when we first recorded it. That was the section where Sister Jeanne meets Madeleine at the gate of the nunnery. I had talked to Ken Russell and decided it would perhaps be lovely to have a dance under the scene, but not just a seventeenth century dance. Why not do some-thing completely crazy and do it in 1920's style! We thought of some send-up music for the scene that follows where Mignon arrives. We recorded it. It turned out beautifully. It was splendid and characterized the scene very well. When it came in context it stuck out like a sore thumb, so the music had to go. In the final film the music does in fact start a good few bars later than we intended it to.

A shot-by-shot breakdown of this scene, with Peter Maxwell Davies's notes is as follows:

Shot	Footage	Duration
Madeleine runs out	39	26 secs
Jeanne at bars exhausted	43½	26 8 secs
sinks down	56½	37 6 secs
Jeanne gets mirror out	65	43.3 secs
Sister Agnes interrupts	86½	57.6 secs
Jeanne thinks "it's Grandier!"	97	I min. 4.6 secs
Jeanne runs through corridor	104	I min. 9.3 secs
Jeanne into chapel	120	I min. 20 secs
Jeanne sees Mignon	129½	I min. 26.9 secs

(Note by P.M.D.: This could, if it doesn't cut exactly at end in right place, be notched up).

Next music starts after "Yes help me father" 0 to 24 ft 16 secs track Madeleine and Grandier in bed.

Peter Maxwell Davies made the following notes for this scene: Dance music under fight from scream (fox-trotty). As Jeanne sinks down becomes more reflective. As Jeanne takes out mirror, soppy music, sentimental, "Young girl's dream". Death chord

252

at climax as Mignon is seen at top of stairs. Stop. Death motif after "Yes, help me father".
(Dissolve into Grandier and de Brou asleep).

2001: A Space Odyssey

This, the most ambitious science fiction film to date, even including the brilliantly low-keyed Soviet film *Solaris*, occasioned an enormous amount of musical response. The film relies heavily on music from Richard Strauss' *Also Sprach Zarathustra*.

Here Kubrick reinforces a current trend to use existing, already recorded music, classical—Mahler in *Death in Venice*, or pop—*Zabriski Point*, rather than commission a composer to write a special work for a film. Is this a retrograde step, a return, in fact, to the silent film? Griffiths unhesitatingly used Beethoven and any other existing compositions for the music to be played during the showing of his "silent" films. Kubrick's choices are generally brilliant. *Zarathustra*, based on Nietzche's superman philosopher has strange overtones of the super race and when we see the ape man, his mind blown further into man's intellectual future, learning to grasp and use a bone as a weapon, the slow motion image, plus the inexorable Strauss, is one of the great moments in cinema.

Each step forward for mankind is accompanied by the appearance on earth of a monolithic black slab, emitting vocal sounds of just the right avant-garde futurist genre. Ligeti, the composer, was surely precisely the right choice, even though his work had already been composed and certainly was never remotely conceived in terms of 2001.

As the astronaut travels from earth to a satellite in a luxurious space craft—complete with luxurious stewardess—and as we see the satellite swing into view, what more surprisingly appropriate music than the *Blue Danube*, superbly recorded on Deutsche Gramophon by the Berlin Philharmonic. What does Kubrick mean by this? Is he giving us a super Muzak—the sort of happy-music background for space travellers, the kind of music they want as a colour, rather like the no-doubt-scented air conditioning? Is the lush sound of a Viennese waltz, thick with the opulent Vienna, fun loving, extravagant, 19th century Pleasure Dome, to give us a bitter sweet comment on the aseptic space craft and the even more empty, humanless universe? Or is it simply a suitable, well known dance rhythm to go with the steady movement of spacecraft, satellite and universe. Would *Eine Kleine Nacht Musik* have done as well?

Or again, is it a quotation from *Dr. Strangelove* where a gay tune accompanies the atomic extinction of mankind? About this, Kubrick said:

> Don't underestimate the charm of the *Blue Danube*. Most people of under 35 think of it in an objective way, as a beautiful composition. Older people associate it with a Palm Court orchestra or have another unfortunate association and generally, therefore, criticize its use in the film. It's hard to find anything better than the *Blue Danube* for depicting grace and beauty in turning. It also gets about as far away as you can get from the cliche of space music.

Many composers were in fact approached to write the score before Kubrick decided on what Alex North—who was one of them—thought:

> The Victorian approach (Strauss) with Mid-European (Ligeti) overtures was just not in keeping with the brilliant concept of Clarke and Kubrick.

The "temporary tracks" of Strauss et al which Kubrick had been using during editing and which he gave to Alex North as guide lines, turned up as the director's final choice. The score composed especially was abandoned. North's comment was, "Well, what can I say? It was a great frustrating experience."

It must be said that most film contracts with composers stipulate that the composer will be paid an agreed commissioning fee, but that the production company need not use the music. It would be most interesting to hear Alex North's score now, after the event.

Second Best

The camera slowly zooms down a hill in Derbyshire into the doorway of a small cottage. A young girl, Anne, about fourteen, comes out of the cottage and goes to join her older sister Fran in the garden. Fran, in the words of D. H. Lawrence, on whose story of the same title this film is based, is "much older, about twenty three, and whimsical, spasmodic. She was the beauty and clever child of the family". Just now she has been crying, but will not tell Anne why she was doing so. "Let's go for a walk", she says.

Music is heard on the sound track in the latter part of this scene. Two instruments are used—the guitar and the flute. They were chosen after considerable discussion between the director Steven Dartnell and composer Richard Arnell. Originally Dartnell had wanted electronic music only for the film. He had in mind something similar to Beaver and Krause's record *In a Wild Sanctuary* which is not a heavy electronic piece. It is rather soft with many airy and watery sounds and has only a very slight melody. After shooting in discussion it was decided to use electronics solely for the mole hunt in the film and for Richard Arnell to compose various pieces for guitar and flute. These instruments were arrived at after considering others, including the harpsichord. Richard Arnell says:

I took an operatic point of view of the film and did what I do if I was writing an opera on the same story. I chose specific instruments for specific characters. This is something I do not only in films. I tend to associate the flute with attractive little girls like Anne in the film. I used the guitar for the older girl Francis because it is a Spanish instrument. If struck in a certain way it has an unconscious association with cruelty and bull fights. It sounds slightly absurd but I think it works and is the right instrument to underline Francis' character.

Steven Dartnell explains the choice of the instruments:

We chose the flute as expressing solitude, sadness and loneliness—Anne's predominant moods. The guitar expressed the warmth and comfort of the earth, and the possibility of Francis somewhere in the depths of her soul, to be able to give and love.
I do not think the instruments indentify particularly with the girls. I feel they express states of mind; such as loneliness and separation with the flute, and blood and the earth with the guitar.

At the beginning of the film Richard Arnell introduces the theme of the music in a shortened form. In the opening minutes Anne in fact hums the tune that Arnell uses. She hums it intermittently throughout the film.

The two girls go for a walk slowly through the lush summery countryside and past a brook. Everything seems to have a double meaning as the famed Lawrence symbols are visually introduced— the images of the brook, fields, trees are all part of human life and at the same time, entirely remote from it. Filming Lawrence has often posed difficulties for directors. The generally bucolic settings of his stories when photographed in colour often look too pretty thus undermining the basically human conflicts that Lawrence was after in setting his stories in the countryside. The danger of making the film too pretty comes in theory to a knife edge with the choice of the flute with all its lyric associations and possibilities. Such over-lyricism is cunningly avoided by using very "breathy notes" and the generally unresolved nature of the melody in the music.

Richard Arnell was against Steven Dartnell's idea to use exclusively electronic music because he thought such would dehumanize the whole film and spoil its particular flavour.

255

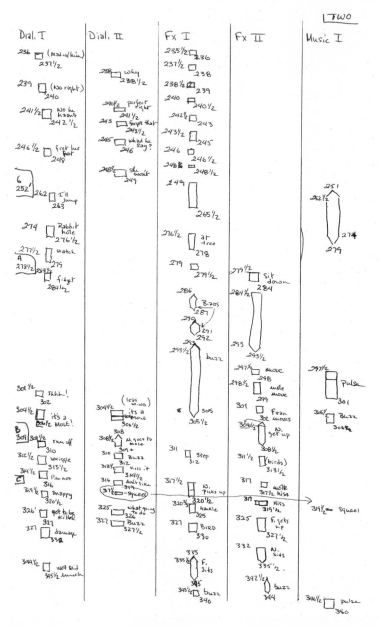

First draft dubbing cue sheet for *Second Best*. Directed by Steven Dartnell. Music by Richard Arnell. The music track is indicated on the right hand column. A horizontal line indicates immediate entrance of the music on the sound-track and two sloping lines indicate a fade-in of the music.

The director does not think that the ravishing beauty of the Derbyshire countryside leads the viewer astray from the inherent point of the story, not without extreme nastiness in the character of Francis. He says:

> The story is set in the Derbyshire area. I feel rather that the beauty of the countryside emphasizes the point—the mixture of the apparent prettiness of nature concealing the relentless process of decay and rebirth. I think the music might lead the viewer astray from these inherent points. If I were making the film again I would seriously consider not using music.
>
> My worry with *Second Best* was that although the psychological implications were great the symbols that are used could appear to be slight and the music does help an audience to maintain its interest. This goes for the whole film. Whereas the long walks through the countryside are always descriptive for Francis' state of mind I can understand that this isn't the case for everyone so I think the music helps them.

Anne pokes a stick in a hollow tree. A mole emerges and she catches it in her handkerchief. She asks about Francis' love in Liverpool from where she has just returned. She replies that she has been jilted. The mole suddenly bites Anne and she kills it with a stick. Francis is horrified and fascinated. They walk on through the fields. In Lawrence's words, "The brown turf seemed in a low state of combustion, the leaves of the oaks were scorched brown". They pass a farm and meet the farmer, Tom. Anne shows him the dead mole. A kind of rough, teasing flirtation goes on between Francis and Tom to the puzzlement of a not quite awakened Anne. She teases Francis about not being able to kill a mole herself. She says "Why would you like me to kill moles?"

Tom replies: "They do us a lot of harm".

Francis: "Well, I'll see the next time I see one".

The part of Tom, played by Alan Bates, was thought too small to warrant the use of an instrument in the music for him as the two girls have. Originally Richard Arnell planned that in the final sequence of the film, with Tom and Francis united, always unresolved melody of his music would be resolved, thereby using the resolved melody for Tom. The music was composed but ultimately not used because Steven Dartnell thought that the ending with the music might have made the film appear too sweet and lacking the viciousness it does in part convey.

Francis the next day sets out at dawn on her bicycle. She leaves her bicycle and walks through the fields full with cows, calves suckling and insects humming. She is out to catch a mole. Eventually

258

she finds one, hunts it down and viciously beats it to death.

During this mole hunt electronic music is used. The director's intention was to use music here with the express intention of heightening the dramatic impact of the scene. He says:

> I do not think the natural sounds were strong enough for the mole hunt but I wanted as well to add more dramatic drive, to lift the sequence out of the purely naturalistic rendering, to heighten it a little.

During shooting this sequence neither the director nor editor-cameraman, Chris Arnold, thought that they would be using music over this section. Chris Arnold relates:

> When shooting the mole hunt my feeling was that we could concentrate on effects. To some extent this came from the electronic music we had thought about prior to shooting. This music was very earthy in sound with crunching, watery sounds. We had thought that in terms of effects in the mole hunt we might perhaps use music. I did not separate instrumental music and electronic music or even natural effects. During the filming we were very conscious that we wanted to get a sound orientated scene and we chose images with sounds that approximated the mood of the scene. We thought the sounds that existed belonged there and anything that would go on the sound track would take those sounds and use them, go further with them, perhaps treat them electronically. If there was to be music it would not only take in the spirit of the scene but also the sounds inherent in the scene. We tried to make a symphony of natural sounds. We shot lots of extra sound all the time just in case we needed it—like the sounds of flies and water dripping.
>
> It was only later during the editing that we thought music could exist with those sounds without throwing them out or giving just an overlay. I could see during the editing that the mole hunt was getting too long. The natural sounds were not presenting themselves as dramatic elements as we had hoped. We had to cut the mole hunt down in length or orchestrate the tracks in another way.
>
> It was at this stage that we went to Lawrence Cassily to get some electronic stuff. We more or less told him what type of sounds we wanted. It was not so much precisely where we wanted it. He saw the film and made some suggestions including a type of "boom" sound. Basically we knew we wanted some sounds treated electronically and some had to be created. We wanted as much sound as possible for potential use. In the end we used only a small amount of electronic material plus natural effects for the mole hunt.

The use of electronic music for a pastorally located film, and a D. H. Lawrence film at that, might seem curious. Industrialism is an inherent theme in many of D. H. Lawrence's stories.

Steven Dartnell points out that *Second Best* is one of the few Lawrence stories that does not directly deal with Lawrence's concern with industrialization.

> As I have kept closely to the story I believe it would have been an arbitary decision to introduce any sense of industrialization, particularly as what interested me more was the story's uncompromising obsessions with the earth.

259

It would certainly be wrong to associate electronic music exclusively with either horror films or films about industry—in both such groups electronic music is extensively used. The range of electronic music is massive. The electronic sounds heard in *Second Best* are essentially very earthy sounds whereas the electronic music in Antonioni's *Red Desert* is more that of the machine. That film was woven around the psychological implications and effect of industry on people and nature. The presence of machine type noises brilliantly orchestrated into an electronic music track seems particularly apt.

The appearance of the electronic music in *Second Best*, however earthy the sound, and the type of instrumental music which is hardly folksy tends to place the film on another level—that of timelessness. This is also paralleled in that the costumes and decor in the film are essentially timeless. There is no period flavour, more a simple country flavour which defines precise location in any period of time. This was the director's intention.

Zabriskie Point

Mike Curb, president of MGM Records, writing on the sleeve of the long playing record, the soundtrack of Zabriskie Point (MGM 2315002) says:

Today's artists, such as Antonioni, deal in the presentation of total concepts. There cannot be any loose ends, for each factor must have the power to provoke and to evoke. Therein lies the importance of the music in *Zabriskie Point*. It is more than just a case of a film of today demanding the music of today. Contemporary music doesn't merely tell a story or set a mood; it *is* the story and it *is* the mood.

In an interview during the shooting of *Blow-Up* in 1965 Antonioni remarks: "I hope to do a film in New York this winter. It will be on violence." In 1968 amidst a blaze of publicity and hope Antonioni made his film in America. The film that eventually emerged from his work there on the West Coast was *Zabriskie Point*. The critics and public in America acted in nearly unanimous hostility to it.

This is certainly not the place to discuss the commercial failure of *Zabriskie Point*. It is, however, an interesting film from a major director with an exclusively pop score which include a somewhat surprising choice of groups—The Rolling Stones (incidentally not included in the LP album), The Pink Floyd, The Kaleidoscope, The Grateful Dead (also featuring solo Jerry Garcia), Patti Page,

The Youngbloods, Roscoe Holcomb, John Fahey and on its release in San Francisco the print also had an end-credit sequence song by none other than Mike Curb Generation (this was later removed from the soundtrack and does not appear on the LP).

Talking at the Centro Sperimentale di Cinematografia in Rome in 1961 Antonioni was asked about his opinion of the contribution music could make to a film. Antonioni, after first stating that music could have a great function in film, discussed his own reluctant use of music in his films "for the simple reasons that I prefer to work in a dry manner, to say things with the least possible means." And adding that "I have a need to draw upon sound, which serves an essentially musical function."

In *Zabriskie Point* the music is tightly woven in to the plot of the film. This is best seen in how much the radio plays a part in the film. Doria during her long drive through the desert is ever tuning her radio into rock stations which belt out a variety of songs, yet even these by their lyrics seem to have been carefully chosen to be appropriate to her mood at the time. The radio not only serves her as a source of entertainment, but it also provides her with news. From these news bulletins she learns of the white student wanted by the police in connection with the shooting of a policeman during a campus riot. She learns of the aeroplane stolen by a young man and later of the shooting of the 'plane's hijacker. The music is also tied up with the plot in another way, that of mirroring the mood of the scene—for example the use of Patti Page's *Tennessee Waltz* after the scene in the small roadside cafe that Doria visits during her drive through the desert, with its clientele of old men in cowboy outfits and its ex-world boxing champion with his nostalgia. As we leave the cafe we see an aged crony hunched over a beer at the bar and the Patti Page enters on the soundtrack—a classic piece of Middle America.

One might justifiably fear that *Zabriskie Point* is yet another American "bike movie" with long journeys through open spaces, breathtakingly photographed, and wild pop on the soundtrack such as one gets in *Easy Rider*. This is not the case. Antonioni is never frightened to let silence, or certainly a silent music track, appear in large sections of the film—the scenes of Mark "buzzing" Doria in her car with his stolen 'plane are near totally silent save for the very muted sound effects.

Zabriskie Point is a film about America, about young America, about the culture of young America which has its strange paradox of peace, pot, free love and yet violence. The music of the pop

261

generation is a mixture of those ingredients. Antonioni himself said of the film: "I was trying to feel something about the country, to gain an intuition . . . my film touches on just a few themes, a few places."

The most significant musical contribution of the film is the original music composed and performed by the English pop group The Pink Floyd. Their music appears in three passages: the opening credit sequence entitled *Heart Beat, Pig Meat; Crumbling Land* during Mark's aeroplane flight up into the sky and over the city towards the desert; and *Come in Number 51, Your Time is Up* which accompanies the abstract sequence of the contents of the house exploding.

Heart Beat, Pig Meat opens with a steady heart beat from the hand-drums, then an electronic cry, a near inaudible news bulletin, electronic organ also pumping out the heart beat, muted winds, then a descending piano scale and further news bulletins. Shot with a strong yellow filter, the visuals (plus introductory titles) are close-ups, the camera meandering across teenagers obviously in a meeting. The scene, losing its yellow filter and the music, turns into a meeting between black and white campus radicals. The music adds a nervous, perhaps undue seriousness to the very confused nature of the meeting.

Crumbling Land is something quite different. It is something far more electronic with its almost country-and-western guitar introduction and rattling beat from the percussion. The vocals are very descriptive as Mark flies his stolen aeroplane up, up and away over a city with its massive system of motorways, hazy smog and into the clouds towards the unknown.

Come in Number 51, Your Time is Up is again something different with its slow moaning introduction building up to its violent crescendo. The scene is at the end of the film. Doria has arrived at the luxurious modern retreat of her boss (this seems to be the purpose of her journey away from the city and through the desert). Her boss (Rod Taylor) is in the process of a multi-million dollar land deal to turn the desert into a sunshine paradise garden suburb. The men discuss business. Their wives laze under the pretty sun umbrellas beside the swimming pool. Mark, with whom Doria has made love, has taken the stolen aeroplane back to the airfield from where he stole it. Doria now knows he is the young man sought by the police in connection with the shooting of a policeman during a campus riot. As enigmatically as she came, she leaves the house, set as it is amidst cacti and boulders. She returns to her car and drives it down the hill. She switches on the car radio to hear that Mark has been shot dead on returning the aeroplane.

In a seeming death wish, a wish to destroy all around her, all the symbols of capitalist America, she sees the house, the National Geographic Magazine flapping in the breeze, blown up. We see the house explode, then see that this is her fantasy for it is still standing. To the sounds of terrific explosions it explodes again and again from various angles, blowing up into the sky a huge mushroom cloud of smoke and flames. A cut to the tableau around the swimming pool and it explodes in slow motion. Here the slow organ and muted cymbals beat of *Come in Number 51, Your Time is Up* enters on the sound track which is devoid of any effects. A slow electronic cry enters the music, more like a wail. A long rack of clothes explodes, again in slow-motion, with an accompaniment of electronic gurgles. This long-shot is followed by a close-up of the same scene. Then follows a living room scene with its television set (and talking head programme) which explodes and sends its mechanism slowly drifting through the sky. Four fridges follow, exploding their varied contents into the sky. A giant size lobster floats by, then various foodstuffs in close-up such as a huge olive and a turkey. Finally, a library is shown in long-shot. Suddenly, the books concertina and unfold as a loud electronic cry with lots of echo screams from the music followed by the single word "DIE" held for a long time as the music, at this point violent and loud, closes abruptly. A cut back to Doria entering her motor car and driving off into the sunset brings up "The End".

AN OUTLINE HISTORY OF FILM MUSIC

A RECORD of the principal events and film music compositions from 1895–1972, giving details of film titles, composers, and countries of origin. This index is based on details and recommendations from: *Film Music Magazine, Sight and Sound, Films in Review*, the *Bulletin* of the British Film Academy, the Academy Awards (U.S.A.), the authors and committee of the present book. Individual films have been noted as follows: (1) Title of Film. (2) Name of the Composer. (3) Country of Origin. (4) Name of the Director or other details in cases where more than one film has been made under the title in question.

1895
Lumière Programme in Paris (28th December) in a basement café in the Boulevard des Capucines, Paris. The programme was accompanied by a piano.

1896
20th February. The first public film performance in Great Britain by Felicien Treuwé of the Lumière Brothers' programme. Given at the Regent Street Polytechnic. There is a reasonably well-authenticated story that the programme was accompanied by an old harmonium (with three notes missing), brought in from the Polytechnic chapel. To imitate engine noises a cylinder of compressed air is supposed to have been used for the scene of *The Arrival of a Train in a Station*.
April. Empire and Alhambra Music Halls ran film shows. The music-hall orchestras provided a full musical accompaniment.

1900
Little Tich and his Big Boots (Britain). Early experiment in sound films, using an orchestral gramophone record.

1901–6
Various experiments in musical and singing films, using gramophone records, e.g., Vesta Tilley in *The Midnight Sun*, Lil Hawthorn in *Kitty Malone*, Alec Hurley in *The Lambeth Cake Walk*, and films of the Royal Italian Opera, Paris. A forty-six minute version of *Faust*. (Exact dates not known.)

1907
Specially composed score by Camille Saint-Saëns for *L'Assassination du Duc de Guise*. Produced by Film D'Art, Paris, from a script by Henri Lavedan. Opus 128, for strings, piano and harmonium, consisting of one Introduction and five Tableaux; each part was carefully cued.

1909–12

A schedule of about 300 short musical films exists for this period, with full details of titles, equipment and lists of cinemas in which they were shown.
First "Suggestions for Music" sheets issued with Edison films (1909).

1911

Arrah-na-Pough: specially arranged score by Walter Cleveland Simon (U.S.A.).

1913

Sam Fox Moving Picture Music Volumes by J. S. Zamecnik. A book of pieces for silent film pianists.

1915

Birth of a Nation: music arranged and orchestrated by Joseph Karl Breil, in collaboration with D. W. Griffith (U.S.A.).
Dream Street: directed by D. W. Griffith. It was presented with synchronized records of music at the Town Hall, New York.
Le Retour d'Ulysée. Georges Hue (France).

1918

The Rubaiyat of Omar Khayyam. Charles Wakefield Cadman (U.S.A.). (A Prelude exists in the Philadelphia Library.)
Hearts of the World. Carl Elinor and D. W. Griffith (U.S.A.).

1922

Foolish Wives. Sigmund Romberg (U.S.A.).

1923

Puritan Passions. Frederick Shepherd Converse (U.S.A.). (Score marked *Scarecrow Sketches* in Philadelphia Library.)
Die Nibelungen (*Siegfried* and *Kriemhild's Rache*). Gottfried Huppertz (Germany).

1924

Ballet Mécanique. George Antheil (Germany).
A Quoi Rèvent Les Jeunes Films. (France.) This film by René Clair is said to have had "orchestration by Roger Desormière".
Lee De Forrest produced experimental sound films in New York, including Una Merkel in *Love's Old Sweet Song.*
Entr'acte. Eric Satie (France).
The Thief of Baghdad. Mortimer Wilson (U.S.A.).
The Iron Horse. Erno Rapée (U.S.A.).

1925

Battleship Potemkin. Edmund Meisel (U.S.S.R./Germany).
The Big Parade. William Axt (U.S.A.).
Lee De Forrest produced sound films, with effects, dialogue and music in a studio at Clapham, London. They were shown at the Wembley Exhibition.
L'Inhumaine. Darius Milhaud (France).
The Merry Widow. Franz Lehar, arranged by David Mendoza and William Axt (U.S.A.).

1926

Don Juan: incidental music and arrangements by William Axt (U.S.A.). Conducted by Henry Hadley in New York.
Fox-Movietone News produced with sound-track.
British Acoustic produced sound films, including *A Wet Night* with Arthur Chesney, at Weissensee studios, Berlin.

266

Don Q, Son of Zorro. Mortimer Wilson (U.S.A.).
Napoleon. Arthur Honegger (France). Made by Abel Gance.
Metropolis. Gottfried Huppertz (Germany).
Rien Que Les Heures. Yves de la Casinière (France).
Ben Hur. William Axt and David Mendoza, orch. Baron (U.S.A.).

1927

Berlin. Edmund Meisel (Germany). Silent film made by Walter Ruttmann.
The Wedding March. L. Zamecnik (U.S.A.). Music recorded on discs.
The Spy. Werner R. Heymann (Germany).
Italian Straw Hat. Jacques Ibert (France). (A piano score exists.)
Krazy Kat at the Circus. Paul Hindemith (France).
Changing of the Guard, a sound film, produced at Lime Grove, Shepherd's
  Bush, on British Acoustic equipment.
The Jazz Singer with Al Jolson, produced by Warner Bros. (New York première
  in October.)

1928

Woman in the Moon. Willy Schmidt-Gentner (Germany).
Filmstudie. (Germany.) First presented to music by Ernst Toch; later recorded
  to a fragment of Darius Milhaud's *La Creation du Monde.* Hans Richter
  film.
October: original music by Edmund Meisel (U.S.S.R./Germany).
Actualities. Darius Milhaud (France). (Score in the Philadelphia Library.)
Opus 3. Hanns Eisler (Germany). Walter Ruttman "absolute" film.
New Babylon. Dimitri Shostakovitch (U.S.S.R.).
The Jazz Singer, with Al Jolson, had its London première at the Piccadilly
  Theatre (September).
Steamboat Willie. (U.S.A.) First Walt Disney sound cartoon.

1929

Berlin Carnival. Walter Gronostay (Germany). Hans Richter film.
Weltmelodie. Wolfgang Zeller (Germany). Sound film by Walter Ruttmann.
Vormittagspuk. Paul Hindemith (Germany). Hans Richter film.
Blackmail. Hubert Bath (Britain).
Pays du Scalp. Maurice Jaubert (France).
Rain. Lou Lichtveld (Holland).
Kitty. Hubert Bath (Britain). The first British part-sound film. Music in the
  traditional silent film style, transferred to the sound-track.
Overture 1812. Hugo Riesenfeld's interpretation of the Tchaikovsky Overture
  (U.S.A.).
Skeleton Dance. (U.S.A.) First Walt Disney *Silly Symphony.*

1930

All Quiet on the Western Front. A. Brockman (U.S.A.).
Romance Sentimentale. Alexandrov (France).
The Blue Angel. Friedrich Hollaender (Germany).
Song of Life. Hanns Eisler (France).
Accompaniment to a Cinema Scene. Arnold Schoenberg (Germany). An experi-
  ment in strict twelve-tone technique for an imaginary film.
War is Hell. Hanns Eisler (Germany).
Alone. Dimitri Shostakovitch (U.S.S.R.).
Broadway Melody. (U.S.A.).
King of Jazz. (U.S.A.) Paul Whiteman.
Sous les Toits de Paris. Raoul Moretti and Armand Bernard (France).

1931

The Road to Life. Stoliar (U.S.S.R.).
The Bells. Gustav Holst (Britain). Produced by A.S.F.I. at Wembley.
A Nous La Liberté. Georges Auric (France).
Golden Mountains. Dimitri Shostakovitch (U.S.S.R.).
Tabu. Hugo Riesenfeld (U.S.A.).
City Lights. Charles Chaplin (U.S.A.).
Le Million: Armand Bernard, Philippe Pares and Georges Van Parys (France).
Threepenny Opera. Kurt Weill (Germany).
Brahms's Hungarian Dance. (Germany.) Oscar Fischinger.
In the Night. Schumann (Germany). Interpretation by Walter Ruttman.
Minuet by Mozart. (Germany.) Oscar Fischinger.
Surf and Seaweed. Marc Blitzstein (U.S.A.). (Score in the Philadelphia Library.)
Mor Vran. Alexis Archangelsky (France).
Le Sang d'un Poète. Georges Auric (France).
Congress Dances. (Germany.)

1932

M. (Germany.) Used Grieg theme for murderer.
Poil de Carotte. Alexander Tansman (France).
Prague Castle. Ferdei Bartos (Czechoslovakia).
Le Quatorze Juillet. Maurice Jaubert (France).
Passer-by. Dimitri Shostakovitch (U.S.S.R.).
Counterplan. Dimitri Shostakovitch (U.S.S.R.).
King Kong. Max Steiner (U.S.A.).
L'Affaire est dans le Sac. Maurice Jaubert (France).
Extase. Giuseppe Beece (Czechoslovakia).

1933

Lilliom. Jean Lenoir and Franz Waxman (Germany).
Borinage. Hans Havska (Belgium).
Lot in Sodom. Louis Siegel (U.S.A.).
Acciaio. Georges Malipiero (Italy). Walter Ruttman.
Rising Tide. Clarence Raybould (Britain).
Zéro de Conduite. Maurice Jaubert (France).
Contact. Clarence Raybould (Britain). Paul Rotha.
The Constant Nymph. Eugene Goosens (Britain).
Carmen. Bizet (Germany). Lotte Reiniger silhouette film.
Scarface. Adolph Tandler (U.S.A.).
Deserter. Y. Shaporin (U.S.S.R.).
Forty-Second Street. (U.S.A.)

1934

The Lost Patrol. Max Steiner (U.S.A.).
Le Dernier Milliardaire. Maurice Jaubert (France).
L'Idée. Arthur Honegger (France).
Man of Aran. John Greenwood (Britain).
New Earth. Hanns Eisler (Holland).
Song of Ceylon. Walter Leigh (Britain).
The Private Life of Don Juan. Mischa Spoliansky (Britain).
Lieutenant Kije. Sergei Prokofiev (U.S.S.R.).
L'Hippocampe. Darius Milhaud (France).
Night on the Bare Mountain. Moussorgsky (France). Visual interpretation by Alexieff and Parker.
Easter Island. Maurice Jaubert (France).
Three Songs of Lenin. Y. Shaporin (U.S.S.R.).

One Night of Love. (U.S.A.) (Academy Award to Columbia Music Department.)
Jazz Comedy. (U.S.S.R.) Alexandrov.
L'Atalante. Maurice Jaubert (France).
Pett and Pott. Walter Leigh (Britain).

1935
Aerograd. Dimitri Kabalevsky (U.S.S.R.).
Colour Box. (Britain.) Len Lye "abstract" to music.
Crime et Châtiment. Arthur Honegger (France).
B.B.C.: The Voice of Britain. (Britain.) Appearances by Sir Adrian Boult, Henry Hall, etc.
Escape Me Never. William Walton (Britain).
The Informer. Max Steiner (U.S.A.). (Academy Award, 1935.)
Mutiny on the Bounty. Bronislau Kaper (U.S.A.).
Things to Come. Arthur Bliss (Britain).
The Turn of the Tide. Arthur Benjamin (Britain).
Sanders of the River. Mischa Spoliansky (Britain).
Papageno. Mozart (Germany). Lotte Reiniger silhouette film.
The Wave. Silvestre Revaeltas (U.S.A.). (Score in the Philadelphia Library.)
Coalface. Benjamin Britten (Britain).
Top Hat. (U.S.A.) Astaire-Rogers musical.
Keyboard Talks. (Britain.) Mark Hambourg in a lecture on piano technique.
Book: *Music for the Films* by Sabaneev, published by Pitman, London.

1936
Modern Times. Charles Chaplin; arranged by Alfred Newman (U.S.A.).
Dawn of Iran. Walter Leigh (Britain).
Rainbow Dance. (Britain.) Len Lye "abstract" to music.
Anthony Adverse. Erich Wolfgang Korngold (U.S.A.). (Academy Award, 1936.)
As You Like It. William Walton (Britain).
Night Mail. Benjamin Britten (Britain).
The Plow That Broke the Plains. Virgil Thomson (U.S.A.).
San Francisco. Bronislau Kaper (U.S.A.).
The Robber Symphony. Friedrich Feher (Britain). An experimental film, specially composed screen opera.
The Future's In the Air. William Alwyn (Britain).
The Saving of Bill Blewett. Benjamin Britten (Britain).
The Plainsman. George Antheil (U.S.A.).
Maxim Gorki's Return. Dimitri Shostakovitch (U.S.S.R.).
Midsummer Night's Dream. Erich Wolfgang Korngold (U.S.A.).
Green Pastures. Erich Wolfgang Korngold (U.S.A.).
Book: *Film Music* by Kurt London, published by Faber and Faber, London.

1937
Conquest of the Sky. Darius Milhaud (Switzerland).
Trade Tattoo. (Britain.) Len Lye "abstract" to music.
Un Carnet de Bal. Maurice Jaubert (France).
Fire Over England. Richard Addinsell (Britain).
Lost Horizon. Dimitri Tiomkin (U.S.A.).
Love from a Stranger. Benjamin Britten (Britain).
Mayerling. Arthur Honegger (France).
Spanish Earth. Marc Blitzstein and Virgil Thomson (U.S.A.).
Victoria the Great. Anthony Collins (Britain).

Wings of the Morning. Arthur Benjamin (Britain).

Elephant Boy. John Greenwood (Britain).

New Worlds for Old. William Alwyn (Britain).

Les Maisons de la Misère. Maurice Jaubert (Belgium).

South Riding. Richard Addinsell (Britain).

One Hundred Men and a Girl. Charles Previn (U.S.A.). (Academy Award, 1937.)

Snow White and the Seven Dwarfs. Paul Smith (U.S.A.).

The Edge of the World. Lambert Williamson (Britain).

La Mort du Cygne. (France.) Directed by Jean Benoit-Lévy and Marie Epstein.

Le Quai des Brumes. Maurice Jaubert (France).

We Live in Two Worlds. Maurice Jaubert (Britain).

1938

U and Me. Kurt Weill (U.S.A.).

Europe-Radio. Walter Gronostay (Holland).

Hello Everybody. Darius Milhaud (Holland).

From Lightning to Television. Walter Gronostay (Holland).

The Face of Scotland. Walter Leigh (Britain).

Adventures of Robin Hood. Erich Wolfgang Korngold (U.S.A.). (Academy Award, 1938.)

La Femme du Boulanger. Vincent Scotto (France).

The Four Feathers. Miklos Rozsa (Britain).

Pygmalion. Arthur Honegger (Britain).

The River. Virgil Thomson (U.S.A.).

Volga-Volga. I. O. Dunayevsky and A. Alexandrov (U.S.S.R.).

Village Harvest. Benjamin Britten (Britain).

Conquest of the Air. Arthur Bliss (Britain). Performed as a Suite at the Promenade Concerts 1938.

The Tocher. Benjamin Britten (Britain).

The Islanders. Darius Milhaud (Britain).

Alexander's Ragtime Band. Alfred Newman (U.S.A.). (Academy Award, 1938; musical score.)

Entrée des Artistes. Georges Auric (France).

La Bête Humaine. Joseph Kosma (France).

The Goldwyn Follies. (U.S.A.) Balanchine/Zorina.

1939

Shors. Dimitri Kabalevsky (U.S.S.R.).

North Sea. Ernst Meyer (Britain).

The Four-Hundred Million. Hanns Eisler (U.S.A.).

Alexander Nevsky. Sergei Prokofiev (U.S.S.R.).

The City. Aaron Copland (U.S.A.).

La Fin du Jour. Maurice Jaubert (France).

Goodbye Mr. Chips. Richard Addinsell (Britain).

Night Must Fall. Edward Ward (U.S.A.).

Stagecoach. Richard Hageman (U.S.A.). (Academy Award, 1939.)

Stolen Life. William Walton (Britain).

The Wizard of Oz. Herbert Stothart (U.S.A.). (Academy Award, 1939; best scoring.)

The Proud Valley. Ernest Irving (Britain).

Le Jour se Lève. Maurice Jaubert (France).

The Fourth Estate. Walter Leigh (Britain).

1940

One Tenth of a Nation. Roy Harris (U.S.A.).

Of Mice and Men. Aaron Copland (U.S.A.).

Our Town. Aaron Copland (U.S.A.).

Pinocchio. Leigh Harline, Paul Smith and Ned Washington (U.S.A.). Walt Disney full-length cartoon. (Academy Award, 1940.)

Pride and Prejudice. Herbert Stothart (U.S.A.).

Squadron 992. Walter Leigh (Britain).

Gaslight. Richard Addinsell (Britain).

Men of the Lightship. Richard Addinsell (Britain).

Merchant Seamen. Constant Lambert (Britain).

Men and Ships. Gail Kubik (U.S.A.). (Score in the Philadelphia Library.)

The Long Voyage Home. Richard Hageman (U.S.A.).

The Westerner. Dimitri Tiomkin (U.S.A.).

Ninotchka. Werner Heymann (U.S.A.).

Tin Pan Alley. Alfred Newman (U.S.A.). (Academy Award, 1940; musical score.)

1941

Dangerous Moonlight. Richard Addinsell (Britain).

49th Parallel. Ralph Vaughan Williams (Britain).

Love on the Dole. Richard Addinsell (Britain).

Major Barbara. William Walton (Britain).

Target for Tonight. Leighton Lucas (Britain).

The Land. Richard Arnell (U.S.A.). (Score in the Philadelphia Library.)

Village Music. Douglas Moore (U.S.A.). (Score in the Philadelphia Library.)

General Suvorov. Y. Shaporin (U.S.S.R.).

Dumbo. Frank Churchill and Oliver Wallace (U.S.A.). (Academy Award, 1941; musical picture.)

All That Money Can Buy. Bernard Herrmann (U.S.A.). (Academy Award, 1941.)

Fantasia. (U.S.A.) Famous Walt Disney experiment in cartoon interpretation of concert hall music by Beethoven, Schubert, Bach, Stravinsky, Dukas.

1942

Hangmen Also Die. Hanns Eisler (U.S.A.).

Native Land. Marc Blitzstein (U.S.A.).

Citizen Kane. Bernard Herrmann (U.S.A.).

Coastal Command. Ralph Vaughan Williams (Britain).

The First of the Few. William Walton (Britain).

The Foreman Went to France. William Walton (Britain).

I Married a Witch. Franz Waxman (U.S.A.)

Malta G.C. Arnold Bax (Britain).

Next of Kin. William Walton (Britain).

Now Voyager. Max Steiner (U.S.A.). (Academy Award, 1942.)

Went the Day Well? William Walton (Britain).

The Jungle Book. Miklos Rozsa (U.S.A.).

Fires Were Started. William Alwyn (Britain).

The People's Land. Ralph Vaughan Williams (Britain).

The Talk of the Town. Friedrich Hollaender (U.S.A.).

Bambi. Edward Plumb (U.S.A.).

Yankee Doodle Dandy. Ray Heindorf and Heinz Roemheld (U.S.A.). (Academy Award, 1942; musical score.)

Listen to Britain. (Britain.) Includes Myra Hess playing the Mozart Concerto in G Major (K.453).

Paratroop. Gail Kubik (U.S.A.).
World at War. Gail Kubik (U.S.A.).
To Be or Not to Be. Werner Heymann (U.S.A.).
La Symphonie Fantastique. Life of Hector Berlioz (France).
Four Steps in the Clouds. Alessandro Cicognini (Italy).

1943

Desert Victory. William Alwyn (Britain).
The Flemish Farm. Ralph Vaughan Williams (Britain).
Madame Curie. Herbert Stothart (U.S.A.).
North Star. Aaron Copland (U.S.A.).
World of Plenty. William Alwyn (Britain).
The Forgotten Village. Hanns Eisler (U.S.A.).
Close Quarters. Gordon Jacob (Britain).
The Song of Bernadette. Alfred Newman (U.S.A.). (Academy Award, 1943.)
This is the Army. Ray Heindorf (U.S.A.). (Academy Award, 1943; musical score.)

1944

Dreams That Money Can Buy. Paul Hindemith, Darius Milhaud, Edgar Varese, Paul Bowles (U.S.A.). Hans Richter film.
Hymn of Nations. (U.S.A.) Toscanini and the N.B.C. Symphony Orchestra in works by Verdi.
Les Enfants du Paradis. Thiriet and Joseph Kosma (France).
L'Eternel Retour. Georges Auric (France).
Flesh and Fantasy. Alexander Tansman (U.S.A.).
Halfway House. Lord Berners (Britain).
Hotel Reserve. Lennox Berkeley (Britain).
Maintenance Command. Gordon Jacob (Britain).
The Mask of Dimitrios. Adolph Deutsch (U.S.A.).
The Memphis Belle. Gail Kubik (U.S.A.).
None But the Lonely Heart. Hanns Eisler (U.S.A.).
The Seventh Cross. Roy Webb (U.S.A.).
Since You Went Away. Max Steiner (U.S.A.). (Academy Award, 1944.)
Tunisian Victory. William Alwyn and Dimitri Tiomkin (Britain and U.S.A.).
The Way Ahead. William Alwyn (Britain).
Out of Chaos. Lennox Berkeley (Britain).
Our Country. William Alwyn (Britain).
Laura. David Raksin (U.S.A.).
For Whom the Bell Tolls. Victor Young (U.S.A.).
Battle for Music. Story of the London Philharmonic Orchestra (Britain). Many concert hall excerpts.
A Song to Remember. Miklos Rozsa (U.S.A.). Life of Chopin. Piano recording by José Iturbi.
Frenchman's Creek. Victor Young (U.S.A.).
Saludos Amigos. (U.S.A.).
Lermontov. Sergei Prokofiev (U.S.S.R.).
Cover Girl. (U.S.A.).
Song of Russia. (U.S.A.) Musical score based on Tchaikovsky and other Russian composers.
Love Story. Hubert Bath (Britain).

1945

Storm Warning. David Raksin (U.S.A.).
The True Glory. William Alwyn (Britain).
Burma Victory. Alan Rawsthorne (Britain).

Dead of Night. Georges Auric (Britain).
A Defeated People. Guy Warrack (Britain).
Guest in the House. Werner Janssen (U.S.A.).
Henry V. William Walton (Britain).
Keys of the Kingdom. Alfred Newman (U.S.A.).
The Lost Weekend. Miklos Rozsa (U.S.A.).
Open City. Renzo Rossellini (Italy).
The Rake's Progress. William Alwyn (Britain).
The Seventh Veil. Benjamin Frankel (Britain). Contained a central waltz
    theme, as well as many extracts from concert-hall repertoire, including Grieg
    Piano Concerto and Rachmaninov Second Piano Concerto.
Spellbound. Miklos Rozsa (U.S.A.). (Academy Award, 1945.)
The Way to the Stars. Nicholas Brodzsky (Britain).
Western Approaches. Clifton Parker (Britain).
Blithe Spirit. Richard Addinsell (Britain).
A Walk in the Sun. Frederic Efrem Rich; ballads by Earl Robinson (U.S.A.).
Cyprus is an Island. From the Greek suite by Petro Petrides (Britain).
Johnny Frenchman. Clifton Parker (Britain).
Stricken Peninsula. Ralph Vaughan Williams (Britain).
Myra Hess. Beethoven's *Appassionata Sonata* (Britain).
Journey Together. Gordon Jacob (Britain).
Caesar and Cleopatra. Georges Auric (Britain).
The Southerner. Werner Janssen (U.S.A.).
Rhapsody in Blue. Biography of George Gershwin (U.S.A.).
Music for Millions. (U.S.A.) Included many extracts from popular Dvořák,
    Debussy, Handel and Grieg concert works. With José Iturbi.
Anchors Aweigh. Georgie Stoll (U.S.A.). With José Iturbi. (Academy Award,
    1945; musical score.)
Sylvie et la Fantôme. René Cloerec (France).
The Three Caballeros. (U.S.A.) Walt Disney musical feature cartoon.
Brief Encounter. Rachmaninov's Second Piano Concerto No. 2 (Britain).
A Diary for Timothy. Richard Addinsell (Britain). Includes Myra Hess playing
    Beethoven's *Appassionata Sonata.*
Toronto Symphony. (Canada) Works by Tchaikovsky, Arthur Benjamin and
    Kabalevsky.
Farrebique. Henri Sauguet (France).
Ivan the Terrible. Sergei Prokofiev (U.S.S.R.).

1946

The Best Years of Our Lives. Hugo Friedhofer (U.S.A.). (Academy Award,
    1946.)
La Belle et La Bête. Georges Auric (France).
The Captive Heart. Alan Rawsthorne (Britain).
Devotion. Erich Wolfgang Korngold (U.S.A.). 'Cello Concerto.
Instruments of the Orchestra. Benjamin Britten (Britain).
Men of Two Worlds. Arthur Bliss (Britain).
The Overlanders. John Ireland (Britain).
Escape Me Never. Erich Wolfgang Korngold (U.S.A.).
Spectre of the Rose. George Antheil (U.S.A.).
Make Mine Music. (U.S.A.) A Walt Disney film; includes a performance of
    "Peter and the Wolf" by Prokofiev.
La Symphonie Pastorale. Georges Auric (France).
Un Revenant. Arthur Honegger (France.)
Paisa. Renzo Rossellini (Italy).
Odd Man Out. William Alwyn (Britain).

273

Their's is the Glory. Guy Warrack (Britain).

A Matter of Life and Death. Allan Gray (Britain).

The Jolson Story. Morris Stoloff (U.S.A.). (Academy Award, 1946; musical score.)

Of Human Bondage. Erich Wolfgang Korngold (U.S.A.).

Concerto. (U.S.A.) Arthur Rubenstein playing Rachmaninoff, Beethoven, Chopin, etc.

The Magic Bow. (Britain.) A film on the life of Paganini; recordings by Yehudi Menuhin.

1947

Panique. Jacques Ibert (France).

Six Juin à l'Aube. Jean Grémillon (France).

A String of Beads. Elisabeth Lutyens (Britain).

The Cumberland Story. Arthur Benjamin (Britain).

Midvinterblot. Bjorn Schildknacht (Sweden).

The World of Paul Delvaux. André Souris (Belgium).

Germany Year Zero. Renzo Rossellini (Italy).

The Search. Robert Blum (Switzerland).

Children's Concert. Eugene Kash (Canada).

Humoresque. Isaac Stern (U.S.A.). Dvořák, Wagner, Chopin, etc.

Carnegie Hall. (U.S.A.) New York Philharmonic Symphony Orchestra; Stokowski, Rodzinski, Arthur Rubenstein, Jascha Heifetz, etc.

The Barber of Seville. Rossini opera (Italy). Tito Gobbi.

Spanish Serenade. Life of Albeniz (Spain).

The Treasure of the Sierra Madre. Max Steiner (U.S.A.).

Monsieur Vincent. J. J. Grunenwald (France).

Fiddle-de-dee. (Canada) Norman McLaren abstract film.

Cadet Rousselle. (Canada) Puppet presentation of folk music.

Nicholas Nickleby. Lord Berners (Britain).

The Private Affairs of Bel Ami. Darius Milhaud (U.S.A.).

Song of Love. Schumann, Brahms and Liszt. Arthur Rubenstein, MGM Studio Orchestra. Bronislau Kaper: music director (U.S.A.).

Forever Amber. David Raksin (U.S.A.).

Mourning Becomes Electra. Richard Hageman (U.S.A.).

Take My Life. William Alwyn (Britain).

The October Man. William Alwyn (Britain).

A Double Life. Miklos Rozsa (U.S.A.). (Academy Award, 1947.)

Mother Wore Tights. Alfred Newman (U.S.A.). (Academy Award, 1947; musical score.)

Ballerina. Vanyamin Puskov (U.S.S.R.). With Ulanova.

Aubervilliers. Joseph Kosma and Jacques Prévert (France).

Book: *British Film Music* by John Huntley, published by British Yearbooks, London.

1948

Rubens. Raymond Chevreville (Belgium).

Nettezza Urbana. Giovanni Fusco (Italy).

Steps of the Ballet. Arthur Benjamin (Britain).

Paris 1900. Guy Bernard (France).

Scott of the Antarctic. Ralph Vaughan Williams (Britain).

The Glass Mountain. Nino Rota (Britain).

The History of Mr. Polly. William Alwyn (Britain).

Queen of Spades. Georges Auric (Britain).

Christopher Columbus. Arthur Bliss (Britain).

Louisiana Story. Virgil Thomson (U.S.A.).
Bicycle Thieves. Alessandro Cicognini (Italy).
Hamlet. William Walton (Britain).
The Fallen Idol. William Alwyn (Britain).
Rigoletto. Verdi opera. (Italy.) Tito Gobbi.
Oliver Twist. Arnold Bax (Britain).
Begone Dull Care and *Boogie Doodle* (Canada). Abstract films by Norman McLaren.
The Iron Curtain. Shostakovitch, Khachaturian, Prokofiev and Miaskovsky, arr. Alfred Newman (U.S.A.).
The Red Shoes. Brian Easdale (Britain). (Academy Award, 1948.)
Easter Parade. Johnny Green and Roger Edens (U.S.A.). (Academy Award, 1948; musical score.)
A City Speaks. William Alwyn (Britain). John Barbirolli and the Halle Orchestra.

1949

Lost Boundaries. Louis Applebaum (U.S.A.)
The Heiress. Aaron Copland (U.S.A.). (Academy Award, 1949.).
On The Town. Leonard Bernstein with Roger Edens and Lennie Hayton (U.S.A.). (Academy Award, 1949; musical score.)
The Red Pony. Aaron Copland (U.S.A.).
The Third Man. Anton Karas (Britain).
Trottie True. Benjamin Frankel (Britain).
Dim Little Island. Ralph Vaughan Williams (Britain).
The Rocking Horse Winner. William Alwyn (Britain).
She Wore a Yellow Ribbon. Richard Hageman (U.S.A.).
The Magic Canvas. Matyas Seiber (Britain).
Twelve O'Clock High. Alfred Newman (U.S.A.).
Young Man of Music. Ray Heindorf and Harry James (U.S.A.).
Ichabod and Mr. Toad. Oliver Wallace (U.S.A.).
Daybreak in Udi. William Alwyn (Britain).
Macbeth. Jacques Ibert (U.S.A.).

1950

Gerald McBoing Boing. Gail Kubik (U.S.A.).
Moussorgsky. (U.S.S.R.)
Pablo Casals. (France.)
State Secret. William Alwyn (Britain).
Orphée. Georges Auric (France).
Prelude to Fame. (Britain.) Includes a number of concert hall works.
Stage Fright. Leighton Lucas (Britain).
Sunset Boulevard. Franz Waxman (U.S.A.). (Academy Award, 1950.)
The Wooden Horse. Clifton Parker (Britain).
La Vie Commence Demain. Darius Milhaud (France).
Family Portrait. John Greenwood (Britain).
The Dancing Fleece. Alan Rawsthorne (Britain).
Il Trovatore. Verdi opera. (Italy.)
Tanglewood Story. Serge Koussevitsky, Aaron Copland, Boston Symphony Orchestra (U.S.A.).
La Ronde. Oscar Straus (France).
Of Men and Music. Arthur Rubenstein, Jan Peerce, Jascha Heifetz, Philharmonic Symphony Orchestra conducted by Dimitri Mitropoulos. (U.S.A.)
Beaver Valley. Paul Smith (U.S.A.).
Seven Days to Noon. John Addison (Britain).

Teresa. Louis Applebaum (U.S.A.).
Ballerina. Robert Le Febvre (France).
La Beauté du Diable. Roman Vlad (France).
Miss Julie. Dag Wiren (Sweden).
Annie Get Your Gun. Adolph Deutsch and Roger Edens (U.S.A.). (Academy Award, 1950; musical score.)

1951

Le Sel de la Terre. Guy Bernard (France).
Goya: The Horrors of War. Jean Grémillon (France).
The Boy Kumasenu. Elisabeth Lutyens (Gold Coast).
Loony Tom. Howard Brubeck (U.S.A.).
Fra Brne. Boris Papandopulo (Yugoslavia).
The Medium. Gian-Carlo Menotti (U.S.A.).
Nature's Half Acre. Paul Smith (U.S.A.).
Quo Vadis. Miklos Rozsa (U.S.A.).
An American in Paris. George Gershwin with Johnny Green and Saul Chaplin (U.S.A.). (Academy Award, 1951; musical score.)
Around is Around. Louis Applebaum (Canada). 3-D production by Norman McLaren.
Royal River. William Alwyn (Britain). 3-D production with stereophonic sound.
Pacific 231. Arthur Honegger (France).
The River. K. N. Dandayuhapani and M. A. Partha Sarathy (India).
St. Matthew Passion. Bach (Austria/U.S.A.). Elizabeth Schwarzkopf. Vienna Philharmonic Orchestra conducted by Herbert von Karajan.
A Streetcar Named Desire. Alex North (U.S.A.).
The Magic Box. William Alwyn (Britain).
The Great Caruso. (U.S.A.) Mario Lanza. Selections from operas.
The Young Chopin. (Poland.)
A Beethoven Sonata. (Britain.) Dennis Brain and Denis Matthews.
Outcast of the Islands. Brian Easdale (Britain).
Opera School. (Canada.)
Glasgow Orpheus Choir. (Britain.)
His Excellency. Ernest Irving's arrangement of Handel's *Scipio* (Britain).
Rashomon. Taknashi Matsuyama (Japan).
Miracle in Milan. Alessandro Cicognini (Italy).
The Tales of Hoffmann. Offenbach (Britain). Royal Philharmonic Orchestra conducted by Thomas Beecham.
The Man in the White Suit. Benjamin Frankel (Britain).
A Place in the Sun. Franz Waxman (U.S.A.). (Academy Award, 1951.)
Encore. Richard Addinsell (Britain).
Where No Vultures Fly. Alan Rawsthorne (Britain).
Painter and Poet series. Matyas Seiber (Britain).
Pool of London. John Addison (Britain).
No Resting Place. William Alwyn (Britain).
Henry Moore. William Alwyn (Britain).
El Dorado. Elisabeth Lutyens (Britain).
The White Continent. Peter Racine Fricker (Britain).
Waters of Time. Alan Rawsthorne (Britain).

1952

Mirror of Holland. Max Vredenburg (Holland).
The Magic Garden. Ralph Trewala and Tomany Ramokgopa (South Africa).
Daphni. Howard Brubeck (Greece).
Viva Zapata. Alex North (U.S.A.).

Singin' in the Rain. Arthur Freed and Nacio Herb Brown (U.S.A.).
Cry the Beloved Country. R. Gallois Montbrun (Britain).
High Treason. John Addison (Britain).
The Quiet Man. Victor Young (U.S.A.).
High Noon. Dimitri Tiomkin (U.S.A.). (Academy Award, 1952.)
The Thief. Herschel Burke Gilbert (U.S.A.).
Robin Hood. Clifton Parker (Britain).
The Bad and the Beautiful. David Raksin (U.S.A.).
Journey into History. Arnold Bax (Britain).
The Stranger Left No Card. Alfven's *Midsommarvarka Suite*, arranged by
  Doreen Carwithen (Britain).
Titfield Thunderbolt. Georges Auric (Britain).
Les Belles de Nuit. Georges van Parys (France).
The Cruel Sea. Alan Rawsthorne (Britain).
Sadko. Rimsky-Korsakov (U.S.S.R.).
Shane. Victor Young (U.S.A.).
Glinka, Man of Music. (U.S.S.R.)
The Card. William Alwyn (Britain).
Gift Horse. Clifton Parker (Britain).
Mandy. William Alwyn (Britain).
The Sound Barrier. Malcolm Arnold (Britain).
Opus 65. Richard Arnell (Britain).
Limelight. Charles Chaplin (U.S.A.).
Corroboree. John Antill (Australia).
Aan. Naushad (India).
Casque D'Or. Georges van Parys (France).
Gala Festival. (U.S.S.R.) With Ulanova.
With a Song in My Heart. Alfred Newman (U.S.A.). (Academy Award, 1952;
  musical score.)

1953
The Pleasure Garden. Stanley Bate (Britain).
The Bandit. Gabriel Migliori (Brazil).
The Drawings of Leonardo Da Vinci. Alan Rawsthorne (Britain).
Salome. Daniele Amfitheatrof (U.S.A.).
Moulin Rouge. Georges Auric (Britain).
Julius Caesar. Miklos Rozsa (U.S.A.).
Return To Paradise. Dimitri Tiomkin (U.S.A.).
Victory At Sea. Richard Rodgers, arranged by Robert Russell Bennett (U.S.A.).
The Band Wagon. A. Schwartz-Dietz (U.S.A.).
The Beggar's Opera. John Gay, arranged by Arthur Bliss (Britain).
The Robe. Alfred Newman (U.S.A.).
The Million-Pound Note. William Alwyn (Britain).
Powered Flight. Malcolm Arnold (Britain).
Hobson's Choice. Malcolm Arnold (Britain).
The Maggie. John Addison (Britain).
The Story of Gilbert and Sullivan. (Britain.)
Genevieve. Larry Adler (Britain).
Johnny on the Run. Antony Hopkins (Britain).
The Juggler. George Antheil (U.S.A.).
Malta Story. William Alwyn (Britain).
Melba. (Britain.)
The Man Between. John Addison (Britain).
The Conquest of Everest. Arthur Benjamin (Britain).
World Without End. Elisabeth Lutyens (Britain).

Call Me Madam. Alfred Newman (U.S.A.). (Academy Award, 1953; musical score.)

Lili. Bronislau Kaper (U.S.A.). (Academy Award, 1953.)

1954

From Here to Eternity. George Dunning (U.S.A.).

The Tell-Tale Heart. Boris Kremenliev (U.S.A.).

Rhapsody. Tchaikovsky, Rachmaninov, etc. (U.S.A.). Claude Arrau and Michael Rabin.

Cinemascope orchestral films. Cappricio Italien; Overture: *The Merry Wives of Windsor*; Overture: *Poet and Peasant*; Finale: Tchaikovsky 4th Symphony; Polovetsian Dances from *Prince Igor*; *Street Scene* (Newman); *Farewell Symphony* (Haydn). (U.S.A.)

Seven Brides For Seven Brothers. Adolph Deutsch and Saul Chaplin (U.S.A.). (Academy Award, 1954; musical score.)

Suddenly. David Raksin (U.S.A.).

Romeo and Juliet. Roman Vlad (Britain/Italy).

On the Waterfront. Leonard Bernstein (U.S.A.).

The Living Desert. Paul Smith (U.S.A.).

The High and the Mighty. Dimitri Tiomkin (U.S.A.). (Academy Award, 1954.)

1955

Richard III. William Walton (Britain).

French Cancan. Georges van Parys (France).

Madame Butterfly. Puccini opera (Italy/Japan).

Oh, Rosalinda. Adaptation of *Die Fledermaus* by Johann Strauss (Britain).

East of Eden. Leonard Rosenman (U.S.A.).

Marty. Roy Webb (U.S.A.).

A Kid For Two Farthings. Benjamin Frankel (Britain).

The Ship That Died of Shame. William Alwyn (Britain).

The Rose Tattoo. Alex North (U.S.A.).

Love is a Many-splendored Thing. Alfred Newman (U.S.A.). Best score and Best Song Academy Awards. Best Song composed by Paul Francis Webster.

Oklahoma! Robert Russell Bennett, Jay Blackton, Adolph Deutsch (U.S.A.). Academy Award for Best Musical Score.

White Vertigo. Francesco Lavagnino (Italy). Award in 1956 Nastri d'Argento per la Musica (The Italian "Silver Ribbons" for the best composer of the previous year).

The Kentuckian. Bernard Herrmann (U.S.A.).

1956

Kanal. Jan Krenz (Poland).

Aparajito. Ravi Shankar (India).

Gervaise. Georges Auric (France).

War and Peace. Nino Rota (Italy/U.S.A.) 1957 Nastri d'Argento per la Musica.

Picnic. George Dunning (Britain).

La Sorcière. Norbert Glanzberg (France).

The Burmese Harp. Akira Ifukube (Japan).

Il Terroriere. Carlo Rustichelli (Italy).

The King and I. Music Director Alfred Newman. Songs Rogers and Hammerstein (U.S.A.). Best Musical Picture Academy Award.

Moby Dick. Philip Sainton (Britain).

Giant. Dimitri Tiomkin (U.S.A.).

Les Grandes Maneuvres. Georges van Parys (France).

Calle Mayor (Main Street). Joseph Kosma (Spain/France).

Seventh Seal. Erik Nordgren (Sweden).

Alexander the Great. Mario Nascimbebe (Italy).
Around the World in 80 Days. Victor Young. Academy Award for Best Dramatic or Comedy Score.
The Man with the Golden Arm. Elmer Bernstein (U.S.A.).
Anything Goes. Music James van Heusen and words by Sammy Cahn (U.S.A.).

1957
Throne of Blood. Masaru Sato (Japan).
The England of Elizabeth. Ralph Vaughan-Williams (Britain).
Donzoko (Lower Depths). Masaru Sato (Japan).
The Bridge on the River Kwai. Malcolm Arnold (Britain). Academy Award Score.
The Sweet Smell of Success. Elmer Bernstein (U.S.A.).
Uomini e Lupi. Mario Nascimbene (Italy).
White Nights. Nino Rota (Italy). Nastri d'Argento per la Musica 1958.
Il Grido. Gioranni Fusco (Italy).
Nata di Marzo. Piero Piccioni (Italy).
The Joker is Wild. "All the Way" Academy Award Song by James van Heusen (music), words by Sammy Cahn (U.S.A.).
Wild Strawberries. Erik Nordgren (Sweden).

1958
Hiroshima, Mon Amour. Giovanni Fusco and Georges Delerue (France/Japan).
Rio Bravo. Dimitri Tiomkin (U.S.A.).
Gigi. Frederick Loewe, Alan Jay Lerner. Academy Award for Best Song "Gigi". Also Academy Award for Best Musical Score (André Previn) (U.S.A.).
The Old Man and the Sea. Dimitri Tiomkin. Academy Award for Best Score (U.S.A.).
The Bolshoï Ballet. Yuri Faier and G. Rozhdestvensky (Britain).
L'Uomo di Paglia (Strawman) Carlo Rustichelli (Italy), Nastri d'Argento per la Musica 1959.
Montparnasse 19. Paul Misraki (France).
Vertigo. Bernard Herrmann (U.S.A.).
The Horse's Mouth. Kenneth V. Jones (Britain).
Inn of the Sixth Happiness. (Malcolm Arnold) (Britain).
God's Little Acre. Elmer Bernstein (U.S.A.).
The Lefthanded Gun. Alexander Courage (U.S.A.).
The Vikings. Marco Nascimbene (Italy).
Ajaantrik. Ali Akbar Khan (India).
Paris Holiday. Words and Music by Sammy Cahn and James van Heusen (U.S.A.).
Sait-on Jamais? John Lewis. Played by The Modern Jazz Quartet (France).

1959
North by Northwest. Bernard Herrmann (U.S.A.).
Hole in the Head. Words and Music by Sammy Cahn and James van Heusen. Academy Award for Best Song ("High Hopes"). (U.S.A.).
Ben Hur. Miklós Rozsa. Academy Award for Best Score. (U.S.A.).
Porgy and Bess. André Previn and Ken Darby. Academy Award for Best Musical Score. (U.S.A.).
On the Beach. Ernest Gold (U.S.A.).
Le Testament du Docteur Cordelier (called "The Testament of Doctor Cordelier" or "Experiment in Evil"). Joseph Kosma (France).
Apur Sansar (The World of Apu). Ravi Shankar (India).

Estate Violenta (Violent Summer). Mario Nascimbene. Nastri diArgento per la Musica. 1960.
Can-Can. (Cole Porter) (U.S.A.).
Calypso. Angelo-Francesco Lavagnino (Italy).
Look Back in Anger. John Addison (Britain).
Sudba Celoveka (The Destiny of Man). Veniamin E. Basner (U.S.S.R.).
Blind Date. Richard Rodney Bennett (Britain).
Les 400 *Coups* (400 Blows). Jean Constantin (France).
Some Like It Hot. Adolph Deutsch (U.S.A.).
Anatomy of a Murder. Duke Ellington (U.S.A.).
Pociag (*Night Train*). Andrzej Trzaskowski (Poland).
Šinel (*The Overcoat*). Nikolai Sidelnikov (U.S.S.R.).
Dama S Sobačkoj (The Lady and the Little Dog). Nudeja Simonian (U.S.S.R.).
Bonjour Tristesse. Georges Auric (France).

1960
L'Avventura. Giovanni Fusco (Italy). Nastri d'Argento per la Musica 1961.
The Magnificent Seven. Elmer Bernstein (U.S.A.).
Psycho. Bernard Herrmann (U.S.A.).
Never on Sunday. Manos Hadjidakis (Greece). "Never on Sunday" Academy Award for Best Song.
High Time. Words and Music by Sammy Cahn and James van Heusen (U.S.A.).
Let's Make Love. Words and Music by Sammy Cahn and James van Heusen (U.S.A.).
Oceans II. Words and Music by Sammy Cahn and James van Heusen (U.S.A.).
Exodus. Ernest Gold (U.S.A.). Academy Award for Best Score.
Spartacus. Alex North (U.S.A.).
Elmer Gantry. André Previn (U.S.A.).
Song Without End. Morris Stoloff and Harry Sukman. Academy Award for Best Musical (U.S.A.).
Judgement at Nuremberg. Ernest Gold (U.S.A.).
La Dolce Vita. Nino Rota (Italy).
The Adventure of Huckleberry Finn. Jerome Moross (U.S.A.).
Kapo'. Carlo Rustichelli (Italy).

1961
The Innocents. Georges Auric (U.S.A.).
Sirènes. Luciano Berio (France).
Lola. Michel le Grand (France).
Aktion 5. Hans Eisler (Germany).
Through a Glass Darkly. J. S. Bach. Suite No. 2 in D minor for Cello (Sweden).
Lines Horizontal. Pete Seeger (Canada).
La Notte. Giorgio Gaslini. Nastri d'Argento per la Musica 1962. (Italy).
Jules et Jim. Georges Delerue (France).
Yojimbo. Masaru Sato (Japan).
West Side Story. Leonard Bernstein, Saul Chaplin, Sid Rawin, Irwin Kootal, Johnny Green (U.S.A.). (Academy Award for Best Musical).
Breakfast at Tiffany's. Henry Mancini and Johnny Mercer (U.S.A.). (Academy Award for Best Song "Moon River".
Kovanshchina. Dimitri Shostakovich (U.S.S.R.).
Paris Blues. Duke Ellington (U.S.A.).

1962
The Wrong Arm of the Law. Richard Rodney Bennett (Britain)
Salvatore Giuliano. Piero Piccioni. Nastri d'Argento per la Musica 1963. (Italy).
Cantata. Bela Bartók and Bálint Sárosi (Hungary).

The L-shaped Room. John Barry (Britain).
Days of Wine and Roses. Henry Mancini and John Mercer (U.S.A.). (Academy Award for Best Song "Days of Wine and Roses").
Lawrence of Arabia. Maurice Jarre (Academy Award for Best Score) (Britain).
Mutiny on the Bounty. Bronislau Kaper (U.S.A.).
Freud. Jerry Goldsmith (U.S.A.).
The Music Man. Ray Heindorf (U.S.A.). (Academy Award for Best Adaption or Treatment).
To Kill a Mockingbird. Elmer Bernstein (U.S.A.).
Hung Sik Leung Dje Ching. ("The Red Detachment of Women). Collective Composing. (Peoples' Republic of China).
Arte Programmata. Luciano Berio (Italy).
I Giorni Contati. Ivan Vandor (Italy).
Vivre Sa Vie. Michel Legrand.
Eva. Michel Legrand (Britain).
Noche de Verano. Antonio Perez Loea (Spain).
L'Eclisse. Giovanni Fusco (Italy).

1963
Billy Liar. Richard Rodney Bennett (Britain).
8½. Nino Rota (Italy), Nastri de'Argento per la Musica 1964.
The Leopard. Nino Rota (Italy).
Machorka-Muff. J. S. Bach (Musical Offering BWV 1079 Ricercar a 6) and François Louis (Transmutations) (Germany).
This Sporting Life. Roberto Gehrard (Britain).
Irma La Douce. Andre Previn (U.S.A.). (Academy Award for Best Adaptation or Treatment).
L'Immortelle. George Delerue (France).
The Birds. Berand Herrmann (U.S.A.).
Tom Jones. John Addison (Britain).
Sundays and Cybele. Maurice Jarre (France).
It's a Mad, Mad, Mad World. Ernest Gold (U.S.A.).
The Silence. J. S. Bach's the Goldberg Variations (Sweden).
Papa's Delicate Condition. Words and music by Sammy Cahn and James van Heusen (U.S.A.). (Academy Award for Best Song "Call me Irresponsible").
The Servant. Johnny Dankworth (Britain).
List of Adrian Messanger. Jerry Goldsmith (U.S.A.).
Lancelot and Guienevere. Ron Goodwin (U.S.A.).
The Chalk Gardens. Malcolm Arnold (Britain).

1964
Fall of the Roman Empire. Dimitri Tiomkin (U.S.A.).
The Pink Panther. Henry Mancini (U.S.A.).
Red Desert (Deserto Rosso). Music by Giovanni Fusco sung by Cecilia Fusco. Electronic Music by Vittoria Gelmetti (Italy).
Gertrude. Jorgen Jersild plus songs by Grethe Risbjerb Thomsen (Denmark).
The Silencers. Elmer Bernstein. Lyrics by Mack David. Theme song "The Silencers" sung by Vikki Carr (U.S.A.).
Hard Days Night. Music by The Beatles arranged by George Martin (Britain).
Underground Centenary. Kenneth V. Jones (Britain).
Sing of the Border. Muir Mathieson (Britain).
Hamlet. Shostakovich (U.S.S.R.).
My Way Home. Bartók's Allegro Barbaro and folk songs. Zoltán Jenei (Hungary).
Seance on a Wet Afternoon. John Barry (Britain).

281

Fistful of Dollars. Ennio Morricone (Italy). Nastri d'Argento per la Musica 1965.

Mary Poppins. Richard M. Sherman and Robert B. Sherman. (Best Musical Academy Award and also Academy Award for Best Song "Chim-Chim Cher-ee").

My Fair Lady. André Previn. (Academy Award for best Adaptation and Treatment) (Britain).

Gospel According to St. Matthew. Music J. S. Bach, W. A. Mozart, Sergei Prokofiev, Webern and Luis E. Bacalov (Italy).

Dead Ringer US (called *Dead Image* in Britain). André Previn (U.S.A.).

Jason and the Argonauts (Bernard Hermann) (U.S.A.).

Cheyenne Autumn. Alex North (U.S.A.).

1965

Vaghe Stelle Dell'orsa. Cesar Franck, Choral Prelude and Fugue (Italy).

The Bible. Toshiro Mayuzumi (Italy).

The Battle of Algiers. Ennio Morricone and Gillo Pontecorvo (Italy/Algeria).

Wild Wings. Edward Williams (Britain).

Thunderball. John Barry (Britain).

Sound of Music. Rogers and Hammerstein (U.S.A.). (Academy Award for Best Adaptation to Irwin Kostal). The largest grossing musical to date.

The Sandpiper. Johnny Mandel (U.S.A.). (Academy Award for Best Song "The Shadow of Your Smile" with Paul Francis Webster.

The Umbrellas of Cherbourg. Michel Legrand and Jacques Demy (France).

Doctor Zhivago. Maurice Jarre. (Academy Award for Best Score) (Britain).

Sette Uomini D'Oro (Seven Against the Sun). Armando Trovajoli. Nastri d'Argento per la Musica, 1966.

Inside Daisy Clover. André Previn (U.S.A.).

The Ipcress File. John Barry (Britain).

Those Magnificent Men in Their Flying Machines. Ron Goodwin (Britain).

Duel at Diablo. Neal Heft (U.S.A.).

Marnie. Bernard Herrmann (U.S.A.).

The Pawnbroker. Quincy Jones (U.S.A.).

Mirage. Quincy Jones (U.S.A.).

The Third Secret. Richard Arnell (Britain).

1966

Fahrenheit 451. Bernard Herrmann (Britain).

The Blue Max. Jerry Goldsmith (U.S.A.).

La Guerre Est Finie. Giovanni Fusco (France).

Born Free. (Academy Award for Best Song "Born Free" John Barry and Don Black) (Britain).

Love for a Stranger. John Bath (Uruguay).

A Funny Thing Happened on the Way to the Forum. Ken Horne (U.S.A.). (Academy Award for Best Adaptation).

Who's Afraid of Virginia Woolf. Alex North (U.S.A.).

Persona. Lars-Johan Werle (Sweden).

L'Armatat Brancaleone. Carlo Rustichelli Nastri d'Argento per la Musica 1967.

The Sandpebbles. Jerry Goldsmith (U.S.A.).

Stagecoach. Jerry Goldsmith (U.S.A.).

Luciano, Una Vita Bruiata. Luciano Chailly (Italy).

Torn Curtain. John Addison (Britain).

A Fine Madness. John Addison (Britain).

Morgan: A Suitable Case for Treatment. Johnny Dankworth (Britain).

Seconds. Jerry Goldsmith (U.S.A.).

282

Cul-de-sac. Krzysztof Komeda (Poland/Britain).
Chappaqua. Ravi Shankar (U.S.A.).
The Marat/Sade. Richard Peaslee (Britain).
The Wrong Box. Dudley Moore (Britain).
Un Homme et Une Femme. Francis Lai (France).
The Slender Thread. Quincy Jones (U.S.A.).
Walk, Don't Run. Quincy Jones (U.S.A.).

1967
Deadfall. John Barry (Britain).
Pas De Deux. Maurice Blackburn (Canada).
Labyrinthe (Expo '67). Eldon Rathburn (Canada)—a multi screen film for Expo '67. (Recording LAB-650S).
Billion Dollar Brain. Richard Rodney Bennett (Britain).
Far From the Madding Crowd. Richard Rodney Bennett (Britain).
Half a Sixpence. David Henneker (Britain).
Valley of the Dolls. Songs by Dory and André Previn (U.S.A.).
Oedipus Rex. Rumanian and Japanese folk music plus original music co-ordinated by Pier Paolo Pasolini. Music Director Fausto Ancillai (Italy).
Reflections in a Golden Eye. Toshiro Mayuzumi (U.S.A.).
The Graduate. Simon and Garfunkel (U.S.A.).
The Bride Wore Black. Bernard Herrmann (France).
Ahes. Markowski (Poland).
1812. Tchaikovsky's Opus 49 (U.S.S.R.).
St. Matthew's Passion. J. S. Bach (Hungary).
Casino Royale. Burt Bacharach lyrics Hal David (Britain).
The Trip. Electric Flag (U.S.A.).
Dr. Dolittle. Leslie Bricusse (U.S.A.). (Academy Award for Best Song "Talk to the Animals").
Cool Hand Luke. Lalo Schifrin (U.S.A.).
Camelot. Alfred Newman and Ken Darby (U.S.A.). (Academy Award for Best Scoring of Music).
In Cold Blood. Quincy Jones (U.S.A.).
Pronto, C.è Una Certa Giuliana Per Te. Mario Nascimbene. Nastri d'Argento per la Musica 1968 (Italy).
In Like Flint. Jerry Goldsmith (U.S.A.).
In the Heat of the Night. Quincy Jones (U.S.A.).
Banning. Quincy Jones (U.S.A.).
Enter Laughing. Quincy Jones (U.S.A.).
Thirty is a Dangerous Age Cynthia. Dudley Moore (Britain).
Vivre Pour Vivre. Francis Lai (France).

1968
Secret Ceremony. Richard Rodney Bennett (Britain).
Chronicle of Anna Magdelena Bach. Music of J. S. Bach (Germany/Italy).
Jigsaw. Quincy Jones (U.S.A.).
Rachel, Rachel. Jerome Moross (U.S.A.).
The Rise and Fall of the Third Reich. Lalo Schifrin (U.S.A.).
Dandy in Aspic. Quincy Jones (U.S.A.).
Theorem. Ennio Morricone (Italy).
Hour of the Wolf. Lars-Johan Werle (Sweden).
Planet of the Apes. Jerry Goldsmith (U.S.A.).
2001: A Space Odyssey. Aram Khatchaturuan (Gayane Ballet Suite), György Ligeti (Atmospheres, Lux Aeterne, Requiem), Johann Strauss (The Blue Danube), Richard Strauss (Thus Spake Zarathustra) (Britain).

The Thomas Crown Affair. Michel Legrand, Alan and Marilyn Bergman (U.S.A.). (Academy Award for Best Song "The Windmills of your Mind".
The Lion in Winter. John Barry. (Academy Award for Best Score) (Britain).
Oliver! Lionel Bart. John Green Academy Award for Best Musical (Britain).
Oh! What a Lovely War. Musical director Alfred Ralston (Britain).
Barbarella. Bob Crewe and Charles Fox (France).
Un Soir, Un Train. Freddy Devreese (Belgium).
Baisers Volées (Stolen Kisses). Antoine Duhamel (France).
Rosemary's Baby. Krzystzof Komeda (U.S.A.).
Funny Girl. Isobel Lennart (U.S.A.).
Sweet Charity. Music director Ralph Burns. Songs by Cy Coleman and Dorothy Fields (U.S.A.).
Chitty Chitty Bang Bang. Music director Irwin Kostal, songs Richard and Robert Sherman (U.S.A.).
Romeo and Juliet. Nino Rota. Nastri d'Argento perla Musica 1969 (Italy).

1969
The Italian Job. Quincy Jones (Britain).
The Madwoman of Chaillot. Michael Lewis (Britain).
If. . . . Marc Wilkinson (Britain).
Zabriskie Point. Various artistes including The Pink Floyd, The Kaleidoscope, The Rolling Stones, The Grateful Dead, Patti Page, The Youngbloods, John Fahey (U.S.A.).
Je T'Aime, Je T'Aime. Krzysztof Penderecki (France).
Z. Mikis Theodorakis (France).
Wonderwall. George Harrison (Britain).
The Wild Bunch. Jerry Fielding (U.S.A.).
Yellow Submarine. The Beatles and George Martin (Britain).
Sotto il Segno Dello Scorpione (Under the Sign of Scorpio). Vittorio Gelmetti (Italy).
Keep on Rockin' (Also called *Sweet Toronto*). Bo Didley, Jerry Lee Lewis, Chuck Berry, Little Richard and others (Canada).
Easy Rider. Music from Steppenwolf, Jimi Hendrix, The Byrds, Fraternity of Man, Roger McGunn, The Electric Prunes and others (U.S.A.).
San Francisco. The Pink Floyd (Britain).
Jaunpuri. Jugalbandi music (Britain).
Hello Dolly. Lennie Hayton and Lionel Newman (U.S.A.). (Academy Award for Best Musical).
Sierra Maestra. Vittorio Gelmetti (Italy).
Necropolis. Gavin Bryars (Italy).
Bob and Carol and Ted and Alice. Quincy Jones (U.S.A.).
John and Mary. Quincy Jones (U.S.A.).
Metti, Una Sera a Cena (One Night at Dinner). Ennio Morricone. Nastri d'argento per la Musica 1970.
Figures in a Landscape. Richard Rodney Bennett (Britain).
The Confrontation. Songs by Aladar Komjath and Paul Arma, and the March of the International Brigade (Hungary).
More. Pink Floyd (Luxembourg).
Midnight Cowboy. John Barry and featuring songs by Nilsson, The Group, Leslie Miller and Elephants Memory (U.S.A.).
Butch Cassidy and the Sundance Kid. Burt Bacharach and Hal David (U.S.A.). (Academy Award for Best Song "Raindrops Keep Falling on My Head" and Best Score (U.S.A.).
Justine. Jerry Goldsmith (U.S.A.).
Alice's Restaurant. Arlo Guthrie and Woodie Guthrie (U.S.A.).

Anna Karenina. Rodion Scredrin (U.S.S.R.).
A City for All Seasons. Edward Elgar's Cockaigne Overture (Britain).

1970

The Music Lovers. Tchaikovsky (Britain).
Cotton Comes to Haarlem. Galt McDermott (U.S.A.).
Reggae. Horace Ove (Britain).
Soldier Blue. Roy Budd (U.S.A.).
Double Suicide. Toru Takemitsu (Japan).
Death in Venice. Mahler 3rd and 5th Symphonies (Italy).
Woodstock. Various artistes including John Sebastian, Canned Heat, Richie Havens, Country Joe and the Fish, Arlo Guthrie, Sha-Na-Na, Joan Baez, Crosby, Stills and Nash, Joe Cocker, Ten Years After, The Who, Jimi Hendrix, Sly and the Family Stone, Santana (U.S.A.).
Love Story. Francis Lai (U.S.A.).
Ryan's Daughter. Maurice Jarre (Britain).
The Horsemen. Georges Delerue (U.S.A.).
Anonimo Veneziano. Stelvio Cipriani. Nastri d'argento per las Musica 1971 (Italy).
The Three Sisters. William Walton (Britain).
Deep End. Cat Stevens and The Can (Britain).
Patton. Jerry Goldsmith (U.S.A.).
Cromwell. Frank Cordell (Britain).
Let It Be. The Beatles. (Academy Award for the Best Musical) (Britain).
Valerie and the Week of Wonders. Jan Klusak (Hungary).
Moment. Gavin Bryars (Britain).
Lovers and Other Strangers. Fred Karlin, Robb Wilson and Arthur James (U.S.A.). (Academy Award for Best Song "For All We Know").
Chicago Blues. Johnie Lewis, Floyd Jones, Muddy Waters, J. B. Hutto, Buddy Guy (Britain).
Blues Like Showers of Rain. Otis Span, Little Brother, Lonnie Johnson, Henry Townsend, Sam "Lightin" Hopkins, etc.) (Britain).

1971

A Well Spent Life. Mance Lipscomb (U.S.A.).
Dearest Love. Sidney Bechet, Charlie Parker (France).
The Heist. Quincy Jones featuring Little Richard and Roberta Flade (U.S.A.).
French Connection. Don Ellis (U.S.A.).
Red Psalm. Ferenc Sebo, popular and revolutionary songs (Hungary).
Nicholas and Alexandra. Richard Rodney Bennett (Britain).
Gimme Shelter. The Rolling Stones (U.S.A.).
Whoever Slew Auntie Roo. Kenneth V. Jones (Britain).
Sacco e Vanzetti. Ennio Morricone and Joan Baez. Nastri d'Argento per las Musica (Italy).
Cabaret. Music John Kander, lyrics Fred Ebb (U.S.A.).
200 Motels. Frank Zappa and the Mothers of Invention and Royal Philharmonic Orchestra (Britain).
Plumb-Loco. Library music! (Britain).
Macbeth. The Third Ear Band (Britain).
King Lear. Shostakovich (U.S.S.R.).
Clockwork Orange. Walter Carlos, Beethoven 9th Symphony, Rossini, Elgar, Freed, Nacie, Herb Brown.
La Pacifista (The Pacifist). Giorgio Gaslini and revolutionary songs (Italy).
Tchaikovsky. Tchaikovsky. Arranged by Tiomkin (U.S.S.R.).

285

The Boyfriend. Based on musical play by Sandy Wilson. Music by Ian Whittaker and some by Peter Maxwell Davies (arrangement) (Britain).
Summer of '42. Michel Legrand. (U.S.A.). (Academy Award for Best Score).
Walkabout. John Barry and Stockhausen (Britain).
The Devils. Peter Maxwell Davies and period music arranged by David Munrow (Britain).
Domicile Conjural. Antoine Duhamel (France).
The Cow. Farhat Hormoz (Iran).
L'Eden e Après. Michel Fano (France).
Grissom Gang. Gerald Fried (U.S.A.).
Escape from the Planet of the Apes. Jerry Goldsmith (U.S.A.).
Shaft. Isaac Hayes. (U.S.A.). (Academy Award for Best Song "The Theme from Shaft").
Fiddler on the Roof. John Williams (U.S.A.). (Academy Award).
Times For. Gavin Bryars (Britain).

1972
Brother Sun, Sister Moon. Donovan (Italy).
Dyn Amo. Gavin Bryars (Britain).
Jesus Never Fouled Me Yet. Gavin Bryars (Britain).
Cisco Pike. Music supervisor Bob Johnston. Songs by Kris Kristofferson, Sonny Terry, A. Allen and K. Fowley (U.S.A.).
Dirty Harry. Lalo Schifrin (U.S.A.).
Frenzy. Ron Goodwin (Britain).
The Frogs. Les Baxter (U.S.A.).
How to Steal a Diamond in Four Easy Lessons (called also *The Hot Rock*). Quincy Jones (U.S.A.).
Lady Caroline Lamb. Richard Rodney Bennett (Britain).
Second Best. Richard Arnell. Electronics by Lawrence Casserley (Britain).
La Vallée. The Pink Floyd (Music "Obscured by Clouds") (Switzerland).
The Bitter Tears of Petra Von Kant. Verdi. The Platters, Walker Brothers (Germany).
The Godfather. Nino Rota (U.S.A.).
San Michele Aveva un Gallo. Benedetto Ghiglia (Italy).
Jeremiaha Johnson. John Rubinstein (U.S.A.).
Solaris. Edward Artemyev. Bach Chorale (U.S.S.R.).
Jazz is Our Religion. Langston Hughes, Ted Joans, Jazz poetry and Music of Johnny Griffin, Dizzy Reece, Art Blakey, John Hendricks, The Clarke-Boland Big Band (U.S.A.).

286

FILM MUSIC CRITICISM

The special appreciation and critical analysis of film music has not yet been more than tentatively approached in the English language except for a few specialists such as Gerald Pratley and Louis Applebaum in Canada, Hans Keller in England and Professor Frederick Sternfeld in the U.S.A. Examples of criticism by Louis Applebaum and Professor Sternfeld may be found in this book on pp. 150–2 and 153–4 respectively. The authors are grateful to Gerald Pratley and Hans Keller for permitting examples of their work to be reproduced below.

A CONSIDERATION OF FILM MUSIC
AWAY FROM THE SCREEN

by GERALD PRATLEY
(Canadian Broadcasting Corporation)

Film music should be recognized by the musical world as a new form of composition, equal in rank to the older-established schools, and music critics worth their calling should go to see a film if they receive part of an important score to review, irrespective of who the composer may be. (I say this because there is a tendency on the part of some critics to recognize the film work of the concert hall composer, but to ignore Steiner, Newman, Duning, Rozsa, and other studio composers who write only for films.) In most cases, critics know of an opera and a ballet before reviewing records or orchestral versions of them. Their opinions are obviously influenced by this knowledge. I have heard it said that this is confusing mediums; that opera and ballet are non-realistic musical forms of expression, whereas the film drama is purely realistic, with music used to help create mood, character, settings and atmosphere for emotional purposes; taken away from the visual pattern of the film it has no meaning and does not "stand alone". This is not true. Well written music will always be expressive and meaningful, even when heard in non-functional performance. Certain sections of film scores, mainly music written to underline dialogue sequences, mean little when heard separately; but to criticize film music in this instance as "not standing on its own" is like criticizing, for example, the piano accompaniment to a Schubert song as having no meaning when heard by itself. Music written to accompany dialogue scenes in films is like music written to accompany an art song. But the remaining parts of film scores are musically self-sufficient.

Because everybody knows that film music was written to accompany a story, listeners hearing it away from the visuals feel that, as it was originally closely integrated with them, it cannot be "parted", that they must know every development of the plot to appreciate fully the composer's work, and that they must think of the pictorial narrative when listening to the score.

Should one remember the scene the music accompanied and think only of the story? If the listener is unacquainted with the picture, should he make an attempt to find out what the story is about? This depends on the individual. It is not always necessary to remember in what scene in an opera a certain aria is sung, or at what stage in a ballet a certain melody occurs to enjoy listening to operatic or ballet excerpts. I find myself able to listen, for instance, to Aaron Copland's wistful, sad music from *Our Town* in two ways: it can recall to me quite vividly the conversation at the soda fountain between William Holden and Martha Scott, or I am conscious only of the music, enjoying the pleasure that comes with hearing any form of beautiful and well-written music.

Music critics, I feel, should make a regular practice of analysing important scores, such as Walton's for *Richard III*, but not because the composer is of the concert hall rather than the film studio. They should also consider Alwyn, Frankel, and the many others who write consistently for motion pictures. Where recordings are concerned, such long-playing records as Newman's *The Robe* and *The Egyptian*, Smith's *The Vanishing Prairie*, Steiner's *Gone With The Wind*, or North's *A Streetcar Named Desire* and *The Rose Tattoo*, should be as fully analysed by the serious critics as the new compositions for the concert hall. The classics have been reviewed many times previously, the film scores are new music. They may not all be good, but only by regular and constructive criticism in distinguished journals like *The Gramophone* will any appreciable improvement come about. Men like Mathieson, Rozsa, Alwyn, Bernstein, Copland and their colleagues, who have fought alone within their world of endeavour to improve film music, should receive recognition and support from the influential critics.

I look forward to the day when the standard of criticism applied by critics in responsible journals may have the effect of influencing a producer to choose a master rather than a hack to score his next picture; and when those artists who are composing for films today will be encouraged in the knowledge that their work will receive in these journals the attention it warrants.

FILM MUSIC: SPEECH RHYTHM

by HANS KELLER

Whenever the word "surprise" occurs in critical or analytical writings about music, a favourable judgment seems to be implied. The news that the earth was flat was surprising: surprise is incidental to the communication of something new. It may also be essential to such a communication, which is to say that a creator may use his audience's anticipated surprise as a means of expression, as a pointer to a piece of news which might otherwise be missed or doubted. Surprise shocks, and a shock makes you jump, watch out, concentrate. It need not be loud, of course. The interrupted cadence, emphasized by the entry of the woodwind, towards the end of the main theme's recapitulation in the Adagio of Mozart's "celebrated" A major piano concerto, K.488, is very soft indeed, but it nevertheless is a shock that puts you on the alert and thus prepares you for the ensuing thematic skip of two octaves and a fifth (which also recurs in the coda).

Measured against its context, the loudest shock we know is probably the one in Haydn's "Surprise" symphony. But it does not introduce any immediate news; on the contrary, the fortissimo chord and drumtap seem but a jocular variation on the perfect cadence of the period's first statement. "That will make the ladies jump", was the composer's comment. Yet it would be unwise to think that there is nothing else behind it. The revolutionary events in the tonic (C) minor variation, from the abrupt drop to A flat onwards, might have made the gentler men jump too much if the crash chord on the unaccented beat of the cadential bar had not prepared them for every sudden eventuality. The new developments, then, need not ensue at once; but the creative principle of every intended surprise seems to remain the same, at any rate in good music.

The first half of William Alwyn's C major score for the Ealing film, *The Ship that Died of Shame*, gradually sent me to sleep; in fact, the most impressive part of the sound-track was the opening section of the title credits, which were introduced not by music, but by the din of the sea. The music itself harped on a primitive basic theme in common time that proceeded from a dominant upbeat to the mediant (dotted minim) and, by way of another major sixth on the tonic, in dotted rhythm and on the last beat of the bar, back to the dominant an octave higher. The variations of this basic idea confined themselves on the whole to changes of mode and scale-degrees (VI–V transposed to II–I), and to elementary rhythmic transformations (inversion of dotted motif, augmentation). Opportunities for genuine extensions were simply thrown away, in that the time available for their development was squandered on repetitions and episodical stuff. By the fourteenth entry, which regrouped the notes of the theme in a thoroughly foreseeable manner, I had come to the somniloquous conclusion that this was an utterly conventional and eclectic score by a composer who wrote too much film music. The fifteenth entry with its consquences, however, made me jump.

A realistic fog horn had just sounded an ominous C sharp, which anon assumed the significance of the dominant of the distant key of F sharp minor, where a three-note motif (C♯–D–E♯), consisting of the distinguishing degrees of the harmonic F sharp minor scale, seemed to present the first interesting, if not indeed puzzling, development of the basic theme, whose consequent (C–A–G in C major) it varied lavishly, to the point of mystification. Both these three-note motifs, that is, started on the dominant and consisted of a two-note upbeat and a concluding main beat; and the first two notes of the new motif (dominant-submediant) presented, in the minor mode, the retrograde version of the last two notes of the old motif (submediant-dominant). Since the motifs consisted of three notes each, their pivotal middle notes remained identical, i.e. the submediants of their respective keys. The rhythm of the upbeating two-note group, on the other hand, had for some reason become de-characterized: what had been a sharply dotted rhythm in the first place appeared now as a couple of equal note-values, literally undistinguished. An element of envelopment was thus introduced into the development which, one felt, required an explanation.

The explanation came with a bang. Richard Attenborough, the ship's evil captain, had arrived at the hiding-place of the murderer whom he was about to help to escape. His suppressed shout to the murderer, "Come on out!",was the exact spoken counterpart, in both rhythm and intonation, of the new three-note motif. A dotted "Come on" obviously would not have done.

From this surprising juncture onwards the score proved novel and fascinating. Attenborough's trisyllabic sentence was crucial from the dramatic standpoint: the ship had not behaved all too decently before, but now its real shame had begun, its doom was sealed. By acquiring the rhythm of the dialogue's most operative sentence, the score proved able to replace film-musical tautology by genuinely musico-dramatic interpretation. The sixteenth entry resumed the speech motif, developed it in a passage for solo violin, and transformed it back into the basic theme. The twentieth entry reintroduced the basic theme's dotted rhythm into a chromatic version of the speech motif; and the last, twenty-third entry, finally reunited the two in a triplet ostinato of an inversion of the speech motif on a new harmonic level: VI♭–V–III♭. The motif's augmented second had now become a major third, thus showing even that interval's ultimate derivation from the basic theme, in which the major third figured not only as second interval, but also as melodic background on the same scale-degrees as the last two notes of the triplet ostinato: the two accented notes of the theme were the mediant and the dominant, i.e. the harmonic inversion of its upbeat.

289

Owing to the unusual origin of the three-note motif, all these developments impressed themselves pungently upon the mind, and in the end I wondered guiltily whether I had not missed many a relevant point while drowsing during the first half of the score; unfortunately I had no opportunity of hearing it a second time.

In my article on "British Film Music" for Grove V, I drew attention to the revolutionary "evolving of a musical organism from speech rhythm" in William Alwyn's music for *The Rocking Horse Winner*—the only precedent for the present structure known to me. What I had not yet grasped when I wrote the piece was the importance of the element of surprise which, indeed, is both intenser and subtler in the composer's latest experiment, because the musical imitation of "Come on out!" precedes the enunciation of the verbal model.

In the first of his two recent Third Programme talks on "Writing for the Voice", Mr. Peter Pears has described the eternal struggle between song and words, sound and sense. Alwyn's achievement, hardly imaginable outside the cinema, consists in unifying the two belligerent parties at the very stage where their differences are at their acutest, where speech remains speech and music remains wordless; and the incisive contrast between the two sharpens our wits for the understanding of new musico-dramatic unities between them. There have been previous speech-rhythmic surprises, of course, but none so extreme. Benjamin Britten has proved particularly adroit at musicalizing the rhythm and intonation of speech beyond their actual use in a vocal line; in *The Turn of the Screw* there are two memorable instances, i.e. his utilization of the Governess's "Who is it?" and of Flora's "I can't see anything". Thanks to his "speaking voice" technique, Arnold Schoenberg was able to go yet several steps further in his creation and unification of violent contrasts between speech and music. In *Pierrot Lunaire* the interested reader will find innumerable cases in point; in No. 17 ("Parody"), for example, the viola's opening theme of what is to become a multiple canon turns out to be modelled on the speech rhythm of "Stricknadeln, blank und blinkend . . .', the speaking voice being itself a canonic part. In the context of the canon, the speaking voice imitates the viola, but underneath and against time, the viola imitates the sound and rhythm of the words: as with Alwyn's anticipation of "Come on out!", the imitation precedes the model.

Thanks to the cinema, Alwyn has been able to go all the way, nor will his shock treatment easily wear off, for the eternal struggle between music and speech is not likely to become any less eternal in future. The only way to appreciate a new expressive means is to examine it for a moment, not in its context against other contexts, but apart from its context and out of proportion, compared only with other means of expression that serve a similar purpose. And here it must be said that Alwyn's surprise action is more original than Mozart's deceptive cadence; subtler and more exclusively to the point even than Haydn's joke, with which it shares its function of awakening you to more distant musical event; and yet more revolutionary than Schoenberg's instrumental imitations of the spoken melody.

Returning to a more balanced point of view, we might be tempted to suggest that the novelty of Alwyn's device is itself out of all proportion to the actual content which it serves, but I think it ill becomes a critic to be chary in praising a new means of expression if it really expresses something; later composers— or Alwyn himself at a later stage—may be able to avail themselves of it more fully. Meanwhile, we must not forget that the instrumental version of "Come on out!" is, after all, a surprise of the most genuinely artistic order, for it is a necessary consequence of the extreme contrast to whose extreme unification it draws our attention.

SELECT BIBLIOGRAPHY

Note: Since 1968 regular articles under the title "Records" have appeared in the monthly magazine *Films and Filming* Other regular articles have appeared in *Films in Review* again on film music available on record Tantivy Press' *International Film Year Book* too has annual reports on film music These articles are not listed in the bibliography.

PART I. BOOKS ON FILM MUSIC

1935

Music and the Film. (Leonid Sabaneev.) Pitman, London.

1936

Film Music. (Kurt London.) Faber and Faber, London.

1946

Incidental Music in the Sound Film. (Gerald Cockshott.) British Film Institute pamphlet.

1947

The Need for Competent Film Music Criticism. (Hans Keller.) British Film Institute pamphlet.

British Film Music. (John Huntley.) British Yearbooks, London.

Composing for the Films. (Hanns Eisler.) Oxford University Press, New York and Dennis Dobson, London.

1948

Music for the Movies. (Louis Levy.) Sampson Low, London.

1950

La Musica nel Film. (Ed. Luigi Chiarini.) Includes contributions by Enzo Masetti, Alessandro Cicognini, Roman Vlad, Franco Ferrara, Marius François Gaillard, Ernest Irving, Daniele Amfitheatrof, and others. Bianco e Nero Editore, Rome.

1953

The Blue Book of Hollywood Musicals. (Jack Burton.) Century House, New York.

1954

Film Composers in America. (Clifford McCarty.) Valentine Press, California, U.S.A.

1956

How to Choose Music. (F. Rawlings.) Focal Press, London.

1959

Musica e Film (S. G. Biamonte.) Edizioni dell'Ateneo, Rome.

1960

Underscore (Frank Skinner.) Criterion Music Corp, New York.

1963

Defénse et illustration de la musique dans le film. (H. Colpi.) Sociéte d'édition de Recherche et de Documentation Cinématographique, Paris.

1966

A Filmhang Esztétikája (The Sound of the Film) Ferenc Lohr.) Budapest. A Hungarian book with short english summary and good multi-lingual bibliography.
All Talking! All Singing! All Dancing! A Pictorial History of the Movie Musical (John Springer.) Citadel Press, New York.

1967

A Selected List of Recorded Musical Scores from Radio, Television and Motion Pictures (James L. Limbacher.) Dearborn Public Library.
The Musical Film (Douglas McVay.) Zwemmers, London.

1969

Présence de la Musique à l'Écran (F. Porcile.) Éditions du Cerf, Paris.
Komposition für den Film (Theodor W. Adorno and Hanns Eisler.) Verlag Rognner und Bernhard, Munich. Reprint in French by *L'Arche Editeur*, Paris.

1970

Gotta Sing, Gotta Dance: A Pictorial History of Film Musicals. (John Kobal.) Hamlyn, London. Good bibliography.
The American Musical (Tom Vallance.) Tantivy Press, London. Filmographies and career data of those concerned.
Sounds for Silents (Charles Hofmann—foreward by Lilian Gish.) D.B.S. Publications, New York.

1971

The Hollywood Musical (John Russell Taylor and Arthur Jackson.) Secker and Warburg, London. Survey by J.R.T. plus list of films and career data.
Scoring for Films: A Complete Text (Earle Hager.) Criterion Music Corp, New York.
Hollywood Studio Musicans (Robert R. Faulkner.) Aldene-Atherton, Chicago and New York.

1972

Jazz In The Movies (David Meeker.) British Film Institute Publication. Index of jazz musicians' work for the cinema.
The Golden Age of Movie Musical: the M.G.M. Years (Lawrence B. Thomas.) Columbia House.

PART II. ARTICLES AND REPORTS ON FILM MUSIC

1928

Picture-House Beethoven and the Gramophone. (Alice Green.) The Gramophone. Vol. VI. August. A typical example of the more serious article on silent film music.

1931

Film Synchronization. (Stanley Chapple.) The Gramophone. Vol. XI. June.

1933

Music and the Synchronised Film. (Clarence Raybould.) Sight and Sound. Vol. 2, No. 7.

1934

Music in Films. (Alfred Hitchcock.) Cinema Quarterly. Vol. 2, No. 2.
The Musician and the Film. (Walter Leigh.) Cinema Quarterly. Vol. 3, No. 2.
Music and the Sound Film. (Leonid Sabaneev.) Music and Letters. Vol. XV, p. 147.
Sound Rhythm and the Film. (Ernest J. Borneman.) Sight and Sound. Vol. 3, No. 10, pp. 65–67.
Music and the Film. (A review of Clarence Raybould's music for *Rising Tide*.) Sight and Sound. Vol. 3, No. 11, pp. 98–99.

1935

Music and the Film. (M. D. Calvocoressi.) Sight and Sound. Vol. 4, No. 14.
Music and the Film. Harpers Magazine. July.
Background Music is a Help. (Louis Levy.) Flickers Magazine, 1935.
Classical Ballet and the Cinema. (Alexandra Danilova.) Sight and Sound. Vol. 4, No. 15.

1936

Film Music. (Muir Mathieson.) Royal College of Music Magazine. Vol. XXXII, No. 3.
Film Music. (Darius Milhaud.) World Film News. April.
Music and Film. (Hans Eisler.) World Film News. May.
Music and Film. (Maurice Jaubert.) World Film News. July.
Music and Microphones. (Walter Leigh.) World Film News. August.
Absolute Music. (V. Solev.) Sight and Sound. Vol. 5, No. 18.

1937

Music in Films. (Leslie Perkoff.) World Film News. April.
Music in Films. (Cavalcanti.) World Film News. July.
Film Music. (Arthur Benjamin.) Musical Times. July.
The Story of British Film Music. (Ralph Hill.) Radio Times. 31.12.37.
Music and the "Cellulose Nit-Wit". (Alan Frank.) The Listener. 29.12.37.
Il Problema della Musica nel Film Storico. (Herbert Stothart.) Cinema, No. 17. Rome.

1938

Music from the Movies Radio Programme. (Louis Levy.) Radio Pictorial. 21.1.38.

1940

Music and the Film. New Statesman. 13.4.40.
Film Music. (Muir Mathieson.) Documentary News Letter. September.

1941

The Functions of Music in Sound Films. (Marion Hannal Winter.) Musical Quarterly, Vol. XXVII.
"Film Music Notes", an American publication, first appeared in 1941, and has continued to be issued at regular intervals to date (1957). There are nine issues per year, containing articles and score quotations on films of current musical interest.

1943

Recent Film Music. (John W. Klein.) Musical Opinion. June.
Music in Films. (Ernest Irving.) Music and Letters, Vol. XXIV, No. 4, p. 223.

1944

Film Music. (John Huntley.) Sight and Sound. Vol. 12, No. 48.
Film Music. (Darrel Catling.) Sight and Sound. Vol. 12, No. 49.

British Film Music. (Hubert Clifford.) Tempo. September.
Film Music. (Ralph Vaughan Williams.) Royal College of Music Magazine. Vol. XL, No. I.
Background Music to the Fore. (Sam Heppner.) Sound. December.
Walton's "Henry V" Music. (Hubert Clifford.) Tempo. December.
Aspects of Film Music. (Muir Mathieson.) Tempo. December.
Music and World News. (John Huntley.) Sound. December.
Music and the Cinema. (Alexander Brent Smith.) Piping Times, Vol. IV, No. 3.
Film Music. (Ralph Vaughan Williams.) Piping Times, Vol. IV, No. I.
Film Music. (Ken Cameron and Muir Mathieson.) Piping Times, Vol. IV, No. 2.
La Musique dans le Film. (Maurice Jaubert.) Cahier du Cinema, Idhec. No. I.
Collaboration between the Screen Writer and the Composer. (Adolph Deutsch.) Proceed-
    ings of the Writers' Congress. Los Angeles.

1945

Film Scores. (Arthur Kleiner.) Sight and Sound. Vol. 13, No. 52.
Music and the Film. (Harold Rawlinson.) British Journal of Photography. 16.3.45.
Music for the Films. (Hubert Clifford.) Tempo. March, June and December.
Music of the Cinema. (Arthur Unwin.) Music Parade.
Dramatists in Music. (Muir Mathieson.) Talkabout.

1946

Film Music. (John Huntley.) Penguin Film Review. No. I.
Music from the Films. (Ernest Irving.) Tempo. June and September.
Film Music: A Teacher's Attitude. (Music Master.) Music in Education. July.
Putting in the Sound Track. (Edward Silverman.) Our Time. October.
Fitting the Music to the Picture. (Walter Goehr.) Sound. October.
How a Music Recording Theatre was made from a Sound Stage. (Cyril Crowhurst.) Kine-
    matograph Weekly. 26.9.46.
Film Music: Some Objections. (Hans Keller.) Sight and Sound. Vol. 15, No. 60.
Literature on Music in Film and Radio. (Robert U. Nelson and Walter H. Rubsamen.)
    Hollywood Quarterly. Supplement to Vol. I.
British Film Music. (Ernest Irving.) Kinematograph Weekly. 19.12.46.
Film Music and the Gramophone. (John Culshaw.) The Gramophone. September.

1947

Notes on Film Music. (John Huntley.) Penguin Film Review.
Scoring for Films. (Muir Mathieson.) Penguin Film Review.
Film Music Reviews. (Ernest Irving.) Tempo.
Background for British Pictures. (Muir Mathieson.) Musical Express. 3.1.47.
The British Musical Film. (Muir Mathieson.) Melody Maker. January.
A Film Analysis of the Orchestra. (Hans Keller.) Sight and Sound. Vol. 16, No. 61.
Film Music. (Hans Keller.) Music Survey, Vol. II, No. 6, pp. 196–7.
Music and the Future Films. (Frederick W. Sternfeld.) Musical Quarterly, Vol. XXXIII,
    p. 517.
Music in New British Films. (John Huntley.) Cinema and Theatre, Vol. XV, No. I.
The Music in the Background. (William Alwyn.) Music Parade.
Stage One Music Theatre, Denham. (John Huntley.) Film Industry, Vol. II, No. 2.
British Film Music and World Markets. (John Huntley.) Sight and Sound. Vol. 15, No. 60,
    p. 135.
British Film Music. (Stuart Keen.) Sight and Sound. Vol. 15, No. 63.

1948

Hollywood Music: Another View. (Hans Keller.) Sight and Sound. Vol. 16, No. 64.
Music by Appointment: Sir Arnold Bax and "Oliver Twist". (John Huntley.) Band Wagon.
    Vol. 7, No. 2.
Louisiana Story. (Hans Keller.) Music Survey. Vol. II, No. 2 and Vol. II, No. 3.
Music for the Olympic Games Film. (John Huntley.) Sound. September.
Music for the film "Hamlet". (Hans Keller.) Monthly Film Review. Vol. 6, No. 7.
The Film Music of Sir Arnold Bax. (John Huntley.) Musical Express. 25.6.48.

"Oliver Twist": *Music for the Film*. (Derick M. Green.) Music in Education. September–October.
Music and the Film: "Oliver Twist". (Harold Rawlinson.) British Journal of Photography. 6.8.48.
Music and Films. (Laszlo Lajtha.) The Chesterian. Vol. XXIII, p. 155.
Film Music Orchestras. (John Huntley.) Penguin Film Review, No. 5. Special Reference: *The October Man* (William Alwyn.)
British Film Music. (John Huntley.) Penguin Film Review. No. 6. Special reference: *Henry V* (William Walton.)
The Year in Film Music. (John Huntley.) Film Industry. 30.12.48.
British Film Composers: William Alwyn. (John Huntley.) Music Parade. Vol. I, No. 7.
The Question of Quotations. (Hans Keller.) Music Survey. Vol. II, No. I.
Louisiana Story. (Frederick W. Sternfeld.) Film Music. Vol. VIII, No. 2.
The Music of Hamlet. (William Walton.) Film Music. Vol. VIII, No. 4.

1949

Film Music. (Ernest Irving.) Proceedings of the R.M.A. Vol. LXXVI, 1949–50.
The Music of "Hamlet" and "Oliver Twist". (John Huntley.) Penguin Film Review. No. 8.

1950

La Musica nel Film. Proceedings of the Congresso Internazionale di Musica, Florence, Italy.
Film Music Congress at Florence. (Antony Hopkins.) Sight and Sound. Vol. 19, No. 6.
Film Music. (Bernard Stevens.) Music Survey. Vol. II, No. 3.

1951

Film Music. (Donald Mitchell.) Music Survey. Vol. III, No. 3.
The Film Music of Michael Powell's Productions. (John Huntley.) Sight and Sound. Vol. 19, No. 9.
Sound Effects and Music. (John Huntley.) Sight and Sound. Vol. 19, No. 10.
Film Music Recordings. (John Huntley.) Sight and Sound. Vol. 20, No. I.
Louisiana Story: Recordings. (John Huntley.) Sight and Sound. Vol. 21, No. I.
Theme Songs. (John Huntley.) Sight and Sound. Vol. 21, No. 2.
Film Music on Records. (Gerald Pratley.) Quarterly of Film, Radio and Television. Vol. VI, No. I.
Film Music Orchestration. (Lawrence Morton and Antony Hopkins.) Sight and Sound. Vol. 20, No. I.

1952

Film Music on Records: Part 2. (Gerald Pratley.) Quarterly of Film, Radio and Television. Vol. VII.
The M.G.M. Studio Orchestra. (John Huntley.) Sight and Sound. Vol. 21, No. 3.
Quo Vadis. (John Huntley.) Sight and Sound. Vol. 21, No. 4.
Singin' in the Rain (John Huntley.) Sight and Sound. Vol. 22, No. I.
Caruso on the Movies. (William Ludwig.) Sight and Sound. Vol. 21, No. 4.
The Composer and Crown. (William Alwyn.) Sight and Sound. Vol. 21, No. 4.
Poetry in Fast and Slow Motion. (Douglas Newton.) Sight and Sound. Vol. 22, No. I.

1953

Chaplin's Film Music. (John Huntley.) Sight and Sound. Vol. 22, No. 3.
Music for Ealing Comedies. (John Huntley.) Sight and Sound. Vol. 22, No. 3.

1954

Music on Everest. (Hans Keller.) Musical Opinion. January.
Tales from the Vienna Hollywoods. (Hans Keller.) Music Review. Vol. XV, No. 2.
Twelve-Note Music on Television. (Hans Keller.) Musical Times. February.
How Not to Write Film Music. (William Alwyn.) British Film Academy Journal. Autumn.
Film Music on Records. (Gerald Pratley.) Quarterly of Film, Radio and Television. Vol. IX.

1955

Carmen à la Hollywood. (Hans Keller.) Music Review. May.
The Arthur Benjamin Annual. (Hans Keller.) Musical Opinion. September.
Film Music : Speech Rhythm. (Hans Keller.) Musical Times September.
Film Music: Problems of Integration. (Hans Keller.) Musical Times. July.
Music For Cinerama. (Arthur Jacobs.) Sight and Sound. Vol. 24, No. 3.
Film Music on Records. (Gerald Pratley.) Quarterly of Film, Radio and Television. Vol. X.

1956

The Films were never Silent (John Huntley.) Kine Weekly, 3.5.56.

1958

Composing for Films (Hans Eisler.) Film 58, No. I.

1959

Composing for Screen (William Alwyn.) Films and Filming, March 1959. Based on his National Film Theatre lecture.

1960

A Credit list of most well-known film music composers (Chaplin.) No. II May 1960—Swedish.
Music of 'Hiroshima Mon Amour'. Cahiers du Cinema No. 103.

1961

The Significance of Film Music—on the purpose of film music score using Miklos Rozsa as an example. American Cinematographer. May.

1962

Article describing the use of film music and basic technical processes involved. American Cinematographer. April.
Music of Hans Eisler and his experimentations. Films in Review May. Translated into French Cahiers du Cinema February, 1964.

1963

The New School of American Film Composers (Ermanno Comuzio.) Bianco e Nero, No. 5, May.
The Law and the use of music in film. Film Comment. Autumn.

1964

The New French Film Composers (Ermanno Comuzio.) Bianco e Nero No. 10. Interview with Roman Vlad. Rivista del Cinema. June Interview with Valentino Bucchi. Rivista del Cinema. July.
On the use of music in the films of Pasolini and stimulus to his vision of reality. Filmcritica. No. 151–152 November and December.
The College Film (Lord Birkett.) Royal College of Music Magazine,Winter, Volume LX, No. 3.
A series of interviews and filmographies of French composers and survey of French film music. Cinema 64, No. 89.

1966

The Weight of Tradition in British Film Composers (Ermanno Comuzio.) Bianco e Nero, No. 12, December.
Elmer Bernstein and Jerry Goldsmith. Films and Filming, September.

1967

Music for Films (Kenneth V. Jones.) Royal College of Music Magazine, Summer, 1967.

296

1968

Essay on Giovanni Fusco (Ermanno Comuzio.) Bianco e Nero, No. 5 and 6, May and June.
Minimal Cinema: Chronicle of Anna Magdalene Bach (Richard Roud.) Sight and Sound, Summer.
French Film Composers and details of their work from 1964 to 1967. Film Français, Cannes Special Nos. 1244 to 1245.

1969

Use of music in films—its contribution. Film Quarterly, Volume 22, No. 4, Summer. Some references to publications on the subject.
An interview with Alex North (Joel Reisner and Bruce Kane.) Cinema, Volume 5, No. 4.

1970

Russian Film Composers: the old and the new. (Ermanno Comuzio.) Bianco e Nero, No. 7, 8, 9, 10. July to October.
Composing for Films—an interview with Michael H. Lewis. Screen, March/April.
There has been a revolution in the composition of original music (Keith Robinson.) Making Films in New York, December.
Interview with Jean Marie Straub (Andi Engels.) Cinemantics, No. I, January.
Shock Treatment (Gordon Gow.) Interview with Ken Russell about his film on Tchaikovsky. Films and Filming, No. 10, Volume 6, July.
Long Shot (John Cutts.) Report from Hollywood. Deals extensively with career of Alfred Newman who died in 1970. Films and Filming, July.
Modern Revolutionary Dance Drama: Red Detachment of Women (Anon.)Whole issue of China Pictorial, Special issue No. 10.

1971

The Colour of Music: an interview with Bernard Herrmann (Ted Gilling.) Sight and Sound, Winter 1971/1972, Volume 41, No. 1.
Fantasia—impromptu: the editor in conversation with Leopold Stokowski (Donald Francke.) Royal College of Music Magazine, Easter, Volume LXVII, No. 1.
Music-Film. Film-makers Newsletter, Volume 4, No. 6, April. Whole issue devoted to the subject of film music.

1972

Contemporary use of background music (Alfred Perry.) American Cinemeditor, Vol. 22, No. I, Spring.
*Notes for documentary film music—*discussion of its problems. A.I.D. News, No. 3.
Music in Westerns. Relation to its origin the folk song. Image e Son, No. 258, March.

PART III. SILENT FILM MUSIC PUBLICATIONS

1909

Suggestions for Music. First "suggestions" sheets for music issued by the Edison Company as part of their film booking service.

1913

Sam Fox Moving Picture Music. (J. S. Zamecnik.) Volumes of piano music for silent film accompanists. Sam Fox Music Co., New York.

1914

Playing to Pictures. (W. Tyacke George.) A guide for pianists and conductors of motion picture theatres. E. T. Heron and Co., London.

1919

Kinobibliothek. (G. Beece.) First volume of the series by Beece, published in Berlin.

1920

Musical Accompaniment of Moving Pictures. A Practical Manual for pianist and organists picture, (Edith Langand George West) Boston. Divided into three sections. and an exposition of the principles underlying the musical interpretation of moving Equipment; Musical Interpretation; and the Theatrical Organ. Contains checklist of basic repertoire and explains how to create special orchestral effects on the organ.

1924

Motion Picture Moods for Pianists and Organists. (Arr. Erno Rapee.) G. Schirmer Inc., New York.

1925

Encyclopaedia of Music for Pictures (Erno Rapée.) New York.

1927

Allgemaines Handbuch der Film-Musik. (H. Erdmann and Giuseppe Beece.) Berlin.

PART IV. BOOKS CONTAINING FILM MUSIC REFERENCES

1934

The Secrets of Nature. (Mary Field and Percy Smith.) Section on music. Faber and Faber, London.
Music Ho! (Constant Lambert.) Section on "Mechanical Music and the Cinema". London.

1935

Plan for Cinema. (Dallas Bower.) Sections on music. Dent, London.

1936

Things to Come. (H. G. Wells.) Section on the music by Arthur Bliss. Cresset Press, London.
Documentary Film. (Paul Rotha.) Many references to film music. Faber and Faber, London.

1937

Music in the Modern World (Rollo H. Myers.) Section on film music. Edward Arnold, London.
Footnotes to the Film. (Ed. Davy.) Article: "Music for the Screen" by Maurice Jaubert. Lovat Dickson, London.

1939

Film and Theatre. (Nicoll.) Sections on music. Harrup, London.
Behind the Screen. (Ed. Stephen Watts.) Article: "Film Music" by Herbert Stothart. Barker, London.
Talking Pictures. (Keisling.) Sections on music at M.G.M. Studios. Spon, London and New York.

1940

Our New Music. (Aaron Copland.) Section on film music. McGraw Hill, New York.

1941

Sound Motion Pictures: Recording and Reproducing. (James Ross Cameron.) Full section on music recording and reproduction. Woodmont, Conn., U.S.A.

298

1943

Music For All of Us. (Leopold Stokowski.) Chapter on "Music and Motion Pictures". Simon and Schuster, U.S.A.

1944

The Art of Walt Disney. (Robert Field.) References to music. Collins, New York and London.

1945

Henry V. (C. Clayton Hutton.) Section on William Walton's music. Punch Bowl Press, London.

1946

Meeting at the Sphinx. (Marjorie Deans.) References to the music by Georges Auric. MacDonald, London.
Translantic Jazz. (Peter Noble.) References to the jazz film. British Yearbooks, London.
Winchester Screen Encyclopedia. (Ed. Maud Miller.) Contains article by Muir Mathieson and check lists on important film music compositions. Winchester Press, London.
British Film Yearbook. (Ed. Peter Noble.) Contains check lists and material on film music. British Yearbooks, London.

1947

The Film Sense. (Sergei Eisenstein.) Sections on music, especially Prokofiev's music for *Alexander Nevsky.* Harcourt, Brace, London.
British Film Yearbook. (Ed. Peter Noble.) Article: "Music and the Film Script" by Ernest Irving. Numerous references to film music. Check lists. British Yearbooks, London.
Sound and the Documentary Film. (Ken Cameron.) Numerous references to music; section on music recording. Pitman, London.
Composers in America. (Claire R. Reis.) Check lists of film composers, including some film scores. Macmillan, New York.

1948

The Film "Hamlet". (Ed. Brenda Cross.) Article: "The Music of Hamlet" by William Walton. Article: "Recording the Music" by Muir Mathieson. Saturn Press, London.
The Red Shoes Ballet. (Monk Gibbon.) References to the music by Brian Easdale. Saturn Press, London.
The Art of the Film. (Ernest Lindgren.) References to music and chapter on Film Music. George Allen and Unwin, London.
Experiment in the Film. (Ed. Roger Manvell.) References to the experimental use of music in films. Grey Walls Press, London.

1949

Film Form. (Sergei Eisenstein.) Numerous references to music and further sections on the music for *Alexander Nevsky.* Harcourt, Brace, London.
Descriptive Music for Stage and Screen. (Walter Rubsamen.) Extensive material on film music. Los Angeles, U.S.A.
The History of the British Film, 1906–1914. (Rachael Low.) Section on sound effects and music for silent films. George Allen and Unwin, London.
The Film Till Now. (Paul Rotha and Richard Griffiths.) References to film music. Vision Press, London.

1950

Ballet for Film and Television. (A. H. Franks.) Extensive sections on music, with check list of ballet films. Pitman, London.

Diary of a Film. (Jean Cocteau.) References to film music. Dennis Dobson, London.
Spotlight on Films. (Egon Larsen.) Section on film music. Max Parrish, London.
Music: An Art and a Business. (Paul S. Carpenter.) A chapter on film music. University of Oklahoma Press, U.S.A.

1951

The Tales of Hoffman: a Study of a Film. (Monk Gibbon.) Extensive references to the music by Offenbach. Saturn Press, London.
Film and its Techniques. (Raymond Spottiswoode.) References to film music. Berkeley, California, U.S.A.; Faber and Faber, London.

1952

Making a Film: "The Secret People". (Lindsay Anderson.) References to film music. George Allen and Unwin, London.

1954

The Animated Film. (Roger Manvell.) References to music for the cartoon film. Sylvan Press, London.
Film Techniques and Film Acting. (V. I. Pudovkin.) References to film music. Vision Press, London.
Cocteau on the Film. (Ed. André Fraigneau.) References to film music. Dennis Dobson, London.
London Symphony. Extensive notes by Humphrey Jennings on a proposed film on the London Symphony Orchestra. Naldrett Press, London.
Grove's Dictionary of Music and Musicians. (Ed. Eric Blom.) 18 pages on "Film Music" (Volume III, F–G). The sections include material on: (1) History; (2) Technical Procedures; (3) The Composer's Task; (4) British Music: Perspective; (5) Thematic Organization; (6) Tonal Organization; (7) Tonal Texture: Melodrama; (8) Style; (9) Prospect; (10) The Musical Problem; (11) American Music; (12) Continental Music; (13) Film Opera and Film Cartoon; (14) Bibliography. The contributions were made by Ernest Irving, Hans Keller and Wilfred H. Mellers. MacMillan Press, London.

1955

The Film and the Public. (Roger Manvell.) Chapters on "Music and the Silent Film" and "Music and the Sound Film". Numerous references to music. Pelican Books, London.

1959

Memories and Commentaries (Igor Stravinsky and Robert Craft.) A section dealing with Stravinsky's thoughts and feelings on the subject of film music. Faber and Faber, London.

1960

The Odyssey of a Film Maker. Robert Flaherty's Story.

1963

Federico Fellini (Gilbert Salachas.) Edition Seghers Cineam d'aujourd'hui. Paris. Translated into English by Rosalie Siegel and published by Crown Publishers, New York (1969). Fellini talks about how and Nino Rota compose Fellini's film music.
The Innocent Eye: the life of Robert Flaherty (Arthur Calder-Marshall.) W. H. Allen, London. Harcourt, Jovanovich, New York, 1966.
National Music and other Essays (R. Vaughan-Williams.) Complete chapter on composing for film. Oxford Paperbacks, No. 76.

1964

My Autobiography (Charlie Chaplin). Bodley Head, London. Pocket Books, New York, 1966.

300

1965

The Films of Akira Kurosawa (Donald Richie.) University of California Press, Berkeley.
Dictionnaire des Cinéastes (Georges Sadoul.) Éditions du Seuil, Paris.
Dictionnaire des Film (Georges Sadoul.) Éditions du Seuil, Paris.
The Filmgoer's Companion (Leslie Halliwell.) MacGibbon and Kee Ltd. and Paladin
  Paperbacks, London.

1966

Le Cinéma selan Hitchcock (François Truffaut.) Robert Laffort, Paris. Published in English
  (1968) by Secker and Warburg.

1967

Interviews with Film Directors (edited by Andrew Sarris.) Bobbs-Merrill Company Inc.,
  New York Interviews culled from numerous periodicals with numerous references
  to film music
Film Makers on Film Making (edited by Harry M Geguld.) Indiana University Press.
  Reprint by Penguin Books, London. Antonioni particularly talks on music in his
  films. Some references too from Kenneth Anger.
The Life that Late he Led: a biography of Cole Porter (George Eels.) W. A. Allen, London.

1968

The Making of Kubrick's 2001 (edited by Jerome Ageel.) Signet Books, New York.
  Numerous reviews of the film with much reference to its music Also Alex North
  writes about his abortive compositions for the film.
Walt Disney (Richard Schnickel.) Weidenfeld and Nicolson, London.
The Parade's Gcne By (Hollywood in the Silent Days) (Kevin Brownlow.) Secker and
  Warburg, London. Much mention of music for the silents and talk from accom-
  panists.
Film Essays with a Lecture (Sergei Eisenstein.) Translated by Jay Leyda. Denis Dobson,
  London. Praeger, New York (1970).

1969

Pasolini on Pasolini (Oswald Stack.) Thames and Hudson in collaboration with The
  British Film Institute, London Pasolini talks extensively on his films with references to music used in *Oedipus Rex* and *Accatone*.

1970

Second Wave (edited by Ian Cameron.) Studio Vista, London. Chapter on Jean-Marie
  Straub by Andi Engels Much attention to his *Chronicle of Anna Magdelena Bach.*
Alice's Restaurant: a screenplay (Venable Herndon and Arthur Penn.) Doubleday and
  Company Inc., Garden City, New York. *Alice's Restaurant* was based on the Arlo
  Guthrie Song Arthur Penn talks about how he came to film this song, plus
  screenplay.
The Work of the Film Director (A. J. Reynertson.) Focal Press, London and New York.
  Small section on film music.
A Nous la Liberté and Entr'acte (Rene Clair.) Lorrimer, London. Introduction by Rene
  Clair talks at length about Satie's work on *Entr'acte.*
Wild Strawberries: a film by Ingmar Bergman. The screenplay translated by Lars Malm-
  strom and David Kushner with introduction by Bergman which deals with film
  music. Lorrimer, London.

1971

The Making of Feature Films—a Guide (Ivan Butler.) Pelican Original, London. George
  Sidney on the Musical. Whole chapter on The Composer (John Barry, Richard
  Rodney Bennett and Dimitri Tiomkin) and chapter on Sound.

Straub (Richard Roud.) Secker and Warburg in association with The British Film Institute, London. Extensive chapter on Straub's *Chronicle of Anna Magdelena Bach* and full list of works performed in that film, plus musicians used.

The History of the British Film (Rachael Low.) Covers the period from 1918 to 1929. George Allen and Unwin, London.

The Tales of the Tales (Rumer Godden.) Fred Wayne, London. The story of the filming of the Beatrix Potter Ballet with superficial treatment of all the aspects including choreography and music.

Portrait of a Director: Satyajit Ray (Marie Seton.) Dennis Dobson, London.

Kino: A History of Russian and Soviet Film (Jay Leyda.) George Allen and Unwin, London.

1972

The Making of No, No Nanette (Don Dunn.) Citadel Press, New York.

International Encyclopedia of Film (general editor Roger Manvell, advisory editor Lewis Jacobs.) Michael Joseph, London.

The Apu Trilogy (Robin Wood.) November Books, London. About Ray's Trilogy with some reference to music.

The World Encyclopedia of Film (associate editors Tim Cankwell and John M. Smith.) Studio Vista, London.

INDEX

(This Index covers pages 15 to 263 only)

Addinsell, Richard, 73–4, 150
Addison, John, 88, 114, 232, 237, 246
Adler, Larry, 111, 151
Adomian, Lan, 166
Age of Gold ballet, 183
Aida, 71
Alderson, John, 114
Alexander Nevsky, 136
Alexandrov, Grigori, 180
Alice's Restaurant, 236
All Quiet on the Western Front, 33, 49
Allefex machine, 22
Alwyn, William, 23–4, 59, 109, 113, 135, 221, 222, 224, 225, 227, 229, 211, 228–90
Amahl and the Night Visitors, 67
American Academy of Motion Pictures screen awards for Music, 53, 55, 165, 171, 229
American in Paris, 82–4
Amos and Andy, 25
Anchors Aweigh, 161
Anger, Kenneth, 181, 197
Animal Farm, 171–6
A Nous la Liberté, 162
Antheil, George, 53
Antonioni, Michelangelo, 240, 242, 244, 260–63
Apache, 226
Applebaum, Louis, 166–8
Archangelsky, Alexis, 180
L'Arlesienne, 18
Arnell, Richard, 246, 254–60
Arnheim, Rudolf, 50, 63
Around the World in Eighty Days, 195
Arnold, Chris, 258
Arnold, Malcolm, 135, 154–8, 222, 224, 225, 226
Asquith, Anthony, 29, 33
L'Assassinat du Duc de Guise, 22

Astaire, Fred, 82
As You Like It, 53
Auric, Georges, 90–1, 150–1
Austrian Radio, 68
Avanzo, Renzo, 181
Ave Maria 55 (See also *The Devils*)
Avakian, Aram, 78
Avzaamov, 186–7

Bach, Johann Sebastian, 70, 91, 159, 181, 182 (See also *The Chronicle of Anna Magdelena Bach*)
Bad and the Beautiful, The, 226
Ball, The, 50
Bath, Hubert, 32
Baraza (*Men of Two Worlds*), 109, 161
Barber of Seville, The, 72
Barron, Louis and Bebe, 182
Barry, John, 234–235
Bartosch, Bertold, 412
Battleship Potemkin, 27–8, 35
Bax, Arnold, 90, 114, 219
Becce, Giuseppe, 26
Beethoven, Ludwig van, 25, 43, 76
Beethoven Sonata, 76
Beethoven's *9th Symphony*, 69, 70, 75
Belle et la Bête, La, 65, 90–1
Belles of St. Trinians, The, 154, 227
Belles of Atlantis, 182
Bells, 17
Belshazzar's Feast, 126
Ben Hur, 49
Benjamin, Arthur, 53, 67
Belson, Jordon, 183
Bergman, Ingmar, 240
Berlin, 28, 180–1
Berlioz, Hector, 149
Bernard, Armand, 32, 39
Bernstein, Leonard, 70, 71, 83–4, 85

Best Years of Our Lives, 165–170
Beta Films, 69, 70
Bicycle Thieves, 162–3
Big Combo, The, 226
Birds, The, 241
Blackburn, Maurice, 184, 185, 191
Blackmail, 31–2
Black and White, 177–8
Black Top, 181
Bleak Moments, 238
Blinkety-Blank, 184–5
Bliss, Sir Arthur, 52, 53–4, 68, 74,
    109, 161–2, 231–2
Blithe Spirit, 150
Blonde Women, 46
Blow Up, 259
Blue Angel, The, 33, 46
Boehm, 71
Bohéme, La, 70, 71, 163
Boogie Doodle, 182
Bop Scotch, 186
Boris Godunov, 66
Borneman, Ernest, 27
Bornoff, 68
Bosch, Hieronymus, 128, 178–80
Bout de Souffle, A, 78
Brahms, Johannes, 182
Brief Encounter, 75
Briel, Joseph Carl, 25
British Broadcasting Corporation,
    68, 70, 195–6
British Broadcasting Corporation
    Choir, 128
British Broadcasting Corporation
    Television Unit, 177
British International Symphony
    Orchestra, 32
Britten, Benjamin, 52, 53, 68, 70, 77
Broadway Melody, 36, 40, 53
Brock the Badger, 44
Bryars, Gavin, 197–8
Buckle, C. E., 191
Burge, Stuart, 72
Burke, Sonny, 171
Burma Victory, 114, 135
Bute, Mary Ellen, 183

Cabaret, 86
Café Mozart Waltz (*The Third
    Man*), 110
Call Me Madam, 181
Cameron, Ken 76, 77
Capriccio Italien, 129
Captain's Paradise, 154
Caravan, 183

Carmen, 66, 70, 71, 72, 108, 138
Carmen Jones, 66–7
Carnet du Bal, Un, 162
Caron, Leslie, 82–3
Carrie, 226, 229
Cary, Tristram, 240–2
Castellani, Renato, 128
Cavalleria Rusticana, 72
Celluloid, 49
C'Est l'Aviron, 183
Chant d'Amour, Un, 197–8
Children of Hiroshima, 159
*Chronicle of Anna Magdelena
    Bach*, 79–80
Cicognini, Alessandro, 162–3
Cinechordeon, 22
Cinema Quarterly, 49–50
Cinfonium, 22
Citizen Kane, 65, 136–7
City Lights, 160
Changing Year, The, 43
Chaplin, Charles, 36, 160
Chaplin, Saul, 82
Charell, Erik, 37
Churchill, Frank, 171
Clair René, 32–3, 35, 36, 38–9,
    53, 90, 162, 198
Clavitist-Violina, 22
Click-track, 153
Clifford, Hubert, 93
Coal Face, 52, 171
Cocteau, Jean, 47, 90–1, 237.
    On Film: 91, 196
"Colonial Boy", 160
Colour Box, 182
Composing for the Films, 28
Congress Dances, 37–8
Constant Husbands, The, 154
Contact, 47
Copland, Aaron, 112–3, 167, 223,
    224, 225, 227, 230
Cottage on Dartmoor, 29
Chronophone, 21
Crown Film Unit, 77, 114
Cukor, George, 87
Curb, Mike, 259–60
Czinner, 69, 71, 72

Dahl, Ingolf, 173
Daily Dozen at the Zoo, 44
Dance Macabre, 40, 183
Dangerous Moonlight, 68
Danny Boy, 161
Dartnell, Steve, 241, 245, 254–60

Davies, Peter Maxwell, 234, 235, 246–53
Daybreak in Udi, 109
Deadfall, 236
Debussy, Claude, 108
Depart, Le, 237–8
Deserter, 48
Desert Victory, 66, 135
Devils, The, 234, 235, 245–252
Dickinson, Thorold, 74, 109, 161–2
Dietrich, Marlene, 46
Disney, Walt, 39–40, 42–3, 171, 182
Diversions, 183
Divertissement, 182
Divertissement Rococo, 183
Dixie, 25
Dr Who, 195
Dods, Marcus, 128
Don Giovanni, 68
Don Juan, 31
Double Life, A, 128
Dowland, John, 134
Drake, E. A., 128, 215
Drei von der Tankstelle, 36
Dunham, Katherine, 91
Dwoskin, Steve, 197–8

Ealing Studios, 114
Eames, Charles and Ray, 181
Easy Rider, 239, 261
Eaux d'Artifice, 181
Edison, Thomas, 21, 22
Eisenstein, Sergei, 27, 127–8, 180
Eisler, Hanns, 28, 47
Ekk, Nikolai, 33
Eldorado, 114
Elephant Boy, 109
Elgar, Edward, 95
Ellit, Jack, 187
Elvey, Maurice, 28
Emmer, Luciano, 128, 177, 178–180
Enfants Terribles, Les, 91
Entr'acte, 198
Eroica, 71
Escape Me Never, 51
Experimental Animation, 182

Falk, Ake, 72
Fallen Idol, The, 109
Falling in Love Again, 46
Fantasia, 182
Faust, 21
Fellini, Frederico, 243, 242
Felix the Cat, 40
Fiddle-de-dee, 183

Field, Mary, 43–4
Film d'Art, Le, 21
Film, 50
Film Music, 26, 36
Film Music Notes, 129, 137, 153, 166–8, 175
Film Techniques, 48
Finian's Rainbow, 86
Firebird, The, 72
Fires were started, 65
Fischinger, Oscar, 182, 187
Flaherty, Robert, 53, 109, 115
Forbes, Bryan, 234, 242
Ford, John, 160–1
Forever Amber, 226
Forty-second street, 36, 53
49th Parallel, 219
Formichi, 70
Fosse, Bob, 86
Foster, Norman, 71
Fountains of Rome, 181
Friedhofer, Hugo, 165–70, 204–5, 221, 222, 229

Gallone, 71
Galway Bay, 161
Gance, Abel, 27
Gavoty, 71
General Post Office Film Unit, 52, 182
Genet, Jean, 196–8
Genevieve, 111, 151
Gerald McBoing Boing, 171, 172–3
Gershwin, George, 81–3, 167
Gilbert and Sullivan Opera, 67
Giotto, 128
Giselle, 73
Gluck, C. W., 91
Goldberg Variations, 181
Goldblatt, Charles, 47
Gordon, Douglas, 177
Grafe, Ferde, 80–1
Grammar of the Films, A, 63
Granowsky, 50
Grapes of Wrath, The, 161
Gras, Enrico, 178–80
Great Waltz, The, 78
Green, Johnny, 80–1
Greenwood, John, 53, 109
Greig, Edward, 25, 40
Grierson, John, 52
Griffith, D. W. 24–6
Griy, Mara, 180
Gross, Anthony, 40
Guthrie, Arlo, 236

Haanstra, Bert, 177
Half a Sixpence, 86
Halas, John, 176
Hamlet (Olivier), 91–3, 126, 165
Hamlet (Kozintsev), 244
Ham, Dick, 183
Hamson, Nina, 181
Handel, George, Frederick, 187
Harsanyi, Tobor von, 41, 171
Harry Lime Theme (*Third Man*), 110
Harvey, Lilian, 37
Hávy-Janos, 72
Hayworth, Rita, 67
Hawthorn, Lil, 21
Heavenly Puss, 173–6
Hello Dolly, 86
Hell's Angels, 49
Henneker, David, 86
Henri, Pierre, 177
Henze, 69
Henry V, 87, 92–107, 126–7, 165
Hepworth, Cecil, 20, 21
Herrmann, Bernard, 136, 221, 223, 227, 241–4
L'Hippocampe, 47
Hirsh, Hy, 183
History of the British Film, The, 1906–14, 22
History of Mr Polly, The, 151
Hitchcock, Alfred, 31, 33, 49, 50, 223, 241, 243
Hobson's Choice, 154–158, 227
Hodgson, W. E., 43–5
Hollaender, Friedrick, 33, 46
Hollywood Quarterly, 185
Honegger, Arthur, 41, 53, 126, 171, 182
Hopkins, Anthony, 151
Hoppin, Hector, 40
Hoppity Pop, 182
Howard, Leslie, 16
Hue and Cry, 150
Hugo, Ian, 182
Hungarian Dances, 182
Hurley, Alec, 21
Huston, John, 78, 243

I am a Camera, 154, 227
Iberia Suite, 108
Ibert, Jacques, 182
L'Idee, 41–2, 47, 53, 171
Ifukube, Akira, 159
Images pour Debussy, 181
In der Nacht, 180

In the Hall of the Mountain Kings, 25
Informer, The, 53, 55, 229
L'Inhumaine, 27
Instruments of the Orchestra, 76, 77, 202
Ireland, John, 114
Irving, Henry, 16–7
Ivan the Terrible, 65, 127
Ivens, Joris, 47

Jameson, Arthur, 20
Jammin' the Blues, 75
Jancsó, Miklós, 238
Jaubert, Maurice, 47–8, 162
Jazz Comedy, 180
Jazz Singer, The, 31, 40
Jennings, Humphrey, 65, 110
Jesus Blood Never Failed Me Yet, 197
Johnny's Walk (Odd Man Out), 109
Johnson, Celia, 75
Joie de Vivre, 40, 171
Jolson, Al, 31
Jones, Kenneth V., 233, 234, 243
Julius Caesar, 128, 129–135, 137–8
Just Once for All Time, 37

Kameradschaft, 34, 45, 65
Kander, John, 86
Karas, Anton, 110, 151
Kean, Edmund, 16
Keller, Hans, 288–90
Kellogg, Edward, 206
Kelly, Gene, 82–3
Kentner, Louis, 74
Kid for Two Farthings, A, 109
Kind Hearts and Coronets, 65
King David, 126
King Lear, 244
King of Jazz, 36, 49
Kinobibliothek (Kinothek), 26
Komeda, Krzysztof, 237–8
Korda, Alexander, 52, 53, 231
Korngold, Erich Wolfgang, 53
Kozintsev, 244
Kubelik, 71
Kubik, Gail, 171, 172–3
Kubrick, Stanley, 240–1, 252–3
Kultur Film in Germany, 67

Lady and the Tramp, The, 171–2
La Franchi, 71
Lambart, Evelyn, 191
Landowska, Wanda, 181

Largo (Handel), 187
Last Laugh, The, 34
Lawrence, D. H., 253
Lauderic Caton's West Indian
  Orchestra, 177
Laura, 226
Lean, David, 89, 154
Lee, Peggy, 171–2
Leigh, Mike, 238
Leigh, Walter, 47, 48, 50–2, 53, 108
Leonardo da Vinci, 183–4
Lerner, Irving, 152
Les Girls, 87
Levy, Louis, 22, 26–7, 29, 36
Leyda, Jay, 180
Lieutenant Kije, 53
Lights of New York, The, 31
Limelight, 160
Listen to Britain, 110
Little Caesar, 34
Little Tich and his Big Boots, 21
London, Kurt, 26, 36, 38
London Symphony Orchestra, 54,
  74, 77
London Weekend Television, 70
Loren, Sophia, 70, 71
Louisiana Story, 66, 115–125
Love on the Wing, 182
Love Your Neighbour, 193
Loves of Carmen, The, 67
Lumière Family, 21
Lutyens, Elizabeth, 109, 114, 164,
  225, 229,
Lye, Len, 182

Mackey, Percival, 20
Madame Butterfly, 71
Madeline, 226
Magic Bow, The, 75
Magic Canvas, The, 176
Magic Flute, The, 46
Mahler, Gustav, 70
Malta, G. C., 114, 219
Mambo, 183
Man Between, The, 109
Man of Aran, 53
Man with the Cloak, 226
March of Time, The, 66
Marriage of Figaro, The, 72
Mary Rose, 19
Marx Brothers, 153
Mathieson, Muir, 52–4, 74, 77,
  90, 93, 233
Medium, The, 66, 233
Meisel, Edmund, 27, 28

Melodrama, 17
Mendelssohn, 129
Men of Two Worlds, 74, 109, 161,
  162, 231
Menotti, Gian-Carlo, 66, 67, 233
Merry Wives of Windsor, 71
Messiah, The, 202
M.G.M. Studio Orchestra, 83
Mickey Mouse, 40, 42, 43, 90
Mickey's Moving Day, 42–3
Midsummer Night's Dream, 129
Mikado, 72
Milhaud, Darius, 27, 47
Milestone, Lewis, 33
Million Le, 162
Minuet, 182
Miss Julie, 65
Mitry, Jean, 181, 182
McLaren, Norman, 64, 182, 183,
  184, 185–192
Mockridge, Cyril J., 163
Modern Times, 36
Moholy-Nagy, 186, 187
Moment Musical, 187
Moore, Henry, 177
Morelli, 71
Moretti, Raoul, 32, 39
Moulin Rouge, 78
Mozart, Wolfgang, 46, 75
Muscle Beach, 75, 152
Musical Quarterly, 166, 168, 169
Music for the Movies, 22, 26–7
Music for Strings, 54
Musique Concrete, 177, 183–4

Napoleon, 27
National Film Board of Canada,
  185, 193
Nature's Double-Lifers, 44
Nedda, 70
Neighbours, 183
New Babylon, 27
New Detergents, 177
New Earth, 47
Niebeling, Hugo, 73
Nightingale, The, 44
Night Mail, 52, 171
North, Alex, 254
Now is the Time, 191
Now, O Now, I need must part
  (Dowland), 134

October, 27
Odd Man Out, 109, 137, 139–149,
  229

Of Mice and Men, 112, 113, 225
Oliver Twist, 89–90, 219
Olivier, Laurence, 91, 93, 94–5, 165
Olson, 205
Ondes, Martenot, 41, 42
One Night of Love, 53
O'Neill, Norman, 16–19, 230
On the Town, 65, 81, 83
Orchestrion, 22
Orphée, 65, 91
Our Town, 112, 113, 225
Overlanders, The, 114
Owen Wingrave, 68
Ox-Bow Incident, The, 65, 110, 163

Pabst, G. W., 33
Pacific, 231, 182
Pagliacci, 70, 72
Painlevé, Jena, 47
Parker, Clifton, 114
Paradise Lost, 178
Pasolini, Pier Paulo, 233, 245
Passion of Joan of Arc, 34
Passport to Pimlico, 150
"Pastoral Symphony" (Beethoven),
    43
Pathé, Charles, 21
Pearson, George, 28–30
Peer Gynt, 25
Penn, Arthur, 236
Pepys, Samuel, 15
Pett and Pott, 47, 53
Pfenninger, Rudolph, 187, 191
Phantasy, 191
Philharmonic Orchestra, 90
Pink Panther, The, 195
Pink Floyd, The, 259–262
Pinocchio, 171
Piper, John, 177
Pipes of Pan, 159
Pixilation, 183
Playtime at the Zoo, 44
Plow that Broke the Plains, 111
Plutarch, 15
Poet and Peasant, 23
Polka Graph, 183
Pool of London, 114
Pop goes the Weasel, 45
Pratley, Gerald, 285–6
Prehistoric Man, (On the Town),
    84
Prelude in C Sharp Minor, 187
Previn, André, 70
Privatesekreterin, Die, 36
Prokofiev, Sergei, 72, 136

Puccini, 71
Pudovkin, V. I. 48
Purcell, Henry, 77

Quick Millions, 34
Quiet Man, The, 161
Quo Vadis, 128, 227

Rachmaninov, Serge, 67, 68, 69,
    70, 187
Rain People, The, 239
Rake's Progress, The, 113, 114
Raksin, David, 24, 171, 221, 222,
    223, 224, 225, 226, 228
Rawsthorne, Alan, 114, 135
Ray, Satyajit, 233, 243
Raybould, Clarence, 47
Reed, Carol, 109, 160
Red Desert, 259
Red Pony, The, 112–3
Réflets sans l'eau, 181
"Reflexion Faite", 33, 90
Reichenbach, 71, 72
Reiniger, Lotte, 41
Renoir, Claude, 181
Resnais, Alain, 243
Respighi, 181
Reynders, John, 32
Rhapsody in Blue, 32
Rice, Elmer, 34
Richard III, 93
Ride the Valkyries, 25
Rimsky-Korsakov, G. M., 186, 187
Rival World, The, 176
Road to Life, The, 33
Robinson, Earl, 152
Rogers, Ginger, 87
Romance Sentimentale, 180
Rome Symphony Orchestra, 181
Romeo and Juliet, 72, 128
Ronnell, Ann, 153
Rossini, Gioachino Antonio, 25, 162
Rota, Nina, 234
Rotha, Paul, 7, 49, 164
Roue, La, 27
Royal College of Music Magazine,
    219
Royal Irish Animated Pictures Co.
    Grand Orchestra, 20
Royal Philharmonic Orchestra, 128
Rozsa, Miklos, 129–34, 137–8, 221,
    223, 227, 229
Rubenstein, Anton, 23
Rubinstein, Arthur, 71
Russell, Ken, 80–2, 234, 246–253
Ruttmann, Walter, 28, 180

St Joan, 41
St Matthews Passion, 70
Saint-Saëns, Camille, 22, 40, 183
Salinger, Conrad, 82
Salzburg, 69
Sam Fox Moving Picture Music, 26
Sang d'un Poète, Le, 47, 91, 171
Sargent, Malcolm, 70 77
Schaeffer, Pierre, 183
Scholpo, E. A., 186, 171
Schubert, 30, 187
Schumann, Robert, 27, 180
Scorpio Rising, 197
Scott of the Antarctic, 114, 159–60,
    163
"Seascape", 114
Second Best, 241, 245, 246, 253–9
Secrets of Nature, 43–5
Seiber, Matyas, 171, 176
Shakespeare, William, 92–3, 126,
    127, 128, 129–34, 165,
Shane, 113
Shaporin, Y., 48
Shaw, George Bernard, 19, 230
Shell Film Unit, 176
She Wore a Yellow Ribbon, 161
Ship that Died of Shame, 288, 289,
    290
Shooting Stars, 29
Shostakovitch, Dimitri, 27, 183,
    244
Sica, Vittorio de, 162
Sidney, George, 86
Sight and Sound, 27
Silly Symphony, 40
Sinfonia Antarctica, 115
Skeleton Dance, 40, 42, 49
Skolimowski, Jerzy, 237–8
Sleuth, 232
Sloppy Jalopy, 226
Smith, J. B., 128
Smith, Percy, 43
Solaris, 252
Song of Ceylon, 47, 48, 50, 51, 52,
    53, 108
Song of Life, 50
Song of Norway, 78
Song of the South, 171
Song of Schéhérezade, 78
Song to Remember, 78
Sound Barrier, The, 135
Sound of Music, 85
Sous les Toits de Paris, 32 36, 38,
    39, 49
Space Odyssey: 2001, 245, 252–3

Spenser, Norman, 234, 235, 236,
    238, 239–40
Stafford, Harry, 32
Stagecoach, 161
Stars and Stripes, 182
Star-Spangled Banner, 25
Steamboat Willie, 40
Steiner, Max, 53, 55, 221, 225
Stereophonic music, 227
Sternfield, Frederick, 166, 169–70
Stevens, James, 177
Stignami, 70
Stokowski, Leopold, 70
Strange Incident (see also The Oxbow
    Incident) 110, 163
Stravinsky, Igor, 72, 78–9
Strick, Joseph, 152
Suddenly, 226
Sunshine Susie, 36–7
Swan Lake, 73, 163
Sylvie et le Fantôme, 159
Szinetár, Miklós, 73

Talankin, Igor, 81–2
Tchaikowsky, Peter Ilytch, 23, 25,
    80–2, 129, 162
Tebaldi, 70
Technique of Film Animation, The,
    170
Technique of Film Editing, The, 8
Tell England, 33
Tempo, 93
That Dear Old Song, 110
Thérémin, 41
They were Expendable, 161
Thiele, William, 36, 50
Third Man, The, 109,110
Things to Come, 52, 53–5, 74, 231
Thomson, Virgil, 53, 111–2,
    115–125
Three Dawns to Sydney, 109
Three Little Pigs, The, 40, 171
Tilley, Vesta, 21
Tiomkin, Dimitri, 81
Titfield Thunderbolt, 109
Tobias and the Angel, 68
Toch, Ernest, 186
Tom Jones, 88, 246
Tönende Handschrift, 187
Torn Curtain, 232
Tosca, 163
Tovey, Donald Francis, 205
Traumerei, 22
Twirligig, 191
Two Bagatelles, 191

Ultus, the Man from the Dead, 29
Underground, 29
UNESCO, 68–9
Unfinished Symphony, 30
Unicorn in the Garden, The, 171, 226
Unter dem Lindenbaum, 110
UPA, 172, 226
Ustinov, Peter, 151

Valse Grise, 162
Vanishing Point, 238–9
Verdi, Giuseppe, 25, 71, 162
Vice Versa, 151
Vigo, Jean, 47
Vionov, N. W., 186, 187, 191
Virginian, The, 49
Virgin Martyr, The, 15
Vivaldi, 181
Vivaphone, 21
Vlad, Roman, 89, 128, 178, 221,
  223, 225, 229, 231, 237
Volga, Volga, 180
Von Karajan, 69, 70, 71, 72, 73
Von Sternberg, Josef, 33, 46
Voyage to Purilia, 24

Wagner, Richard, 25, 219,
Walk in the Sun, A, 65
Walton, William, 53, 87, 91–3,
  96–107, 126–7, 165
Waltzes from Vienna, 49–50
Warhol, Andy, 196
Warner Brothers, 31
Warsaw Concerto, The, 68–9
Waters of Time, 114
Watkins, A. W.,
Watts, Stephen, 49
Way Ahead, The, 109
Welles, Orson, 136, 223, 243
Wells, H. G., 53, 231

Western Approaches, 114
Westfront, 1918, 33
West Side Story, 85
When you wish upon a star, 171
White Chrysanthemums, 110
Whiteman, Paul, 82
Whitney, John, 183, 187
Who's afraid of the big bad wolf,
  40, 171
Williams, Edward, 177
Williams, Ralph Vaughan, 94–5,
  115, 159, 160, 163, 219, 220, 223,
  227, 232–3
William Tell Overture, 23, 39
Wiren, Dag, 222, 225, 227
"Wonderful Town," 83
World of Plenty, 66
World without End, 109, 164
Wright, Basil, 47, 51, 114, 164
Wurlitzer Organ, 34

Yanovsky, B. A., 187
Young Chopin, 78
Young, Victor, 113
*Young Person's Guide to the
  Orchestra, A.*, 70, 77
*You're Awful-awful nice to
  know, dear*, 84
You were meant for me, 40

Zabriskie Point, 239, 244, 259–262
Zamecnik, 26
Zampa, 23
Zanuck, Darryl, F., 223
Zeffirelli, Franco, 71
Zéro de Conduite, 47–8
Zohlinsky, N. Y., 186
Zip-a-dee-do-dah, 171
Zither, 109, 110, 151, 160

THE TECHNIQUE OF LIGHTING FOR TELEVISION AND MOTION PICTURES

by Gerald Millerson

This unique study of the art and techniques of creative lighting runs from basic principles to specialised applications in TV and motion pictures.

366 pages, 39 colour plates, 206 photographs, 471 diagrams

THE TECHNIQUE OF FILM EDITING

Compiled by Karel Reisz and Gavin Millar

The British Film Academy appointed a committee of ten outstanding film editors to summarize their views and experience in this book.

2nd. edn., 412 pages, 325 photographs, 21 diagrams

Case bound & Paperback

THE TECHNIQUE OF THE MOTION PICTURE CAMERA

By H. Mario Raimondo Souto

A comprehensive study of the modern film camera in all its forms.

3rd edn., 322 pages, 191 diagrams

THE TECHNIQUE OF DOCUMENTARY FILM PRODUCTION

By W. Hugh Baddeley

How to plan, budget for, produce and present documentaries.

3rd edn., 268 pages, 63 diagrams

THE TECHNIQUE OF FILM AND TELEVISION MAKE-UP

By Vincent J-R. Kehoe

This book is intended primarily for the professional make-up artist, but the amateur also will find invaluable its practical advice.

3rd edn., 280 pages, 131 photographs, 182 diagrams

THE TECHNIQUE OF SPECIAL EFFECTS CINEMATOGRAPHY

By Raymond Fielding

The first professional work in English to bring together and describe every special effects technique in use throughout the world.

3rd edn., 426 pages, 283 photographs, 222 diagrams

THE TECHNIQUE OF FILM ANIMATION

By John Halas and Roger Manvell

This is the first comprehensive work to demonstrate the aims and organization of making animated films on an industrial level.

4th edn., 360 pages, 191 photographs, 56 diagrams

THE TECHNIQUE OF THE SOUND STUDIO

By Alec Nisbett

This book is intended for all those who are concerned with putting sound programmes together.

3rd edn., 560 pages, 242 diagrams

THE TECHNIQUE OF TELEVISION PRODUCTION

By Gerald Millerson

This book presents the first comprehensive survey of the mechanics, art, method and techniques used in television studio work.

9th edn., 440 pages, 1,150 diagrams   Case bound & Paperback

THE TECHNIQUE OF THE TELEVISION CAMERAMAN

By Peter Jones

Primarily intended to help the newcomer to the field, others co-operating with the cameraman will also find it of great value.

3rd edn., 244 pages, 120 diagrams   Case bound & Paperback

THE TECHNIQUE OF TELEVISION ANNOUNCING

By Bruce Lewis

A complete manual for all who appear or aspire to appear " on camera" —not only announcers but actors, politicians and others.

264 pages, 43 diagrams

THE TECHNIQUE OF EDITING 16mm FILM

By John Burder

This is a practical book on a vital phase of creative film-making at a down-to-earth level of craftsmanship.

3rd edn., 152 pages, 169 diagrams

THE TECHNIQUE OF THE FILM CUTTING ROOM

By Ernest Walter

This book is concerned with the physical side of editing. It describes in detail the functions of the editor and his assistants in relation to each stage in the production of a large scale film.

2nd edn., 316 pages, 167 diagrams

THE TECHNIQUE OF SPECIAL EFFECTS IN TELEVISION

By B. R. Wilkie

This unique work covers everything—from the popping champagne cork to bullet and bomb effects, collapsing floors to animated captions. The treatment is detailed, giving full descriptions of equipment, working principles, safety precautions and type of effect obtained.

392 pages, 169 photographs, 51 diagrams